"The Gautreaux case not only shook housing policy in Chicago to its core, but also introduced working principles which have redirected national policies and transformed housing practices in cities across the country. Only the lawyer whose courage, tenacity, and keen sense of justice guided the legal battle could tell the story as it must be told."

—HENRY CISNEROS, chairman, CityView, and former secretary of the U.S. Department of Housing and Urban Development

"*Waiting for Gautreaux* is a powerful personal history of the decades-long effort to desegregate public housing in the Chicago metropolis. Polikoff's message is clear and compelling: isolating low-income Americans in neighborhoods where the schools don't teach and jobs are absent is a recipe for disaster. Gautreaux teaches us a powerful lesson: housing policy needs to promote mobility and choice, not reinforce concentrated poverty."

—BRUCE KATZ, vice president, Brookings Institution

"I highly recommend this book as a valuable truth-teller, which makes a timely, urgent plea and cogent argument to dismantle the ghettos. That's right, dismantle them— once and for all. In the pursuit of ending discriminatory habits and practices, and creating a society where equality can actually be achieved, and flourish, we don't need no stinking ghettos."

—MICHAEL MEYERS, executive director, New York Civil Rights Coalition

"At last: a definitive insider's account of the landmark legal saga that redefined housing choice for low-income people and that cast the dilemma of community segregation in a radically new light. Gautreaux's importance is singular and profound, and Polikoff's memoir makes a significant contribution to the political history of civil rights and social policy in America. Among other virtues, this must-read book will be a terrific resource for educating the next generation committed to social change."

—XAVIER DE SOUZA BRIGGS, editor of *The Geography of Opportunity: Race and Housing Choice in Metropolitan America*

DOROTHY GAUTREAUX, 1927–68

WAITING FOR GAUTREAUX

WAITING FOR GAUTREAUX

A STORY OF SEGREGATION, HOUSING, AND THE BLACK GHETTO

ALEXANDER POLIKOFF

Foreword by Clarence Page

NORTHWESTERN UNIVERSITY PRESS | EVANSTON, ILLINOIS

Northwestern University Press
www.nupress.northwestern.edu

Copyright © 2006 by Alexander Polikoff.
Foreword copyright © 2006 by Clarence Page.
Published 2006 by Northwestern University Press.
All rights reserved.

First paperback printing 2007

Printed in the United States of America

10   9   8   7   6   5   4   3   2   1

ISBN-13: 978-0-8101-2420-2
ISBN-10: 0-8101-2420-3

"The Ballad of Rudolph Reed" reprinted by consent of Brooks Permissions.

The Library of Congress has cataloged
the original, hardcover edition as follows:

Polikoff, Alexander.
    Waiting for Gautreaux : a story of segregation, housing, and the
black ghetto / Alexander Polikoff.
        p.   cm.
    Includes bibliographical references and index.
    ISBN 0-8101-2344-4 (cloth : alk. paper)
    1. Discrimination in housing—Law and legislation—Illinois—
Chicago—History. 2. African Americans—Housing—Illinois—
Chicago. 3. Public housing—Law and legislation—Illinois—
Chicago—History. 4. Gautreaux, Dorothy. I. Title.
KFI1660.5.D5P65 2005
344.773'110636351—dc22

                                                            2005018738

⊗ The paper used in this publication meets the minimum requirements
of the American National Standard for Information Sciences—
Permanence of Paper for Printed Library Materials,
ANSI Z39.48-1992.

To the memories of Dorothy Gautreaux, Charles Markels, and Bernard Weisberg; to the thousands of families who braved the unknown to make "housing mobility" a reality; to the countless lawyers and paralegals who have given of themselves to the Gautreaux litigation for nearly four decades; and to Barbara, my wife and friend of more than half a century

CONTENTS

FOREWORD

Clarence Page

While the civil rights revolution was knocking down the walls of American apartheid across the South, racial segregation by neighborhood and income persisted in northern cities like Chicago—with taxpayers' help.

By the early 1960s, public housing in Chicago had deteriorated into a swamp of problems and pathologies. High-rise developments like the Robert Taylor Homes, the nation's largest public housing project, became no-go zones of gang activity, violent crime, low marriage rates, high unemployment, and low student achievement.

While high-rise public housing worked for senior citizens across the nation and for mixed-income families in densely populated New York City, stacking low-income families into the air or segregating them horizontally in sprawling low-rise developments created problems wherever it was tried.

Nonetheless, in Chicago, as my late colleague Mike Royko described in his urban classic *Boss,* strongman Mayor Richard J. Daley kept as many poor African Americans as possible segregated into the neighborhoods in which poor African Americans already lived when he took office in 1955. It worked. By the late 1960s, a third of the city's population, the black third, was penned up in less than a fifth of the city's land, the black fifth.

The unofficial but very real patchwork of racial and ethnic apartheid in Chicago and other big northern cities was invented long before "Hizzoner" came along. But Daley was more than willing to perpetuate it, with the help of federal dollars.

The Civil Rights Act of 1964, the Voting Rights Act of 1965, and earlier hard-won victories against America's legal apartheid opened unprecedented opportunities for my generation of African Americans but left the de facto neighborhood segregation of northern cities like Chicago virtually untouched.

The projects fit well into a system of "plantation politics," as black reformers like the late Mayor Harold Washington would later call it. Public housing served as a form of government-sponsored population control, forming and preserving ghettos of neighborhood segregation for blacks akin to the reservations for Native Americans.

Segregation, from this vantage point, was what "the neighborhoods" wanted. The white neighborhoods wanted to prevent "invasion" and more "white flight." The black ward bosses didn't want to upset a system that kept their poor African American constituencies reliably dependent and compliant.

As a kid I grumbled about such injustices. My father would shrug and tell me, "You can't fight city hall." Little did either of us know that by the end of the 1960s I would hear about people like Alex Polikoff and his colleagues who saw injustice, took on city hall—and won!

In the early 1970s, as a reporter on the streets of Chicago, I covered clashes over insurance redlining, mortgage discrimination, panic peddling by real-estate salespeople, and the other practices and prejudices that built the ghetto and kept it humming. I wrote about the early days of the Rev. Jesse Jackson and the last days of Black Panther leader Fred Hampton. But, from my perspective, the activists who had the most impact on the lives of low-income black families may well have been Alex Polikoff and the rest of his pro bono team of lawyers.

When I saw the headlines for the Gautreaux v. CHA decision, I could hardly believe my eyes: black public housing applicants would no longer be herded into neighborhoods populated only by other blacks. They would be offered housing in white neighborhoods in the city and suburbs!

When I figured out, after my third or fourth reading of the story, that my eyes were not deceiving me, I thought about my father's words and smiled. So, you could fight city hall after all—even Mayor Daley's city hall.

And as Polikoff battled all the way to the Supreme Court, arguing against his law school classmate Robert Bork, at that time the Solicitor General, he showed us that dedicated public-interest lawyers could beat the White House, too. They could change the nation's housing policy and, more important, change lives.

By the late 1980s, I was covering a different kind of housing story. The "Gautreaux children" were growing up. The first generation of low-income black children to benefit from racially and economically mixed rent-subsidized housing were graduating from school—and they were graduating at a substantially higher rate and with higher grade point averages than their counterparts left behind in segregated black neighborhoods. Environment does make a difference. The results of Gautreaux have proved it.

I have been waiting a long time for this book.

Here, for the first time, Alex Polikoff describes what happened behind the scenes during all of these stories and more. In a dramatic yet also instructive narrative worthy of Hollywood, he describes the tick-tock of a forty-year legal battle. He places this drama within its historical context of the larger struggle for civil rights and housing rights and offers his own recommendations for where the nation's housing policy needs to go from here.

Martin Luther King tried with demonstrations and boycott threats to break down racial and economic housing segregation in Chicago. In one of many powerful episodes described in this book, Daley either outfoxed or double-crossed King, depending on your perspective. But, where King suffered a rare setback, the Gautreaux decision succeeded mightily, showing how the legal system can be used to change a city and visibly improve lives.

Today Chicagoans are seeing something few anticipated: high-rise public housing is being demolished and residents are being relocated in mixed neighborhoods throughout the city and suburbs, following the pattern established by Gautreaux. In 1998, the Gautreaux judge ordered the CHA to stick with that pattern by building half its replacement public housing outside depressed black neighborhoods, as a way of continuing to reverse years of discrimination. It was yet another important Gautreaux victory, thirty years after the death of Dorothy Gautreaux, the public housing resident after whom the case was named.

Leading national trends, Chicago is now, at the dawn of the new century, experiencing a real-estate boom. In the wake of lower crime rates, reduced housing density, and other improvements, market confidence has grown, spurring even more development. This poses new challenges for housing the poor. The fight has not ended, but the challenges don't seem so intractable anymore. Gautreaux has succeeded before. It can succeed again.

Polikoff shows how in this book. His recommendation for—at long last—facing up to and doing something about the nation's black ghettos merits serious consideration. If it is followed, to the lasting benefit of all Americans, Dorothy Gautreaux will have won again.

PREFACE: A CHRISTIAN FOR THE LIONS

To-morrow, when I wake, or think I do,
what shall I say of to-day?

—Vladimir (*Waiting for Godot*)

January 20, 1976, dawned sunny but cold. A rare snow had laid a white patina on the streets. Barbara, our three children, and I had taken the train from Chicago. My colleague Bernie Weisberg had flown in earlier. We had stayed at Jay Miller's place—he headed the ACLU in Washington—and the house overflowed with well-wishers. Everyone was ridiculously solicitous, which only served to make me feel like a Christian being readied for the lions.

I had pared my argument down to seven key points. Even were I allowed to speak for the allotted half hour without interruption, it would have been a challenge to make all seven with clarity and coherence. But interruptions were certain. The idea was to make the "affirmative" points while answering questions. Barbara and the kids had a list—they were to keep score on how many of the seven points I was able to make before the red warning light on the podium signaled I was out of time.

We rose early. Through breakfast and our cab ride, I tried to appear nonchalant. Actually, I was pretty nervous. My briefcase, stuffed with papers I would never use, was absurdly heavy.

The marbled Supreme Court building was imposing. So was the hearing chamber, dominated by a great curving desk on a raised platform. Behind the desk were arrayed the massive swivel chairs in which the justices would sit, or slouch, or revolve slowly—until they pounced. Relegated to a level below the curved desk, the lawyers' tables looked pitifully insignificant. The podium, from which one addressed the justices, seemed more a witness box than a pulpit. Sloping down to the space before the great desk, the crowded gallery reminded me of an amphitheater.

And there was Robert Bork, my former law school classmate, splendid in his gray morning coat with tails. I had learned only minutes before that the solicitor general himself would argue. During our time in law school he and I had worked together on the law review. Occasionally, in the lingo of the '50s, we and our wives had "double-dated." But except for my unsuccessful mission of the previous year, we had had no contact since graduation.

After a parting kiss from Barbara, I threaded my way down the aisle to a seat at the front with Bernie at my side. He would join me at the lawyers' table when our turn came. I nodded to Bork and Robert Elliott, HUD's general counsel, who would sit with Bork at the government's table.

The argument in another case came first. I didn't even try to focus on what was being said except to note that Rehnquist was asking most of the questions. Finally, it was over. John Paul Stevens collected his papers, rose, and made his way purposefully out the side door. He must have been recusing himself, probably because he had ruled on motions in our case in the Seventh Circuit Court of Appeals, before President Ford's recent selection of him to fill William O. Douglas's former seat.

Bork and Elliott, Bernie and I quickly moved to the lawyers' tables. I extracted my oral argument notebook from my briefcase and slid it noiselessly to the table before me. White-haired Chief Justice Warren Burger, looking regal as always, intoned, "We'll hear arguments next in 1047, Hills v. Gautreaux. Mr. Solicitor General." Exuding confidence, Bork rose smartly and strode to the podium.

The day was precisely one short of ten years from the snowy lunchtime when it had all begun. As I had no way of knowing at the time, Hills v. Gautreaux was to be the beginning of a run of over two decades during which some 25,000 black Americans would cross America's class and color lines, changing the way we think about public housing and even about the urban poor. The overly enthusiastic *Baltimore Sun* would call it a more important case than Brown v. Board of Education. Patrick Buchanan, Richard Nixon's erstwhile speechwriter and later sometime presidential candidate, would rail in his syndicated column that it was tyranny, justifying a little rebellion. The *New York Times* would liken the blacks crossing the lines to pioneers settling the West. On television, *60 Minutes* would offer praise instead of its usual exposé.

When all is said and done—which it isn't—history will someday render judgment. Until then, the task is to tell the story, which I'll do in three stages. Part 1 (chapters 1 through 3) recounts our ten-year tramp—1966 to 1976—through a litigation jungle in which we barely escaped being blown up by a booby trap fashioned by Richard Nixon. Part 2 narrates our adventures along the three paths we explored upon emerging from the jungle: scattered sites (chapter 4), rent subsidies (chapter 5), and public housing "transformation" (chapter 6). Finally, part 3 (chapter 7) considers the implications of the whole Gautreaux journey for race relations in America, particularly from Alexis de Tocqueville's point of view that racial inequality will one day bring America to disaster.

And so to the story, which begins in Chicago on January 21, 1966, my thirty-ninth birthday.

WAITING FOR GAUTREAUX

PART ONE

CHAPTER ONE

UP WITH A LADLE

A dog came in the kitchen
And stole a crust of bread.
Then cook up with a ladle
And beat him till he was dead.

—Vladimir (*Waiting for Godot*)

1

January 21, 1966. The moist snowflakes, melting as they hit the pavement, were hardly a storied Chicago blizzard. But they were enough to have made driving downright unpleasant had we not been feeling so upbeat. As it was, the slap-slap of the windshield wipers and the rattling of the heater fan were like background applause to our hyped-up talk. Chuck Markels and I were heading for a pizza at Edwardo's in Chicago's Hyde Park.

What had happened that morning in Waukegan explained our animated conversation. Judge Parker was treating us fairly—exactly what we had hoped for and all we needed. More than wet snow would have been required to dampen our spirits. Two pro bono lawyers were about the business of righting at least one Waukegan wrong. Soon they would be talking about frying bigger fish.

The Waukegan wrong was that Whittier Elementary School, surrounded by four all-white schools, was a black island in a white sea. The schools were so close together that all five could easily have been integrated by redrawing boundary lines—no busing required. Yet the Waukegan School Board refused to act even though Illinois law directed school boards to revise boundaries periodically to prevent segregation. Shirley Tometz, a plucky mother of one of the few white kids in Whittier, had risked the ire of friends and neighbors by complaining to the American Civil Liberties Union. As a volunteer ACLU attorney, I had taken her case, then talked Chuck, a good friend from childhood, into joining me. We had been assigned to Charles Parker, a crusty, conservative judge of the circuit court of Lake County, Illinois. Now, in the pretrial maneuvering, he was proving the truth of his reputation for fairness. We were looking forward with anticipation to a trial in the spring.

With thirteen years of law practice under my belt, I was a partner in the Chicago firm of Schiff Hardin & Waite. Fresh from the University of Chicago Law School (after giving my lawyer-father pause by first detouring for a master's degree in English literature), I had joined Schiff in 1953. My starting salary of $4,500 a year looked pretty good at a time when a tuna fish sandwich cost about thirty-five cents.

I did well at Schiff in litigation, corporate, and securities work. From the beginning I also handled a fair amount of pro bono cases—working as a volunteer lawyer for some public interest cause. My preferred cause was the ACLU, to whose board meetings I had been invited by two acquaintances who had preceded me through law school, Abner Mikva and Bernard Weisberg. Why the ACLU? Partly because a favorite professor, Harry Kalven Jr., was an inspiring scholar who instilled in me a great respect for the First Amendment. And partly because, in our conversations about public matters, my father had always seemed to side with the underdog and the outsider.

Schiff was tolerant of pro bono so long as the firm's work was done satisfactorily. Over the years I handled a number of ACLU cases. In one, Henry Miller's supposedly obscene *Tropic of Cancer* had been summarily stripped from bookstands in Lake County, Illinois. We quickly got the books restored to the racks. Another was a notable losing effort (with Kalven, Weisberg, and others) on behalf of George Anastaplo, a fellow law student. A committee of the Illinois Supreme Court had denied George permission to practice law because he refused to answer the familiar McCarthy-era question, Are you now or have you ever been a member of the Communist Party?

Eventually the Anastaplo case wound up in the U.S. Supreme Court.

George acted as his own attorney and a 5–4 vote went the wrong way. Five of the justices concluded that George's refusal to answer the "material" question had obstructed the committee's ability to determine George's fitness to practice law. Four of the justices—but only four— said that the evidence of George's good character was overwhelming. They could think of no reason for the committee's decision other than that "this young man should not be permitted to resist the committee's demands without being compelled to suffer for it."

In the 1960s, encouraging pro bono was a useful arrow in a law firm's recruiting quiver. Competition to hire the best students from the best schools was keen, and many students were interested in a firm's views on pro bono. So it was not surprising that Schiff tolerated my forays into such matters as the Tometz, Tropic of Cancer, and Anastaplo cases, and I felt comfortable exploring still another possibility. I had no idea that the scope and longevity of what was to be discussed at Edwardo's would make Shirley Tometz's case look like a flyspeck.

On a cold day, Edwardo's hot pizza seemed especially tasty. So, in a manner of speaking, did the conversation. Chuck and I were meeting with Zoe Mikva, Abner's wife, who was a member of the Civil Rights Committee of the Illinois division of the ACLU, and Harold Baron, research director of the Chicago Urban League. In arranging our meeting, Mikva had told me very little. I knew only that Baron had asked her whether the ACLU would look into the Chicago Housing Authority construction program. All the new public housing, he had said, was going into black neighborhoods. If discrimination was prohibited in public schools, wasn't it also prohibited in public housing?

At Edwardo's, Baron added some detail. The complaint about the CHA had come from the West Side Federation, an umbrella group of black organizations. The city's pattern of building virtually all of its new public housing in the black ghetto had long been obvious and long been objected to—without effect—by civic groups and even the press. But there was a new factor here: the West Side Federation complaint was based on a recently enacted civil rights law. More public housing for the ghetto was being planned; maybe now there was a legal tool to break the pattern.

It is easy to become specialized in the practice of law. At Schiff I had started in litigation, then added corporate and securities work. For the ACLU I had worked on First Amendment issues. But I did not dig into school desegregation until Shirley Tometz came along. Although I now knew something about that subject, I had never considered segregation in housing—the public housing program was utterly foreign to me. Chuck was in a similar state of ignorance. And what, really, could be done about the CHA's bricks and mortar already implanted on Chicago's cityscape? Waukegan could be solved by redrawing some boundary lines. No remedy that simple would work for high-rise towers.

Yet Chuck and I were feeling hopeful about Waukegan. Litigation was turning out to be an effective lever for social change. Besides, it was my birthday, an auspicious time to begin something new. What fun! "Let it snow, let it snow, let it snow" ran the refrain of a popular song. Yes, we would take a look at the CHA and its public housing ghettos.

2

So our next pro bono sortie would involve ghettos and housing discrimination against black Americans. In the America of 1966, these were matters freighted with a heavy history. Chuck and I thought we had better read some of that history.

Schoolchildren soon learn that the hallowed Declaration of Independence phrase penned by Thomas Jefferson—"all men are created equal"—was not meant to include blacks. In the southern part of the new nation, where most blacks lived, blacks were viewed as property, not "men." Though he believed slavery was morally wrong, the slaveholder Jefferson did nothing about it. In 1863, the Emancipation Proclamation formally ended slavery's reign, but it would take more than a proclamation to confer "created equal" status on black Americans.

Reconstruction lasted barely a dozen years. The Republican Party's commitment to black freedom in the South was no match for southern whites' commitment to the reestablishment of white supremacy. Historian Adam Fairclough explains that three key elements were missing: (1) land—the promised forty acres and a mule never materialized; (2) education—two-thirds of the former black slaves were illiterate, but public schools were left under local, predominantly white, control; and (3) enforcement of racial equality—the federal effort to combat white terror and violence petered out in weariness and a calculation that the Republican Party could control the White House with northern votes alone. The Republicans, says Fairclough, allowed the Democrats to "redeem" the South.

Redemption included disfranchisement by systematically purging blacks from voting rosters, and by pervasive segregation, initially by custom but soon by law. These "redemptive" policies were backed not only by terror and violence but also by what today would be called a propaganda campaign. Its purpose was to gain national acceptance of the view that blacks were an inferior race whose relegation to inferior status was therefore justifiable.

The campaign succeeded brilliantly. By 1896, the Supreme Court, upholding the segregated seating of rail travelers, pronounced: "If one race be inferior to the other socially, the Constitution of the United States cannot put them upon the same plane." A few years later President Theodore Roosevelt himself opined, "A perfectly stupid race can never rise to a very high plane."

By 1900, the South's black population was once again utterly powerless. Yet powerlessness was but one part of the picture. Blacks were also subjected to a loss of humanity second only to slavery itself. Virtually every aspect of black life in the South—schooling, housing, work, marriage, even walking down the public street—was governed by Jim Crow's implacable and humiliating law of white supremacy and black subjection. Upon leaving the House of Representatives in 1901, George H. White, the last black congressman from the South for seventy years, chose to retire to New Jersey, explaining, "I can no longer live in North Carolina and be a man." Not often had the losing side in war snatched so complete a victory from the jaws of its defeat.

Given the ubiquity of Jim Crow and the acquiescence of the rest of the country, it is unsurprising that the new servitude persisted for generations. Lynchings were not only the symbol but the harsh reality of the enforcement of white supremacy—"essentially state-sanctioned events," one historian calls them. A congressional report listed 3,377 lynchings from 1899 to 1921.

So successful was the continuing propaganda that the victims were blamed. The greatest cause of lynching, President Roosevelt told Congress in 1906, was "the perpetration, especially by black men, of the hideous crime of rape." In 1915, the wildly successful film *The Birth of a Nation* cast blacks as Reconstruction oppressors and rapists lusting for white women, the Ku Klux Klan as heroes. Following a private screening in the White House, President Woodrow Wilson commented, "My only regret is that it is all so terribly true."

Two hopeful moments flickered across the screen of black life in the South during the first half of the new century. World War I brought military training and service for some black men, the first wave of the Great Migration of blacks to wartime factory jobs in the North, and the widespread belief that the war for democracy abroad would somehow erode white supremacy at home. But the moment of hope was quickly squelched in postarmistice red-baiting. "Bolshevist agitation has been extended among the Negroes, especially in the South, and . . . is bearing its natural and inevitable fruit," said the *New York Times.* The "fruit" was a particularly harsh wave of violence, justified as patriotism, against newly assertive blacks, who were to be kept in their place.

The second war for democracy was something of a repeat performance—an even bigger migration, with over 900,000 blacks in uniform, and once more hope that black support of the war effort would be rewarded. It was not to be. Military service was largely segregated, and southerners who dominated Congress saw to it that the war's rhetoric about democracy had little application to blacks at home. The war fueled hopes, and staffing the arsenal of democracy gave some blacks unprecedented work opportunities. But the postwar reality in the South was more racial tension and violence, much of it to squelch postwar assertiveness, especially by veterans. In the end, the basic situation of southern blacks was hardly changed.

Until about 1950, says Fairclough, blacks in the South had little choice but to make the best of a bad situation. "Sharecroppers could be evicted, employees fired at will, and businessmen refused credit." With virtual impunity, whites could also employ more drastic "sanctions"— arrest, beating, banishment, and murder.

But stirrings there were, and change—so long in coming—finally bubbled to the surface. With the end of sharecropping, rural blacks streamed into the cities where their numbers and relative anonymity provided a degree of safety. Slowly, painfully, against fearful odds, and at great personal cost, more blacks registered to vote. The NAACP began to win some cases in its early challenges to white supremacy in the courts.

Of great importance, the ideology of white supremacy was now being undermined. Nazi racism, and Soviet cold war exploitation of America's brand of it, meant that the federal government could no longer endorse the most extreme practices, or even the theory, of the South's hegemony. In 1946, after vicious racial violence was directed at black veterans in the South, President Truman appointed a committee on civil rights whose recommendations included terminating segregation in the military. Two years later, against strong opposition from the generals, Truman issued an executive order that eventually put a legal end to armed forces segregation.

In these and other ways the stage was being set for the epic struggle of the civil rights movement. In fewer than a dozen dramatic years, from 1954 to 1965, the South's white supremacy system, solidly in place since the demise of Reconstruction, would be swept away.

The 1954 Brown decision, ordering an end to segregation by law in schools and effectively undermining it elsewhere, was but the beginning of the epic. The next year it moved from the courtroom to the streets. In December 1955, in Montgomery, Alabama, Rosa Parks refused to obey a bus driver's order to vacate her seat. She was promptly arrested and jailed. Within days, as if by spontaneous combustion, some 50,000 Montgomery blacks were refusing to ride the buses. Exactly 381 days later, after selecting as its leader a twenty-six-year-old minister who had recently moved from Atlanta, and receiving the good news that the Supreme Court had applied the Brown decision to bus segregation laws, the Montgomery Bus Boycott ended in resounding victory. Blacks returned to the buses, sitting wherever they pleased, and the next month, January 1957, the Southern Christian Leadership Council (SCLC) was formed.

Loosening the fetters of Jim Crow remained slow, hard, dangerous work, even in the wake of Montgomery. But 1960 saw another spontaneous leap forward, this one across the entire South. On February 1, at a Woolworth lunch counter in Greensboro, North Carolina, four black college students sat down and ordered coffee. Within days there were student sit-ins in other North Carolina cities, and within weeks in states throughout the South. Before the year was over tens of thousands of students, braving mobs, serious injury, and arrest, were ordering coffee in establishments that had never before served blacks. The story became national news, the economic consequences grew increasingly severe, and by the end of the year merchants and municipal officials in nearly a hundred towns and cities had capitulated—"a massive dent in the structure of segregation," Fairclough calls it.

The next year another region-wide effort at last involved a reluctant federal government. On May 4, 1961, under the aegis of the Congress of Racial Equality, thirteen black and white volunteers, among the first "Freedom Riders," boarded Greyhound and Trailways buses for a trip from Washington, D.C., to New Orleans. Their interstate journey would penetrate the Deep South, where the riders intended to ignore segregated bus terminal arrangements.

The predictable happened. Mobs in southern cities accosted and beat the riders, who were then arrested and jailed. Much of this was viewed by avid reporters and photographers following what had become—like the sit-ins—another national story. Eager to remove the "distraction" of the Freedom Rides from the president's agenda, Attorney General Robert Kennedy had his staff draft a petition to the Interstate Commerce Commission. The result, after unprecedented hounding from the Department of Justice, was that the commission banned segregation in interstate travel effective November 1, 1961.

Then, in 1963, from early April to May 10, the SCLC led a successful, multipronged campaign in white supremacy's most impregnable bastion—Birmingham, Alabama. The sit-in technique was employed, as was the boycott (this time of stores), together with mass meetings and marches. Some 3,300 protesters wound up in jail, including Martin Luther King Jr. himself—from whence he wrote his "Letter from Birmingham Jail." At the end, the SCLC had a written agreement with business leaders to desegregate store facilities and to hire black sales clerks.

It wasn't a lot, but it was Birmingham and that meant a lot. It meant, indeed, opening the floodgates to black protest all across the South—a "feverish, fragmented, almost uncontrollable revolution" as *Time* put it—more boycotts, more sit-ins, walking straight into white restaurants, theaters, playgrounds, and parks. More than 20,000 people were arrested, but by the end of the year merchants in more than 300 cities had more or less given in rather than continue to suffer the business disruption the turmoil was causing.

Most important, Birmingham and its aftermath frightened the federal government into entering the civil rights struggle. Bobby Kennedy's hand had been forced, but only briefly, by the Freedom Riders. With that crisis resolved, the administration had lapsed back into standoffishness. Now there was real fear about *Time*'s "almost uncontrollable" revolution. King's letter from the Birmingham jail had warned that unless whites supported the civil rights movement, millions of frustrated blacks might lead the country into a "frightening racial nightmare."

On June 11, 1963, barely a month after the Birmingham accord, President Kennedy spoke to the country on television and asked Congress to enact a sweeping civil rights law. Even though a quarter of a million people marched in Washington on August 28, 1963, and heard King's "I Have a Dream" speech, the bill seemed to be going nowhere in a Congress whose key committees were still dominated by southerners. Three months later Kennedy was assassinated, and Lyndon Johnson made enactment of the civil rights bill one of his priorities, a tribute, he said, to Kennedy. When it finally happened, in July 1964, segregation in public facilities and discrimination in federal programs were barred. If the sit-ins had put a massive dent in Jim Crow, the Civil Rights Act of 1964 came close to totaling it.

Voting rights, however, were barely touched. Most southern blacks still could not negotiate their way past the South's voting registrars. One more round in the movement's battle would be required to truly enfranchise southern blacks. The Mississippi Freedom Summer of 1964 employed the stratagem of bringing hundreds of college students from the North to help with voter registration. That had the potential to capture the attention of the whole country, including the administration. Which it promptly did, when one of the student volunteers and two civil rights workers were arrested, murdered by the Ku Klux Klan, and buried in a dam.

The disappearance of James Chaney, Michael Schwerner, and Andrew Goodman, and the eventual discovery of their bodies, immediately became national news and put enormous pressure on Johnson to provide federal protection for civil rights workers. The president did order FBI director J. Edgar Hoover to solve the murders and hound the Klan, but that didn't prevent a terrible summer during which some thirty-five black churches were burned, over a thousand people arrested, and several more murders committed.

After his landslide defeat of Barry Goldwater in November, and with voting rights in Mississippi and elsewhere a festering sore, Johnson decided he would have to do something more. He told King, however, that enactment of another civil rights measure so soon after the last one would not be easy. For his part, King laid plans for a nonviolent campaign in Dallas County (which included Selma), Alabama, where of 15,000 blacks eligible to vote only some 335 had been able to register.

When a young black man, Jimmie Lee Jackson, was shot to death in one of its marches, the SCLC decided on a fifty-four-mile march from Selma to the Alabama capital in Montgomery, where arch-segregationist Governor George Wallace could be "held responsible" for Jackson's death. Selma's sheriff, Jim Clark, known for using force against blacks and civil rights workers, lived up to his reputation.

The marchers, about 600 of them, got as far as a bridge over the Alabama River. There they were met by Clark and a posse, backed by Wallace's state troopers, some on horseback. When the marchers refused to disperse, they were set upon with clubs, whips, and tear gas, trampled and ridden down in what *Time* called an "orgy of police brutality." By playing out their orgy in front of the press, Wallace and Clark had made one of the South's greatest blunders in its battle against civil rights.

Perhaps it was mostly the television pictures that did it. In any event, the reaction was immediate. Picketers appeared at the White House. Protesters marched in most major cities. Recruits, including clergy from numerous denominations, streamed to Selma for further marches. One of them, Jim Reeb, a Unitarian minister from Boston, was attacked by a group of whites and died from a blow to the head. The National Council of Churches promptly held a rally in Washington to which 15,000 people came.

On March 15, 1965, a week and a day after the orgy on the bridge, Johnson asked a joint session of Congress to pass the voting rights bill he had not, until then, been ready to introduce, electrifying the nation by closing his address with, "We shall overcome." On March 25, marchers finally reached Montgomery under federal court order and the watchful eyes of federal troops. Their ranks had now swelled to 25,000. In August, the voting rights bill passed; with King at his side, Johnson signed it on August 6, 1965. Among other things the new law gave the attorney general power to appoint federal voting registrars in seven states of the Deep South.

The Voting Rights Act at last assured southern blacks of the ballot and the opportunity to translate their numbers into political power. The crowning achievement of the civil rights movement, it has been called. One hundred years after the end of the Civil War, the act finally ended Jim Crow and brought formal democracy to the South.

Especially during its climactic final years, the civil rights movement was a tremendous victory of the human spirit. In a battle that had lasted for generations, an entire people—blacks who had lived, suffered, and many of whom had died under the lash of white supremacy and the badge of black inferiority—had triumphed against pitiless, seemingly insurmountable odds. And they had done so in a struggle in which their principal weapon had been nonviolence. Garry Wills, reviewing a history of the King years, wrote, "There is no time in our country's history of which we can be more proud." One would have thought that blacks all over America would have been bursting with pride at the achievement of their people.

They were not. In the very month the Voting Rights Act became law, the Watts neighborhood in Los Angeles flamed into one of the worst racial conflagrations the country had ever seen. It lasted for six days, spread over forty-five square miles, and destroyed some $200 million worth of property. Thirty-four people were killed, 4,000 arrested. How could two such dramas play in the American theater in the same month?

The answer is that America was two theaters, not one. The century-long civil rights struggle was mostly a drama of the South. The civil rights movement was a southern movement. The story of black Americans outside the South had an entirely different script.

3

Free blacks long had lived in the North, but their numbers were small. When the Civil War ended in 1865, roughly 90 percent of the nation's five million black Americans were in the South. By 1910, when the black population had doubled, nearly 90 percent still lived there. Slavery and Jim Crow were the anvils upon which the life circumstances of nine of every ten black Americans had been forged.

The Great Migration, catalyzed by the Great War, began in earnest in 1915. Exactly half a century later, when the culminating victory of the Voting Rights Act was won, nearly half of black Americans (more than 45 percent) were living outside the South, mostly in the cities. What were the experiences of these blacks who escaped Jim Crow by moving away?

An old folk saying captures the essence of the answer: "The South doesn't care how close a Negro gets just so he doesn't get too high; the North doesn't care how high he gets just so he doesn't get too close." For a long time southern whites didn't worry about blacks getting too close because Jim Crow prevented them from getting too high. In many southern cities, whites lived on broad avenues with their black servants and laborers housed nearby on side streets and in alleys.

Lacking Jim Crow to keep "their" blacks down, whites outside the South were indeed concerned about blacks getting too close, particularly as black numbers swelled. Some 174,000 blacks departed the South in the last decade of the nineteenth century, another 197,000 during the first ten years of the twentieth. With the start of the first wave of the Great Migration, the numbers in the next decade grew to 525,000, followed by 877,000 more between 1920 and 1930. The Depression staunched the flow somewhat, but the river swelled to a flood with the onset of World War II. In the second wave of the Great Migration, which lasted through the 1960s, some five million black Americans spilled from the South into the cities of the Northeast, Midwest, West, and border states.

The overall numbers do not reveal what the migration meant for individual cities. In the Northeast and Midwest, in just the two decades of the 1940s and 1950s—after, that is, the already huge growth of the preceding half century—the black population of New York City increased 137 percent, of Chicago 193 percent, of Buffalo 301 percent, of Milwaukee 607 percent. In the West, the Los Angeles increase was 425 percent, Seattle's 592 percent, San Diego's 721 percent, San Francisco's 1,425 percent. In border states, Baltimore's increase was 96 percent, Dallas's 156 percent. The sheer numbers, said sociologist Philip Hauser, "made the Negro in-migratory stream relatively unassimilable—economically, socially and politically."

The careful, "relatively unassimilable" language of the social scientist was hardly adequate for whites in the "receiving" cities. To them, the enormous inflow of black families was a black tide that threatened to engulf them, a "black plague," as a Philadelphian put it. Their reaction was as reflexive as that of a bear protecting her cubs. It was displayed by women as well as men, by the middle class as well as by the working class, in all sections of the nation. It was not confined to one period or decade or generation, but persisted throughout the entire duration of the white supremacy war in the South.

There is a considerable literature about exactly how whites outside the South tried to prevent blacks from getting too close. One of the most recent additions is a book by Stephen Grant Meyer, *As Long As They Don't Move Next Door.* (The title comes from a line in a Phil Ochs song: "I love Puerto Ricans and Negroes / As long as they don't move next door.") A long essay about Meyer's book by a law professor, Leonard Rubinowitz, and his coauthor, Imani Perry, focused on violence and the criminal law aspects of what whites did. Taken together, Meyer and Rubinowitz-Perry describe an unremitting struggle outside the South every bit as brutal as the white supremacy one inside it.

Violence wasn't the only weapon. For a time racial zoning—carving up a city by law into black and white zones—was in vogue. After the Supreme Court held that unconstitutional in 1917, although it was decades before the laws were everywhere abandoned, racial covenants that prohibited selling real estate to blacks (and other "undesirables," such as Jews) came into widespread use. In 1948 the Supreme Court finally decided that the covenants couldn't be enforced by courts, but again that didn't stop their continued use for years.

Undergirding these techniques of the law were the segregationist business practices of real estate salespeople. Their national trade organization actually made it a breach of ethics to allow the "introduction" of blacks into a white neighborhood. A model law, drafted by the association and adopted by thirty-two states, authorized state officials to revoke the license of any real estate agent who breached the ethics code. Banks and other lenders followed suit and denied loans to blacks seeking to buy in white neighborhoods.

The result was a dual housing market, one for blacks within their segregated confines, one for whites outside. As more migrants poured into the black ghettos, the only options for most were to double up, triple up, and quadruple up in apartments and homes that were subdivided into ever smaller compartments. Prices in the blacks' market rose compared to those for whites. And with demand so great, landlords didn't have to spend money on maintenance and repair. Where they could find it, blacks paid more for their housing than whites, and for their money they got poor housing in poor neighborhoods. A description of Chicago's black ghetto referred to "decaying buildings, leaking roofs, doors without hinges, broken windows, unsanitary plumbing [and] rotting floors."

Hemmed in as they were, under steadily worsening conditions, blacks exerted enormous pressure on adjacent white neighborhoods, building by building, block by block. Escape from intolerable conditions was the blacks' motivation. Floodgates opening was what whites saw. Under these circumstances, it was perhaps predictable that, from the end of Reconstruction through the entirety of the southern white supremacy struggle, violence—a readiness to use it, promptly and viciously—became a defining characteristic of the struggle outside the South to prevent blacks from getting too close.

Resistance to blacks daring to move beyond the ghetto commonly occurred, in Meyer's phrase, as "thousands of small acts of terrorism." What Meyer means is that a burning cross on the lawn, a brick through a window, a Molotov cocktail on the roof, are "small" when placed or thrown by individuals or small groups. The devastation wrought by such acts—psychological as well as physical—obviously did not depend on the numbers of the perpetrators.

Some particulars, mostly from Meyer's account, will help show what the "thousands of small acts" were like.

1910   In Baltimore, whites broke windows in one black's home, tarred the marble front steps of another, stoned a third.

1917   In Kansas City, Missouri, when a first bomb failed to drive out a black homeowner, a second bomb was promptly set off.

1921   In Brooklyn, a note mailed to a black who had moved into a white neighborhood read simply, "Unless you vacate and move, you and members of your black family will be killed."

1924   On Staten Island, a black family's move into a white neighborhood was delayed because fire insurance was repeatedly canceled. Two days after the family finally did move, the windows of the house were methodically smashed in the middle of the night.

1929   In Detroit, a bomb destroyed a black apartment house, leaving nine families homeless.

1944   In Chicago, a black woman purchased a home two blocks outside the ghetto. Returning the next day she found the building totally razed. Little remained but the foundation.

1945   In Fontana, California, whites ordered a new black homeowner to abandon his home. Shortly after his refusal, neighbors reported hearing an explosion and seeing "blobs of fire" around the home. The family fled with their clothes ablaze. (The wife and young children died almost immediately, the husband two weeks later.)

1949   In Chicago, in front of an apartment building into which a black family had moved, whites threw stones, smashed windows, and chanted, "Burn the black bastard out." With a flaming rag a fire was then started that destroyed almost the entire building.

1951   In Cicero, Illinois, a black army veteran tried to move his wife and family into the apartment they had rented. A mob stormed the apartment and threw furniture out the third-story window. The next day the entire building was gutted by a firebomb.

1953   In Los Angeles, a black homeowner came home from work one night to find his house flooded by a garden hose pushed through the mail slot.

1962   In Boston, the public housing authority rented an apartment in a white neighborhood to a lone, elderly black woman. Her apartment was stoned on two successive nights, even before she had finished moving in.

In addition to threats, beatings, and shootings directed at individuals, Rubinowitz and Perry summarized the small acts against property from the experience of Boston in the early 1960s: "damaged cars, ignited papers thrust under apartment doors, fecal material at [blacks'] doorways, racial epithets on their doors, . . . rocks, bricks, bottles, and other debris thrown through their windows, . . . Molotov cocktails, arson, and shootings."

If their numbers failed to match the "thousands of small acts," mobs and riots made up for it in ferocity and deadliness. Houses were ransacked or burned. Rampaging bands of whites attacked, beat, and shot blacks. The search for living space beyond the ghetto wasn't always the trigger, but the ghetto was always the gunpowder—black anger about the conditions and white insistence that blacks stay put. By 1900, New York City had had a full-fledged race riot. In the ensuing six and a half decades what happened in New York was repeated many times outside the South, as a few examples will show.

In Chicago's 1919 riot, some 38 people were killed, 537 injured, more than 1,000 rendered homeless, and entire blocks of the Black Belt left in ruins.

In Tulsa, in 1921, scores of blacks were killed, countless injured, and thirty-four square blocks of black Tulsa reduced to rubble by a white mob of thousands, many deputized by the local police.

In Detroit, in 1925, a series of white mobs ranging from 1,000 to 4,000 "confronted" various black families attempting to move into white blocks. On one occasion nearly 10,000 gathered to celebrate a "victory" by burning crosses. In a nine-month period police shot 55 blacks, 20 fatally.

In Chicago, in 1949, a false rumor that a black family had moved into a white block quickly generated a mob of almost 10,000 that for four days stoned property and brutally beat "strangers," unknown whites and blacks who had happened by the area.

In Cicero, Illinois, in 1951, a mob estimated at 4,000, protesting a black move-in, battled some 450 National Guardsmen and 200 police for four days.

From 1953 to 1957 whites in Chicago resisted the entry of black families into Trumbull Park Homes, a public housing project on Chicago's Far South Side. Crowds sometimes grew to an estimated 2,000, police to 750. During one particularly difficult twenty-four-hour period nearly 1,000 police were on Trumbull Park duty. Almost four years after the disturbances had begun, aerial bombs were still exploding almost nightly, and police had a special 50-man detail assigned to the project.

Fairclough observed that in the southern war to preserve white supremacy, whites acted with virtual impunity. Rarely did they have to worry about the police or the law. The same "ground rules" prevailed in the war to preserve white neighborhoods outside the South. Illustrative is what two historians say about law enforcement at Trumbull Park Homes. One refers to the beating of a black and vandalism "under the steady but unconcerned gaze of the police." The other tells us that most of those arrested were charged with disorderly conduct and fined five or ten dollars.

Summarizing the criminal law aspects of this war, Rubinowitz and Perry say that the criminal justice system "did little to prevent, pursue, prosecute, or punish," that the police made "few efforts" to arrest white perpetrators, that prosecutors prosecuted "very few" of those arrested, that they secured "still fewer" convictions, and that the rare punishment reflected the courts' view that the offenses were of a "trivial nature." One may conclude that if southern lynchings were state-sanctioned events, and if southern whites could engage in criminal acts with virtual impunity, the thousands of small acts and the mob actions outside the South had like sanction and impunity.

4

Describing how whites confined blacks to ghettos does not reveal what it means to be a black ghetto dweller. For that Chuck and I turned to other sources.

The great black intellectual leader W. E. B. DuBois used the metaphor of a dark cave. Looking out from inside, DuBois wrote, one sees the world passing and speaks to it of how the "entombed souls" are hindered in their natural movement and development, and how their release from their prison would help not only the prisoners themselves but all the world.

The talk is courteous and logical, but the prisoners notice that the passing throng either does not turn its head, or merely glances at them and walks on. Gradually the prisoners realize that the outsiders do not hear, that a thick sheet of invisible glass stands between them and the world. The prisoners get excited, talk more loudly, gesticulate. Some of the passing world stop in curiosity, then laugh and move on. They either do not hear, or hear but dimly and do not understand.

Eventually, the prisoners become hysterical, screaming and hurling themselves against the glass, hardly realizing in their bewilderment that they are unheard, and that their "antics" may seem funny to those outside. Here and there they may even break through in blood and disfigurement. When that happens they find themselves "faced by a horrified, implacable, and quite overwhelming mob of people frightened for their own very existence."

On the centennial of the Emancipation Proclamation in 1963 came James Baldwin's national best seller, *The Fire Next Time*. The book consisted of two "letters" to James, Baldwin's nephew and namesake. You were "set down in a ghetto," Baldwin writes James, "because you were black and *for no other reason*," born into a society in which your countrymen "have destroyed and are destroying hundreds of thousands of lives and do not know it and do not want to know it." They have spelled out with brutal clarity that you are a "worthless human being." Your grandfather, Baldwin adds, who never saw you, was defeated long before he died because, "at the bottom of his heart, he really believed what white people said about him."

In 1965, Kenneth B. Clark published *Dark Ghetto*, a book that soon achieved the status of a classic. Clark had served as a research associate on the *American Dilemma* project, Gunnar Myrdal's massive 1945 study of blacks in America, and Myrdal returned the favor by contributing a foreword to Clark's book. The foreword described *Dark Ghetto* as another effort by one of the DuBois cave dwellers to speak so loudly, though calmly, that their voices would pierce the invisible glass and make known the conditions of American color caste.

In an early chapter, "The Invisible Wall," Clark describes both the "objective" and "subjective" dimensions of the ghetto. The objective are bad housing, high infant mortality, crime, disease, and the like. The subjective are resentment, hostility, despair, apathy, self-deprecation, and its "ironic companion," compensatory grandiose behavior. Collectively, they comprise a "pervasive pathology."

The remainder of *Dark Ghetto* describes and explains each ghetto dimension, including how "the pathologies of the ghetto community perpetuate themselves through cumulative ugliness, deterioration, and isolation and strengthen the Negro's sense of worthlessness, giving testimony to his impotence." *Dark Ghetto* can be read as an explanation of how and why the black ghetto gives birth to the sense of impotence and worthlessness. The explanation does not make for pleasant reading.

Underlying the familiar symptoms—unemployment, bad schools, crime, drug addiction, alcoholism, family instability, illegitimacy, illness, early death—are hatred, despair, and corrosion of personality, a "human debasement [that] can only be comprehended as a consequence of the society which spawns it." The spawning society, Clark writes, is "institutionalized pathology," chronic and self-perpetuating. What happens to its residents—who come to doubt their own worth and eventually to believe in their own inferiority—is to be understood as symptomatic of the "contagious sickness of the community itself." From these seeds of a "pernicious self- and group-hatred" grow constricted lives that become "purposeless" and "irrelevant."

✦   ✦   ✦   ✦   ✦

In January 1966, as Baron, Mikva, Chuck, and I downed hot pizza and fancied challenging the CHA's ghettos, black slavery in America had been defunct for over a hundred years. Yet with little exaggeration one might say that, in the same hundred years, Americans had been treating blacks seeking housing outside the ghetto not much better than, in Vladimir's nonsense rhyme, cook treated the dog who sought a crust of bread. The CHA's public housing ghettos were part of a relentlessly somber history.

CHAPTER TWO

ECSTASY AND SOBRIETY

To-morrow everything will be better.

—Vladimir (*Waiting for Godot*)

1

For six months Chuck and I worked on the facts and the law. But not alone. The CHA was a bigger fish than the Waukegan School Board, and we needed help. We enlisted recruits.

First was Milton Shadur, a partner in the firm formerly called Goldberg, Devoe and Brussell. The Goldberg name was now gone because a few years earlier President John Kennedy had appointed Arthur Goldberg to the Supreme Court. Abraham Brussell, Goldberg's partner, had been a fine state court judge. Milt was of their stripe, brilliant, efficient, hardworking (each morning he boarded a 5:41 A.M. train to work). Years later, in the tradition of his firm, Milt would be appointed a federal district court judge.

Next came Bernard Weisberg, a shining light in a good-sized Chicago law firm but best known for two other activities. One was his devotion to the ACLU, for which he handled a number of important cases. The other was his voracious reading. Wherever he went, Bernie would carry a book. A few years earlier he had joined my brother-in-law and me in a whitewater rafting trip down the Green River in Utah. I've never forgotten the image of Bernie, humped at the aft end of the small raft, floating through magical copper and gold canyon country with his nose buried in a paperbound copy of Dostoyevsky's *The Idiot*.

Our final recruit was Merrill Freed, a classmate of mine in law school, also then practicing with a Chicago firm. Merrill was deceptively quiet, with a steel-trap mind. He had been number one when the grades were posted after our first law-school year. That prompted my hard-to-please father to ask, only half in jest, what had gone wrong when I told him I was number two. What I didn't tell him was that I was a distant second to Merrill, whose analytical skills seemed to put him in a separate rank from the rest of the class.

Chuck was the only one of our starting quintet in a struggle with the practice of law. Milt, Bernie, Merrill, and I had each had the good fortune to sign on with highly regarded firms, and we were all doing well. Chuck, in a firm with a lesser reputation, was not having the satisfactions the rest of us were enjoying. In an unthinkable way I was later to learn that our pro bono work was the only part of his professional life that gave Chuck much pleasure.

2

To begin gathering the facts, Chuck and I arranged for a long visit in his book-strewn Urban League office with the wiry, bespectacled Baron, who delivered the information we absorbed that day with constant gesticulation and great passion. Sometimes Chuck and I felt like students in a lecture hall, sometimes like the audience in a theater.

Baron showed us an August 1965 letter from the West Side Federation, the group he had mentioned at Edwardo's, to Robert C. Weaver, the federal government's top housing official. The letter asked Weaver to disapprove the CHA's latest group of proposed sites, pointing to the "pervasive pattern" of segregation in CHA projects—"There exists no ascertainable reason why the [new] sites were selected in the Negro ghetto." Choosing those sites, the letter argued, amounted to "discrimination" under Title VI of the 1964 Civil Rights Act, which barred federal funding of racially discriminatory programs.

Next Baron laid on the table the reply to the federation's letter— seven single-spaced pages from Marie McGuire, commissioner of the Public Housing Administration. The gist of the government's response was that most CHA applicants wanted to live in black neighborhoods, as the "location preferences" in their applications showed. The CHA's proposed sites therefore complied with federal rules on site selection. In typically opaque government prose the rules said the idea was to select "from among otherwise available and suitable sites those which will afford the greatest acceptability to eligible applicants."

Baron pointed one of his bony fingers at a key sentence in McGuire's letter: "We are also advised that sites other than in the south or west side [the black ghetto areas], if proposed for regular family housing, invariably encounter sufficient objection in the [City] Council to preclude Council approval." In other words, because Chicago's aldermen—whose approval was required by state law—refused to agree to locations outside the ghetto, nonghetto sites were not "otherwise available." Therefore, the McGuire letter implicitly asserted, there was no violation of law.

Raising his voice, Baron honed in on his key point. McGuire's reasoning would encourage other state and local governments to impose local approval requirements on federal programs. Under the McGuire theory, agencies receiving federal funds would not have to comply with Title VI because they would be acting under orders from other local bodies not themselves receiving federal money, and therefore not subject to the law. That stratagem—Baron concluded his oration with a flourish— would neutralize Title VI; federal funds would continue to flow to local agencies whose practices reinforced segregation.

"Read, read," Baron admonished (his degree was in history) as Chuck and I said our good-byes. We did, and slowly filled the vast void of what we didn't know about this thing called public housing.

Public housing began in the Great Depression. It was built by local agencies, called "authorities," with federal funds under federal oversight. Its dual purpose at the outset was to provide badly needed jobs and to serve as a way station for working families down on their luck. Families on welfare, or with social problems or criminal records, were not accepted. When World War II came along, public housing began to serve factory ("war") workers and, for a few postwar years, returning veterans and their families.

Like the America of those years, public housing was racially segregated. Of the ten early Chicago developments, four were for whites in white areas, four for blacks in black areas, and two were intended for mixed occupancy. These arrangements were prescribed by the federal government's "neighborhood composition rule"—the racial occupancy of a public housing development should mirror the racial composition of the host area. In Chicago, "host area" usually meant inside the black ghetto, hence black, or outside, hence white.

Chicago's ghetto grew rapidly during the first wave of the Great Migration of blacks from the South, roughly from 1890 to 1930. It then grew even more quickly after the Great Depression, as southern blacks streamed to the wartime factories of the North and West. When cotton picking was mechanized in the early 1940s, the plantations of the South no longer needed large numbers of black workers (each mechanized picker did the work of fifty people), and the streams became torrents. By 1950 Chicago's black population had more than doubled from its 1930 level, leaping from 234,000 to 490,000.

From the earliest days of the Great Migration, fabled, job-rich Chicago was a natural destination out of the Jim Crow South. During the labor shortage years of World War I, Chicago stockyards and meat packing plants had hired agents to recruit strong-backed laborers from the cotton fields. The country's leading black newspaper, the *Chicago Defender,* exhorted southern blacks to come to Chicago not only to make money but also to gain the legal benefits of citizenship denied them in the South. In one tale about the migration, after their trains crossed the Ohio River the migrants "signalzed the event by kissing the ground and holding prayer services."

As they quickly learned, Chicago was not exactly the promised land the migrants had dreamed of. Its residential segregation practices—including firebombings and riots—were as rigid and ubiquitous as the South's Jim Crow. The result was that ghetto borders on Chicago's South and West Sides were sharp and clear. Within them lived a population crammed to the bursting point into dilapidated slum tenements.

At the end of World War II, white Americans too faced a severe housing shortage. After much controversy, in part because of its racial implications, in 1949 Congress passed a housing act that set a national goal of "a decent home and a suitable living environment" for every American family, and authorized 810,000 units of public housing to be built over six years. In the early 1950s, therefore, public housing began to sprout in cities and towns across the country. Because it helped keep Chicago's burgeoning black ghetto population from spilling into white neighborhoods, most of Chicago's new public housing was slated to replace black slums. The black ghetto quickly became public housing's location of choice.

The story of that choice is one of the most fateful in the history of a storied city. For the first two years of the new public housing program the federal government allotted 21,000 units to Chicago, more than to any other city. The CHA's chairman was Robert Taylor, an African American who managed a large apartment building for the Julius Rosenwald Foundation. (Hoping to attract private philanthropy to the black housing problem, Rosenwald had in 1929 built the model private housing project in the South Side ghetto.) Taylor had studied architecture at Howard University and graduated from the University of Illinois. He was also the secretary-treasurer of a savings and loan association that encouraged black homeownership. He wanted to use Chicago's public housing allocation to provide—at long last—some decent housing for slum-dwelling blacks outside their ghetto confines.

So did Elizabeth Wood, the CHA's staff director. Before her appointment at the CHA's founding in 1937, Wood had received degrees in English literature from the University of Michigan and then taught at Vassar College. The daughter of a lay missionary, she was frequently described as "progressive." To Wood and Taylor, the task of developing 21,000 badly needed public housing apartments in Chicago was not just a technical challenge but a social opportunity. They prepared a list of sites for the new housing consisting mostly of vacant parcels in the City's outlying—white—areas.

In October 1949, Taylor asked Mayor Martin Kennelly to send the CHA's proposed sites to the city council with a strong endorsement. Kennelly had been elected in 1947 to succeed Chicago's longtime political boss, Edward J. Kelly. Under the powerful Kelly the CHA had been able to build its projects where it chose (and Kelly approved). In the immediate aftermath of World War II, Kelly had actually supported Taylor and Wood in their controversial and only partly successful effort to house some returning black veterans temporarily on government-owned land in outlying white areas. Then, however, Kelly had been forced to retire, mostly because of a corruption scandal but also partly because of his support of Taylor and Wood.

Kennelly was a "reform" businessman with no political experience and little influence with the city council. Relatively docile under Kelly but feeling their oats as he departed, Chicago aldermen were not about to allow an independent housing agency—which had never worked closely with them but had relied instead on Kelly's dominating power—to have the final word on bringing public housing into their wards. In 1949, the powerful chairman of the city council's Housing Committee, William Lancaster, arranged for the state legislature to enact a law that gave the Council power to approve—and disapprove—CHA's purchases of real estate. Unsympathetic to Taylor, Wood, and their policies, the legislature passed the new law without a dissenting vote. Taylor later said he knew the battle to distribute public housing throughout the city was lost the moment the legislature acted.

Kennelly—who was not supportive of either public housing or racial integration—rebuffed Taylor and sent the CHA's proposed sites to the council without his endorsement, saying only that it was an important matter that deserved prompt attention. After four days of hearings in February 1950—attended by hundreds of whites in raucous opposition—the Housing Committee recommended only two of the CHA's proposed sites, both extensions of existing ghetto projects. Lancaster and Alderman John J. Duffy, chair of the council's Finance Committee, then took matters into their own hands and, after informal meetings with key colleagues, proposed the "Duffy-Lancaster compromise." The so-called compromise provided for 10,000 units inside the ghetto but only 2,000 outside. Since it would displace almost as many families—nearly all black—as units it would build, Duffy-Lancaster would add fewer than 100 net units to the housing supply, doing virtually nothing to alleviate the shortage of decent housing for blacks.

Taylor and the other commissioners resisted for weeks, but came under increasing pressure to accept Duffy-Lancaster. As time dragged on, concern grew that the city council might not approve any new public housing at all. Washington, fearful of losing its entire Chicago program, was no help. The *Chicago Sun-Times*, which had supported the CHA in the early stages of the controversy, now called for acceptance of what was viewed as the council's final "offer."

Finally, in June 1950, after minor tinkering with Duffy-Lancaster, Taylor and all the other commissioners save one succumbed. Three months after the city council gave the compromise its final approval, a dejected Taylor resigned. When his term expired, the one dissenting commissioner was not reappointed by Kennelly. In the ensuing years, a number of the CHA's most infamous projects were built on the approved ghetto sites. Of the five approved nonghetto sites, only three were ultimately used, and two of these were enlargements of existing projects. The ghetto die on the location of Chicago's public housing had been cast.

Chicago's prewar public housing was low-rise, mostly two-story row houses. In the postwar years, the ideas of the Swiss architect Le Corbusier led to a radical change. Le Corbusier's vision for urban living was a "vertical garden city" of blocks of apartments stacked atop one another, surrounded by parkland. A few low-rise developments would still be built in Chicago in the early postwar years. But the Le Corbusier vision was beginning to dominate much of the architectural world, including the design of Chicago's public housing.

Following approval of Duffy-Lancaster, the CHA soon began building towers of fourteen and fifteen stories. Because so many of the new sites were adjacent to existing ghetto projects, many of the new towers were "extensions"—new projects cheek-by-jowl with old ones. Chicago's very first public housing development, the Jane Addams Houses, had about 1,000 apartments. After two extensions nearly doubled its size, another 1,200 units brought the total to some 3,000 apartments spread over twenty-six city blocks. Henry Horner Homes, completed in 1957, had 920 apartments in nine elevator buildings. Four years later an extension added 736 more apartments in seven elevator buildings. In the early 1960s the CHA built Robert Taylor Homes, the world's largest public housing development, with 4,400 apartments in twenty-eight identical sixteen-story buildings.

By the time Taylor was being planned, the CHA had grown skittish about cramming families with many children into Le Corbusier towers. But the Eisenhower administration refused to raise public housing cost ceilings. Only if the CHA used less expensive vacant land would low-rise construction comply. That, however, would have meant reopening Duffy-

Lancaster and trying once again for sites in white neighborhoods. When the alternatives came down to high-rises in black neighborhoods or low-rises in white, there was never any doubt about which would be pursued.

Duffy-Lancaster's slum sites also required an important change in public housing tenancy. Slums could not be cleared without displacing slum dwellers, many of whom were one-parent families on welfare. Because public housing was so directly and visibly displacing them from their tenement homes, welfare and "social problem" families could not be excluded from the replacement housing. No longer a temporary way station for working families hurt by the Depression, Chicago public housing was becoming the landlord for hard-core poverty families.

Housing only poor, black tenants in the enormous projects in black slum neighborhoods was a prescription for disaster. Slum tenements were being replaced with high-rise ghettos. In 1958, Harrison Salisbury of the *New York Times,* fresh from years of assignments in Russia, described what with astonished eyes he saw in New York City's public housing—

> the broken windows, the missing light bulbs, the plaster cracking from the walls, the pilfered hardware, the cold, drafty corridors, the doors on sagging hinges, the acid smell of sweat and cabbage, the ragged children, the plaintive women, the playgrounds that are seas of muddy clay, the bruised and battered trees, the ragged clumps of grass, the planned absence of art, beauty or taste, the gigantic masses of brick, of concrete, of asphalt, the inhuman genius with which our know-how has been perverted to create human cesspools worse than those of yesterday.

Not long after Taylor Homes opened, an anonymous resident supplied a tenant perspective: "We live stacked on top of one another with no elbow room. Danger is all around. There's little privacy or peace and no quiet. And the world looks on all of us as project rats, living on a reservation like untouchables."

3

With Baron's help it didn't take long to assemble these facts about the CHA's history. Soon we learned that more ghetto projects were being proposed for 1965 and 1966. It was time to get moving. We asked Baron to have the Urban League find us some plaintiffs. We needed blacks who lived in public housing (some from the waiting list would be nice too) who were being forced to live in black neighborhoods but would have preferred to go elsewhere.

Baron said the Urban League would, and it did—Odell Jones, Doreatha Crenchaw, Dorothy Gautreaux, Robert Fairfax, Eva Rodgers, James Rodgers. Chuck or I interviewed them all, and they met our criteria and were willing to sign on. We would file the case as a "class action" on behalf of all CHA tenants and applicants, but it was important to have "named representatives" who would stand up under courtroom questioning.

Through the first half of 1966, meeting around the gleaming wood conference table in the Schiff offices, our quintet of Shadur, Weisberg, Freed, Markels, and I wrestled with turning our accumulating information and ideas into a complaint we would file in court. At the same time the duo of Markels and Polikoff had some wrestling to do in Waukegan.

The Tometz trial lasted five days, each one avidly reported on the front pages of the *Waukegan News Sun*. Barbara permitted the children—Deborah, 11, Daniel, 9, and Joanie, 5—to skip school, and they made the drive to Waukegan each day to form a silent cheering section in the courtroom. Deborah and Daniel passed notes back and forth to record their acerbic comments on the mental capacity of the school board witnesses. Our experts, Professors George Foster of the University of Wisconsin and Robert Crain of the University of Chicago, had stayed in our house for two days before the trial, so our family had gotten to know them pretty well. "Foster and Crain, Foster and Crain," became Joanie's newest refrain.

On the witness stand the Waukegan school superintendent, Dr. H. R. McCall, could not give a credible explanation for his failure to redraw the Whittier area boundary lines. It soon became evident that the real reason was a defiant school board that Dr. McCall, a kindly gentleman on the eve of retirement, was unwilling to oppose. With charts, maps, and statistics, Foster and Crain showed that boundary changes could easily be made. And so, at the end of July, Judge Parker ordered a modification of boundaries. Chuck and I were ecstatic. We had won! The CHA had better watch out!

Yet something should have warned us not to blow trumpets prematurely. Then again, maybe it was just as well we didn't then know what was to come. In an eerie foreshadowing of the tortuous path the CHA case was to follow, the victory in Waukegan turned out to be a skirmish, not the decisive battle. The school board appealed to the Illinois Supreme Court, insisting that to redraw school boundaries for racial reasons would violate the American way, specifically the United States and Illinois Constitutions. Our system, they argued, required government to be color-blind. We lost by a 5–2 vote.

Miraculously, however, we won in a rehearing by 4–3. The explanation for the "miracle" was that Chuck and I were able to persuade a goodly number of organizations to file friend-of-the-court statements to support our rehearing request. After the briefs were filed, two of the supreme court judges flip-flopped. The court then returned the case to Judge Parker, who saw to it that his boundary change order was carried out. Shirley Tometz was at last vindicated.

But by then it was the summer of 1968. Two full school years had been consumed by the supreme court appeal. Three years had elapsed since the filing of the Tometz case. There is a saying that the mills of justice grind "exceeding slow." Chuck and I felt that Waukegan illustrated the adage. We did not then remotely imagine how the CHA case would become an archetypal example of grinding "exceeding slow."

4

The first half of 1966 was a busy time for yet another reason— Martin Luther King Jr. came to town to march for what was turning out to be the most difficult civil rights battle of all, "open housing."

America entered World War II with rigid racial segregation as its race relations norm. When I joined the navy in January 1945 as a seventeen-year-old volunteer, I became part of a firmly segregated military. I am not proud that I did not even question the fact that the only blacks I encountered in my service experience were busboys. Like the furniture in the room, segregation of blacks was an accepted part of the environment for myself and many Americans.

Incremental change began toward the end of the war and accelerated in the postwar years as the civil rights movement gained steam. But not in housing. As the flow of whites to the suburbs increased, black ghettos in the cities remained concentrated, accommodating their swelling populations by expanding at their edges into adjacent white neighborhoods. In 1965, when Lyndon Johnson, the nation's first southern president in a century, was intoning, "We shall overcome," the National Committee Against Discrimination in Housing, a leading civil rights organization, said:

> Today, in the very eye of the storm of the Negro revolution the ghetto stands—largely unassailed—as the rock upon which rests segregated living patterns which pervade and vitiate almost every phase of Negro life and Negro-white relationships.

The persistent intractability of housing segregation in the midst of the civil rights gains of the 1950s and early 1960s was dramatically—and poignantly—highlighted by what happened to King in Chicago in 1966 and 1967.

The Watts riot in Los Angeles in August 1965—the worst race riot in the nation since Detroit in 1943—was seminal in King's thought. As he viewed the still-smoldering embers, King came to believe that the plight of millions of black Americans confined in big city ghettos in the North and West was as pressing as the travail of southern blacks. The next major campaign of the Southern Christian Leadership Conference should bring the strategy of nonviolent change to the North.

At about the same time Al Raby, a young high school teacher turned activist, began working hard to lure King and the SCLC to Chicago. Lean, intense, wholly dedicated to his cause, Raby had become the leader of a Chicago civil rights movement focused on public education. Under arrogant, Jim Crowish school superintendent Benjamin Willis, who had always peremptorily brushed aside black demands for higher-quality, less-segregated public schools, Chicago school segregation was a twin of Chicago housing segregation. Faced with severe overcrowding in black ghetto schools, Willis had rejected the course of integrating nearby, sometimes half-empty, white schools. Instead, he put black students on double shifts, eight to noon and noon to four, frequently plunking "Willis Wagons"—trailers converted to temporary classrooms—on their playgrounds.

Yet after several years of struggle, Raby's group, the Coordinating Council of Community Organizations (CCCO), could point to no tangible success. Three school boycotts had produced impressive totals of stay-at-home students. But the numbers for the third, in June 1965, were fewer than half those for the first, twenty months earlier. Dozens of CCCO marches to city hall, some led by the popular comedian Dick Gregory, had brought no change.

In July 1965, Raby filed with the U.S. Office of Education a well-documented complaint charging the Chicago School Board with operating segregated schools. The complaint generated a threat from the U.S. commissioner of education, Francis Keppel, to cut off federal funds to Chicago schools if remedial steps were not taken. Yet a single telephone call from Mayor Daley to President Johnson undid all Raby's hard work. When the irate Daley made his views known, Johnson saw to it that the fund cut-off threat was withdrawn and that Keppel was transferred to a different job—assistant secretary "in charge of nothing," as Keppel put it.

Raby also feared that his troops were weakening. He joked that he was down to fourteen marchers and a dog. With the passion the former schoolteacher had learned to meld with his logic, and with help from his mentor, Edwin "Bill" Berry, head of the Chicago Urban League, Raby marshaled the arguments to bring the SCLC to Chicago.

King didn't need much persuading. Chicago was the capital of northern segregation; King believed that if he and the SCLC could take on Chicago and win, they could succeed anywhere. With near-total power possessed by its dominating mayor, Chicago was unique among northern cities. If Daley could be brought around, things would get done.

The decision was not unanimous. Although James Bevel, one of King's aides, argued that "Black Chicago *is* Mississippi moved north a few hundred miles," Bayard Rustin, the civil rights theoretician, cautioned King that he was underestimating Daley and the Chicago difficulties. "You don't know what Chicago is like . . . You're going to get wiped out." Andrew Young, another King aide, was worried about unfinished business in the South and the SCLC's limited resources. But King was still smarting from his August tour of Watts. He was also savoring the national support for the civil rights movement generated by the Selma to Montgomery voting rights marches in early 1965. The question soon became when and how, not whether, the SCLC would take on Chicago.

King came north in October 1965 for a three-day planning meeting with SCLC and CCCO staff. An alliance was formalized. The Chicago

Freedom Movement was chosen as the name, and King and Raby would be cochairs. Soon King established a residence in a North Lawndale ghetto apartment, began to visit Chicago frequently, and with his aides—Jesse Jackson as well as Bevel, Young, and others—began preparing to confront Chicago and Richard J. Daley.

There was, of course, the need to select the right issue. By now Willis had retired, depriving Raby of his symbolic schools enemy. Slums, another candidate ("I'm not leading any campaign against Mayor Daley. I'm leading a campaign against slums," King had announced), was ultimately rejected. The causes and cures for slums were complex, and the shrewd Daley was already fashioning a slum-buster image for himself with well-publicized strikes against building code violations and rats.

After considerable discussion, in June 1966 "open housing" became the Freedom Movement's issue—a good choice. It was simple; a family should be able to live anywhere it could afford to rent or buy. It was important; if blacks could move outside the ghetto, their circumstances would improve. It was something Daley could act on directly; he could take away the licenses of real estate brokers who violated Chicago's Fair Housing Ordinance. And it lent itself to action; marches could target both segregated neighborhoods and the offices of brokers who refused to serve blacks. By the summer of 1966, King, Raby, and the Chicago Freedom Movement were ready to fight for "open housing" in Chicago.

King was half right about Daley; the mayor was truly the man in charge in Chicago. But "bringing Daley around" on open housing was another matter. Richard J. Daley had been sworn in as mayor of Chicago in April 1955. Until his death in December 1976 he ruled as the most powerful of the nation's big-city chiefs, supported eventually even by Chicago's Republican establishment and its newspaper, the *Chicago Tribune.* Though he had to weather some difficult moments, Daley was indisputably the fount of power in Chicago by the time King came to town.

Daley had been born in Chicago's working-class Bridgeport neighborhood, about four miles southwest of the Loop. He lived there still, in a pink bungalow not far from his birthplace. Bridgeport was commonly thought of as Irish, but Germans, Italians, Lithuanians, and Poles lived there as well. No blacks. That was the way things were when Daley grew up, and that was the way they stayed as the ambitious mayor-to-be steadily climbed the ladder of the Chicago Democratic machine.

In 1956, the year after Daley reached the top rung, Eleanor Roosevelt had suggested that to set an example for the rest of the nation, especially the South, northern cities might desegregate. Academics had thoroughly documented Chicago's black ghetto, and most black Chicagoans who valued life and limb had learned its boundaries. Yet Daley's next-day response to Roosevelt's suggestion was, "We believe that we do not have segregation in Chicago." Seven years later, after Little Rock and Selma, with the South undergoing painful change and rumblings beginning in some northern cities, Daley's views were unchanged. "There are no ghettos in Chicago," he told the NAACP in 1963.

Mike Royko, Chicago's much-beloved journalist and author of a Daley biography, *Boss,* thought that Daley might have believed what he said:

> To Daley, the blacks were merely going through the same onward and upward process of all other ethnic groups, huddling together and waiting for their chance to move up the American ladder. The Irish had done it and so had the other European groups. They put in their time in rickety neighborhoods then moved on. Daley was a firm believer in the bootstrap theory.

Political considerations—as always with Daley—were also at play. In the concentrated ghetto, the black vote could be controlled. If open housing should come to pass, black voters would be dispersed, and whites, with blacks entering their neighborhoods, would be enraged. As one observer put it, "Neighborhood racial transition was the only powerful force at work in the city that posed a real threat to the machine."

Whatever Daley's precise feelings and calculations may have been, his conduct on "open housing" was unambiguous. A few months after his 1955 election, Daley turned a deaf ear upon a delegation of black tenants seeking police protection from a vicious pattern of racial harassment in the CHA's Trumbull Park development. The following year, the city council approved South State Street in the black belt as the site for the world's largest public housing development, Robert Taylor Homes ("It'll Be Segregated," was the *Chicago Daily News* headline). But additional thousands of black families just a few blocks from white neighborhoods to the west posed a threat that the black belt would push westward across its historic Wentworth Avenue border. Soon, however, when the final plans were announced for the new fourteen-lane Dan Ryan Expressway, one of the world's widest highways, the roadway had been realigned to head south along Wentworth Avenue, where it served as a practically impenetrable wall between State Street public housing and the all-white neighborhoods on the other side.

If there was any doubt about the mayor's intention to protect Chicago's white neighborhoods from black "invaders," it should have been dispelled by a 1964 incident Royko relates. A group headed by John Walsh, a high school teacher who was also a civil rights activist, bought a two-flat building three blocks from the mayor's bungalow. Walsh then rented one of the apartments to two young black men, a college student and a mail clerk.

Rioting promptly broke out—complete with bottles and rocks, chanted hate messages, hundreds trying to storm Walsh's building, arrests, and injuries—until after a few days the police and the Bridgeport Democratic Organization peremptorily ended the whole business. The procedure was simple and direct. Police entered the flat during the day and carried the tenants' belongings to their local station. The ward organization summoned the real estate broker who had worked with Walsh, told him the tenants were gone, and insisted on the immediate execution of a lease to two white men from the neighborhood. When the two young blacks returned to "their" apartment that night, they were escorted to the police station, given their belongings, and told to move on. Walsh learned of it all after the fact and, following a flood of inspections and demands for costly improvements from Daley's building department, sold his building.

Throughout the swirling Bridgeport episode, unfolding noisily almost within eyeshot of his home, Daley remained out of sight. When angry crowds tried to speak with him, a police line kept them at a distance. The obliging press largely ignored the story. Soon it was nothing but a historical footnote, relegated to that status by the artistry of the man who believed there was no segregation in Chicago. The man Martin Luther King hoped to bring around on open housing.

5

On a hot July Sunday in 1966, in Chicago's Soldier Field, upward of 30,000 people sat through five hours of entertainment and speeches in over ninety-degree heat. It was the Freedom Movement's kick-off event. Open housing demands directed to real estate boards and brokers, banks and government agencies, were enthusiastically approved, including two for the CHA: (1) halt public housing construction in the ghetto until a substantial number of units were started elsewhere; and (2) create a program to vastly increase the supply of low-cost housing on a scattered-site basis.

King then led thousands of his followers on a march to the Loop, where the Freedom Movement's demands were taped to a city hall door. The next day, July 11, King, Raby, and their aides met with Daley at city hall to discuss the demands. Nearly three hours of talking failed to produce any tangible concession. Afterward, King told the waiting reporters that the Freedom Movement would be forced to "escalate" its activities. An angry Daley accused King of attempting to make the city look bad for political purposes. The problems they had discussed, he insisted, could not be remedied overnight.

The escalation King referred to would take the form of "testing" real estate offices for discrimination (with matched pairs of black and white couples) and conducting prayer vigils outside offending establishments. In response to neighborhood reactions that were not always peaceful—jeering became jostling, which became rock and bottle throwing—the testing and praying soon escalated further. King and Raby announced a series of marches through the city's white neighborhoods, the blue-collar and bungalow belt, a march a day.

To Daley this was a worrisome tactic. The neighborhoods would not react quietly; the city could be subjected to nightly television coverage of violence. But the political implications were even worse. If Daley did not use the police to stop the marchers, he would be seen by his white ethnic political base as siding with its enemies. If he did, he would hand the Freedom Movement the very issue that had crucially aided the civil rights movement in the South—violation of the constitutional right to peaceful assembly and protest.

The marches began on July 16, 1966. For a time they remained peaceful. Under the watchful eyes of the police, neighborhood reactions were confined to taunts and jeers. But soon what Daley had feared came to pass. On July 29, in the all-white Gage Park and Chicago Lawn neighborhoods, the marchers were met with rocks, bottles, bricks, and cherry bombs. On July 30, six persons were injured and seven whites were arrested. The next day, with marchers numbering about 350, the mob of restive whites grew to 4,000. Soon, to cries of "nigger lovers," the missile-throwing began again. Part of the mob surged to where the marchers' cars had been left under police protection in a public park. Twelve cars were burned, two rolled into a lagoon, and many more overturned. In all, some thirty-one people were injured.

On August 5, in Gage Park, 1,200 police tried unsuccessfully to protect 600 marchers against a mob of thousands. King was knocked to the ground by a rock. There were shouts of "Kill him, kill him!" The incident and King's statement, "The people of Mississippi ought to come to Chicago to learn how to hate," were worldwide news. Thirty more people were injured, an additional forty arrested. Daley went on television to ask King to call off the marches and return to the conference table, but offered nothing specific or new. The marches, and the violence, continued.

Finally, a worried Daley, moving behind the scenes, arranged for an assembly of the city's top business, religious, civic, political, and civil rights leaders. The Chicago Conference on Religion and Race (CCRR), chaired by Episcopal Bishop James A. Montgomery, agreed to convene the proposed conference. Daley did not want the city to be the sponsor lest it appear to be negotiating against the Freedom Movement, preferring that the real estate industry be viewed as the opponent of "open housing." The CCRR and the clergy associated with it had backed King's Chicago campaign, but favored ending the marches in exchange for serious negotiations.

On August 11, Raby and Berry flew to Jackson, Mississippi, to consult with King. A decision was soon reached to agree to the proposed conference. Physical exhaustion was taking its toll. The end of summer was approaching and students, who helped man the marches, would be returning to school. Churches and unions, important allies, were in favor of a conference. Defeat in the SCLC's first northern campaign had to be avoided at almost any cost.

On August 12, with assurance that the Freedom Movement would attend, the CCRR issued invitations to a meeting to be convened the following Wednesday, August 17. The date was picked so that King could be there, although discussions about whether to participate continued until the day before the meeting commenced. On the appointed day, some seventy religious, business, labor, government, civil rights, and community leaders gathered around a U-shaped table in the parish house of St. James Episcopal Church for what came to be called the "Summit Meeting."

At the head of the U sat Bishop Montgomery, other religious leaders, and Ben Heineman, of the Chicago and Northwestern Railway, who at Daley's summons had interrupted his vacation to chair the meeting. Ranged around the sides of the U were Mayor Daley and other city officials, King, Raby, and leaders of the Chicago Freedom Movement, the head of the Chicago Real Estate Board, and the business, civic, and labor elite of Chicago. The press was excluded. But after a day of intense discussions the only tangible results were a commitment from the Chicago Real Estate Board to withdraw its opposition to a state fair-housing law, and an agreement to continue negotiations in a committee to be chaired by Thomas Ayers, head of the Commonwealth Edison Company and a civic powerhouse. Well past eight o'clock, after a long day, Heineman finally adjourned the meeting, even though—to Daley's great disappointment—King had made it clear that the marching would not cease. The full summit group would reconvene on Friday, August 26, the agreed deadline for the Ayers committee.

Days of committee meetings in the St. James Parish House ensued, during which the marches—now, however, mostly peaceful—continued. The Freedom Movement was represented by Raby, Berry, Bevel, John McDermott of the Catholic Interracial Council, and Kale Williams of the American Friends Service Committee, a quintet selected by an informal caucus after Heineman had closed the full meeting. King, back in the South for SCLC activities, did not attend. The key participants for the Chicago establishment were Ayers, Edward Marciniak, head of the city's human relations commission, and Charles R. Swibel, head of the CHA. Nominally, Swibel was chairman of the seven-person board of CHA commissioners. In reality, however, he was the dictator of the CHA, selected (as were the other commissioners) by Chicago's all-powerful mayor to do the mayor's bidding.

Swibel came from the humblest of origins—his family had fled the

Polish ghetto of his birth in 1935. As a Yiddish-speaking boy of nine, Swibel had worked after school in a sausage factory, packing mustard into paper cones to be handed out with orders for corned beef and salami. Later, he ran errands and collected rents for a mortgage house, where he made himself indispensable to Isaac Marks, the childless, wheelchair-bound president of the company. When Marks died, Swibel became vice president, then president, while surviving a breach of trust lawsuit (by making a hefty settlement payment) brought by some of the Marks heirs.

Through his friendship with the politically well-connected president of the flat janitors' union, Swibel soon became a prime mover in Marina City, a profitable residential development on the Chicago River near the Loop. In 1956, Daley had appointed the twenty-nine-year-old Swibel to the CHA Board of Commissioners, and in 1963 made him chairman. Now Swibel, handsome, impeccably dressed, a millionaire real estate developer, was a confidant of the most powerful mayor in the country and a power in his own right, at least so long as the mayor approved.

During the weeklong Ayers committee meetings, Swibel operated mostly outside the meetings themselves. Repeatedly he assured movement representatives that the mayor agreed with their principles and would carry them out in city policy. There needn't be too much concern about details, was the message. The mayor, Swibel insisted, would make everything right.

The movement representatives were poorly prepared for the Ayers negotiations. They had so focused on whether to participate at all that sufficient time had not been given to negotiating strategy. The night before the Summit Meeting was to commence, with the decision to attend now finally firm, McDermott, the scholar of the group, had sketched out a list of "talking points." Raby had used McDermott's list in his opening summit speech.

In the committee meetings, Ayers seized upon the McDermott list as the full statement of Freedom Movement demands and insisted that no new issues be raised. Heated exchanges followed, but Ayers was a canny veteran of Edison's union negotiations, experienced in narrowing issues and crafting compromises. Essentially, he got his way. Several times breakdown seemed imminent, particularly when Daley secured an injunction restricting the size and timing of the marches, a step viewed—in the middle of negotiations—as akin to betrayal. The injunction posed a serious threat to the SCLC because violation could result in heavy fines that would put the SCLC's limited financial resources at risk. Concerned about their dwindling strength, the movement representatives reluctantly continued the Ayers discussions even with the injunction hanging over their heads.

Finally, a report was produced to lay before the summit group, although without assurance of support from a divided Freedom Movement. Bevel was especially disdainful. Nothing in the Ayers report required real estate offices to serve blacks, which is what Bevel believed was a central issue. A stormy meeting on August 25, not attended by King, was inconclusive. Kept informed of the Ayers negotiations, King ultimately sided with those who favored returning to the summit.

On August 26, with King present, the Summit Meeting reconvened to consider the Ayers committee report. Discussion ebbed and flowed. On occasion it became rancorous. Only the desire of each side—for different reasons—not to break up in disarray kept the talks going. Finally, with the Ayers report essentially unchanged, Daley called for a vote. Raby demanded a recess for a Freedom Movement caucus.

It was a crucial moment for the Chicago struggle. Movement representatives clustered around King. The talk was intense, passionate. Bevel and Jackson, dissatisfied with the vague language of the Ayers report, were against the proposed agreement. But King and Raby, supported by Young and Berry, felt otherwise, and they prevailed. When the Freedom Movement representatives returned to the meeting, one remaining hurdle was cleared by a compromise suggestion from King. Then the vote Daley had called for was agreed to, unanimously. Heineman closed the meeting with a paean to the "great democratic process." Said one of the Freedom Movement representatives as he exited, "Democratic process shit . . . It was forced out of them."

Throughout the summer King had proceeded by consensus, or as near to it as he could come. But the decision to accept the ten-point Summit Agreement, essentially the Ayers report, reflected his will and authority. In his closing benediction, thanking everyone for all that had been accomplished, King intoned, "We must make this agreement work." John McKnight, who attended both sessions of the Summit Meeting as an observer for the Midwest Office of the U.S. Commission on Civil Rights, was not optimistic. A keen student of civil rights, McKnight wrote in his detailed summit notes that the agreement was "so vague as to be an unreliable instrument for securing significant progress." The dominant feeling among movement representatives was not one of triumph but of regret that their waning strength had precluded them from staying the course.

McKnight's assessment was realistic. The Summit Agreement included promises from the Chicago Commission on Human Relations to enforce the city's fair-housing ordinance against real estate brokers, from the Department of Public Aid to seek housing for welfare recipients throughout the metropolitan area, from the Chicago Real Estate Board to drop its opposition to a state fair-housing law, and from business and religious leaders to form a new organization that would undertake the programs necessary to achieve fair housing. It also included a promise from the CHA:

> It [CHA] recognizes that heavy concentrations of public housing should not again be built in the City of Chicago . . . In the future, it will seek scattered sites for public housing and will limit the height of new public housing structures in high density areas to eight stories, with housing for families with children limited to the first two stories. Wherever possible, smaller units will be built.

Some of the agreement's promises came from ostensibly independent agencies, both private, such as the Real Estate Board, and public, such as the CHA. But the reality was that Daley was in charge. As King believed, Daley could have seen to it that even vague promises were kept. Indeed, the Chicago establishment soon formed the promised fair-housing organization, called the Leadership Council for Metropolitan Open Communities. And the council was given a prestigious board of directors that, in addition to black leaders, included presidents of banks, utilities, and other corporations, as well as the cardinal of the Chicago Archdiocese.

However, while larded with statements of good intention, the Summit Agreement was woefully short on specifics. The public aid department would make a "renewed and persistent effort" to find good housing regardless of location. The Mortgage Bankers Association "affirmed" that the policy of its members was to lend mortgage money without discrimination. The CHA would "seek" scattered sites for public housing. But as for withdrawing federal deposit insurance from financial institutions found guilty of racial discrimination, "the matter is a complex one [but] will be diligently pursued." The Real Estate Board was not required to drop its court attack on the city's fair-housing ordinance. Even though construction had not yet begun, the CHA was not obliged to jettison its pending proposals for new public housing units in the ghetto.

Under these circumstances, the Leadership Council understandably failed to achieve the Freedom Movement's basic goal of opening white neighborhoods to blacks. White real estate offices still would not serve would-be black customers. The CHA moved forward with its plans for new projects in ghetto neighborhoods. The Leadership Council did not even make a serious attempt to require the CHA to perform its promise to scatter public housing.

The following year, 1967, King let it be known that he might return to Chicago to try to achieve the unrealized promise of the Summit Agreement. The response was immediate. He was criticized violently by the mayor, by the United Auto Workers, even by the head of the Leadership Council, and by a group of black clergymen who accused him of creating hatred with his marches and urged him "to keep the hell out of Chicago." Faced with this hostility, King issued a statement praising the council for its hard work and said there would be no repetition of his open housing marches as long as "progress" continued. On that ignominious tone, with perhaps a grace note of hope that, over time, the Leadership Council might be able to do more, concluded the efforts of Martin Luther King and the Chicago Freedom Movement to end residential segregation in Chicago.

Hindsight can be harsh. The Urban League was helping with the CHA case and Bill Berry, head of the League, was an important Freedom Movement leader and summit negotiator. Why didn't we try, through Berry, to urge the Freedom Movement to insist on specifics from the CHA, including dropping its plans for more ghetto high-rises on which construction had not yet begun?

Whether talking to Berry or anyone else would have made a difference, we will never know. Given the movement's weakness by summer's end, it might not have. In any event, we were a small group of volunteer lawyers working on a specific case; they were national civil rights leaders engaged in high-stakes political action. None of us thought to connect the two. In the long course of the Gautreaux case I have had numerous regrets about paths not explored and ideas not pursued. Our failure even to try to influence the summit negotiations on the CHA is one of the regrets.

6

In the late spring and early summer of 1966, as the Chicago Freedom Movement drama was unfolding, our quintet of lawyers pushed on with fact gathering and legal analysis, blending them into the complaint we would soon be filing in court. Some tasks were easy, such as describing the core facts that public housing in Chicago had steadily become a black institution, and that virtually all the newer CHA sites were in the black ghetto. We also quickly decided to put the Gautreaux name first in the list of plaintiffs. Dorothy Gautreaux was a tenant leader who would be an especially good spokesperson. In addition, a case usually becomes known by the first name on the list of plaintiffs, and we were attracted by the unusual Gautreaux name.

Other decisions were more difficult. Would it be enough to show that virtually all CHA projects were located in predominantly black neighborhoods? That the effect of CHA site selection had been to deny black tenants access to white neighborhoods? Or did we have to prove that the CHA intended to discriminate? If we could prove intention, we would in theory have an easy win. Brown v. Board of Education had said that government officials could not intentionally segregate the races in schools, and the Brown principle should apply to public housing as well. But could we uncover evidence that segregating blacks was the reason the CHA had chosen its sites?

Not likely, we feared. Almost certainly there would be plausible explanations, such as land costs, land availability, slum clearance, and the like. And in the early years the CHA had really tried, under Robert Taylor and Elizabeth Wood, to do the right thing, only to be blocked by the city council. In the end we decided to advance both theories, although the cases seemed to lean to a discriminatory intent requirement. If that proved to be so, we faced a daunting prospect.

Another troublesome issue was how to handle the U.S. Department of Housing and Urban Development, of which Marie McGuire's Public Housing Administration was a division. HUD had given the CHA the money to build its segregated system, and McGuire's letter to the West Side Federation showed that the federal government knew what was going on. We should be suing HUD too. Yet suing the federal government could be a steep uphill climb. The "feds" had all sorts of legal defenses not available to the CHA, and we would be opposed by the always resourceful lawyers of the U.S. Department of Justice. We were also uncertain about whether, for technical reasons, we could sue HUD and the CHA in a single lawsuit. We finally decided to file two similar complaints, Gautreaux v. CHA and Gautreaux v. HUD, as "related cases," so both would be assigned to the same judge.

On August 9, 1966, five days after Judge Parker's final order in Tometz and three before the CCRR issued its invitations to the Summit Meeting, we filed what came to be known as Gautreaux in the federal district court in Chicago. The complaint was a simple document, belying the time spent on it. The CHA was now a black system. Its tenants and applicants were mostly black, and its developments were practically all in black neighborhoods. Some 85 percent of Chicago's one million blacks lived in neighborhoods that were all or substantially all black, and compact and contiguous, not scattered. Borrowing from the Brown opinion, we said that segregation in the black ghetto had detrimental effects on the blacks who lived there, including isolation from the larger society and school segregation for the children.

On the question of intent versus effect we held to our tentative decision to advance both theories. In the first count of the complaint we said the CHA had selected its public housing sites "because" it wished to avoid placing blacks in white neighborhoods—the intent theory. Then, in the third count, we omitted the "because" statement and said only that the CHA sites "have been" in the black ghetto—the effect theory.

We had four counts rather than two because we had two legal theories. The first was that the CHA and HUD's conduct violated the U.S. Constitution, specifically the equal protection and due process clauses of the Fourteenth Amendment that formed the legal underpinning of the Brown decision. The second was that it violated the 1964 Civil Rights Act prohibiting racial discrimination in programs that received federal funding. Each of the two legal theories had an intent and an effect count—hence, four counts in all.

Merrill Freed walked the papers over to the courthouse to file our complaint and learn who our judge would be. (Chuck and I were in Waukegan for some last-minute adjustments to Judge Parker's order.) The lottery system of the federal district court in Chicago used stacks of gummed labels with the name of a judge printed on the down side of each label. After the clerk examined the papers to be filed to verify that they complied with court rules, he would peel back the next label, paste it on the first page of the complaint and the judge for the case would be identified and assigned. Federal judges are lifetime presidential appointees who range from liberal to conservative and across the spectrum of human qualities. It would be a vast understatement to say that the assigned judge had a great deal of influence over the course of a case. So it was with proverbially bated breath that Merrill awaited the peeling back of "our" label. Then, as we had agreed, he called my office immediately and left his message. The Gautreaux judge would be Richard B. Austin.

Austin was a former prosecutor and state court judge with a no-nonsense, law-and-order reputation. He had been narrowly defeated in 1956 in a race for the governorship of Illinois for which Daley had hand-picked him. In 1961 he had been appointed to the federal district court by President Kennedy with, of course, Daley's support. He was known as a "tough little scrapper" with a sarcastic wit. Five feet four inches tall, sporting a bristly white crew cut that made him look, as one reporter wrote, as if he had an acrylic rug on top of his head, one of his proudest accomplishments was having sentenced Jimmy Hoffa to prison for fraud. On the door to his chambers in the federal courthouse he displayed a cartoon with the caption, "Yea, though I walk through the valley of the shadow of death, I shall fear no evil because I am the meanest SOB in the valley."

Austin lived in the affluent white suburb of Flossmoor. On the question of race, as on most other matters, he was not considered a liberal. When I first appeared in Austin's courtroom to set a schedule for filing, and told him generally what the case was about, he immediately shot back, "Where do you want them to put 'em [the CHA projects]? On

Lake Shore Drive?" It appeared that whatever progress we might make in Gautreaux would have to be earned the hard way.

7

Kathryn Kula was tall, slim, intense, and never without a hat, although over the course of our numerous encounters I did not see her wear the same hat twice. She was also never without a cigarette, a habit that would eventually kill her. "Cancer cures smoking," she remarked some years later from her hospital bed. Entirely devoted to the CHA, she transformed her otherwise attractive features into granite whenever the CHA's conduct was questioned. As CHA general counsel it was Kula's job to deal with the Gautreaux complaint, and she promptly hired an outsider to help. He was John Hunt, an experienced, well-respected, bow-tied lawyer from the small but prestigious firm of Todhunter & Hunt. Kula and Hunt promptly set to work to head us off at the pass.

Two of the ways lawyers perform this Wild West maneuver are the motion to dismiss and the motion for summary judgment. Kula and Hunt tried both. The motion to dismiss asserts that a complaint is so grievously flawed that it should be killed off immediately—"dismissed" with the back of a judicial hand. The motion for summary judgment says no relevant facts are disputed and so there is no need for a trial; given what the facts clearly are, the other side must lose. It took Kula and Hunt just two months to file both motions. When their documents arrived in mid-October, together with a thick legal memorandum, it was plain that getting over the pass would be arduous.

The first of the two most worrisome Kula and Hunt arguments was that Dorothy Gautreaux and the other plaintiffs had no right to complain about not having a chance to live in public housing in white neighborhoods. The reason was that, in their written applications to the CHA, each had expressed a "location preference" for specific projects in black neighborhoods. A sworn affidavit from Harry Schneider, the CHA's director of management, described in distressing detail what each of the location preferences had been. Gautreaux, for example, had opted for Dearborn Homes, in a 95 percent black neighborhood; her second preference had been for "any" housing. At the time, Schneider's affidavit went on, the CHA operated projects in locations other than black neighborhoods "where this plaintiff could have been housed had she so requested."

The location preference argument was not a surprise. It had appeared in Marie McGuire's letter to the West Side Federation, and McGuire had presumably gotten it from the CHA. When Chuck and I had interviewed our plaintiffs and questioned them on the location preference point, they had all said they asked for housing where they understood they had the best chance of getting accepted quickly. We had not explored the matter further.

The other troublesome CHA argument was that it was a lie—"clearly and demonstrably untrue"—to say that the CHA had chosen black neighborhoods for public housing sites. The affidavit supporting this argument was from C. E. Humphrey, the CHA's deputy executive director. With a detailed historical chart, Humphrey showed that of the nearly 20,000 public housing apartments the CHA had developed since 1950, almost 30 percent were in neighborhoods that had had white majorities at the times the CHA had acquired the sites.

The Schiff conference room lights burned late as we pondered how to respond. The answer to Humphrey's "clearly and demonstrably untrue" argument eventually emerged from Philip Hauser, an esteemed professor of sociology at the University of Chicago, who had once been acting director of the U.S. Census Bureau. As he read the Humphrey affidavit, the portly, good-natured Hauser guffawed loudly.

Humphrey's chart was based on Chicago's seventy-seven "community areas" that ranged in population up to 140,000 persons. Some were so large, Hauser said, that were they to be incorporated as municipalities they would have bigger populations than any city in Illinois except Chicago itself. Most were so big that, although they had some historical identity as regions, they were made up of many local neighborhoods that differed greatly from one another. Two key paragraphs of our complaint asserted that confining the CHA's public housing within the black ghetto led to highly detrimental consequences for CHA families, including school segregation, lack of social contact with the larger community, and, ultimately, feelings of inferiority. Hauser was willing to say that as to these consequences community areas were too large and disparate, and that census tracts were much better for determining the racial composition of the relevant "neighborhood."

The second and final step in dealing with Humphrey's "community area" chart was to have Baron prepare a chart of our own, this one based on census tracts. When Baron's detailed chart was finished, it radically transformed the Humphrey-drawn picture of racial diversity: of thirty-three CHA projects since 1950, thirty-two were, when completed, in census tracts that were over 84 percent black, and for twenty-six of the thirty-three the figure was over 95 percent.

With the Hauser and Baron affidavits we felt we could parry Humphrey's "demonstrably untrue" thrust, at least for summary judgment purposes. To defend against summary judgment we needed only a legitimate dispute about some relevant and important fact. Hauser's opinion and Baron's census tract chart gave us that. Whether census tracts would ultimately "win" over community areas when it came to a trial was something we didn't have to worry about now.

The "location preferences" were a different matter. We would never reach trial if we couldn't figure out a way to handle those. With something approaching fear and trembling we began to explore the question of how, if our plaintiffs had really asked to be housed in black neighborhoods, they could still complain about not being given a chance to live elsewhere. Over the next weeks the answer slowly emerged. Yes, the plaintiffs had expressed their location preferences as Schneider's affidavit had said, but why had they done that? We were beginning to learn that Schneider's affidavit hadn't told the whole story.

Dorothy Gautreaux was desperate when she filed her CHA application in 1953—she, her husband, and their four children had only a single bedroom and they would have gone almost anywhere to get more space. The CHA clerk helping her fill out the application form said her best chance of getting housed "promptly" was in Dearborn Homes. Gautreaux therefore listed Dearborn as her first choice and "any" as her second. What about white neighborhoods? We knew there were a few white projects, Gautreaux said, but we also knew that the CHA excluded blacks from them and limited the number of blacks in the few projects in mixed neighborhoods. We believed we could not "promptly" get into any CHA apartment in a white or mixed area.

Odell Jones had filled out his CHA application in 1955 when he was living with his wife, three children, and innumerable rats in two rooms, with the bathroom as the cooking area. He did not see his location preference sheet at the time of his interview, and it was not in his handwriting. When he was later told an apartment in Henry Horner was available, he snapped it up. He too did not believe the CHA would move a black family to a project in a white neighborhood.

Doreatha Crenchaw lived with her three children in one and a half rooms. She shared a bathroom with six other families, rats, and roaches. Like Jones, she did not see her location preference sheet at the time of her interview, and it too was not in her handwriting. She later was told she had two choices, Altgeld Gardens or Henry Horner. She chose Horner. She too believed she would not be admitted to white projects.

And so on. But would these statements be enough? Would Judge Austin side with the self-serving recollections of Dorothy Gautreaux, Odell Jones, and the others against the "hard" evidence of the application forms they had signed? We got in touch with J. S. Fuerst, who had been the CHA's director of research and statistics from 1946 to 1952. A balding, passionate man who loved to talk and always seemed to do so as if he were addressing a large audience, Fuerst told us two things of great importance. The first strongly supported the "beliefs" of our plaintiffs about getting into white or mixed area CHA projects. During Fuerst's six years with the CHA, the staff had admitted no black families to CHA's four projects in white neighborhoods, and the staff had been instructed to and had maintained low black quotas at two other "mixed" projects. Those were the facts, Fuerst said, slamming his pudgy fist on his desk for emphasis, and yes, he would sign an affidavit.

The second was that we needed to find and talk to Tamaara Tabb, who had been in charge of CHA tenant selection in the 1950s and really knew the story. Would she talk to us? Fuerst thought she might, and he thought she was now in New York. He turned out to be right on both counts.

It was pouring rain on Manhattan's Upper West Side, and I was badly in need of a warm, dry spot when I walked into Tamaara Tabb's small apartment. Tabb provided it, along with a chopped chicken liver sandwich that I gratefully wolfed down at her chrome and Formica kitchen table. While I was drying off, Tabb, a short, graying woman with a ready smile, warmed me with her story of the CHA's tenant selection practices. She had actually been the supervisor—the boss—of tenant selection at the CHA from 1953 to 1961, and the facts behind "location preferences" were not exactly what Kula, Hunt, and Schneider would have had Austin believe.

While I furiously scribbled notes at the kitchen table, Tabb unfolded her tale. First she took me through the details of the process, from initial registration to moving in, describing the several steps and various CHA forms. Then she told me about the "coding" system. When a family registered with the CHA its registration card was marked to classify each family according to three factors: a letter showing "priority status" (displaced, emergency, or nonpriority); a number showing "veteran preference" (veteran or not); and a letter showing "race" (white or black).

The next step was an interview at which a full application was filled out by the interviewer and signed by the applicant. Tabb said that for almost all "A" (white) families, without regard to priority status or veteran preference, interviews were promptly scheduled and eligible families were immediately referred out for housing. But for "B" (black) families, exactly when an interview would be scheduled depended on priority status, veteran preference, and "location preference."

Then came the key point. Central Rental Office interviewers had orders to "guide" the "B" families in stating their location preferences. They were also told how to do the guiding. They were to suggest that housing could be obtained quickly in some projects, and they were not to mention others. The not-to-be-mentioned group consisted of the white projects, in which only "A" families could be housed, and the mixed-neighborhood projects, in which "A" families were to be—as the CHA lexicon put it—"maximized."

I was warm now, and practically dry too. A little too dry in the mouth, perhaps, for I was working up to the crucial question. It was clear that if Tabb would sign an affidavit, the odds on the believability of our plaintiffs' self-serving recollections would be markedly changed in our favor. When we had finished going over the last detail—by now I was stalling, putting off the moment of truth, trying to be charming—I finally asked Tabb as casually and matter-of-factly as I could, "Tamaara, will you sign an affidavit about this?" Her brief hesitation seemed to last a hundred years. Then, she replied, "I guess so. Why not? It's true."

At that moment I believed Gautreaux had been saved from premature demise. I was reluctant to leave the apartment without some tangible evidence of the last two hours, fearful that the whole episode might turn out to be a rainstorm fantasy. I composed a short affidavit then and there and Tabb signed it, though of course we had no notary public and affidavits were supposed to be notarized. A signed but unnotarized statement, I thought, was better than none at all.

Tamaara Tabb was not fantasy. We soon had a detailed affidavit typed up, signed, and notarized. Then, with affidavits from Philip Hauser, Hal Baron, J. S. Fuerst, and the plaintiffs, plus our own—also thick—legal brief, we filed our response to the CHA motions in mid-December. It had been an eventful two months.

8

At the beginning of March 1967 we received in the mail a gratifying surprise from the judge whose snap initial sarcasm had been to ask if we thought CHA projects should be built on Chicago's Gold Coast. Austin ruled, briefly but deliciously, in our favor. On the location preferences, he wrote that the particulars of the CHA's contacts with individuals were not at stake. Whether or not the CHA's site selection policy had been administered without regard to race was the issue, and that "transcended" any individual's relationship to the CHA system. The reasoning followed the school desegregation cases we had cited in our brief, which said that the purpose of the school suits was not to gain admission to specific schools for particular children, but to end a system-wide segregation policy. Though Austin made no reference to Tamaara Tabb or to A and B families, I said a silent thank-you to Tabb anyway, convinced that but for her affidavit the case would not have survived.

Austin also quickly disposed of the "clearly and demonstrably untrue" argument. Once again he did not refer to the affidavits, to Humphrey, Hauser, and Baron, but he did say that summary judgment was rarely appropriate where an issue of intent was involved and where serious questions of fact remained unresolved—"for example, the racial composition of the neighborhoods involved."

There were, however, some casualties. We lost two of our four counts. Dismissing each of our "effect" counts, Austin said we had to show that the CHA had selected sites at least in part because of "a desire to maintain concentrations of Negroes in particular areas or to prevent them from living in other areas." Under the Constitution, he wrote, so long as it was free of a "design" to concentrate black or white tenants in some areas to the exclusion of others, the CHA was free to pick sites based on such factors as "need, cost, and rehabilitation of deteriorating neighborhoods," that is, slum clearance.

So we had succeeded in getting over the pass, not a small feat. But beyond us loomed another. Would we be able to show the CHA "desire" or "design" Austin had said we must prove?

Surviving a motion to dismiss entitles the survivor to "discovery"—to require the opposing side to open its files and submit its employees to questioning under oath ("depositions"), thereby to try to prove what was merely asserted in the complaint. We promptly began our discovery to try to prove the CHA's "desire" and "design."

First we asked the CHA to turn over all its files having anything to do with site selection. Kula was outraged. We were talking about nearly thirty-five years of records. Our request was ridiculous. To Austin, Kula complained that it would take thousands of hours and tens of thousands of dollars to comb years of CHA records for documents relating to site selection. "We'll do the job ourselves," I quickly responded (having not the least idea how), "and save the CHA all that time and money." All the judge had to do was order the CHA to open its records. Austin agreed, and a reluctant CHA was forced to let us peer into its file cabinets.

Baron helped us address our new challenge. Through the good offices of the Urban League half a dozen college students were hired, instructed about what sorts of documents to look for, and set loose with mimeographed forms to record what they found. During a good part of the summer of 1967, in dingy basements and storage rooms, our "jeans brigade" burrowed industriously through CHA filing cabinets and folders. Most of the documents they examined were useless, but a few were not.

The most important find was a copy of a 1955 agreement between General William B. Kean, then the CHA's executive director, and Alderman Murphy, chairman of the city council Housing Committee. Its stated purpose was to ensure "close coordination" between the CHA and the committee "to provide for the selection of the most satisfactory sites." But what the agreement really did was to turn the CHA's site selection responsibility over to the city council's Housing Committee. CHA staff, working with a subcommittee, would make "initial selections" of sites, and then the subcommittee would make recommendations to the full committee. Only sites recommended by the full committee would be formally submitted by the CHA to the city council. The agreement said its procedures would enable the subcommittee to "clear" with the alderman in whose ward a proposed site was located, and to determine "community attitudes which should be recognized in site selection."

Kean, a retired army general, had replaced Elizabeth Wood in 1954. Wood's attempts to foster integration in CHA projects had put her at odds with the more conservative CHA Board that had finally ousted her. Kean felt differently than did Wood on the "Negro question," and one of his first acts in his new position had been to agree with Chairman Murphy on a procedure that would help avoid controversy on that matter.

Armed with the documents unearthed by the jeans brigade, we began to interrogate CHA officials, including Swibel, Alvin Rose (Kean's successor as executive director), Humphrey (who had succeeded Rose), and Kula. Thousands of pages of sworn testimony were produced. Many were as useless as most of the CHA's documents, but some answers were revealing.

Rose and Humphrey both testified that they knew the city council wanted to keep blacks out of white neighborhoods, and that in its formal site submissions the CHA "went along" with the council. Rose said that even though the council was "guilty of practicing to a certain degree segregated housing," the CHA wasn't going to "waste time" proposing sites in white areas. Humphrey agreed that the CHA didn't believe in spending money to propose sites outside black areas which it knew the council would not approve—"We don't find sites where we know there will be resistance." From Kula's deposition we learned that she had told Swibel she was concerned that the CHA wasn't getting more sites approved outside ghetto areas. She thought there might be merit in submitting sites directly to the council, without preclearance, and "letting the chips fall where they may."

We also learned of a practice under the Kean-Murphy agreement that wasn't apparent from the face of the document. Humphrey testified that, at the request of the aldermen, the CHA began to submit twice as many sites to the Murphy subcommittee as its federal funding would allow to be developed, so that, as the aldermen put it, "if we knock some [sites] out you can still carry the ball." Humphrey acknowledged that, by avoiding any risk of not using all available federal funding, this practice gave the aldermen greater "flexibility" in picking and choosing among sites, that is, to eliminate those in white areas.

With the depositions at last concluded, we thought we had a theory about CHA "intent" that just might carry the day. The deposition testimony and the Kean-Murphy agreement clearly showed that the CHA was playing ball with a city council it knew would cull white locations out of proposed sites. In fact, if census tracts were viewed as neighborhoods, the council had approached perfection: of some 21,000 CHA apartments completed or under development since 1949, over 98 percent were in black neighborhoods. "Playing ball" meant that the CHA was making the culling easy and more or less private. Because of Kean-Murphy and the "twice-as-many-as-needed" practice, there would be no angry council debates and messy publicity. Yet the law cases we were reading seemed to bar a government agency from knowingly playing along with segregation. A good example came from Little Rock, Arkansas, the city that became the testing place for violence in resisting the Brown decision.

In its now-legendary Supreme Court phase, the Little Rock case had begun when, under a court-approved desegregation plan, a moderate school board, in a moderate city of the South, carefully planned the admission of a few black children to Central High School as a way to begin school desegregation gradually. The designated starting date was Tuesday, September 3, 1957. On Monday night, in a wholly unanticipated—and never satisfactorily explained—statement on television, Governor Orval Faubus said it would not be possible to maintain order if "forcible integration" were carried out the next day. He then posted the National Guard to see to it that it didn't happen. The ensuing events—the mobs, Faubus's frantic and erratic negotiations with President Eisenhower, the president's eventual dispatch of a thousand riot-trained paratroopers (the first federal troops sent to the South to protect blacks since Reconstruction), and an academic year that included soldiers patrolling Central High's corridors—climaxed in a defiant legal challenge to Brown.

On June 27, 1958, because of an "unfavorable community attitude" that led to "intolerable" tensions, the federal judge in Little Rock, Harry J. Lemley, granted the beleaguered school board's request to suspend its desegregation plan for two and a half years. Two months later, Cooper v. Aaron (Cooper was a school board member, Aaron one of the black students) was heard in an extraordinary special session of the U.S. Supreme Court, followed by a second day of argument two weeks later.

The day after the second argument the Court unanimously overruled Lemley, not even waiting to complete its written opinion, which, some two weeks later, set out the reasoning we hoped we might persuade Austin to apply to the CHA. The opinion accepted the "entire good faith" of the Little Rock School Board. It also recognized the public hostility to Central High desegregation and the violence and disorder stimulated by the governor and, later, by the Arkansas legislature. But, the Court said, hostility to racial desegregation was not relevant. The school board simply could not operate a segregated school system. Even though implementation was rendered difficult or impossible by other state officials, those in charge could not use good faith as an excuse for declining to implement federal constitutional rights.

We imagined we could hear Austin, echoing the Little Rock decision, saying that the hostility of the city council was irrelevant. That the CHA simply could not operate a segregated public housing system. That the CHA's good faith was not a legal excuse for failing to implement the rights of Dorothy Gautreaux and the others just because the city council was making implementation difficult or even impossible.

In fact, didn't we have a stronger case than Cooper v. Aaron? After all, the Little Rock School Board had really tried to desegregate Central High. In the face of public hostility to school desegregation, it had proceeded with its plan, only to be stopped by no less a force than the governor and the National Guard. Not so with the CHA. The CHA had not tried to desegregate public housing, which in its case would have meant submitting white sites to the city council, arguing for them, and—as Kula had put it to Swibel—letting the chips fall. No, with the Kean-Murphy deal and the twice-as-many-as-needed practice, the CHA had played the city council's game. The argument that accommodation was necessary as a practical matter to avoid dire consequences—violence in Little Rock or site vetoes in Chicago—was not an acceptable defense under the law.

Our research also turned up another "intent" argument. We found a few cases in which statistics showing that blacks had never served on juries were accepted by the Supreme Court as proof of intentional discrimination. The Court had said that even without other evidence of discrimination, proof that blacks were a substantial part of the population and that some of them met the qualifications for jurors, but that over a long period of time none had been called for jury service, was a situation that "bespeaks discrimination." In one case, where the exclusion of blacks was not complete but nearly so, practices were employed that presented an opportunity for discrimination—using differently colored paper slips for printing the names of prospective jurors, white for whites, yellow for blacks. Supreme Court Justice Felix Frankfurter had said that, under those circumstances, to attribute the absence of blacks from a jury to fortuity, "the mind of justice, not merely its eyes, would have to be blind."

Well, we told ourselves, sitting around the Schiff conference table in our interminable discussions of the cases, we too have nearly total exclusion. And we also have practices—Kean-Murphy and twice-as-many-as-needed—that lend themselves to discrimination. Besides, we said, in the jury cases the only evidence of discrimination was statistics, or statistics coupled with practices (such as colored juror slips) that lent themselves to discrimination. We have both of these and more, we gleefully concluded. The CHA's own officials had acknowledged in their depositions that the city council wanted to keep blacks from entering white neighborhoods via public housing. No one in the jury cases had testified that the jury commissioners wanted to keep blacks off juries. We announced we were ready for trial.

Perhaps fearing the publicity a trial would generate, the CHA once again asked Austin for summary judgment. By now it had augmented its legal team with another experienced lawyer. He was James Otis, an able, jovial partner in a large Chicago law firm. (He, like John Hunt, also wore bow ties.) Kula, Hunt, and Otis argued that the materials developed during discovery proved that the CHA had no discriminatory intent, and that any discrimination came from elsewhere. The centerpiece of the CHA's new motion was another affidavit from Humphrey that played a variation on the "demonstrably untrue" theme. Humphrey now adopted Hauser's definition of "neighborhoods"—that is, census tracts—and with another chart, this time tract-based, showed that the CHA's site recommendations to the city council's Housing Committee had included a goodly number of white sites. That proved, the CHA argued in its brief, that the CHA had no intent to discriminate. If white sites were later eliminated, that was the council's doing. Lacking any discriminatory intent of its own, the CHA was entitled to summary judgment.

The Humphrey affidavit was a big surprise. From the beginning, we had feared we would lose for cost and slum clearance reasons. The CHA would show that no affordable sites could be found in white areas, and, besides, all the slums the CHA wanted to clear were in black areas. But here was Humphrey saying, no, there were lots of white sites the CHA wanted to use. It had actually recommended to the Housing Subcommittee many white sites that met all of the CHA's own criteria. It was just that the council screened them out. We were beginning to believe that we actually had a chance to win!

Since we were about to be delayed by another summary judgment motion, we thought, why not file one of our own? If we were right about our intent theory based on Cooper v. Aaron and the jury cases, the discovery materials proved our case. If we were wrong, if the council "excuse" let the CHA off the hook, why not learn that now? So, in mid 1968, with voluminous briefs from each side, not one but two summary judgment motions were delivered to Austin.

9

While all this "motioning" and briefing was going on during 1968, in quick succession momentous events unfolded on the national stage. First, on March 1, 1968, came the Report of the National Advisory Commission on Civil Disorders—the Kerner Commission. In the summer of 1967, black ghettos in Newark, Detroit, and a dozen and a half other cities had exploded in race riots. Police and National Guardsmen were able to quell the disturbances only after scores of deaths and the leveling of entire city blocks—the Detroit riot alone caused forty-three deaths. Some 4,700 federal troops had been flown in to restore a kind of order. On July 28, 1967, President Johnson had appointed an eleven-person commission, headed by Illinois Governor Otto Kerner, to answer three questions: What happened? Why did it happen? What can be done to prevent it from happening again? Reporting five months early because of the "gravity of the problems and the pressing need for action," the Kerner Commission described what had happened and why. Its "basic conclusion" was, "Our nation is moving toward two societies, one black, one white, separate and unequal." Segregation and poverty, it said, had created in the racial ghetto a distinctive environment totally unknown to most white Americans. "What white Americans have never fully understood—but what the Negro can never forget—is that white society is deeply implicated in the ghetto. White institutions created it, white institutions maintain it, and white society condones it." Answering the president's third question, the report said:

> Federal housing programs must be given a new thrust aimed at overcoming the prevailing patterns of racial segregation. If this is not done, those programs will continue to concentrate the most impoverished and dependent segments of the population into the central-city ghettos where there is already a critical gap between the needs of the population and the public resources to deal with them. This can only continue to compound the conditions of failure and hopelessness which lead to crime, civil disorder and social disorganization.

In April, only weeks after issuance of the Kerner Report, Martin Luther King Jr. journeyed to Memphis to help striking janitors. There, as he stepped onto the balcony outside his room in the Lorraine Motel, he was felled by an assassin's rifle shot. Outrage and more rioting immediately swept the nation. One consequence was that open housing legislation, filibustered to death in the Senate two years earlier, was enacted within a week. The Fair Housing Act was a milestone. It outlawed most housing discrimination, even in purely private transactions. For a country in which private property rights were practically sacred, limiting an owner's freedom to sell or rent was a major step for both American law and American social policy. The new act also obligated the federal government to administer its housing and urban development programs "affirmatively" to further fair-housing policy. "Affirmative administration" was undefined, but the reach of the new provision, relating as it did to a broad array of federal programs, could be considerable.

Later in the summer, Congress passed yet another housing law. As he signed the 1968 Housing and Urban Development Act on August 1, President Johnson grandly called it "a Magna Carta to liberate our cities." The law was indeed grandiose. The 1949 housing act had given the nation a housing goal—a decent home in a suitable environment for every American family. Now the 1968 act quantified the goal—26 million units of new and rehabilitated housing were to be provided over the ensuing ten years, 20 million by the private sector and 6 million by federally subsidized programs. Public housing was dealt with handsomely. Authority was provided for more than 300,000 new units over three years, a figure that amounted to nearly half the units built in the thirty-year life of the program. Two new programs engaged private developers on a significant scale in the construction and ownership of subsidized housing. If "Magna Carta" was an exaggeration, the 1968 act was still the biggest, most imaginative housing program the country had ever adopted.

In December, ending the momentous 1968 year, two presidential task forces on housing delivered their reports to the White House. The charge of the first, headed by industrialist Edgar F. Kaiser, was to determine how housing construction costs could be reduced, especially for low-income housing. Its report, *A Decent Home,* warned that new subsidized housing "should not be concentrated in the present slums but scattered throughout the metropolitan areas." Where necessary, the report said, the federal government should be empowered to preempt local zoning ordinances, subject only to a governor's veto. Although reluctant to suggest reducing local powers, the Kaiser Commission was convinced that "wide-spread abuses of zoning . . . make it necessary for local prerogatives to yield to the greater common good."

The other task force, chaired by former Illinois Senator Paul H. Douglas, was to look at slum and urban growth problems. The Douglas Commission concluded that the most "explosive" of our urban problems was the "almost unyielding pattern of [residential] segregation." The overwhelming majority of future nonwhite population growth, it said, was likely to be concentrated in central city slums, leading to increased tension and violence, further racial polarization, and the flight of more and more businesses and jobs from the central city. These were "suicidal consequences." Housing the poor and eliminating housing segregation were therefore of such supreme national importance that, if all else failed, the federal government should do the job itself.

Collectively, the Kerner Report in March, the housing laws of April and August, and the Kaiser and Douglas reports in December laid the rhetorical groundwork for a historic reversal of federal policy toward the black ghetto. While the Great Migration was pumping millions of southern blacks into constricted urban ghettos, the federal government had barely moved beyond its neighborhood composition rule of the 1930s. Neither the civil rights laws of the early 1960s nor the antipoverty programs of the Kennedy and Johnson administrations had been designed for or had had the effect—as the Kerner Report had put it—of "overcoming the prevailing patterns of racial segregation." Distributed through a mass-market paperback, the Kerner Report had now inscribed an impassioned yet reasoned statement of what had to be done. The housing acts of April and August provided legal tools. And the Kaiser and Douglas reports showed precisely what else was needed.

The Kerner, Kaiser, and Douglas commission members were all moderates. Of Johnson's appointments to the Kerner Commission, Tom Wicker had observed that had the commission included militants, it could not have spoken with a voice so sure to be heard. What had to be said, he wrote, had been said at last, not by radicals, but by representatives of white, moderate, responsible America. At the end of 1968 such representatives had delivered the same message twice more.

The message was not to be heeded. Sandwiched between the Kerner Report and the housing laws which preceded them, and the Kaiser and Douglas reports which followed, came the Republican and Democratic national conventions in August and the presidential election in November. In Miami, in what turned out to be an easy, first ballot victory over Nelson Rockefeller and Ronald Reagan, the Republicans nominated Richard Nixon. In Chicago, amid tear gas and what some called "police rioting," the Democrats nominated Minnesota Senator Hubert Humphrey.

Long a leading figure in supporting housing and civil rights legislation, Humphrey might well have listened to Kerner, Kaiser, and Douglas and used the tools of the 1968 housing acts "affirmatively." Nixon, who had campaigned vigorously in the traditionally Democratic South and made commitments to southern segregationists in the process, particularly about school busing, was unlikely to do the same. When Nixon beat Humphrey with a comfortable electoral college majority (although with less than a 1 percent popular vote margin), instead of an administration likely to heed 1968's messages about its black ghettos, the country would have one almost certain to turn a deaf ear. Our quintet of Gautreaux lawyers was sorely disappointed, but mercifully was spared foreknowledge of what the election of Richard Nixon would mean for our case.

Amid the momentous national events of 1968, a momentous event occurred in the Gautreaux case. On August 15, 1968, Dorothy Gautreaux died at the age of forty-one. The cause was kidney failure, brought on by a hypertensive condition that had plagued her for years. In the morning before what was to be her last hospital visit, Gautreaux was on the telephone, making arrangements for a block club meeting that night.

Of all our named plaintiffs, Gautreaux had been the most articulate about ghetto isolation. When, in the early 1960s, the Chicago civil rights movement had focused upon school issues, it was Gautreaux who had pushed—successfully—to include housing on the agenda. In part, at least, it was the passion of Dorothy Gautreaux that had led to the open housing banner under which Martin Luther King had marched in Chicago. Baron later wrote:

> I can still visualize this intense, yet wonderfully warm, brown-skinned woman as she participated in the planning and strategy meetings of the coordinating body of the Chicago civil rights movement during the 1960s. Dorothy always brought to the often rancorous debates a sense of hope and possibility. When discussion became stymied over abstract principles or personalities, she punctured the posturing by quietly stating what she and her small band of tenant organizers were going to do—specifically. For many of us, Dorothy's judgment was the touchstone of whether a proposal had merit and should be acted upon.

Court rules require that when a named plaintiff dies a paper is to be filed "suggesting" that the death has occurred. The name of the deceased is then to be deleted from the title of the case. We duly filed the suggestion of demise, but it seemed "sacrilegious" to delete the Dorothy Gautreaux name from the title of the case. We "forgot" that step, no one raised a question, and the case continued to be known as Gautreaux.

10

February 1969. The unbelievable happened. Ruling on each side's summary judgment motions—through an opinion simply mailed to the lawyers—Austin denied the CHA's and granted ours! The facts were not really in dispute, said the opinion. The CHA's own documents and testimony showed intentional discrimination. The Equal Protection Clause of the Constitution had been violated. Ecstasy fought with disbelief as I fingered the few pages that had arrived with the day's mail in an ordinary-looking envelope. We had a nearly complete victory without even having to go to trial! In my phone calls to the others, I came close to adolescent glee. Milt and Bernie were much better at sounding professional. Merrill was still unbelieving, and kept repeating, "I didn't think it would happen." With Chuck the refrain was, "We did it. We really did."

The opinion was strong. Austin concluded that the statistics alone proved a deliberate intention to discriminate. He said that no criterion other than race could plausibly explain the location of the CHA's projects. He added that the testimony of CHA officials corroborated the fact that there had been a deliberate intention to segregate. Neither the laudable goal of providing needed housing nor the possibility that the aldermen were not personally racist but were simply reflecting the sentiments of their constituents could justify a governmental policy of keeping blacks out of white neighborhoods.

Austin specifically addressed the city council "excuse." The CHA could not escape liability because the impetus for the policy against white sites came from the council. Incorporating the Kean-Murphy agreement—we gave special thanks to the jeans brigade—into the CHA's site selection procedure resulted in a racial veto before the CHA formally presented the council with its sites. The CHA thereby made the policies of the aldermen its own and deprived opponents of the opportunity for public debate. But even if the CHA had not participated in the informal elimination of white sites, it was bound by the Constitution not to build on sites chosen by some other agency on the basis of race.

The closing paragraph of Austin's opinion conveyed a sense of urgency:

> Existing patterns of racial separation must be reversed if there is to be a chance of averting the desperately intensifying division of Whites and Negroes in Chicago. On the basis of present trends of Negro residential concentration and of Negro migration into and White migration out of the central city, the [Kerner Commission] estimates that Chicago will

become 50 percent Negro by 1984. By 1984 it may be too late to heal racial divisions.

Front-page headlines announced the decision. Pointing out that "public housing is being objected to by many people in all wards," Daley said the ruling could slow up public housing construction. Then, sounding a theme that was to occupy us for years to come, he added, "There is no public housing in the suburbs. Surely the metropolitan area should open up if we are going to answer the problem."

Jesse Jackson opined that Austin's decision "validated" Martin Luther King's 1966 open housing marches. Editorials discussed the "public housing dilemma" at length. "The realities of changing neighborhoods and of whites fleeing to the suburbs are eloquent testimony to the difficulties that still lie ahead," said the *Daily News*. "Mayor Daley Must Lead," demanded the *Sun-Times*. Hoping, perhaps, as had Martin Luther King, that Daley could be "brought around" on housing, the editorial called upon the mayor to act "vigorously and positively."

Denying that the CHA's actions had ever been discriminatory, Swibel emphasized that opposition to public housing by a community might be based on economic and cultural factors as well as on race. He said that the CHA's great goal had been to build urgently needed housing for low-income families and that the CHA had proceeded "where the community welcomed public housing and where the need for slum clearance was the greatest." Austin's decision, he concluded, placed the responsibility for the location of public housing squarely where it belonged—"on the entire community."

11

Austin's opinion had merely pronounced a dispersal objective. Still remaining was the job of drafting a specific remedial order, a challenging task that took over four months. We consulted with countless groups and individuals in both Chicago and Washington about what to do, and tried hard to engage HUD in the process. For its part, the CHA sought advice from a research center at Loyola University, as well as from Richard C. Wade, a professor of urban history at the University of Chicago who had recently been appointed to the CHA Board of Commissioners.

Our efforts with HUD went nowhere. HUD's position, and the posture of the Justice Department lawyers representing it, was awkward because HUD was still itself a Gautreaux defendant. In the middle of 1967, after receiving scores of pages of briefs on HUD's motion to dismiss the separate Gautreaux case against it, Austin had postponed that case until after he ruled on the CHA. Whatever he did with the CHA, he reasoned, might either end or "facilitate" the case against HUD. Now HUD and its lawyers were leery that any suggestions they made about relief against the CHA might hurt them in the HUD case.

There were long discussions with Austin in his chambers to which each party brought the views of outsiders, sometimes in person, sometimes by letter, reflecting the widespread interest in what the judge would do. Many of the letters, of course, were solicited by one side or the other. Rancor ran high. Kula, perhaps smarting from her loss, declined to engage in serious discussion with us about the shape of the order to come.

From all the conferring and discussing, two major, intertwined issues emerged. The first was whether the CHA should be subjected only to a general prohibition against "discrimination," or whether a specific "formula"—a required ratio of white area to black area construction—should be imposed on future CHA development. (At that time Chicago was a white and black city; the population of other minorities, including Latinos, was minuscule.)

The CHA badly wanted an order that merely prohibited it from discriminating, without specifics governing future conduct, and without saying how the past location imbalance was to be redressed. Swibel and Kula were passionate about the risks to the public housing program should anything more be done. A Swibel memorandum to Daley said that the formula we had proposed (four new units in white neighborhoods for each one in a black) could mean the end of public housing. Later, sensing perhaps that the judge was leaning against them on this issue, Kula and Swibel suggested that instead of an imposed formula the CHA would bring each of its future development proposals to the judge for approval.

Wade wrote a strong letter to Austin in support of the CHA's position. "The breaking up of the ghetto is the central domestic issue of our time." But two aspects of our proposals, Wade's letter went on, would have the opposite effect. First, our proposed definition of white and black neighborhoods (some definition was an essential element of our specific formula proposal, by now reduced to three to one) was an "open invitation to block-busting on a grand scale." We defined census tracts with 30 percent or more black population as the "limited public housing area," but that was just a euphemism for predominantly black. This definition, Wade wrote, would play into the hands of blockbusting real estate agents. They would canvas white neighborhoods, door to door, saying, "the court itself has declared [your] community to be black." Wade also argued that our "buffer-zone" proposal—treating areas within a mile of a 30 percent black census tract as if they too were "limited"—would have the same effect. That too would lead to panic and "accelerate the process of ghettoization."

Wade's letter merited thoughtful consideration, not only because, coming from a well-known urban analyst, the views he expressed commanded respect, but also because we had labored through identical concerns before arriving at our proposal. Our 30 percent number had originated in "tipping point" analysis. When the black population of a neighborhood rose to a certain level, whites would leave and the neighborhood would "tip" to all black. The CHA's own witnesses had put the tipping point at 30 percent, and Hauser had confirmed that it was a good number to use. So we asked Hauser to consider Wade's letter with us.

Hauser responded that if public housing were built in neighborhoods whose black population was already 30 percent or higher, the transition from white to black would simply be speeded up. So too, he thought, with our buffer zones. These were areas where residents were already nervous about their proximity to heavily black neighborhoods. Hauser's suggestion was that, if anything, our proposal should be strengthened: before more public housing was permitted even in black or buffer areas—our proposal would allow 25 percent in such areas so long as the "matching" 75 percent in white areas were also being built—the CHA should be required to establish that the stability of the particular neighborhood would not be affected by its proposed development.

Wade's recommendation was that the judge should review each CHA development proposal for conformance with the court's goal, an alternative we viewed as entirely impractical. Without objective standards, each court hearing on each CHA proposal would be like tramping directionless through a swamp. Nor would the judge conceivably consent to becoming Chicago's public housing czar, granting or denying approval, after endless hearings on the facts, to each and every CHA proposed development.

Concerned as we were about Wade's fears, Wade's letter left our views unchanged. The alternatives of leaving everything either to the CHA or to the judge, in either case without standards, were both unsatisfactory. Some tipping point number had to be used, and we could do no better than use the one both the CHA and Hauser agreed upon. So we persisted in arguing for a formula that would require a majority of future CHA units to be located in white neighborhoods. In one of our conferences the judge himself indicated that in future construction some "imbalance" in favor of white areas might be necessary.

The second major issue to emerge from all the discussion was "metropolitanization." Given what was happening to the nation's big cities in the 1960s, Chicago most emphatically included, there was no way that enough scattered-site public housing could be provided inside Chicago in white neighborhoods. At least that could not be done without precipitating the exodus of whites that Wade feared, thereby intensifying the very condition we were trying to correct. As if to emphasize Wade's views, new Census Bureau estimates, released about the time of Wade's letter, showed that whites were leaving the nation's central cities three times as rapidly as in the previous six years of the 1960s.

Several years earlier, in 1965, President Johnson had urged Congress to recognize that central cities and their suburbs were really single metropolitan areas. He had suggested that Congress might condition federal aid to state and local governments upon metropolitan-wide planning. Congress had not acted, but there was widespread recognition that the poor and minorities were disproportionately concentrated in central cities, as was public housing, while jobs were moving to the suburbs. A 1967 *Sun-Times* headline captured the essentials: "Jobs Move Away From City, Negroes Lack Access."

Just days before Austin's February 1969 opinion had arrived in the mail, John Gardner, former secretary of health, education, and welfare in Johnson's cabinet, had advanced a significant policy proposal at a congressional committee briefing on cities. Referring to the 1968 housing act's directive to build six million housing units for low- and moderate-income families, he emphasized that, because of where available land was to be found, two-thirds of the new units would have to be built outside central cities. Yet the suburbs, Gardner said, "unyieldingly resist" federally assisted housing. His proposed way around this blockage was aggressive use of the "affirmatively administer" provision of the Fair Housing Act to "open up" the suburbs. Under the authority of that provision, Gardner said, HUD could and should deny grants—including crucial funding for sewer and water facilities and federally insured mortgages—to communities that failed to shoulder their fair share of housing for poorer families. Extra money should be given to those that did.

Gardner's proposal fell short of the Kaiser and Douglas Commission recommendations, for it involved neither tampering with local zoning powers nor authorizing the federal government itself to build the needed housing. Instead, it relied on the "leveraging" power of the federal purse to induce local communities themselves to do what was required. It was "conservative" in another important respect, too, for it did not require Congress to pass any more laws. Through "affirmative administration" of already enacted programs, HUD could itself pull the financial levers.

It was of course unlikely that the Nixon administration would follow Gardner's approach, much less swallow the even stronger medicine prescribed by the Kaiser and Douglas commissions. But we fantasized that for the Chicago area the Gautreaux case presented another possibility. Suppose we could persuade Austin that some of the CHA's future housing had to be scattered into the suburbs because his goal could not be achieved in the city alone. And suppose he therefore ordered the CHA to do the scattering. That, however, would require suburban consent. Illinois law required a public housing authority wishing to develop public housing beyond its borders to obtain the agreement of the "outside" public housing authority. And federal law called for a "cooperation agreement" with the local municipal government if building was to be within an incorporated area. The CHA long had had its cooperation agreement with Chicago, but to move into surrounding Cook County would require the consent of the Cook County Housing Authority and, for housing proposed within a municipality, an agreement with the municipal government as well.

The prospects for obtaining such agreements voluntarily lay somewhere between zero and nil. But we reasoned that the refusal of suburban consent would amount to frustration of a court order intended to remedy a federal constitutional wrong. Couldn't Austin then remove the frustration by setting aside the legal requirements that the CHA obtain suburban consents before it embarked on development in the suburbs? This "set-aside" approach seemed to be our only hope for metropolitan-wide public housing.

It was a long-shot idea, and we knew from our meetings with Austin that he would not enter such an order at our request. In fact, our gentle suggestion that it would be fine with us if some of the CHA's scattered-site housing were placed in the suburbs had elicited an acerbic response about letting the CHA "off the hook." From talks with HUD I also knew there was no chance that HUD would ask Austin to enter that kind of order. But if the U.S. Department of Justice should propose it, or even agree to support it, maybe Austin would then listen.

In March, full of anticipation if not hope, I spoke to an acquaintance in a Washington law firm who had entree to the Justice Department and agreed to do some exploring for us. The report came back that nobody could or would tell us what, if anything, Justice might be thinking about. We were whistling in the dark about the Justice Department. The metropolitan issue, which would necessarily involve white suburbs, was fraught with racial implications and therefore political obstacles. The best we could do was to urge that the order against the CHA should permit some of the CHA's future units to be located in Cook County, sidestepping for the time being how on earth the CHA would ever be able to put them there.

Austin himself invited HUD, as the federal government's housing expert, to submit its suggestions as to what his order should say. HUD was impossibly slow to respond. Apart from the awkwardness that the agency was a defendant in a related case, there were differences of view between HUD and its Justice Department lawyers that led to prolonged negotiations and delayed the government's response. In the end a joint HUD–Justice Department memorandum was delivered to Austin late in the day on June 30, even though the judge had earlier advised that he would issue his order on July 1. The government's memorandum was probably too tardy to affect Austin's thinking—by then we all pretty well knew what the order would say—but it was good to have the federal government agree that the kind of general order proposed by the CHA "will not serve the Court's purpose." Indeed, HUD and Justice said specifically, "We accept the Court's intention to lay down specific requirements for dispersed and desegregated housing . . ."

Yet the memorandum walked on eggs. It was "concerned" that Austin's order be "realistic," but gave the judge precious little advice on how "realistically" to achieve desegregated public housing. It supported the objective of developing public housing outside Chicago, but quickly added that, "in light of the probable difficulty of obtaining the required cooperation of local governments, that appears unlikely to be a major factor in the immediate future." So much for our hopes that the Justice Department would be imaginative on metropolitanization. The largest part of the government's memorandum described HUD-funded programs for new housing in black areas (such as urban renewal and model cities) and worried that Austin's forthcoming order might constrict those programs. It could not "evaluate the workability" of our proposed ratio of white to black sites.

If a bureaucracy may be said to have a heart, what HUD felt deep in its bureaucratic heart was expressed a few months later in a speech by its top trial lawyer, Arthur J. Gang, assistant general counsel for litigation. Gang noted that we intended to reactivate the case against HUD, an effort HUD would oppose, he said, with all the "usual legal and policy arguments." The reason? Gang was worried that Austin's decision would lead courts around the country to supervise HUD's activities to "speed the pace of integration in housing." However, he went on, it was the secretary of HUD, not the courts, who was responsible for administering the nation's housing policy; the judiciary should stay out of the "complexities of site selection."

Moreover, it was an event of "utmost gravity" when the secretary of HUD, whose duty it was to make and police rules on equal opportunity in housing, was charged with "complicity in a scheme to perpetuate segregation in housing." It was a little like "finding the policeman with his hand in the till," something that could "undermine the confidence of the American people in the processes of law." Responsible lawyers should weigh the consequences carefully before participating in such "rash action."

Yet Gang's speech acknowledged that the evidence of CHA discrimination was "overwhelming." And Marie McGuire's letter showed that

HUD, knowing what was going on, had continued to pump fuel into the CHA's discriminatory engine. So the policeman's hand *was* in the till. Gang's speech conspicuously omitted any discussion of a court's responsibility to deal with that circumstance.

***

As Austin's draft order was shaped and honed in the long discussions in the judge's chambers, it became in one respect less restrictive than the CHA had feared. Presumably because the CHA had already invested much planning time and secured HUD approval, Austin decided to rule that a dozen ghetto projects could move forward. Only future CHA proposals would be governed by his order. Of the 1,458 "exempted" units, about half were in six more elevator buildings. Three of them, with some smaller buildings, plus another nearby cluster which included an elevator building, added to an already massive CHA concentration near the southside lakefront, which would now aggregate more than 5,000 units with close to 20,000 residents. This was an unhappy loss for us, reminiscent of the Summit Agreement, which had not stopped the CHA's planned ghetto projects even though construction had not yet begun.

On the other hand, Austin clearly agreed with us on the question of a specific formula for future construction—three-quarters of future units were to be located in white areas. He even indicated that to "match" by about half the 1,458 ghetto area units he intended to exempt, the first 700 new units would all have to be located in white neighborhoods. It also became clear that the order would require half the tenants in new projects to be local community residents who were not CHA tenants or applicants, although they had to be poor enough to meet public housing eligibility rules. This was an approach we strongly favored because in white neighborhoods the local residents would be whites, leading to integration within buildings as well as within neighborhoods. We also hoped that giving half the new units to present neighbors would make for greater community acceptance of the new scattered sites, or at least lessen community opposition.

Other provisions of the draft order prohibited high-rises and large projects, or concentrating units in any one neighborhood. Our hope was that small-scale developments in stable communities, with half the apartments occupied by neighbors already living in the community, would generate positive experiences that would counter blockbusting fears. Our unopposed recommendation that up to one-third of the new units be permitted in Cook County was also acceptable (though there was no mechanism to get them there). Finally, the CHA was to use its "best efforts" to develop as much public housing as possible under the new ground rules.

The morning of July 1 was our last scheduled conference with Austin, the day he had earlier said he would sign an order. People crowded into Austin's chambers for the climactic moment, ranging around the judge's table and filling an outside row of extra chairs—Kula, Hunt, Otis, our quintet of Gautreaux lawyers, HUD's lawyers, some "outsiders" such as John McKnight. The discussion was over details, the fine-tuning of an order that had already been through countless drafts. As the noon hour approached Austin suggested a break for lunch. As if it were a comment on the weather, he added that he thought he would sign the order that afternoon.

In the corridor outside the courtroom Kula told Hunt and Otis that she had better call Swibel to give him the news. Putting down the phone after delivering her message, Kula said Swibel wanted to talk—he would meet the CHA lawyers at Fritzel's, one of Chicago's best-known restaurants. Fritzel's was notable not only for its food but for its ability—uncommon in those days—to provide telephone hookups at individual tables. After hearing Kula's story, Swibel called for a phone and telephoned the mayor. As the conversation ended, Swibel—downing the receiver—announced, "He wants me to talk to the judge."

"I don't think that's a good idea," Kula immediately rejoined. The order had been worked over for months, she said, the die was cast, and nothing more could be accomplished at this late stage. But Swibel had his orders and, when the participants reconvened in Austin's chambers, the CHA chairman was present to receive a seemingly warm "Hello, Charley" and handshake from the judge.

After everyone had found chairs (Swibel at the table near Austin), the judge turned to Swibel and asked him what he had to say. With the earnestness and passion he could always turn on like a faucet, Swibel launched into a plea that lasted nearly half an hour. Give us some time, he urged. We can work this out. It's a tough problem, but we can come up with the right answer. More time, without specifics, was the refrain.

Austin listened impassively throughout. He uttered not a word during the entire oration. When Swibel had finally finished, Austin fixed him with a stare. "Do you have anything more to say, Mr. Chairman?" Swibel looked startled. "No," he managed weakly, and seemed to slump in his chair as if spent from his rhetorical effort. "Then," said Austin, "I think I'll sign this order." Which he proceeded to do, while everyone stared at his scratching pen making the only sound in the otherwise completely silent room.

<hr />

The order was headline news. Editorial comment was generally favorable but somber. Whatever happened, said the *Daily News*, "one thing that Judge Austin has done is to put Chicago face to face with its most crucial issue—whether it is to be a city united or a city divided." It added: "The [City] Council, under the leadership of Mayor Richard J. Daley, must act in the full knowledge that if the decision is for a divided city, that can only be a stop gap on the way to a city in social and economic ruin." The *Sun-Times* editorialized that Austin's ruling opened the way for "some truly imaginative planning for a viable bi-racial city." The somber tone was best illustrated by a *Sun-Times* editorial cartoon: a seated, gloomy, Abe Lincoln, eyes closed, chin resting on one hand, the other holding the day's front page with the headline, "Court Rules CHA Biased on Sites."

Other comments emphasized foreseeable problems. The *Tribune* opined that the housing dispersal ordered by Austin "is something more easily said than done." *Time* magazine quoted the leader of a white homeowner group as threatening: "If the construction really starts, we'll take action of some sort, and not letters or petitions." A *Daily News* article was headlined, "Backlash looms for CHA."

It had been three and a half years since the pizza at Edwardo's on January 21, 1966. In many ways we were in a new era—the civil rights revolution was over and the Nixon age (it was now six months past inauguration) was upon us. Yet, carryover as it was from the former era, in two respects the Gautreaux case was just beginning. First, how would Austin, and we, deal with a recalcitrant city council and "backlash" in the neighborhoods? Second, with whites streaming out to suburbia and the housing problem clearly metropolitan, how could we "engage" the suburbs?

Perhaps, had the CHA, the city, the Justice Department, and HUD all been willing to work together with Austin, a strategy along the lines of our set-aside approach could have been crafted. But Swibel and Daley were not open to working with the judge on Gautreaux. The hubris of Gang's speech would show how little creative thinking could be expected from HUD. The unhappy reality was that we had achieved a city remedy for a metropolitan disease.

The night Austin signed the judgment order, Barbara, the children, and I went out for a celebratory dinner. We picked a local Italian restaurant, informal enough so that I could wear—at Deborah's insistence—the Peanuts sweatshirt she had given me after the Tometz win. In bold letters the back side of the shirt posed Charlie Brown's query, "How can we lose when we're so sincere?" Our talk was upbeat, befitting the occasion. It had been an exciting run. Victory was sweet. We were going to make a difference—make things better. And we were now free to take on HUD in its separate Gautreaux case.

Yet a sober note insinuated itself into all the bravura. The reality was that the way ahead in Gautreaux—indeed, in the country, under its new president—was far from clear. The HUD case would probably be a bruising battle. Nor could it be assumed that Austin's paper order against the CHA would be effortlessly transformed into scattered-site construction. After all, we reminded ourselves, there were two ways to read Charlie Brown's question.

CHAPTER THREE

THROUGH THE JUNGLE

Things have changed here since yesterday.

—Vladimir (*Waiting for Godot*)

1

July 10, 1969, ten days after Austin signed the final judgment order, the CHA commissioners voted not to appeal. What an unexpectedly positive development! The vote was on Swibel's recommendation, no doubt blessed by the mayor. It had to signify, we thought, a good faith effort to comply. And through the grapevine—now the source of most of our knowledge since Kula had erected a stony wall between us—we heard that the CHA had asked HUD for 5,000 new public housing units. After some delay, it had received approval for 1,500. That was a start. We also learned that the CHA was "working up" sites to submit to the city council—even 1,500 units would require many scattered sites.

Sitting around and hoping that the CHA would do the right thing wasn't easy. Yet we felt we had no alternative but to give the CHA a reasonable amount of time. So I was especially grateful to be buoyed by an experience at the start of a family camping trip in the San Juan Mountains that seemed, along with the CHA's decision not to appeal, a hopeful omen.

The logistics of our trip with the Sierra Club included advance payment and meeting the camping group at a prescribed time and place. In our case this meant quite a few hundreds of dollars (real money in those days), endless hours—mostly Barbara's—packing backcountry gear for two adults and three children, and a cross-country drive of over a thousand miles to a campground some sixteen miles up a dirt road in a national forest outside Durango, Colorado. We arrived, hot and tired, to find no sign of the Sierra Club. My inquiries produced nothing but puzzled looks. Finally one woman said she might have seen a paper plate on a tree at the campground's upper end. Yes, it might have had "Sierra" penciled on it.

As I half-jogged up the campground road, peering at every tree for a paper plate, I found myself musing about our situation. On the basis of a receipt for our money and a couple of sentences of mailed instructions, we had committed our whole family, financially and emotionally, to this vacation. We had spent many days in careful preparation, and had then loaded the car and driven halfway across the country. Yet it all came down to searching through a forest campground for a paper plate tacked to a tree.

Sure enough, where the road curved back toward the entrance, I spied an ordinary—but to me quite lovely—paper plate on a tree. Indeed, it bore the penciled words "Sierra Club." As I rushed back with my glad news, I thought happily to myself that Murphy's Law was not infallible. Sometimes things worked out. Why not with the CHA and Gautreaux too?

2

From the front, Marshall Patner verged on roly-poly—his impressively rounded stomach pushed his belt buckle well down below his navel. From the rear, however, he looked like a stick, seeming entirely to lack buttocks. Marshall's personality reflected this physical dichotomy. He was kind and generous, and nothing pleased him more than to help his friends and acquaintances by matching them with things—cheap travel tickets, unusual restaurants, used cars, jobs. Yet Marshall could be impatient and dismissive. Once off his list of friends, it was difficult to get back on.

Marshall's favorite activity was conversation, preferably accompanied by food. During 1969 Marshall and I conversed a good deal. Marshall's perambulations through the law, after his 1956 graduation from the University of Chicago Law School, had led him through a succession of jobs. Now he had yet another, executive director of a group called Businessmen for the Public Interest (for obvious reasons soon changed to Business and Professional People for the Public Interest). BPI, the shorthand moniker, was what Marshall and I were talking about.

BPI had been brought to life by an iconoclastic businessman, Gordon B. Sherman. Some years earlier Gordon had created Midas Mufflers, an immensely successful franchise business of which he was now the wealthy president. A gifted orator and knowledgeable music lover, he also headed an anti–Vietnam War organization, tended aviaries in both his home and office, and played the bagpipes. His deep concern for social justice had led him to the idea of a "public interest law firm." Only partly tongue in cheek, Gordon's concept was:

> Since the perpetrators of evil in our society are skilled, experienced professionals who ply their nefarious trades full time, they should be engaged not by callow youths, fresh and unlearned from college, not by part-time volunteers, torn between the demands of their coffers and their consciences, but by equally skilled, equally experienced professionals serving full time in the public interest.

Gordon had started BPI in early 1969. On the recommendation of Jay Miller, then head of the ACLU in Chicago, he had selected Marshall as its director. The organization had a $200,000 annual budget (supplied by Gordon) and four lawyers. At our frequent lunches, Marshall and I were talking about my leaving Schiff and taking over as the BPI director.

Some years earlier I had told Barbara that, by the time I reached forty, I would like to be doing something other than the commercial practice of law. Already behind schedule, I had asked Marshall if he had any ideas. "Come with BPI," had been his immediate response, and I was quickly captured by the prospect. Barbara gave her wholehearted consent and, following an interview with Gordon, the deal was struck. Marshall would become general counsel and I would take over as executive director.

"Interview" with Gordon is not quite accurate; "encounter" would be closer. Barbara and Deborah were there—Gordon wanted to know the family—and the discussion ranged far beyond BPI and the law. My concern was independence; if I were going to head BPI, I wanted to be boss, not Gordon's aide. Marshall had assured me that that was the understanding, but I wanted to hear it from Gordon. For his part, Gordon probably accepted my legal credentials at face value but wanted to size me up as a human being. When I told him that some of my partners at Schiff were urging me merely to take a leave of absence, and that I might like to consider that, Gordon shot back, "Oh, so you like to do your act over a net." Embarrassed, I dropped the leave of absence idea. Otherwise, I passed muster. By the end of our meeting it was clear that I wished to join BPI, and that Gordon was agreeable.

Gordon was true to his word about not interfering, and I have never had the slightest regret about my decision. What I did regret was the brevity of my association with Gordon, who soon found himself engaged in a battle with his father over business matters (Midas was part of his father's still larger empire) and lost a proxy fight. Whereupon he picked up stakes and family and headed for California. There he learned nature photography and earned a master's degree in the oboe. He also contracted cancer, which he fought valiantly for a dozen years before succumbing to hepatitis. The quality of Gordon, both the man and his prose, may be gathered from a letter he wrote to me in 1986, the year before his death:

Dear Alex,

I am stirred out of my customary correspondence lassitude by your tender inference that I am "not well." Lest intimations of my decline compound my doubtful reputation in the city from which I am exiled and, indeed, my true friends brood without cause, I leap to assurances that I am bristling with well-being.

On the very precipice of death, yes, but ill . . . oh, no. I have never, in my life, been better; were it not in poor taste as the world goes, I would make bold to recommend, if not prescribe, some slow, sparing form of cancer to one and all as an elixir, a bracing way to tone up your lives. You, who know of my appetite for enigma, might suppose that I am being characteristically and intemperately playful here, but not so. I used to think my affliction was some form of punishment; now I see it as benevolent compensation from a loving deity and I look with condescending compassion on the rest of you who must proceed through your days without the organizing benefits of a fatal diagnosis.

The truth is, emerging from all of this tedious abstraction, that this late in life, and with doom swaying uncertainly over my head, I have found my true vocation. I tell you because you (and Barbara) are kindred souls: I have become a wildlife photographer. This is no "hobby"; it smacks of high professionalism and provides me with the greatest excitement and steady satisfaction since the formation of BPI (the only near contender in my life). It carries me out of my warm bed hours before dawn, imposes on me skills of stealth, and supplies me with a harvest of exquisite color-slide images of birds (mostly) and rare, illuminating moments in nature. I have become locally celebrated out here and it is refreshing at this late end of my life to be engaged in honest work.

I follow your reports as they arrive . . . I bless your work and hold myself worthy that once I played a small part in it.

> With much affection,
>
> Gordon

At a memorial service in Chicago, Deborah played a Schubert sonata, one of Gordon's favorites. Before sitting down to the piano she reminisced about meeting Gordon and about BPI, particularly her teenager's understanding that social change organizations like BPI existed to fix the world, and her more mature realization that the world might not be fixable. The point, she said, as Gordon had put it, was not about fixing the world, or about conquering death, but about living passionately. She concluded:

> That seems a very important message right now when the world appears to be less fixable than ever. To remember that the energy we summon can create beauty, for ourselves, and for everyone. That Gordon's camera was a mirror up to nature, but also to us, asking us to look into ourselves for the passion we possess and the beauty we can create as its byproduct.

Some of my partners at Schiff were flabbergasted at my proposed move to BPI. The era was one in which a partnership in a big firm was a sinecure, while BPI's future was far from assured. My parents, and my mother-in-law who was living with us at the time, could not forget the trauma of the Great Depression; each thought I had taken leave of my senses.

Still, the decision was not a difficult one. Our lifestyle was not extravagant (our vacations were mostly in tents), and Barbara and I felt we could handle the drop in income and the future uncertainty. We quickly agreed that present desires should trump future prospects. At dinner one night I told fourteen-year-old Deborah that my proposed move to BPI was being called "courageous," and asked her what she thought. Always ruthlessly candid, she replied after only the briefest hesitation, "Dad, you're not being courageous. You're just giving in to temptation."

And so in April 1970 I moved over to BPI's untidy offices in an ancient, down-at-the-heels building on North Dearborn Street, bringing Gautreaux with me. From then on Gautreaux was a BPI, no longer an ACLU, case.

3

After the exhilaration of the San Juan trip, we restarted the case against HUD. I first talked to Frank Fisher, HUD's top Midwest official, a lawyer dedicated to public service, not a career bureaucrat. We thought Fisher would be sympathetic and hoped that through him we might work out a court-ordered approach to metropolitan relief. Fisher would have none of it—probably on orders from Washington *could* have none of it. He tried to persuade me instead that we should let our HUD suit die and rely on the good HUD people, himself included, to do the right thing. We respected Fisher, but he was a transient whom political winds could blow away at any moment.

When the dialogue came to its predictable end and we filed a motion for summary judgment against HUD, we were at once met with all the "usual legal and policy arguments" to which Arthur Gang had referred. Yet it was a hopeful time. The facts—the CHA's discrimination, and HUD's knowledge and funding of it—were not in dispute, and we had a sound legal argument that HUD's actions violated the Constitution's Fifth Amendment too. The federal government could no more approve and fund a discriminatory public housing system than could a local agency like the CHA. If we succeeded in getting a quick guilty ruling, perhaps HUD would then work with us on a metropolitan remedy. For, wonder of wonders, Nixon's secretary of HUD was viewing housing problems through a metropolitan lens. He was former Michigan governor George Romney, who had saved American Motors with the compact Rambler and was now embarking on another savior's mission.

Shortly after assuming office in early 1969, Romney announced that building the housing authorized by the 1968 housing act was the way to overcome the country's domestic crisis. It would ease racial tensions and bring millions of "neglected Americans" into the mainstream of American life. It could save the cities. It was the nation's number one economic opportunity, and it would be Romney's number one priority. By the end of 1969 HUD had broken records for building subsidized housing and was proposing still more. Yet, where to put all the new housing was becoming a challenge. Available land in central cities—just as John Gardner had forecast—was in short supply and expensive.

Romney confronted the location issue with characteristic fervor. It was vital, he asserted, for subsidized housing to be dispersed more broadly than in the past. His undersecretary referred to HUD plans for expanding suburban housing opportunities for low income minority families. Jerris Leonard, head of the Civil Rights Division of the Justice Department, added that past policy had sometimes made government a partner in perpetuating racial discrimination in housing. The Nixon administration, Leonard said, would soon unveil significant policy changes to encourage suburban locations. In the president's Second Annual Report on National Housing Goals, issued in April 1970, Nixon seemed to lend his support to the emerging new policy.

Population growth, the report said, would require enlarging the housing supply beyond crowded city centers. Though sufficient land was available in metropolitan—particularly suburban—areas for building the needed housing, one of the most serious problems in finding housing sites for the poor was opposition by middle-class, white communities. "There must be an end," the report went on, "to the concentration of the poor in land-short central cities, and the inaccessibility to the growth of employment opportunities in suburban areas." The objective was to achieve "open communities" that provided jobs and housing for families of all income levels and racial characteristics. To that end, legislation would soon be proposed to prohibit local governments from discriminating against federally subsidized housing.

Nixon's "opening" to China still lay in the future. But to those concerned about ghettoization in America, the proposed "opening" to the suburbs was of comparable surprise and significance. Although Romney's lawyers were opposing a Gautreaux order against HUD, once HUD liability had been established, didn't all this talk suggest that Romney would be an ally in what came after?

That was April 1970, a time of great optimism, the very month I moved to BPI. HUD's briefs—opposing our summary judgment motion in Gautreaux—were truly nothing but the usual (unpersuasive) arguments about limited court jurisdiction and broad agency discretion. We could not imagine that Austin wouldn't see through them. After what he had written about the CHA it didn't seem possible that Austin would let HUD "off the hook." And once HUD was hooked . . .

But T. S. Eliot was right—April is the cruelest month. In a short time the hopeful picture, both nationally and in Gautreaux, turned to ashes.

4

Romney's undoing was spawned in the industrial Detroit suburb of Warren. With a population of 180,000, Warren housed a grand total of twenty-eight black families. The population of neighboring Detroit was more than 40 percent black, and 30 percent of the workers in Warren's own Chevrolet, Dodge, and Chrysler plants were also black. Frank Fisher was studying Warren with an eye toward developing the "affirmative administration" called for by the 1968 Fair Housing Act. A memorandum he sent to Washington described the unparalleled opportunity Detroit and its suburbs presented for applying a fair-housing strategy:

> Perhaps nowhere else is there the combination of a large central city with a substantial black population (over 40 percent) surrounded by predominantly white large suburbs which use many HUD programs, in which there is extensive black employment, and with a great deal of housing for lower middle income families (suggesting racial rather than economic exclusion).

With Washington approval, Fisher told Warren that if it wanted its pending $3 million urban renewal application approved, it would have to take some fair-housing steps that would lead to "increased housing opportunities for minorities in Warren."

Warren officials were upset, and Mayor Ted Bates arranged a Washington meeting with Romney. On May 7, 1970, Bates and about ten Warren officials were ushered into Romney's large, wood-paneled conference room. Fisher was already seated at the table. The mayor began by saying Warren was an "open city"; it was not against housing for minorities. "We have our colored in Warren. We have no problems there . . ." Interrupting, Romney leaned forward and said, "Mr. Mayor, you do have a problem or you would not be here."

Taken aback, Bates tried a different approach. He explained that Warren had spent $75,000 on police protection for a racially mixed couple that had moved into the city in 1967. Again Romney cut in. "Mayor Bates, I was governor of Michigan when the Bailey family moved in and I had to send the state police in there to protect them because the local officials would not fulfill their responsibilities."

A long silence followed. Finally, Romney broke it:

You can try to hermetically seal Warren off from the surrounding areas if you want, but you won't do it with federal money. You will find it will be impossible to do. We are living in a nation now where everybody is interdependent. Black people have as much right to equal opportunities as we do. God knows, they have suffered so much they may have more right. Inexorably, there is going to be a change, so you might as well face up to it now and agree to these requirements.

Someone asked if Romney was talking about integration. He was, Romney replied. "Well," said a Warren councilwoman, "what you're asking us to do is give up our jobs."

Bates then argued that integration should be a "natural happening," that the community should "wait for nature to take its course." Romney spoke a final time:

The youth of this nation, the minorities of this nation, the discriminated against of this nation are not going to wait for "nature to take its course." What is really at issue here is responsibility—moral responsibility. This problem is the most important one that America has ever faced, is now facing and will ever face, bar none. It must be solved and we, the citizens, must solve it.

As the meeting ended, Bates said he had a better understanding of how Romney felt. He would return home to discuss the situation.

Intense negotiations between Fisher's office and Warren ensued. Finally, on June 16, by a 5–4 vote, the Warren city council approved a compromise—a limited open housing ordinance and a resolution authorizing the mayor to appoint a fair-housing board. The papers were flown to Washington and approved. Warren's check would be written as soon as Mayor Bates appointed the fifteen members of the fair-housing board.

The joy in HUD's offices over this first victory for Romney's metropolitan strategy lasted five weeks. On July 21, 1970, while Bates was still assembling his list of appointees to the fair-housing board, the *Detroit News* published the first of a series of stories on the Warren-HUD negotiations. "U.S. Picks Warren as Prime Target in Move to Integrate All Suburbs," read the initial headline. Weeks of effort, the *News* proclaimed, had enabled it to piece together the full story of how the federal government "intended to use its vast power to force integration of America's white suburbs—and it is using the Detroit suburbs as a key starting point." A step-by-step account on succeeding days throughout the week was promised. As a Warren councilman said, it was like dropping a bomb each day for seven days in a row.

Bates professed outrage. "I won't tolerate Warren being used as a guinea pig for integration experiments, even if it means losing urban renewal." He charged that HUD had "lied about their intentions in wanting open housing guarantees from us," saying HUD had told Warren it would not push "forced integration." The headline for the second day was, "Warren Charges HUD Deceit." So it went for the rest of the week. "How Warren Became Integration Test City," and "Warren Was Given Romney Ultimatum," were headlines on succeeding days. Romney quickly arranged for a public meeting to be held on July 27 at Warren's Fitzgerald High School. The meeting lasted two and a half hours. Inside the auditorium about a hundred officials from Warren and other Detroit suburbs were assembled. Outside, a crowd of about three hundred whites milled around, carrying signs with such sentiments as "Romney is a HUDache" and "Get rid of the dud at HUD."

Romney's prepared statement was conciliatory. There was no policy of "forced integration." Warren was not a testing place. In Warren, as in other cities, HUD's policies were to enforce laws against housing discrimination and to encourage voluntary steps toward more low- and moderate-income housing. The *Detroit News* headlines were "unjustified."

Heated questioning followed. Romney continued to insist on "voluntary," but it was clear that the word meant Warren could "voluntarily" forgo urban renewal dollars if it refused to appoint the fair-housing board HUD was insisting upon. "Romney's speech was just a play on words," a Warren councilwoman was quoted as saying, and she was clearly right. As he left the meeting Romney was booed and police had to clear a path for him through the throng. The crowd pounded on Mayor Bates's departing car, shouting, "Bates is a nigger lover."

Two days after Romney's visit, petitions were circulated for a referendum to abolish the Warren urban renewal program. Within ten days nearly 15,000 signatures were obtained. In November 1970 Warren voted overwhelmingly to kill its urban renewal plan. Warren would forgo the millions of federal dollars being held for it rather than take a small step—well short of actually providing any housing for minorities—in the direction of open housing.

A few weeks later, testifying before a Senate committee investigating the relationship between school segregation and housing discrimination, Romney hedged about supporting a policy of housing dispersal. He was uncertain, he said, about the extent of HUD's power under the civil rights laws. There was also the question of "how far you go from the standpoint of pushing things forward without setting things back as a result of pushing too hard too fast." He now sounded quite unlike the George Romney who had told Mayor Bates that the nation could not wait for nature to take its course, and that moral responsibility was the real issue.

There were portents too of trouble with the White House. Early in the summer John Ehrlichman, a top Nixon aide, had inquired about HUD's reported new initiatives. He hoped HUD was not embarking on a new policy without consulting the White House. As the Warren debacle unfolded, White House anxiety increased. To inquiries about its open communities activities, HUD had been routinely responding that its policies were still in a formative stage. To the White House, HUD insisted it had not embarked upon a scheme to "force integration" on the suburbs and that White House concerns were without foundation. Meanwhile, however, some HUD officials had been talking candidly with writers for a periodical, the *National Journal*, about their hopes for open communities. They understood that the *Journal's* piece on housing would not be published until after the November 1970 congressional election.

In fact, the *Journal* article appeared on October 17. Titled "Romney Faces Political Perils with Plan to Integrate Suburbs," its lead sentence announced that Romney was in the final planning stage of a full-scale effort "to disperse largely black and poor populations of center-city ghettos into largely white and affluent suburbs." Quoting an unnamed HUD official, the article continued, "The Secretary is dead serious about giving low-income people a credible opportunity to live where the jobs are—which often means in the suburbs." A confidential HUD memorandum was cited as saying that the decision to build low-income housing in the suburbs reflected the need for a "major change in past policies whereby HUD funds have been concentrated in the core cities; instead, this Department must now put *greatly increased resources where the solutions are, not where the problems are.*"

The approach, the *Journal* said, was to be essentially the one employed in Warren. But the emphasis would not be on terminating funds for programs already begun, as with Warren's urban renewal program. Instead, new projects would be approved in accordance with priorities determined in part by a community's willingness to accept low-income housing. Though HUD was reluctant to talk openly because of the Warren episode and the November elections, a HUD official—again unnamed—was quoted as saying, "We've been doing our thing quietly, but we really plan to fly after the November election."

If HUD was embarrassed by the *National Journal* article, the White House was angry. "Paranoid" was the word one HUD official used. HUD promptly sent Ehrlichman an analysis of its open communities position, saying that the subject of suburban integration had been sensationalized in the press, that HUD's position-in-formation was not one of "forced integration," that HUD's ideas were soundly based in law, and that the White House was unduly concerned.

The White House, however, decided that the time had come to develop a formal position on housing policy. It was made clear to HUD that any major new initiatives should await the definitive policy statement. On its front page, the *New York Times* reported that Attorney General John Mitchell had visited Romney and ordered him to drop his program initiatives until an official administration position on housing desegregation was formulated.

In December, the blow fell. The definitive administration statement was still six months away but in a televised press conference the president told the country, "I believe that forced integration of the suburbs is not in the national interest." Romney had been at pains, in his missives to the White House and in his meeting with Mitchell, to make clear that the occupants of the low- and moderate-income housing called for by the 1968 housing act were not all, or even mostly, black. Most of the nation's low- and moderate-income housing, his statistics showed, was occupied by white Anglo-Saxons. As the *Wall Street Journal* pointed out, Nixon could have talked of the need to alleviate crowded housing conditions in the central city. By his selection of the phrase "forced integration," said the *Journal,* the president "draped the dreaded race-mixing shroud over the entire Romney effort to move subsidized housing beyond city limits." Moaned a Romney aide, "The president hurt us badly."

In June 1971, with fanfare appropriate to a major presidential pronouncement, the Statement by the President on Federal Policies Relative to Equal Housing Opportunity was formally unveiled. Ehrlichman and special White House Counsel Leonard Garment held a press conference in the presidential briefing room. Romney and Mitchell issued separate statements at a joint press conference of their own. The opening paragraph of the Nixon statement fairly described the racial separation problem. The rest was a disaster.

In the nation's largest metropolitan areas, which accounted for more than half the country's population, the statement began, central cities were growing increasingly black while the suburbs remained overwhelmingly white. In city after city the story was the same; the facts revealed by the 1970 census were "compelling." Such a degree of racial separation engendered mistrust, hostility, and fear, wasted human resources by denying human opportunity, and exacted a direct dollar cost in lost wages when minority families could not find housing near suburban jobs.

The administration had therefore developed a three-part housing policy. First, the federal government would be vigorous in enforcing all laws against racial discrimination. (As it turned out, it wasn't.) Second, after sites for HUD-assisted housing had been selected and acquired by local public or private developers (HUD's role being confined to approval or disapproval), HUD would give funding priority to those proposed projects that would open up nonsegregated housing opportunities. But it was a "basic principle" that a municipality that did not want federally assisted housing "should not have it imposed from Washington by bureaucratic fiat."

Third, local authorities should press forward with innovative approaches to making housing more widely available, thereby reducing racial concentration. However, the federal government would not interfere with local policies, such as zoning laws, unless they demonstrably cloaked racial discrimination. The administration would offer leadership in encouraging local governments to adopt new approaches, but the choices involved were essentially local. For emphasis, again, "This administration will not attempt to impose federally assisted housing upon any community."

It was just about as bad as it could have been. As a way to achieve desegregated housing, funding priority for housing proposals was doomed to failure. John Gardner's idea that sewer and water grants and federally insured mortgages should be denied to communities that refused to provide subsidized housing might have had a chance. But funding criteria for housing proposals was a nonstarter. As in Warren, most suburban communities would forgo federal dollars for housing rather than open their doors to the minority poor.

In a statement on school segregation a year earlier, Nixon himself had defined "freedom" as having two essential elements, "the *right* to choose, and the *ability* to choose." Strikingly, the president had offered a housing illustration of his point: "The right to move out of a mid-city slum . . . means little without the means of doing so." It was perfectly clear that only the federal government, with its subsidized housing programs, could provide that "means." Yet here was the self-same president saying, "This administration will not attempt to impose federally assisted housing upon any community."

Nixon's statement was a defining moment for America. Generations of racist policies had brought the country festering black ghettos and urban riots. The respectable white moderates who made up the Kerner, Kaiser, and Douglas commissions, speaking with authority conferred by presidential appointment, had sounded the alarm and pointed out what the nation must do. Manifesting one of the best strains in the American tradition—"moral responsibility" was what Romney had said to Mayor Bates—the federal government seemed at last poised to begin redressing the most visible current manifestation of the historic wrongs visited upon its black citizens. Now, in an instant, as if it had been a bug on the sidewalk, Nixon had stamped out Romney's initiative.

Shortly after its issuance, the U.S. Conference of Mayors condemned Nixon's statement. The federal government, the conference resolution said, should advise communities "that the future availability of all federal funds depends on the applicant community's commitment to provide low and moderate income housing opportunities." Among many other responses to the president's statement, a group of public interest organizations used a telling medical metaphor: the president had diagnosed a cancer and prescribed aspirin as the remedy. But only one statement counted, the president's, which—for the executive branch, at least—became the formal policy of the U.S. government.

So the door to the executive branch had been closed on metropolitan remedies. The door to the legislative branch had never been opened, and it was doubtful, given the growing political power of white suburbia, that it ever would be. The remaining door was the judicial. Had Austin found HUD liable, perhaps with sufficient creativity we could have alchemized HUD's liability into a metropolitan remedy, at least in the Chicago area. Gautreaux-type suits elsewhere would have followed.

But no, the judicial door had been slammed shut too. In September 1970, Austin mailed us an opinion that had the impact of a sharp blow to the midsection. HUD was *not* liable, he ruled, and he entered an order simply dismissing our complaint against HUD. Ignoring many of the cases to which we had referred, Austin's written opinion said—without citing any authority on the point—that he did not have the power to "direct and control the policies of the United States." The government, he added, "must be permitted to carry out its functions unhampered by judicial intervention." No matter that the policeman had had his hand in the till. As to that, Austin merely noted that HUD faced the tough dilemma of either accepting sites believed to be "lawful but not optimal," or of shutting down Chicago public housing. Why that dilemma excused HUD but not the CHA he did not explain. The excruciatingly disappointing fact was that Gang's "usual" arguments had won the day after all.

We would appeal, of course. But even if we won in the court of appeals, what relief could we then expect from an Austin who was unwilling to tell the federal government what to do? And talk about "exceeding slow." So long as the appeal process—more brief writing!—was grinding along, carrying with it our slim-in-any-event hopes for a metropolitan remedy, we would have no relief but scattered sites confined to Chicago, with all the limitations of such a straitjacketed program.

5

By the spring of 1970, nine months had elapsed since Austin's July 1969 final order against the CHA, enough time to birth a baby. Wasn't the CHA finally ready to submit some white sites to the city council, so at last we could see where the chips would fall? I called Kula and announced that the time for action had come.

A few days later my phone rang. Swibel. He wanted to meet. In his office, he said. Not a big meeting; just the two of us. I demurred. Lawyers weren't supposed to meet privately with the opponent's client. But this was all right, Swibel assured me. Kula had approved the meeting. I should check it out with her, which I did.

Swibel's office was sumptuous, befitting the wealthy real estate developer he had become. He spoke earnestly, as he always did, with an air of admitting his listener into his confidence. The problem the CHA—indeed, the entire city—faced was a difficult one. We knew the CHA was acting in good faith, didn't we? Remember, he, Charley Swibel, had recommended that the CHA not appeal, and that was why we were where we were, not off in court somewhere. Charley Swibel wants to do the right thing. But timing is important. Nobody would want the site selection question to become a political issue, would they? That would be the worst thing for everybody, wouldn't it, Al?

Then, with the sugar coating applied, the pill was presented: the CHA would not submit sites to the city council until after the upcoming mayoral election. Upcoming? The election wasn't until April 1971, nearly a year away! So much for Sierra Club omens. I contained my shock and anger and bid Swibel a civil farewell, telling him we would take our counsel and be in touch with Kula. After a hurried conference our quintet of lawyers agreed that Austin should be informed promptly. I called Kula and the judge's clerk, and was able to arrange a meeting in Austin's chambers for June 2, 1970.

It was the first of what turned out to be five conferences. In the first two, Kula gushed about the CHA's considerable accomplishments, including obtaining the HUD reservation for 1,500 units, looking for and selecting sites, and submitting them to HUD for approval. As if she were playing a trump card, she then told Austin that HUD had recently approved some 263 sites, enough for the entire 1,500 unit reservation.

She also listed a number of conversations the CHA had had with suburban officials and, though not denying what Swibel had told me about holding off until after the mayoral election, advanced a different reason for delay. The problem, everyone agreed, was metropolitan. The CHA wanted to prepare a metropolitan "package" and did not want to make any sites public until suburban as well as city sites could be proposed together. The realities of blockbusting and white flight made that the best way to proceed.

Swibel elaborated in a written statement, which he read aloud at the third, June 26, conference, flanked by the other CHA commissioners. Because the problem was metropolitan, any public announcement of new public housing locations should include both suburban and city sites. As soon as "sufficient feasible sites" for one-third of the proposed units had been located outside the city, the CHA would deliver the Chicago sites to the city council and the suburban sites to the suburban governments. Unless a combined city-suburban list were submitted, "wholesale blockbusting" would result.

When Swibel finished I asked the obvious question. Swibel's answer was lengthy, but it amounted to an acknowledgment that the CHA's conversations with suburban officials had produced not a single site and no tangible prospect of one. Austin then entered the dialogue. He spoke with his usual directness, although he appeared to be musing aloud rather than addressing anyone in particular. Under those circumstances, he said, couldn't the matter be handled just as well by a strong statement of intent to find suburban sites as by a transparently empty announcement of prospective sites that were not "imminent"?

A pregnant silence ensued. It was Wade who then spoke, without however answering Austin's question directly. He would not, he said, want to see an opportunity for integrated housing jeopardized by "temporary political considerations." Swibel hadn't mentioned the Chicago mayoral election, but now Wade did. He believed, he said, with strong emphasis, that submitting sites at the present time would make public housing the "central issue" of upcoming political campaigns.

After that, conversation quickly wound down. Except for asking his unanswered question, Austin had listened silently throughout—unusual for him. At the end of the meeting he scheduled another, for July 13, to give the CHA, he explained, a further opportunity to tell him anything else it wished about why it should delay submitting the HUD-approved sites to the city council.

The July 13 meeting was mostly repetitious. Austin again mostly listened. Then, with the meeting clearly ending, he spoke. Without a change in the conversational tone, or any other indication that he had made up his mind, he said he "believed" he might be entering an order. Making it sound almost like an afterthought, he added that he didn't think the CHA should delay submitting its sites any longer. The room fell silent, as if a tape recording had been interrupted. Finally, Kula spoke. The CHA, she said, might want any order to be in writing. That would be fine with him, Austin responded.

With much of what Wade and Swibel had said, we didn't disagree. The problem was that there was no realistic prospect of even a single suburban site. In all of the rhetoric from Swibel, Wade, and Kula, we could not discern a glimmer of a possibility. The CHA's "conversations" with suburban officials had been just that. Swibel hadn't even said that he was close to agreement with any of them, or suggested a timetable for when he might be, or advanced a reason for believing he ever would be. Not a thing had changed since the HUD–Justice Department memorandum of a year earlier saying that, in light of the "probable difficulty" of obtaining suburban cooperation, constructing public housing outside Chicago "appears unlikely to be a major factor in the immediate future." The reality was that the CHA was arguing not just for indefinite delay, but for abandoning Austin's basic order.

On July 20, at the fifth and final conference, with no further argument, Austin signed an order we had drafted giving the CHA one month to submit sites to the Chicago Plan Commission (a required precouncil step) and another month to deliver its sites to the council itself. The meeting was businesslike and anticlimactic. Swibel didn't even attend.

We should have anticipated what happened next, but it came as a surprise. The CHA trotted out a new lawyer, Patrick W. O'Brien, an acerbic litigation partner in the large firm of Mayer, Brown & Platt. On August 11, 1970, O'Brien filed motions asking Austin to reverse himself by "vacating" his July 20 order, and—failing that—to extend the time for the CHA to appeal. The motions argued that Austin's order had been improper because the CHA had not been given adequate notice and a sufficient opportunity to present evidence.

It looked absurd. Kula had not only consented to the Austin conferences, but had specifically declined the judge's invitation to have a court reporter put everything "on the record." As for "sufficient opportunity," the fourth conference had been scheduled for the precise purpose of giving the CHA another chance to say anything it wished. But O'Brien was a good, if irascible, lawyer. (He too wore bow ties, seemingly a condition of employment for CHA lawyers.) He contended that the consent argument worked only to the point—at the end of the fourth conference—at which Austin had indicated that he would enter an order directing the CHA to submit sites by a specific date. Until then, O'Brien asserted, the conferences were only "informational"; the CHA was entitled to formal notice and procedures if orders were to be entered that changed "best efforts" by imposing a specific timetable.

In truth, O'Brien had a point. Once Austin had started talking about entering an order, it would have been better had we asked to have the proceedings recorded from then on and made them formal. Now, although Austin quickly denied O'Brien's motions, the court of appeals thought enough of the CHA argument to put Austin's order on hold until an appeal could be heard. The appeal was "expedited"—placed on a hurry-up schedule—but the hold meant still more delay.

In mid-December 1970, the court of appeals ruled against the CHA by a 2–1 vote. After trying unsuccessfully to get the entire court to rehear the three-judge decision—adding two more months of delay—O'Brien turned to the U.S. Supreme Court. By now Austin, "unhandcuffed," as he described himself, by the court of appeals ruling, venting that the case was replete with "stalls" and "procrastination," had rescheduled the CHA's site submission to Friday, March 5, 1971. But O'Brien flew to Washington with an emergency motion. Put Austin's order on hold until the Supreme Court could hear the case, the motion asked.

On Thursday, March 4, Justice Thurgood Marshall denied O'Brien's motion. The ever-resourceful O'Brien then asked the Supreme Court clerk to present his motion to Chief Justice Warren Burger for submission to the entire Court at its regular Friday session. The clerk told O'Brien he would do so, but there could be no assurance the Court would actually rule on Friday because it had had no opportunity to study the case.

Hoping against hope for word from Washington, the CHA kept the city clerk's office open past the normal closing time. At last O'Brien received word from the Supreme Court clerk that all the justices had left the Court building in Washington without ruling on his motion. At 5:56 P.M. on Friday, March 5, 1971, Sam Lucchese, public relations director for the CHA, lugged a huge briefcase into the city clerk's office, dutifully filed the CHA's proposed sites, and passed out press releases to the throng of waiting reporters.

Unsurprisingly, the CHA's executive director, C. E. Humphrey, was quoted as saying that the CHA still believed "public identification of these sites is unwise until suitable sites have been identified in suburban communities." The mayor, however, spoke out "live" at a city hall press conference. Forcefully, he denounced the CHA's sites as "detrimental" to the people of Chicago. "These units should not be built," Daley declared. Public housing should be built "where this kind of housing is most needed and accepted."

On March 8, the Supreme Court anticlimactically denied the CHA's motion. On April 8, 1971, the political epilogue to the frantic effort not to disclose the CHA's selected sites until after the election was that Richard J. Daley buried his opponent, Richard E. Friedman, with a tally of more than 70 percent of the vote.

We speculated about the calculus that had led Daley and the CHA not to appeal Austin's basic order, but then to dig in their heels against taking the next logical step. Was the political situation different? Was

Daley angry at being told what to do by his former friend, Dick Austin? Why not let Austin take the "heat" and posture the city and the CHA as having no choice but to comply with a federal court order?

The probable answer was mundane. The decision not to appeal had been tactical, designed to maximize the likelihood that actual implementation of the July 1969 best efforts order would be worked out with Austin in politically palatable ways. Never short on self-confidence, Swibel had probably assured the mayor that he could pull that off. Now, political considerations dictated that the mayor should be perceived as doing everything possible to prevent the building of public housing in neighborhoods that didn't want it.

6

So the deed was done. Two years and a month after Austin had found the CHA liable in February 1969, locations for scattered-site housing in white neighborhoods had finally been selected by the CHA, approved by HUD, and submitted to the city council. Lucchese's briefcase had disgorged 275 proposed sites for 1,746 units of public housing in thirty-seven of the city's fifty wards. The average site had six apartments, and all complied with the judgment order requirements that no buildings should be taller than three stories, and that no group of buildings should raise the public housing portion of a census tract's housing above 15 percent.

The newspaper headlines were as big as those announcing Hitler's invasion of Poland. Comment was predictable. Although the *Daily News* editorial, emphasizing how small and scattered the sites were, said the proposal "cannot be viewed as a threat to any given neighborhood," little attention was paid to how small each proposed development really was, or to the fact that half the units would be occupied by poor families—not the CHA's—already living in the neighborhoods. The precise locations were the big news.

Yet with his easy reelection an accomplished fact, perhaps now Daley would do what the *Sun-Times* had long ago called upon him to do— lead. Perhaps he would now "make it happen." We joked about sending Daley a copy of John Kennedy's book *Profiles in Courage.* The trouble with that idea was that the political leaders Kennedy had profiled all believed in the causes for which they stuck out their political necks. Scattered-site public housing was not a cause in which Daley believed.

Then, however, assistance materialized from an unlikely quarter. Chicago was a participant in Model Cities, a Great Society program that provided money for job training, child care, and the like. For its second year in the program Chicago had prepared a $38 million application. Among Model Cities program requirements was a housing relocation plan that included a minimum supply of housing for the poor. A Frank Fisher task force had determined that Chicago had a housing "deficit" of some 4,300 units.

On May 12, 1971, George Vavoulis, Fisher's successor, signed a "letter of intent" with Daley and Swibel to handle the housing deficit. (The White House had been pressuring Romney to get rid of Fisher. Finally, Romney told Fisher, he could hold out no longer. Would Frank come to Washington as his special assistant? Fisher agreed, but stayed only for a few months.) Of the 4,300 units needed, 1,700 would be supplied through CHA sites awaiting city council approval. The approval was to come in three stages, June 15, September 15, and December 15. The Model Cities money would be released conditionally after the June approval.

This was assistance indeed. Here was the federal government saying to Chicago, give the CHA its site approvals if you want your Model Cities money. For a brief time there were encouraging signs. Before the June 15 deadline the city council actually held hearings on some of the CHA sites and approved a few. Vavoulis released the hostage funds conditionally, presumably expecting the June shortfall to be made up in the September approvals.

July and August came and went without further hearings. What was going on? Had Daley and Vavoulis come to some new, undisclosed arrangement? Then, with exquisite timing, on September 10, 1971, five days before the September 15 approval date, the court of appeals reversed Austin and ruled that HUD *was* liable for funding the CHA's discriminatory program. Gang's usual legal and policy arguments were swept aside. Citing our old friend from Little Rock, Cooper v. Aaron, the court of appeals—this time unanimously—said that HUD's good faith was irrelevant. It would be "unthinkable" that in the operation of a discriminatory public housing system the Constitution would impose a lesser duty on the federal than on the state government. HUD's approval and funding of a system it knew to be racially discriminatory amounted to discriminatory conduct of its own.

We were ecstatic. The way was now open to go back to Austin and try once more for a metropolitan public housing program. And didn't we now have good reason to expect HUD to stick to the Model Cities letter of intent? With four days remaining before the September 15 deadline, I went to see Vavoulis, seeking assurance that HUD would hang tough.

Vavoulis was a former mayor of St. Paul who had spent most of his adult life as a florist. He was a big man, tall, with wavy gray hair, bushy eyebrows, and a vague manner. At least he was vague with me; I could get no commitment from him about what HUD would do if the city council missed the September 15 deadline. I feared the worst.

Shadur, Weisberg, and I held a war council in Shadur's office. If need be, should we go to Austin to force HUD to hold back the Model Cities money? Or was that too much of a stretch? The arguments in favor were strong. The opportunity to put new pressure on Daley and the city council seemed a heaven-sent gift. How could we reject it?

Yet there were good arguments on the other side too. If HUD were to change its mind and release the money without the council approvals, who were we—or Austin—to say that housing was more important than Model Cities jobs and hot breakfasts for schoolchildren? Legally, we might be on shaky ground. And what about the antagonism of those who would lose the jobs, or their children's breakfasts, some of them no doubt our own clients? Finally, why spend our energy on a sideshow? If the council failed to approve the sites called for by the letter of intent in September, and didn't "catch up" in December, we could and would move directly against the council to take its veto power away.

Round and round we went for what seemed an eternity. In the end, we couldn't reach consensus and agreed to abide a majority among the three of us. Milt and Bernie voted for going ahead, I against. So by another divided vote, this one of our own making, we were off on another sortie.

On September 17 we filed a motion and Austin promptly scheduled a hearing that confirmed our worst fears. I asked Vavoulis on the witness stand about his meeting with Daley. He answered that he and the mayor hadn't even discussed the city's plans for dealing with the housing deficit. Then, whether defiantly or defensively was hard to tell, Vavoulis volunteered, "No amount of money that I would cut off . . . would affect the decisions of the city council."

Austin had been listening intently. Now he hunched forward and asked Vavoulis whether, as a former mayor, he had any suggestions about putting pressure on a recalcitrant city council. Vavoulis didn't hesitate. "The name of the game in politics is to win the election . . . and unless you reflect the opinion and the will of the electorate you won't get elected."

Austin was visibly angry, particularly, it seemed, with Daley. Perhaps the mayor's statement in the wake of the March site submission really rankled. After all, the CHA was doing only what Austin had ordered it to do. Yet here was the most prominent mayor in the country saying, "These units should not be built." Was the mayor saying don't obey a court order? Even if that wasn't what he meant, he certainly was not indicating respect for the orders of his old friend, Dick Austin.

Soon after the hearing ended Austin issued a blistering opinion. He compared Daley, with his "wattles flapping," to Alabama Governor George Wallace standing in the schoolhouse door to prevent integration.

> There have been occasions in the past, in other parts of the country, when chief executives have stood at the school house and the state doors with their wattles flapping, and have defied the federal government to enforce its laws and decrees.

It was an anomaly, Austin wrote, that "the 'law and order' chief executive of this City should challenge and defy the federal law." He would, however, give the chief executive and the city council an opportunity to "repent and reconsider their conduct." He would require only 700 units to be approved (not coincidentally, perhaps, the exact number of "matching" white neighborhood units in his July 1969 order against the CHA) before authorizing the release of the Model Cities money. "The court is handing [the City] the key to the funds . . . Only the City of Chicago, by failing to comply with its undertakings, and neither the plaintiffs nor this court, would be responsible" if the Model Cities programs ended.

Austin's opinion was not only intemperate but short on factual analysis and legal reasoning. We had supplied plenty of case law and analysis, but Austin ignored most of it. Nor did he bother to explain why the judge, who but a few months before had written that the federal government "must be permitted to carry out its functions unhampered by judicial intervention," was now so ready to intervene against that selfsame government. Hindsight showed that we should have supplied him with a draft order that crossed the t's and dotted the i's. Now we were stuck with a "wattle flapping" opinion and an order that was skimpy in explaining its factual and legal basis.

HUD and the city appealed immediately. In March 1972, we lost in the court of appeals by a 2–1 vote. Judges Duffy and Swygert didn't view housing as a major element in the Model Cities program. They saw it as jobs and hot breakfasts, programs that were not themselves racially discriminatory. Only six of some fifty Model Cities programs were housing related, they said. It was within HUD's discretion to decide not to terminate over forty programs because the city had so far failed in six. Without a finding of discrimination in the Model Cities program itself, it was "abuse of discretion" for Austin to impose his own judgment on HUD.

Judge Sprecher understood our argument. Housing was an essential part of a Model Cities plan, he wrote. Since HUD clearly had the power to condition funding on performance of that essential part, it was not wrong, under the circumstances, for Judge Austin to take that selfsame step. Lack of housing, Sprecher added, was a "prodigious spawner" of the very kinds of problems the other Model Cities programs were designed to alleviate, including poverty, unemployment, crime, and civil disorder.

But that was the losing argument. We tried for a rehearing by the full court, came close, but lost, 4–3. Not even Milt and Bernie argued for trying the Supreme Court, and thus our Model Cities sortie terminated in a dead end.

Many years later I spent some hours with the Nixon tapes in the National Archives. I shouldn't have been surprised to learn that when he caved in to Daley on the letter of intent conditions, Vavoulis had been under direct orders from Washington. On May 13, 1971, one day after he had signed the letter with HUD, Daley visited Nixon in the Oval Office. Immediately before the mayor arrived, the president was briefed by his aide, John Ehrlichman. Describing the Gautreaux situation, Ehrlichman reported, "Our instructions to HUD have been to cooperate with the mayor right down the line—we didn't want to louse up his election." Daley, Ehrlichman explained, was helping to keep the Illinois congressional delegation in line on Nixon's revenue-sharing proposals.

The conversation between the president and the mayor began with Gautreaux. "How can you force people to accept something they don't want?" Daley asked. "I don't think [public housing] is a racial question—public housing is objected to by many of our black neighborhoods and communities." An understanding Nixon chimed in, "You cannot go into these neighborhoods [with public housing] without destroying the makeup of the community."

Thus spoke the president a month before his formal Presidential Statement on Equal Housing Opportunity set the nation's policy on the location of subsidized housing. His mantra—"This administration will not attempt to impose federally assisted housing upon any community"—was a perfectly logical extension of a personal view that public housing would destroy "the makeup of the community."

7

December 15, the third deadline in the Daley-Vavoulis letter of intent, had come and gone without further city council action. It was time to move directly against the council. But before we could do more than get started with our city council case we suffered a terrible, bewildering tragedy. On February 8, 1972, Chuck Markels, small in build but big in heart, whom I had known since childhood as one of the kindest, gentlest persons ever to have walked the earth, who put in time for civil rights in Mississippi and sang folk songs to his own guitar accompaniment, took his life with an overdose of sleeping pills.

Little was known about depression in 1972. A review of the state of medical knowledge at that time conceded that no satisfactory explanation had been found—there were major unresolved issues regarding the nature and causes of the disease. Treatment was likewise beset with uncertainty; drugs, electric shock, and psychotherapy were all being tried.

Diagnosis itself was a challenge. Studies of suicides in England revealed that most patients had been seen by a family physician a few weeks before the suicide attempt, but the diagnosis of depression had generally been missed. Even when physical disorders were excluded as the cause of symptoms, "the long-suffering patient may be discharged with the physician's cheery assurance that there is nothing physically wrong with him."

Successful suicides followed unsuccessful suicide attempts in a substantial portion of the cases. An article in the *Journal of the American Medical Association* opined that more human suffering had resulted from depression than from any other single disease. Boswell's description of Samuel Johnson's "dismal malady" came to mind: "dejection, gloom and despair, never perfectly relieved; and all his labors, and all his enjoyments, were but temporary interruptions of its baleful influence."

I combed my memory for subtle signs of Chuck's anguish, but could recall none. Had I been unobservant, insensitive? Worse, had I missed opportunities to help? It was some comfort to learn that none of Chuck's friends had been aware of his condition. Apparently only his doctor and his wife had been privy to Chuck's increasingly serious melancholia. I also learned that Chuck's final attempt to take his life was not the first, even though he had a good marriage and three wonderful young sons.

In the late 1960s and early 1970s, Chuck and his family came to our home each year to celebrate Hanukkah. Chuck was beloved by our children, and his guitar playing and singing were the highlight of those happy occasions. Was Chuck, even then, compensating for despair and hopelessness by affecting an ebullient, joyous nature? At what cost to himself was he entertaining us? Deborah captured his double life in a poem:

ELEGY FOR CHUCK

Those were my first expectancies
of winter. While a single blade
of snow fell yellow past the porchlight,
I waited at the window.
Twin cones of lighted snow would ease
Up the drive. His guitar would sway
Beside him on the path. Inside,
He'd whirl me, "Deberino!"

He must have had another life:
The darknesses, the little griefs
Outside a child's imaginings . . .
Somewhere, a wind is ever

Blowing answers: *Got me a wife,*
Kissed her and then a whistle weaves
five hundred miles, Aunt Rhody, winging
grey geese to sleep . . . I never

guessed, sung round in the warm room,
that outside, blanked in the steadily falling
silence, *mi caballo blanco*
was waiting to unbless
my house . . . We bundled the last tunes,
hugged in the hall. I waved, calling,
"Good night," as he walked into snow
whitening out toward darkness.

8

What wrongdoing to charge the aldermen with was a nice question,
especially when the point was what they hadn't done. And perhaps had
no duty to do? Aldermen could offer numerous reasons for not casting a
particular vote. In fact, most of CHA's proposed sites had never come to
a vote, exactly the fate of most proposed legislation in most legislative
bodies.

We drafted our complaint against the aldermen very narrowly. We
did not say they had a duty to act, much less that they were racists. We
said only that the effect of their inaction was to frustrate the vindication
of federal constitutional rights, and that therefore they had a responsibility to explain and justify. We did not contend that inaction could never be
justified. And we marshaled cases saying,

A state law is invalid to the extent that it frustrates the implementation
of a constitutional mandate.

The remedial power of the federal courts under the Fourteenth
Amendment is not limited by state law.

At the hearing on April 4, 1972, we showed that the council had not
considered CHA sites since June 1971. Surprisingly, the city offered no

explanation. The one alderman the city called as a witness said that he had not discussed CHA sites with his fellow aldermen at all. The closest approach to acknowledging the elephant in the room came from Alderman Claude Holman, who had asked to testify "in his own behalf." On cross examination, when I asked Holman why the council had not acted, he responded, "I don't think you could get, right now, an affirmative twenty-six votes [a council majority] to put that many housing units in white neighborhoods."

Six days later Austin signed our proposed order. This time we did the drafting. After reciting that no reason had been given for the council's failure to conduct hearings since June, it said that the effect of the council's inaction "has been and continues to be to thwart the correction of federal constitutional wrongs." The state law requiring council approval, it went on, "shall not be applicable" to CHA steps designed to carry out its "best efforts" duties. And it directed the CHA to proceed, including to acquire sites, "regardless of any action taken or not taken by the Council."

The city appealed immediately and so did the CHA, although in theory the CHA should have welcomed being freed from city council fetters. The usual round of briefs, oral argument, and consideration by the court of appeals consumed a year, until May 18, 1973, when we won in a strange way—three opinions from the three-judge panel. Judge Sprecher ruled for us but on a theory we had been careful to avoid. The "discriminatory" action and inaction of the city council, Sprecher wrote, made it a joint participant in the CHA's discriminatory conduct. Chief Judge Swygert pointed out that we had not made the joint participation argument. Our theory, he wrote correctly, "requires no connection of the Council with CHA and no finding of active discrimination on the part of the Council." It was enough that the council's inaction had the effect of denying the plaintiffs the relief granted them "[without] even a rational basis . . . advanced by the Council for its neglect, much less a compelling governmental interest."

Judge Pell dissented, objecting that the city council was a legislative body entitled to the "ultimate determination as to whether it should provide low-cost housing." There having been no determination that the council was acting unconstitutionally, the court should not "order the legislative function . . . to be ignored." With what I viewed as close to intellectual dishonesty, Pell did not discuss our cases, saying that the acts of local legislative bodies, whether or not unconstitutional, couldn't be interposed to frustrate a remedy for a federal constitutional wrong.

So we had a 2–1 win, and rehearing was soon denied. Six more months were then consumed with the city and the CHA trying to get the Supreme Court to take the case. In January 1974, the Court declined. At long last, just a month short of five years after Austin had granted our summary judgment motion in February 1969, the CHA was free to develop housing in white neighborhoods without city council approval. A milestone.

9

The September 1971 ruling of the court of appeals—that HUD as well as the CHA was responsible for Chicago public housing segregation—entitled us to another shot at persuading Austin to order public housing in the suburbs. Knowing that Austin was unenthusiastic, we proceeded the way porcupines make love—carefully.

First, in December 1971 we persuaded Austin to order HUD, the CHA, and the plaintiffs to prepare a comprehensive remedial plan, allowing us, however, to submit our own, separate plan if the parties couldn't agree. The order we drafted specifically said that the plans could extend beyond the "geographic boundary of the City of Chicago." It was not clear from his acceptance of our language that Austin would be open to metropolitan relief, but it was a mildly hopeful sign.

We expected little from HUD. Milt Shadur and I went to Washington to meet with HUD's general counsel, David Maxwell, but Maxwell made it clear that HUD would not propose a metropolitan plan. HUD's role, he said, was to cooperate with local agencies. If they would take the lead, HUD would cooperate with them. And if the moon were made of green cheese . . .

Sure enough, when HUD responded to Austin's December order, it supplied not a plan but merely a laundry list of its own programs. The city and the CHA would not meet with us, even though both had always insisted that public housing should be a metropolitan matter. Maxwell's reason was undoubtedly political: Nixon could not be perceived as foisting blacks on white suburbs. So, too, must have been Daley's: metropolitan plan or not, the Democrats could not appear to be enabling poor blacks to move into white neighborhoods in the city.

We secured a little foundation money and hired Leonard Rubinowitz, a young lawyer who had worked under Frank Fisher at HUD, to help us fashion a metropolitan approach that Austin might accept. In his thoughtful, deliberate way, Rubinowitz began to analyze how HUD was administering housing programs on a regional basis. We wanted to show not only that HUD "talked" a metropolitan game but that administratively it "played" the housing game that way too.

For expert help, we began a lengthy dialogue with Martin Sloane, a lawyer on the staff of the U.S. Commission on Civil Rights in Washington, who had spent years steeping himself in the history of U.S. housing policy. We also consulted with our "regular" expert, Phil Hauser.

Eventually, a plan emerged, designed in three ways to have special appeal to Austin. First, it looked much like the "plan" Austin already had imposed on the CHA; it used the same format and terminology, had the same restrictions against overconcentration of public housing units, and in every possible way was made to look similar to what Austin had previously ordered. Second, of crucial importance to Austin we thought, the CHA would have to build in the city regardless of what it was able to do in the suburbs. In fact, our proposal required performance in the city *before* the CHA could develop suburban housing.

Third, the suburbs would be required to take only half the amount of new public housing in the city. Blacks were then nearly a third of Chicago's population but only 17 percent of the region's. The poor, regardless of race, were likewise disproportionately concentrated in Chicago. With the city already possessing far more than its "fair share" of the region's black and poor families, the region should have been called upon to "catch up." Yet, ignobly, we catered in this way to Austin's negative attitude about suburban relief.

Ignoble, but justified. It was vital, we believed, to obtain some kind—almost any kind—of order establishing the metropolitan remedial principle. Once entered, an order could be modified. We even wrote some specific, deliberately low, numbers into our plan. Although our proposed order would remain in effect until 60,000 housing units were produced (because that was double the approximately 30,000 units of segregated housing the CHA had produced, and doubling the number was required because half the new units were allocated to non-CHA families already living in the neighborhoods where the new housing was to go), the CHA was then working on a HUD reservation of 1,500 units. Therefore, the initial suburban number would be a mere 750 units, to be spread among the counties of our proposed metropolitan area roughly in proportion to population. Each municipality would have a public housing ceiling of 4 percent of its housing stock, which would be lowered to 2 percent if it acted voluntarily.

A suburban refusal to build our public housing would trigger the key mechanism in our plan—an order from Austin, analogous to the order Austin eventually entered on the city council veto power, setting aside laws that prevented the CHA from building outside Chicago unless it had agreements with the "outside" authorities. Our proposed order said the CHA should use its best efforts to obtain the agreements, but if it could not get them within six months, the CHA was then to "go it alone"—itself apply for HUD financing and ask Austin for set-aside orders to enable it to develop the proposed suburban units without the suburban approvals the law otherwise required.

Everything hinged on Austin's willingness to issue these set-aside orders. We believed he had the power to do so, and we gave him a separate memorandum collecting the cases. One of them, a Supreme Court school desegregation case, said it all:

> State policy must give way when it operates to hinder vindication of federal constitutional guarantees.

It was true that none of the cases involved facts precisely like ours, but the essence of legal reasoning is to apply settled principles to new situations. After all, the constitutional prohibition against unreasonable search and seizure, written against the backdrop of British soldiers invading colonists' homes, had been applied to electronic eavesdropping.

We also argued that the same set-aside approach would apply to the federal law requiring a housing authority to obtain agreement from the local municipal government if it wished to build housing within an incorporated area. Here, however, as our memorandum did not acknowledge, we had no precedent. Strong as were the cases on not allowing state policy to hinder the vindication of federal constitutional rights, we could find no authority applying that principle to a federal statute. But since federal courts could set aside federal laws if they were found to conflict with the

Constitution, we would argue that the same power could be exercised where a federal law conflicted with steps necessary to carry out federal constitutional remedies.

In spite of our careful "packaging" to make the new order look like only a modest extension of what he had already done, Austin remained flinty. We continued to hope he would come around, as he had after his initial remark about putting CHA units on Lake Shore Drive. But, with a single exception, what he kept saying and doing was not encouraging.

At a hearing in February 1972, I reported to Austin about our meeting with David Maxwell and said we had no alternative but to prepare a metropolitan plan of our own. William Warnock, HUD's local lawyer, responded that although HUD endorsed the concept of metropolitan approaches there was a need for local communities to "stand up together and face up to the problems . . ."

Austin interrupted. "How do you propose to bring that about?" "Well," said Warnock, "the most logical approach, the one that is most likely to succeed, is where local communities will initiate this kind of action, and not through . . ."

Again Austin interrupted. "In the event of no initiation, where do you go?" "Well, Judge," Warnock responded, "I think that it is a question of continuing to mold and shape public opinion. And the secretary is hard at work at that goal . . . I don't believe that you are going to achieve any degree of success by trying to hammer it out in the courtroom . . . I think there is a growing recognition on the part of local officials that they have to take account of not only their own little community, but what is happening in the large urban center upon which they are so vitally dependent."

As Warnock finished his little speech, Austin hunched forward. Peering down from under his acrylic rug, dripping incredulity, he said, "I mean, you really believe that?" For a moment the courtroom was silent. Warnock seemed speechless. Then he said the only thing possible under the circumstances, "I really believe that, Judge."

A formal hearing was scheduled for November 1972. Our job would be to persuade Austin that metropolitan public housing relief was both necessary and legally permissible. A logical first step would be to show that we couldn't get all the relief we needed inside Chicago, that there weren't, or wouldn't be, enough white neighborhoods in Chicago with enough developable land to do the job. Hauser, with his knowledge of demography and Chicago neighborhoods, would supply that testimony.

After that, what should we say about suburbia? Sloane had educated us about the federal government's historic double wrong—helping confine blacks to city ghettos and helping whites flee to the suburbs. But what "evidence" to offer Austin on that subject was a nettlesome question.

Confining black Americans to ghettos had been accomplished only in part through public housing, with its neighborhood composition rule and, later, its high-rise ghetto enclaves. Confinement also was a by-product, Sloane explained, of the urban renewal program, dating to the housing act of 1949. Local governments were authorized to buy and clear land in blighted areas and resell it at low prices to private developers. The urban renewal law did not require replacement of housing bulldozed to provide raw land for renewal projects. Instead, it permitted commercial properties and middle-class and luxury apartments to be developed. After eighteen years, urban renewal had destroyed over 400,000 homes and apartments, while building only about one-tenth that number for poor families on urban renewal sites. The evicted poor, who were mostly black (two-thirds of cleared urban renewal units were black occupied), were forced to crowd into other black ghettos. "Negro removal" came to be urban renewal's bitter synonym.

White flight came about through several programs. The first, as Sloane also explained, was mortgage insurance provided by the Federal Housing Administration (FHA). Established in 1934 to help the moribund housing construction industry, the FHA—which later became a part of HUD—offered private lenders insurance against losing their money on loans to home buyers. And it offered these guarantees on unprecedented kinds of loans—greatly increased loan amounts, greatly reduced down payments, and greatly lengthened terms. Later, the Veterans Administration—created in 1944—followed the FHA's lead.

The FHA was remarkably successful in spurring home construction and dramatically increasing home ownership. Over the next thirty years millions of homes and apartments were built with FHA- and VA-insured mortgages. Most, particularly in the postwar years, were in the suburbs. Insuring homes in city neighborhoods was thought to be risky, and FHA property evaluators were told to consider "adverse influences," including "lower class occupancy." Until the late 1960s, when the FHA finally, grudgingly, changed policy, the FHA rarely insured mortgages in slum or adjacent areas. The result was that 90 percent of the FHA's borrowers were middle-class or young, upwardly mobile families. The poor and those on the fringe of poverty were largely excluded from FHA benefits.

Most blacks were too poor to take advantage of suburban, middle-class housing opportunities. The FHA would therefore have had a predominantly white clientele even if its programs weren't discriminatory. But they were. The FHA promoted racial restrictive covenants and was, as a presidential commission later said, a "powerful enforcer" of them. The FHA Underwriting Manual warned that the "infiltration of . . . inharmonious racial groups" would lead to declining property values. As Romney later acknowledged in congressional testimony, in addition to preventing minorities from gaining access to new housing, FHA "redlining" practices put the federal government on record that minority neighborhoods had unfavorable economic futures and were to be treated accordingly. From 1946 to 1959, less than 2 percent of the housing financed with federal mortgage insurance was for blacks.

The FHA's practices survived long past the Supreme Court's 1948 ban on court enforcement of restrictive covenants. When in 1950 the FHA finally announced it would no longer insure property with new covenants, it continued insuring properties with covenants written earlier. Nor did it object to agreements requiring sales to be approved by neighbors or community boards. Redlining did not formally cease until 1965. Not until 1968 did the FHA take effective action to make mortgage insurance available in redlined areas. In 1966, John McKnight spent weeks with FHA appraisers to learn what went into FHA decision-making in the Chicago area. He concluded that there were three kinds of houses the FHA absolutely would not insure—those (1) immediately adjacent to a factory, (2) built on cedar posts, or (3) in a white neighborhood into which a black proposed to move.

The impact of FHA practices, described by one writer as "separate for whites and nothing for blacks," was enormous. The U.S. Commission on Civil Rights concluded that the country's segregated housing patterns were "due in large part to racially discriminatory FHA policies in effect during the post–World War II housing boom." Historian Arnold Hirsch writes that the FHA and its practices did not just create new homeowners. For very many, along with their new homes, came an "assumption of a racially exclusive neighborhood."

Sloane described three other federal policies that also fostered white middle-class suburbia in the postwar years. The vast federal highway building program made central city commercial centers accessible to white-collar suburban residents and permitted the spread of industry and blue-collar jobs to the suburbs. The dispersal of blue-collar jobs was a disaster for central city minorities, who often lacked information about suburban jobs, or found them difficult or expensive to reach because they did not own cars or could not afford commuting costs. "There is no question," Romney's testimony acknowledged, "but what the freeway program in our cities has permitted the jobs . . . and also . . . the people to move out at an accelerated pace [leading to] patterns now of separation based on economic levels as well as racial backgrounds . . ."

The two other policies that encouraged white flight were income tax deductions for property taxes and mortgage insurance worth billions of dollars to homeowners during the post–World War II housing boom and beyond. The tax treatment of homeownership helps homeowners pay housing costs. Since homeownership is less widespread among the poor than the affluent, the homeowner subsidy mostly benefits middle- and upper-income families. This relative exclusion of the poor was only a minor inequity before World War II, when income tax rates were low. But in the postwar years, homeowner deductions quickly became the biggest housing subsidy by a wide margin. By the 1960s they were several times larger than housing subsidies for the poor.

Sloane pointed out that Nixon's 1972 annual housing report acknowledged, "Federal housing programs over the years have contributed to rapid suburbanization and unplanned urban sprawl, to growing residential separation of the races, and to the concentration of the poor in decaying central cities." The report added, however, "While housing programs have *contributed* to these problems and in many cases intensified them, it is important to emphasize that they did not *cause* them. The causes stem from the complex interaction of population migration, community attitudes and prejudices, consumer preferences, local government fragmentation, and the impact of other federal programs such as urban renewal and the highway programs."

Nixon's summary committed the sins of understatement and omission, if not downright distortion. It was true that "residential separation of the races" predated federal housing programs. But residential segregation before the federal programs of the 1930s lacked the scale that came with the population and housing explosions of the post–World War II years. Hirsch distinguishes the "first ghetto" of the 1890–1930 era, fed by the Great Migration of blacks from the South beginning with World War I, from the "second ghetto" that was the response to the massive movement of blacks to the cities beginning in the early stages of World War II. In absolute numbers, this second wave of blacks was far larger than the first. After forty years of the first migration, the Chicago of 1930 had 234,000 blacks. After forty years of the second, Chicago in 1980 had 1.2 million blacks, a fivefold increase. (The figures from other cities are comparable. New York's black population was 328,000 in 1930 and 1.8 million in 1980.) The second ghetto, Hirsch says, "simply dwarfs" the first.

Yet it was precisely during this period of unparalleled growth in the black urban population that the federal government played a leadership role in enforcing the residential segregation that Sloane had described to us. "Private prejudices were now clothed with public powers," Hirsch writes. And the federal tailor was stitching up all this segregatory clothing just as crowds of guests were arriving for the ball. The sophistry of Nixon's "complex interaction" contrasts with Hirsch's summary:

> With the emergence of Federal supports for the private housing industry, public housing, slum clearance, and urban renewal . . . government took an active hand not merely in reinforcing prevailing patterns of segregation, but also in lending them a permanence never seen before. The implication of government in the second ghetto was so pervasive, so deep, it virtually constituted a new form of de jure segregation.

What should we do with this "evidence" Sloane had laid out for us? Here was the federal government, implicated for more than thirty-five years in helping to confine blacks to city ghettos, while simultaneously keeping them out of the burgeoning suburbs to which it was facilitating the exodus of city whites. Yet HUD was our defendant, and HUD wasn't building interstate freeways or granting income tax deductions. It would require a new complaint against other federal agencies to bring these matters before Austin, a prospect that was chilling both because of the time it would consume and the degree of success it promised. Yes, the urban renewal program was administered by HUD. But we already had a "confinement" case against HUD based on public housing.

That left the FHA mortgage insurance program, deliberately fostering white segregated suburbs. But not for public housing families. Our CHA families hadn't tried to buy homes in the suburbs; they weren't the blacks who had been denied FHA insurance. How, then, could the FHA story be made relevant to public housing metropolitan relief in Gautreaux? Rubinowitz's work did show a "mini-CHA" pattern of public housing segregation in the suburbs—ten of twelve public housing projects in predominantly black areas, serving virtually all blacks. But it would be tantamount to starting our case all over again to try to prove that the location of each of these projects had been the result of intentional discrimination. Six years after filing our cases against the CHA and HUD, having "won" both of them, would it be sensible to begin entirely new suits against the FHA and the suburban housing authorities?

We decided instead to try to apply our city council set-aside approach to suburbs that declined to cooperate. Our approach hadn't required proof of council discrimination. Here too, therefore, we shouldn't be required to show suburban discrimination. We would offer the FHA and suburban public housing facts as "background." Since we wanted Austin to order HUD and the CHA to build in the suburbs, we could explain that it was relevant to show that suburbia was an appropriate geographical area for them to enter, because suburbia—including its public housing—was as segregated as the city, in good part because of HUD's (the FHA's) own doing. It was hardly the daring new legal initiative that Hirsch's "new form of de jure segregation" seemed to call for. But in our context, given Austin's apparent leanings, it seemed the best way to go.

The hearing on our proposed metropolitan order began on November 27, 1972, and lasted for three days. It did not go well. From my opening statement, the swimming was upstream. First, Austin balked at the analogy to the city council set-aside order. "There was some evidence," he said, "that it was used to bring about segregation. I have no knowledge of any laws [in the suburbs] that have been passed or used to bring about segregation . . ."

I argued that we had not tried to prove *why* the city council hadn't approved white neighborhood sites. "[The cases] have not found that laws were passed or used with a subjective racially discriminatory intent. They have found that the effect . . . has been to prevent the Court from remedying segregation, and for that purpose have set the law aside."

Austin shot back, "There is such a thing as . . . circumstantial evidence." Okay, I said, as to circumstantial evidence we could show that ten of twelve suburban housing projects were in black neighborhoods and had only black tenants, a pattern that "virtually duplicates the pattern you found in the city . . ." But he was like a fencing opponent, not a referee. When I said set-aside orders would only be required "down the road" if the suburban housing authorities declined to cooperate, Austin virtually smirked, "That is down the road until you run into a roadblock, then you come in and set aside this and set aside that, none of which was adopted to bring about the keeping of blacks out . . ."

I had another weir to negotiate in my upstream, opening-statement swim—Austin couldn't seem to get it through his head that under our proposed order housing in the city came first—that suburban housing, if developed, would not lessen the CHA's obligations to develop in the city. The suburban set-asides would give the CHA "an opportunity to build less in Chicago than they are obligated to already," he insisted. I explained repeatedly why our proposed order wouldn't allow that, but Austin did not seem persuaded, or even to understand. The only mildly hopeful note was sounded when I told him that to help explain why it was appropriate for our proposed order to be entered against HUD we would show that HUD had "helped to create" the pattern of the black city and the white suburb. "I will be interested in that," Austin allowed.

Hauser, our first of two witnesses, testified that if present demographic trends continued, by the turn of the century Chicago would have no census tracts left with less than a 30 percent black population. That is, there would be no tract in the City within which to locate any remedial housing for Gautreaux families. He also said that building public housing in the suburbs would help stem white flight from the city.

Sloane was our second witness. He began by saying that U.S. Commission on Civil Rights hearings throughout the country disclosed that, with minor variations, "precisely the same pattern" was to be found wherever the commission went—"metropolitan areas . . . separated by the central city versus suburbs, poor versus affluent, black versus white." So far so good. I then asked Sloane to explain what the federal government's role in developing that pattern had been. When Sloane began to talk about the FHA, Austin exploded. The FHA did not build public housing, he practically shouted. Why was I trying to drag it into the lawsuit?

I reminded Austin of his expression of interest. We were trying to show, I said, how HUD had helped create the pattern Sloane had testified to. "If we didn't have . . . white segregated suburbs surrounding an increasingly black segregated city," we would not be asking for the metropolitan relief we were seeking. Finally, Sloane was permitted to testify. But after cross-examination, and in spite of his earlier expression of interest, Austin granted a motion to strike Sloane's testimony about the FHA. Not a good sign.

The hearing ended on November 29, 1972. For better or worse, our metropolitan plan—so we thought—was now ripe for decision. But almost before we could pack up our papers a decision in another case caused us to modify our course. The case was Milliken v. Bradley (the former being Michigan's governor). It was about desegregating Detroit schools, and it presented the question of whether suburban school districts could be required to participate in Detroit desegregation.

We had been citing the Milliken case to Austin ever since the federal judge in Detroit, Stephen Roth, had ruled in late 1971 that Detroit's schools had been deliberately segregated. Because the schools were heavily black, Roth had begun to consider busing plans that would involve the predominantly white suburban school districts. Eventually he had ordered the preparation of a metropolitan plan. Now his decision had been upheld by the Sixth Circuit Court of Appeals—a great victory for metropolitan relief—but with one important change: the suburban school districts were to be brought into the case and given a chance to be heard before any metropolitan plan was ordered. If that was what the law required, didn't it mean we needed to bring the suburban housing authorities into the Gautreaux case now, before Austin ordered—if he would—our metropolitan plan?

It was already a year after Austin's December 1971 order calling for the submission of remedial plans, and we had a keen distaste for further delay. But the alternative of winning a metropolitan order that might later be reversed for the Milliken reason was even worse. And perhaps, with the suburban authorities in the case, and following a procedure specifically approved by a court of appeals, Austin might be more open to metropolitan relief than he had appeared during the hearing. So we quickly filed a motion asking Austin to let us to bring in the suburban housing authorities and hear their views before he ruled on our metropolitan plan.

That done, our metropolitan plan with its suggested Milliken procedure was finally laid before the little scrapper from Flossmoor. We felt we had done all that it was sensible to do. Metropolitan public housing, the holy grail of Gautreaux, was now in the hands of the self-described meanest SOB in the valley. He had, however, "come around" on the CHA and the city. Maybe he would now do the same on the suburbs.

10

The months dragged on. No word. Then, without warning, in September 1973, the blow fell. Exactly three years after he had first dismissed our complaint against HUD, Austin mailed us a devastating ruling.

Once again, exactly as he had done three years earlier, Austin shied from telling the United States what it must do. Instead of the metropolitan public housing plan we had so laboriously crafted, the "relief" Austin gave us was that HUD should use its best efforts to cooperate with the CHA in the latter's efforts to comply with the order against it. Our porcupine approach had gotten us exactly nowhere. In retrospect we could have saved two years by handing Austin a simple, metropolitan motion which, it was now clear, he would have rejected.

Most frustrating was his superficiality, his almost studied refusal to deal with our arguments and cases. The first of the two reasons Austin gave was that Hauser's opinion was "inadequate" to support imposing obligations on suburban housing authorities who were "incapable" of discriminating in Chicago. Austin ignored completely the key fact that our proposed order did not impose any obligations on suburban authorities; if the suburbs declined to cooperate it became *the CHA's obligation* to develop the suburban housing. What Austin said about Milliken in this context was maddeningly unilluminating: "Although [metropolitan] relief may have been justified in [Milliken], it is simply unwarranted here because it goes far beyond the issues of this case."

Austin's second reason was equally wrong—we were letting the CHA "avoid the politically distasteful task before it by passing off its problems onto the suburbs," who had had "nothing to do with this lawsuit." Here, too, Austin ignored what our proposed order actually said—that only development of housing *in the city* would trigger the CHA's obligation to develop in the suburbs.

In the long course of the Gautreaux case, this was—and in retrospect remains—one of the moments of greatest disappointment. Admittedly, our metropolitan plan was an exercise in hope. There were a million reasons why it might not have worked. But it represented a responsible way to try to begin atoning for the public housing ghettos, the racial zoning and covenants, the redlining, the "Negro removal," and the other policies and practices that had given us the two separate and unequal societies described by the Kerner Report. In Tom Wicker's words, it was a way to begin, for Chicago at least, the "largely uncharted course of dispersing poor blacks from isolated urban ghettos and integrating them fully into the national life and economy." For Austin to blow us away as he did, without reasoned analysis and based on what looked like deliberate misreading, was a nadir—the place or time (as the dictionary says) of greatest depression or degradation.

Fearful that the Sisyphus myth was disturbingly apt, we were on our way up to the court of appeals once more. I argued our appeal of Austin's ruling in June 1974, before a three-judge panel consisting of retired U.S. Supreme Court Justice Tom Clark, Walter Cummings, and Phillip Tone. Clark had resigned from the Supreme Court in 1967, a fatherly gift to allow his son, Ramsey, to be appointed attorney general by President Johnson without any appearance of impropriety. Now, as was the usual practice with retired federal court judges willing to keep on working, Clark was helping out in appeals courts around the country.

I was feeling optimistic. The oral argument had gone well, and we had good law on our side, especially Milliken. Austin's opinion was embarrassingly (for HUD) unadorned with legal reasoning. In July, awaiting a decision, Barbara and I took a weekend drive through lovely rolling country near Woodstock, Illinois. Purple thistles grew six feet high in fields of waving grasses and Queen Anne's lace. The insect buzz was like an orchestral background. We left the car and walked the empty, dreamy roads for miles.

As we were driving back, I turned on the car radio. A big mistake. A news commentator was reporting on the decision that morning in Milliken v. Bradley. The Supreme Court, by a 5–4 vote, had reversed the court of appeals and ruled that the suburbs could not be required to participate in desegregating Detroit schools. I was enraged. Not only was our idyllic Woodstock time destroyed, but so were our dreams for metropolitan relief in Gautreaux. I braked the car, got out, and kicked the front tire, hard. A stupid gesture, but the tire was in range, kickable. The Supreme Court was not.

The opinion was as frustrating as the idyll-destroying moment of the radio report. Written by Chief Justice Warren Burger, it said that unless it were shown that segregation in Detroit schools had caused segregation in suburban schools, or that suburban school district boundaries had been drawn to create segregation, a metropolitan remedy could not be ordered. The "condition alleged to offend the Constitution," Burger wrote, was segregation within the Detroit school district. Based on the principle that the remedy for a constitutional wrong should be no broader than the wrong itself, the remedy should be confined to Detroit. The right of Detroit students under the Constitution was to attend an unsegregated school system "in that district," even though nearly two-thirds of Detroit's public school pupils were black.

Each of Burger's two themes was maddeningly opaque. Why was the constitutional right of Detroit students limited to "that district"? Burger's answer was that the remedy had to be tailored to fit the wrong, with heavy emphasis on the administrative difficulty of consolidating school districts. But "tailoring," like beauty, was to be found in the eye of the beholder. It could as easily have been said that the students' constitutional right was to attend desegregated schools, period. If providing Detroit pupils with that right required the involvement of "innocent" school districts, hadn't the Court itself said that political boundaries within states were not matters of sovereignty but of convenience, and could be disregarded to vindicate constitutional rights? Burger's opinion not only failed to explain why the cases stating this principle were not relevant, but did not even mention them.

Burger's second theme was that effective desegregation could be accomplished within the predominantly black Detroit school district because desegregation did not require any particular racial balance. He pointed to previous Supreme Court cases that had approved desegregation plans where 57, 66, and even 77 percent of the student population was black. But the Court's previous cases also had required the "most effective" practical desegregation. Could it be denied that 57 percent was more "effective" than 77 percent, and that if it were "practical" would constitute a more effective remedy?

If the Burger opinion was unsatisfactory as an intellectual matter, in another respect it was totally unfathomable. Judge Roth had made a finding that

> for many years FHA and VA [the Veterans Administration] openly advised and advocated the maintenance of "harmonious" neighborhoods, i.e., racially and economically harmonious. The conditions created continue. The affirmative obligation of the [school] board has been and is to adopt and implement pupil assignment practices and policies that compensate for and avoid incorporating into the school system the effect of residential racial segregation.

In affirming Roth's order in most respects, the court of appeals had said that, except as to school construction programs, "we have not relied at all upon testimony pertaining to segregated housing . . ." For whatever reason, the court of appeals had decided to rely exclusively on school evidence and school law. But given Burger's view that the school evidence failed to show interdistrict effects, the housing evidence was of potentially crucial significance. After all, Burger himself had written in another school desegregation case that segregated residential patterns combined with neighborhood zoning of schools could lock schools into a mold of race separation.

Suppose, for example, the evidence showed that Michigan had participated in deliberate residential segregation throughout the Detroit metropolitan area, which is what Judge Roth had seemed to say, and then drew school boundaries along the "fault lines" of the residential segregation it had helped to create. Wouldn't that amount to an interdistrict effect? At the very least, wasn't this a subject that cried out for Burger discussion?

Instead, noting the court of appeals statement about the housing evidence, Burger said, "Accordingly, in its present posture, the case does not present any question concerning possible state housing violations." But the decision of the court of appeals not to rely on Roth's residential segregation finding did not erase that finding from the case. Roth's order, not the court of appeals' opinion, was the ultimate subject matter the Supreme Court was supposed to be addressing. If the Supreme Court was unwilling to deal with the housing evidence without having it first "filtered" through the court of appeals, it had merely to return the case to that court with directions to consider that evidence. This was a normal procedural step the Supreme Court had taken countless times. To pretend that the court of appeals' treatment of the housing evidence eliminated that matter from the case was like the proverbial ostrich plunging its head into the sand to avoid a fearful sight.

Potter Stewart, writing a separate opinion to explain why he was willing to supply the crucial fifth vote for Burger's ruling, likewise seemed to have sand in his eyes. "Were it to be shown," he wrote, "that state officials had contributed to the separation of the races by . . . purposeful, racially discriminatory use of state housing or zoning laws, [metropolitan relief] might well be appropriate." But, he went on, "No record has been made in this case showing that . . . residential patterns within Detroit and in the surrounding areas were in any significant measure caused by governmental activity . . ." Yet given the evidence in the very case before him— including a specific finding of fact by Roth—that helped to explain these housing matters, why did Stewart fail to discuss the "residential patterns" issue? Even if he viewed the evidence as inadequate or erroneous, on a matter of such importance to his own views he would have been expected to say so.

The frustration level was at boiling point in the dissenting opinions. Pointing out that if the case had involved a sewerage or water or energy problem, there could be no doubt that a metropolitan remedy would be appropriate, Justice Douglas said the Court was in "dramatic retreat" from the 1896 Plessy v. Ferguson decision upholding separate but equal treatment of blacks. Justice White called the majority's interdistrict rule "arbitrary," "fashion[ed] out of whole cloth," and "wholly without foundation." Until today, he wrote, effective enforcement of the Fourteenth Amendment's desegregation obligation had never been limited by political boundary lines created by the very state responsible for the constitutional violation and for remedying it. He also pointed out that the majority opinion did not even challenge Roth's conclusion that any Detroit-only plan would leave many schools 75 to 90 percent black, with the district likely to become progressively more black as more whites left the city, or that a metropolitan plan would in many ways be easier and more practical to administer than a Detroit-only plan.

In his separate opinion, Justice Marshall wrote of the majority's "emasculation" of the constitutional equal protection guarantee. The majority's crucial reliance on the principle that "the nature of the violation determines the scope of the remedy," Marshall found "hopelessly simplistic." "Barring a district court from imposing the only effective remedy," he wrote, "clouds the very principle on which [the court] purports to rely," and "turn[s] a simple common-sense rule into a cruel and meaningless paradox." As to the "innocence" of the suburban school districts, Marshall wrote that even the majority did not place real weight on that consideration. Where a constitutional violation in one district produced a "segregated effect" in another, it would allow interdistrict relief to reach "innocent" districts. Marshall's final paragraph, written by the man who had himself argued Brown v. Board of Education, was somber:

> In the short run, it may seem to be the easier course to allow our great metropolitan areas to be divided up each into two cities — one white, the other black, but it is a course, I predict, our people will ultimately regret.

The White and Marshall opinions seemed to us to destroy Burger and Stewart. It would have been much better for our psyches if the Burger and Stewart opinions had made sense. As it was, we felt violated and betrayed by an incomprehensible ruling that blocked not only effective desegregation of Detroit schools but effective desegregation of Chicago public housing as well. Our feelings of dismay were best captured by Judge Edwards of the Milliken court of appeals. In an extraordinary statement in later Milliken proceedings, Edwards wrote that his conscience compelled him to record how deeply he disagreed with the Supreme Court's decision:

> [It] imbued school district boundaries . . . with a constitutional significance which neither federal nor state law had ever accorded them . . . [It] can come to represent a formula for American Apartheid. I know of no decision by the Supreme Court of the United States since the Dred Scott decision which is so fraught with disaster for this country.

11

Three circumstances—collectively they could be summed up in the two words "Richard Nixon"—made the Milliken decision especially painful. The first circumstance was merely bad luck. But the second was reprehensible conduct, and the third was criminal abuse of power.

The bad luck had enabled Nixon, in a single presidential term, to appoint four of the five majority Milliken justices. In 1968, fearful that a Nixon presidency would be a catastrophe for the country—Nixon had campaigned against the "Warren Court" almost as much as against Hubert Humphrey—seventy-five-year-old Chief Justice Earl Warren submitted his resignation to Lyndon Johnson, effective upon his successor's taking the chief justice's seat. But it was an election year, and the Senate rejected Johnson's attempted elevation of his longtime friend, Abe Fortas, to the chief's position. With Warren's resignation in hand, it would be Nixon, not Johnson, who would name the next chief justice.

Even before he did, however, another seat on the Court unexpectedly opened up, that of Fortas himself, whom the Nixon administration hounded out of office for an unseemly but not illegal financial indiscretion. (The hounding included the spectacle of Nixon sending his attorney general, John Mitchell, to complain to Warren about Fortas's ethics—the same John Mitchell who would in a few short years be indicted, convicted, and jailed for perjury and obstruction of justice in Watergate.) Mitchell and the Justice Department were helping *Life* magazine establish that in 1966 Fortas had accepted a $20,000 payment from a foundation headed by Louis Wolfson, a millionaire financier of questionable reputation, under a contract calling for payments each year for the rest of Fortas's life and then to his widow. A week after a six-page *Life* exposé appeared, and with Republicans clamoring for impeachment, Fortas resigned.

For the position of chief justice, Nixon chose Warren Burger of Minnesota, soon to be our nemesis in Milliken. After serving as an assistant attorney general during the early Eisenhower years, Burger had been appointed in 1956 to the court of appeals for the District of Columbia where, on a liberal court, he had made a reputation as a conservative, especially on criminal law matters. He was sworn in as chief justice on the last day of the Warren Court's last term, June 23, 1969.

Nixon stumbled in the selection of a replacement for Fortas—his first two choices were rejected by the Senate—but by June 1970 he had his man. He was Harry A. Blackmun of Minnesota, a lifelong friend of Burger's who had served as counsel to the Mayo Clinic in Rochester and in 1956 had been appointed to the Eighth Circuit Court of Appeals, where he compiled a strong conservative record.

Then, toward the end of 1971, both eighty-five-year-old Hugo Black and seventy-one-year-old John Harlan fell ill and resigned, and Nixon suddenly had two more seats to fill. Black's place went to Lewis F. Powell of Richmond, Virginia, a former head of the American Bar Association who had for many years been chairman of the Richmond School Board. To Harlan's seat Nixon appointed William H. Rehnquist, who had been active in the Goldwater wing of the Republican Party in Phoenix, and then had gone to work for Mitchell in the Justice Department.

Nixon had carefully checked out both men's views on busing. Speaking of the Black vacancy, Nixon told Mitchell:

> I want you to have a specific talk with whatever man we consider and I have to have an absolute commitment from him on busing and integration. I really have to . . . Tell him we totally respect his right to do otherwise, but if he believes otherwise, I will not appoint him to the Court.

Despite what was viewed as the marked conservatism of their views, particularly Rehnquist's, both Powell and Rehnquist were easily confirmed and took their seats in early 1972. In an uncommonly short time, the fates had given Nixon the opportunity to fill four of nine Supreme Court seats.

Beyond the bad luck of four Nixon appointments was the second painful circumstance—what Nixon did with the presidential pulpit, and with the Justice Department, to create a political and legal atmosphere in which the Supreme Court's Milliken decision became all but inevitable.

The Brown decision had not provided a precise definition of "desegregation." Would it be enough to remove state segregation requirements, giving students the formal freedom to choose their schools, or was elimination of racially identifiable schools required? It took fourteen years to answer that question. For a long time, the Court moved slowly, accepting relatively few cases and leaving most of the decisions to local federal judges. The Justice Department played only a small role.

Then, in 1967, with Lyndon Johnson's appointment of Ramsey Clark as attorney general, the department took a forthright stance and the unresolved question was answered in a case called Green v. New Kent County. New Kent was a small county in rural Virginia with a population of about 4,500, half white, half black. There was no residential segregation; blacks and whites lived throughout the county. New Kent had only two schools, one white, one black, and no attendance zones. Each school served the entire county with twenty-one school buses traveling overlapping routes to bring the black pupils to their school and the whites to theirs.

In 1965, after the Department of Health, Education, and Welfare gained power under the Civil Rights Act of 1964 to withhold federal monies from schools resisting desegregation, New Kent adopted a freedom of choice plan. Under HEW's new regulations, choice plans were acceptable if in operation they proved "effective." Lower courts approved New Kent's plan even though it produced virtually no change in its segregated schools. The Justice Department entered the case as a friend of the court. In a brief written under Clark's direction, it argued, "Effective desegregation is not accomplished so long as there remain all-Negro schools, attended by an overwhelming majority of Negro children." To the contention that formal freedom of choice was enough, the brief said:

> Insecurity, fear, founded or unfounded, habit, ignorance, and apathy, all inhibit the Negro child and his parents from the adventurous pursuit of a desegregated education in an unfamiliar school, where he expects to be treated as an unwelcome intruder.

In February 1968 the Supreme Court ruled unanimously that if other reasonable approaches were available that promised to be more effective, such as school boundary changes, freedom of choice would be "unacceptable." Pointing out that New Kent's segregation could be made to "vanish" by setting nonracial school boundaries, Justice Brennan wrote that the school board should be required to formulate a new plan that promised realistically to convert promptly to a system "without a 'white' school and a 'Negro' school."

In the immediate aftermath of Green, working closely with HEW, the Justice Department brought about more actual school desegregation than had occurred in the many years since Brown. Motions were filed all across the South to require old desegregation plans to be updated. HEW added the pressure of the federal purse. Soon most of the nearly 4,500 school systems in the southern and border states had committed themselves to rapidly ending segregation. After a long period of near dormancy, the prospects for school desegregation suddenly seemed bright.

That reckoning, however, failed to take account of Richard Nixon, who, according to Nixon speechwriter and biographer William Safire, thought the Court was "right on *Brown* and wrong on *Green*." In his memoir, Safire gives us Nixon's exact words:

> If the Court had written *Green* in a way where freedom of choice was permitted when it was honest, breaking down the dual system, and not permitted when it was used as a subterfuge, then it would be okay.

Of course, that was almost precisely what Brennan had said:

> We do not hold that a "freedom-of-choice plan" might of itself be unconstitutional . . . There may well be instances in which it can serve as an effective device [to aid desegregation].

It is hard to believe that even Nixon doubted that in New Kent County freedom of choice was a subterfuge. But no matter; Nixon set out, says Safire, to "affect" and "move" the Court by "mobilizing public opinion."

In his 1968 election campaign, Nixon had endorsed freedom of choice, said he believed judges were not qualified to make local school decisions, and promised to rein in HEW and produce a more conservative Justice Department and Supreme Court. (The Nixon rhetoric included such one-liners as, "The busing of a school child will only destroy that child.") Ramsey Clark and Earl Warren having already been replaced by John Mitchell and Warren Burger, more of the election promises were redeemed during the 1969 Independence Day celebrations.

On July 3, 1969, a new policy was announced by Mitchell and HEW Secretary Robert Finch. The federal government would no longer use fund withholdings to enforce desegregation. The exclusive enforcement mechanism would be Justice Department lawsuits. The HEW-developed plans, many to take effect in a few months, could be delayed as "too rigid." Headlines in southern papers read, "Nixon Keeps His Word," and "School Deadlines Scrapped." The government, said NAACP Executive Director Roy Wilkins, was "breaking the law."

A month later, the Justice Department acted. Plans to desegregate the last thirty Mississippi school districts were before a federal district court, and Justice had told the court that each of the plans was "educationally and administratively sound." Suddenly, Mitchell instructed Justice Department lawyers to file a motion for delay. Finch wrote an extraordinary letter to the chief judge of the Fifth Circuit Court of Appeals, warning that his own department's desegregation plans would lead to chaos and confusion. In an unprecedented public statement, sixty-five of seventy-four "line" attorneys in the Civil Rights Division of the Justice Department protested the abandonment of "clear legal mandates." Jerris Leonard, head of the division, told the leader of the "rebel" group that John Mitchell had decided delay in Mississippi was the right course and that, "around here the Attorney General is the law." He offered the option of resignation or discharge.

Although the Supreme Court in Green had said that delays in implementing desegregation plans were "no longer tolerable," southern judges were happy to acquiesce in the delay the U.S. government itself was now proposing. With unaccustomed haste, the Supreme Court expedited the appeals. Under Mitchell's instruction, the Justice Department argued for delay. On September 29, 1969, Leonard called a press conference to announce that "if the Supreme Court were to order instant desegregation nothing would change. Somebody would have to enforce that order." Said the *New York Times:*

Mr. Leonard's remarks raised the possibility that the Supreme Court could find itself, for the first time since it declared public school segregation unconstitutional in 1954, in the position of issuing a school desegregation order without full expectation that it could or would be enforced by the executive branch.

In October 1969, in a rare rebuke to the Justice Department, the Supreme Court ruled unanimously in the Mississippi cases decided in Alexander v. Holmes that under the Court's previous rulings "the obligation of every school district is to terminate dual school systems at once." But far from settling the controversy, the Alexander ruling only led Nixon to up the ante.

In March 1970, in a formal presidential address on national television, Nixon fed the busing opposition flames he himself had been fanning. Reminding the nation of his consistent opposition to "forced" busing for racial balance, which was not the issue, the president nowhere stated his support for busing needed to eliminate deliberate segregation, which was very much the issue. While opposing "buying buses, tires, and gasoline," and "instant solutions" imposed by "extreme" judges, Nixon repeatedly emphasized that the neighborhood school should be protected even if segregated housing patterns produced segregated schools. Not once did the president say that where busing rather than "normal geographic school zones" was found to be necessary to remedy deliberate school segregation, his administration would enforce such orders. While paying lip service to Brown, the president essentially signaled the country that his administration was solidly behind the neighborhood school and would oppose whatever court-ordered busing it possibly could.

Six Civil Rights Division attorneys resigned. One of them, Arthur Chotin, wrote a letter to the *Washington Post* which began,

> As I sit here watching President Nixon make his statement on school busing I am sickened. Sickened because it is the job of the president to unite and lead the nation to the future, not buckle under the weight of political pressure and retreat to a dark and miserable past.

The next step in Nixon's campaign came the following month, April 1970. A federal district judge had decided that the only way to end unconstitutional school segregation in Charlotte, North Carolina, was a busing plan that would bring approximately equal numbers of black and white students to each school in the consolidated city-county district. In the Fourth Circuit Court of Appeals, Jerris Leonard argued against district-wide desegregation and won. The appeals court ruled that the district court plan involved too much busing. In October, as the case came before the Supreme Court, with the district court's plan already in effect, the Justice Department argued for scrapping the plan and restoring many of the segregated schools.

The decision, Swann v. Charlotte-Mecklenburg Board of Education, in April 1971, was—as in Green and Alexander—unanimous. It upheld the district court's plan, once again pointedly not following the views of the Justice Department. On the facts, it is difficult to see how a different result could have been reached: busing trips under the district court's plan averaged seven miles and less than thirty-five minutes, compared to an average of fifteen miles with travel times over an hour under Charlotte's previous plan.

But Green, Alexander, and Swann could not compete with the presidential pulpit. In August 1971, the Nixon administration further intensified its war on busing. HEW Secretary Elliot Richardson invited a congressional committee to prohibit the use of federal money for pupil transportation. When Alabama Governor George Wallace charged that federal agencies were defying administration policy, White House Press Secretary Ron Ziegler, speaking for the president, announced that federal officials who were not "responsive" would find themselves without jobs. The president once again ordered the Justice Department to oppose busing plans (a public relations gesture since he had clearly done that already), and the department continued to do so in cases all across the country.

With antibusing sentiment running at fever pitch, Congress debated measures to cut off gasoline for school buses, to prescribe how the Supreme Court should handle school desegregation cases, and to permit resegregation of southern schools. Many of the measures were endorsed, or even proposed, by the president. In early 1972, Nixon publicly stated he might support a constitutional amendment against busing unless Congress prohibited it legislatively. In another nationally televised speech in March, the president said he had decided to oppose the amendment approach because it had "a fatal flaw—it takes too long." Instead, he asked Congress to enact legislation sharply limiting courts' desegregation powers. Five hundred law professors signed a letter contending that the proposed legislation was unconstitutional. Roy Wilkins used stronger language than he had three years earlier: "Our President . . . is leading the mob which is tearing at the concept of equal protection of the law."

And so it went for two more years. The extreme forms of antibusing legislation did not pass Congress, but the extreme forms of presidential rhetoric did not abate. In May 1974, the then head of the Civil Rights Division, J. Stanley Pottinger, who long had been a team player in John Mitchell's Justice Department, called for an end to the nation's preoccupation with busing. For emotional and political reasons, he said, the issue had been developed by northern politicians who wanted to survive in a national climate of resistance to desegregation. "Busing is not only right legally, but morally and socially," Pottinger declared. The very same day, however, Nixon restated his "unequivocal opposition to forced busing," and an emissary from the president soon called upon the head of the Civil Rights Division. A few days later Pottinger told a reporter he agreed with the president that busing was "an unsatisfactory tool" and "not a realistic response" to the problem of providing equal educational opportunities.

As the chief law enforcement officer of the land, the president is ultimately responsible for securing equal justice under law for all American citizens. As Arthur Chotin had said, it was his job to unite and lead the nation forward, not backward to a dark past. Yet by fueling antibusing fervor instead of damping it, by labeling federal judges as extremists, and by directing the Justice Department not to enforce the law of Green, Alexander, and Swann, Nixon had deliberately prepared a culture—as surely as if he had been a chemist in a laboratory—in which the Milliken v. Bradley decision would be almost certain to germinate.

(It was politics, not principle, that explained Nixon's conduct. When John Ehrlichman argued that it was ludicrous to put something about school buses in the Constitution of the United States, Nixon responded, "I know it's not a good idea, but it'll make those bastards [in the Democratic Party] take a stand and it's a political plus for us.")

The third, criminal misconduct circumstance that so intensified our pain about the Milliken decision was the Greek-like chorus of Watergate, which provided an eerie accompaniment to the unfolding of Milliken.

Judge Roth's ruling that a metropolitan Detroit busing plan should be considered was issued in June 1972, the very month and year of the Watergate burglary. Milliken was decided on July 25, 1974, just two weeks before Nixon's resignation and helicoptering off the White House lawn. In fact, newspaper coverage of the Milliken decision competed for space with the spectacle of the Nixon impeachment hearings before the House Judiciary Committee.

So the very president who had misused the Department of Justice to defile the law of school desegregation was simultaneously so abusing the powers of his office that virtually the entire inner circle of the executive branch of government wound up in jail—where, but for a presidential pardon, Nixon himself might well have gone. One has to go back to Aaron Burr to find comparable perfidy at the epicenter of power in the country. It was all but unbearable that this miscreant should have been the instrumentality through which the country was effectively disabled from dealing with the apartheid that had been fastened upon the nation's metropolitan regions.

The passage of time has not eased the pain. Because of Milliken even the school desegregation achievements of the late 1960s and early 1970s were eventually rolled back. Harvard professor Gary Orfield reports that at the end of the century, the South—the region of the country with the most desegregated schools—was experiencing accelerating resegregation, and that school segregation was spreading throughout the nation. School desegregation was, in fact, dying. A poignant illustration is that desegregation was not even mentioned in a year 2000 NAACP fund appeal focused on "America's failing public schools."

And over the years—as if history were deliberately refusing to heal the hurt—it became clear that Nixon had probably won the 1968 election only because Humphrey chose not to reveal Nixon's role in sabotaging Vietnam peace negotiations on the eve of the election. Even as he pretended publicly to support the idea of the proposed talks, Nixon tried to persuade South Vietnam's Nguyen Van Thieu not to attend by offering him, through intermediaries, assurances that he would get a better deal from a President Nixon than from Johnson's peace conference and a President Humphrey. (Thieu ultimately did refuse to participate, but Nixon reneged on his pledges anyway.) One of the most "essentially decent stor[ies] in American politics," says Theodore H. White of Humphrey's decision to remain silent. Would that there had been less decency, I mused.

The bitter truth, however, was that in addition to Nixon's 43.4 percent of the 1968 tally, another 13.5 percent of the votes for president went to George Wallace, whose third party campaign transcended the busing issue to tap into fear and hatred of blacks generally. (NBC's Douglas Kiker said that, looking out upon white Americans north of Alabama, Wallace had been awakened by a blinding vision: "They all hate black people, all of them. They're all afraid, all of them. Great God! That's it! They're all southern! The whole United States is southern!") Whether because of Vietnam, 1960s counterculture excesses, weariness with civil rights, or fear and hatred of blacks, some 57 percent of the electorate had voted to turn away from the civil rights policies of Johnson and Humphrey. Though he went too far on Watergate, it could be argued that in giving it Milliken v. Bradley, Nixon had given the country what it wanted and had voted for.

12

We did not have the luxury of gnashing our teeth indefinitely. Our appeal was still pending before Clark, Cummings, and Tone. We had relied heavily in our briefs and oral argument on the now-reversed court of appeals opinion in Milliken. We had to do something—quickly. Perhaps, we thought, we could discern some light at the end of the Burger-Stewart tunnel.

We asked to file an additional brief explaining Milliken, then set to work on a tight time schedule. First, perhaps Milliken could be confined to school desegregation. We emphasized Burger's own words, the "deeply-rooted tradition of local control over public schools" and the disruption of public education that Burger said would result from upholding a metropolitan remedy. We quoted from Stewart's "fifth vote" opinion about what he thought the Court's opinion meant—

that traditions of local control of schools, together with the difficulty of a judicially supervised restructuring of local administration of schools, render improper and inequitable . . . an inter-district response to a constitutional violation found to have occurred only within a single school district.

And we pointed out that White's opinion said the core of the dissenters' disagreement with the majority was that deliberate segregation would go unremedied "because an effective remedy would cause what the Court considers to be undue administrative inconvenience to the state."

Therefore, we said, all nine members of the Court were of the view that the metropolitan remedy was rejected *because* it would interfere with the tradition of local control over schools and would actually require restructuring schools. It was true, we acknowledged, that Burger's opinion also said that interdistrict remedies were permissible only where so-called interdistrict effects were found. But that statement, we argued, citing several of the Court's own cases, was to be taken in connection with what was before the Court, that is, school desegregation, not as a general rule that would apply to all kinds of cases.

Second, having pigeonholed Milliken as a schools case, it was easy to show that housing was different because its roots were federal, not local, and because HUD used an "interdistrict" housing market area approach in its administration. Milliken should not apply at all to such a case. And, of course, we quoted Burger's Milliken statement that in its "present posture" that case did not involve housing violations.

Third, Burger had criticized the lawyers and judges in Milliken for switching midstream to a metropolitan theory, emphasizing that suburban school districts were to be denied any opportunity to oppose metropolitan relief. We on the other hand had been talking about metropolitan relief since Austin's July 1969 order permitted the CHA to build housing in Cook County, and we had proposed a no-holds-barred role for the suburban authorities to be brought into the case.

Finally, we argued "evidence" of suburban discrimination. Our exhibit in the metropolitan hearing before Austin—showing the predominantly black locations and tenancy of the suburban housing projects—had not been offered to prove racial discrimination. But a case our Seventh Circuit Court of Appeals had decided just the previous month, involving selling homes to blacks on contract at unconscionably high prices, had taken "judicial notice" of racial residential segregation in the Chicago metropolitan area and ruled that it was a violation of civil rights to sell property to blacks in a manner that "reflect[ed] or perpetuat[ed] discrimination against black citizens." Couldn't the same thing be said about the suburbs having located public housing projects in residentially segregated neighborhoods?

It is an occupational hazard of trial lawyers that in preparing to persuade a judge or jury they also persuade themselves. By the time we filed our brief we were convinced that, disastrous as Milliken was for school desegregation, metropolitan relief in Gautreaux could survive—if Burger and Stewart meant what they said. I was feeling much more hopeful than when I had braked the car to kick the tire outside Woodstock. Perhaps we were still in the ball game.

And so it was. On August 26, 1974, we won! The opinion, written by Clark, accepted each of our arguments. Milliken, Clark said, dealt with schools only; housing *was* different. Given the facts in Gautreaux, including particularly HUD's housing market area approach, "it is necessary and equitable that any remedial plan to be effective must be on a suburban or metropolitan area basis." Clark's opinion even concluded that our suburban public housing exhibit was evidence of suburban discrimination.

It was only a 2–1 decision. Judge Cummings voted with Clark, but Judge Tone dissented on the ground that Milliken controlled. Yet a motion for rehearing by the full court of appeals was denied. Presumably that meant that a majority of all the judges on the court agreed that Milliken spoke only to schools. We still had to bring Austin around, of course, but maybe now that could be done. Austin would, after all, be obliged to follow Clark's opinion.

There was one possible snag. Always a long shot, the Supreme Court might be persuaded to accept Gautreaux for review. HUD would of course want to take it there, but HUD did not have the power to make that decision. The solicitor general of the United States was *the* Supreme Court lawyer for the entire U.S. government. Although he was subordinate to the attorney general, he had much to say about which cases federal agencies could bring before the Supreme Court. If the solicitor general opposed, an agency's desires might not prevail.

The "SG," as he was called, was Robert Bork. Later Bork became a household name when in 1987 the Senate refused to confirm President Reagan's appointment of him to the Supreme Court. But that was a dozen years in the future; at this time Bork was merely another in a long line of SGs. This SG, however, I knew personally. Bork and I had been classmates during my final year at the University of Chicago Law School. (He had started earlier than I but left for a stint with the Marines.) We had worked together on the law review, and even "double-dated," as the ancient expression went—Barbara and I, and Bork and his wife, would spend an occasional social evening together. As a law student, Bork was extremely bright, and had an incisive, clipped way of talking that made him sound dogmatic. He was, indeed, increasingly under the influence of the University of Chicago School of Economics, led by the Nobel laureate Milton Friedman. One of Friedman's disciples, Aaron Director, taught in the law school and influenced many University of Chicago law students, Bork included, to look at the world through conservatively tinted economics glasses.

After law school, Bork spent a few years with a large Chicago law firm and then went on to a teaching career at Yale Law School. There he made his reputation as a strong and prolific conservative scholar, advocating "strict construction" of the Constitution and opposing "judicial activism." In the early 1970s, while still at Yale, Bork worked with the Nixon administration on its antibusing legislation, virtually alone against the 500 law professors who viewed the proposed legislation as unconstitutional. After Nixon's 1972 reelection, Bork was appointed solicitor general.

One of Bork's early cases had been none other than Milliken. Representing the United States as a friend of the court, Bork had argued that a metropolitan remedy would involve widespread disruption of long-established government units because of racial discrimination found to have occurred only within Detroit. "The government believes that a remedy so disproportionate to the violation found is an improper exercise of judicial power." If those were Bork's views, he was not likely to take kindly to metropolitan relief in Gautreaux.

I had not seen Bork since law school. His reputation and record hardly suggested that I could persuade him to leave Gautreaux alone. But there was no reason not to try, and so I made an appointment. Bork's greeting was cordial, if formal. His hair was thinner, his face fuller, but his small eyes had the focused glint I remembered. I reminisced briefly about our law school days, then observed that his sumptuous wood-paneled quarters were a far cry from the dingy basement room that had served as our law review office. This produced Bork's first and last smile of the meeting. After that we got down to cases—or rather, the case.

I made three points. First, it would be premature for the Supreme Court to take on Gautreaux now. We did not yet have a metropolitan order, and there might never even be one. Clark's opinion had merely authorized—arguably directed—Austin to consider metropolitan relief. It didn't prescribe any specifics, and it would be much better to wait until we had a fully formed metropolitan order before the Supreme Court was asked to consider the issues.

Second, there really was no conflict with Milliken. Clark was right in viewing Milliken as focusing on school consolidation and the tradition of local control. Public housing was different, especially because there was no schools counterpart to HUD's housing market area. HUD's entire market area was really the "district" under Milliken.

Finally, I argued policy. A metropolitan approach was the *right* policy. HUD espoused metropolitanism. Why not go along with the policy HUD itself favored, and work with us in fashioning a metropolitan remedial arrangement that HUD would be happy with?

Bork listened but said not a word of substance. He was attentive and polite—no drumming of the fingers or other sign of impatience—but he gave me absolutely no indication of his views on any of my three points. He was a study in impenetrability, allowing himself neither a raised eyebrow nor the slightest nod of head, vertical or horizontal, to indicate his attitude. It quickly became clear that we were in the monologue part of our meeting, and I did not try to overstay my leave.

We didn't have to wait long to learn how effective I had been. In February 1975, the Office of the Solicitor General filed a petition for Supreme Court review. Milliken governed, it argued, and Clark's decision conflicted with it. So much for persuading Bork. A disappointment, but not unexpected. We worked hard on our opposing brief—convincing ourselves in the process that the Supreme Court should not and would not take the case. Indeed, on the housing market area issue we had been handed another strong argument that had not been available to us when we wrote our brief distinguishing Milliken for the court of appeals.

On August 22, 1974, an entirely new subsidized housing program had been signed into law. It came to be called the Section 8 program, after the section of the law in which it appeared. One of its striking features was that HUD could, if it wished, administer the new program directly through contracts with private developers, without the participation of housing authorities or municipalities.

Section 8's roots went back to 1965. In that year, Congress had enacted a small program allowing public housing authorities to lease homes and apartments from private owners and sublease them to public housing families. Following Romney's production blitz in 1969 and early 1970, the Nixon administration had begun to have second thoughts about building so much subsidized housing; troubling issues needed to be addressed, said the president's 1971 Report on National Housing Goals. The continuing middle-class exodus to the suburbs was emptying out a great deal of city housing, so perhaps all the new subsidized housing wasn't needed. Romney's production was expensive, and there were the usual scandals and administrative problems. An internal HUD report in late 1971, calling subsidized housing production "unquestionably one of the Administration's great success stories," nonetheless warned of negligent administration and inferior projects.

After Nixon's reelection landslide over George McGovern in 1972, the president determined to end the traditional housing subsidy programs while he rethought and reshaped subsidized housing policy. In January 1973, a public housing "moratorium" was declared. In August 1974, after lengthy negotiations with Congress conducted by Romney's successor, James T. Lynn (a disillusioned Romney having departed at the end of Nixon's first administration), the entirely new Section 8 approach to subsidized housing had been enacted.

Conventional public housing was kept technically alive, though appropriations for it were minuscule. The new and virtually exclusive housing subsidy for the future would be a modified 1965 leasing program that relied on shelter in the private market. Section 8 subsidies came in two forms. Under one, "tenant-based," an eligible family was to find a private landlord willing to rent it a home or apartment. The landlord would then enter into a lease with the tenant (not with the housing authority as under the old 1965 program), charging no more than a HUD-established "fair market rent" for the location and size of dwelling. The assisted family would pay 25 percent of its income toward the rent, and the balance would be paid by the local housing authority administering the Section 8 tenant-based program with HUD-supplied funds. Landlords were free to participate or not, and were free to screen tenants. Racial discrimination alone was prohibited.

The other, "project-based" Section 8 program fostered new construction and rehabilitation by private developers, producing new, "hard" housing units. Neither construction nor rehabilitation costs were directly subsidized, but with HUD's approval the contract to make Section 8 rent payments could be pledged as security for construction or rehabilitation loans and the mortgage could be insured by the FHA. Unlike the tenant-based subsidy, which "moved" with the tenant to successive locations, the project-based rental subsidy remained with the dwelling unit.

For us, the vital factor in the new Section 8 program was the elimination of local government veto powers over federally subsidized housing. Section 8 programs could be arranged solely between HUD and private developers or landlords, and they would not be subject to the local approval requirements that had plagued public housing. Local governments were given nothing more than an opportunity to comment on proposals, and the comments could be ignored if HUD determined that the proposed housing was needed.

Adding the Section 8 arrow to our quiver greatly strengthened our Milliken argument. Since Section 8 was a program HUD could administer itself, without local government participation, how could this new remedial capacity, involving no "coercion" or "restructuring" of local government, be denied us? Yet, we feared, the Court could "give" us Section 8, thereby granting some metropolitan relief, while denying the metropolitan public housing remedy we had so long sought because that would be "restructuring."

This was a disturbing prospect, of course, but our decision was never in doubt. With public housing appropriations now dried up, with no assurance when, if ever, they would be resumed, and with Section 8 possibly to become the federal government's major subsidized housing program, it was plain that we couldn't risk omitting the Section 8 argument. So into our brief it went, as a separate point, independent of the multiple reasons why Milliken really did not preclude a metropolitan public housing remedy. And, of course, separate as well from the reasons why the Supreme Court should not take the case at all. And then we waited.

On May 13, 1975, Barbara's birthday, standing at a secretary's desk in the BPI offices, I opened an envelope which, according to the return address, came from the Supreme Court clerk. On the single sheet inside, under the Gautreaux caption, I read the two simple words: "Petition Granted." The disappointment was like a sudden sharp blow. As if in reflex I lashed out with my foot at the metal wastebasket on the floor. Neither it nor the heavy wooden desk against which it rested had much "give." My big toe took the brunt of my displeasure. Ruefully nursing my bruise, I limped through the rest of Barbara's now-ruined birthday, telling myself that I had to stop kicking at tires and wastebaskets. It wasn't getting me, or Gautreaux, anywhere.

Preparing for the Supreme Court argument—eventually scheduled for January 20, 1976, ten years minus one day after pizza at Edwardo's—was arduous. We worked and reworked our brief in Hills v. Gautreaux, the name for the Supreme Court phase of the case. (Carla Hills had succeeded James Lynn as HUD secretary and, as the party seeking Supreme Court review, her name went first in the Court caption.) I even received an unprecedented dispensation from the Polikoff family to do "office work" during our annual summer vacation in the mountains. This time we were backpacking in Wyoming's Wind River Range, adjacent to the Wind River Indian Reservation. We heard that some hikers who had strayed onto the reservation had been jailed by the Indians, and we imagined that if that happened to us it would lead to a unique Supreme Court motion: "Due to an unanticipated incarceration in a Wind River Indian Reservation jailhouse, Respondent's attorney, Alexander Polikoff, respectfully requests an extension of time to file Respondent's Brief."

Once the brief was finished we held numerous "moot courts" in which we practiced the oral argument, complete with interrupting questions from our "justices." I worked over the hardest questions I could imagine and had them typed, with proposed answers, for inclusion in my oral argument notebook. We carried on endless discussions with organizations filing friend of the court briefs to support us—among others, the

National Education Association, the Lawyers Committee for Civil Rights Under Law, the League of Women Voters, and the National Committee Against Discrimination in Housing.

Bork's briefs had been powerful, and there were three of them—the request for Supreme Court review, a reply to our brief opposing the request, and his main brief once the Court had taken the case. We had five ways to avoid losing entirely. Down at "level six" was a complete loss— a decision that refused to enlarge HUD's remedial obligations beyond Chicago.

Level one was prematurity—the Supreme Court shouldn't take the case. We had already lost this argument once. Although the Supreme Court had occasionally changed its mind after accepting a case, that was always unlikely. Bork had written:

> Review is not premature. This case is now at the same stage as was *Milliken v. Bradley* when this Court granted [review]: a court of appeals has ordered a district court to develop a plan of affirmative relief that would effectively consolidate a variety of legally separate governmental entities to remedy a discrimination found in only one of them.

Except for the "consolidation" part, that was largely true; while we would try to keep the door open to the prematurity possibility, we felt it was likely that, having accepted Gautreaux, the Court would not now give it up.

Level two was to confine Milliken to schools, as we had persuaded Clark to do. The Burger and Stewart opinions were certainly open to that interpretation, but so were they to Bork's view. He wrote:

> *Milliken* focused on the lack of evidence of any interdistrict wrong, not on the impracticality of the relief sought. The Court's basic holding was that it was improper to use the population of one governmental unit as a racial reservoir to cure racial discrimination occurring within a different governmental unit—regardless of the presence or absence of administrative problems.

We argued strongly that Milliken should be read only as a case about consolidating school districts. But Burger and Stewart knew what they intended by their Milliken opinions; we were not likely to influence their views by thrusting their own words too strenuously at them.

Level three was to contend that our "suburban exhibit" showed discrimination in the suburbs, and therefore, under Milliken, we were entitled to interdistrict relief. This was a long shot because the case had clearly begun as a "Chicago-only" suit. Austin's opinion had explicitly said, "The wrongs were committed within the limits of Chicago and solely against residents of the city." Only later, as Bork pointed out, did we argue to Clark—in our frantic, last-minute effort to distinguish Milliken— that our suburban exhibit amounted to evidence of segregation in suburban public housing. Philosophically friendly judges, such as Tom Clark or Thurgood Marshall, might see suburban discrimination in what we had offered, but the very judges who had pulled the Milliken rug out from under us were hardly likely to do so.

The real contest was likely to be at levels four and five. Because HUD used a housing market area approach, we would argue that metropolitan relief was not interdistrict as to HUD. Public housing metropolitan relief—level four—would leave us free to try to "restructure" public housing throughout HUD's designated market area. Through our set-aside approach, the CHA could be authorized to build outside Chicago. But better, we thought, to save this issue for another day. The objective now was merely to keep that door from being slammed shut. Emphasizing that we were presently seeking relief only against HUD, we wrote: "The separate question of extending metropolitan relief to CHA, or to CHA and other local housing agencies in the housing market area, is not now before the Court."

A win at the fifth level, that is, Section 8 relief, would allow HUD to run a metropolitan Section 8 program. But it would not leave the door open for the CHA to build public housing in the suburbs. As our strongest metropolitan card—no "coercion" of suburban political units was required for HUD to contract directly with developers and landlords willing to participate in Section 8—this was our best chance to avoid total defeat.

Bork pounded at both levels four and five. Of level four, his brief said that any metropolitan plan involving suburban governments "must perforce coerce" their participation because absent "coerced consolidation" they would be free, "as Congress intended," to accept or reject participation in a metropolitan plan. As to level five, Bork argued that a private Section 8 developer needed to arrange for local services and had to comply with local zoning. "Thus the practical operation of the [Section 8] program remains, in significant degree, under local control."

There was, of course, level six. Relief against HUD must be confined to the place where the proven wrong was perpetrated—Chicago. No metropolitan relief of any kind was permissible because we had not shown an interdistrict violation or interdistrict effects. Clark reversed, Austin affirmed.

As the January 20 argument date drew near, we played the depressing game of counting votes. No matter how we fantasized about the possibilities, we could not imagine a win. Five votes against us seemed a certainty, the four Nixon appointees—Burger, Blackmun, Powell, and Rehnquist—plus Stewart, who had supplied the deciding fifth vote in Milliken. Level six, it seemed, was where our elevator would stop.

13

From the moment we entered the building, I felt like a stranger on a movie set. I had never argued in the Supreme Court before. Bernie had, but his advice had been given in our moot courts. Now I was on my own, nervous, pessimistic. Through the arguments in the case that preceded us, I kept feeling for my briefcase on the floor beside me, fingering it as if it were a security blanket.

Suddenly, when Chief Justice Warren Burger announced, "We'll hear arguments next in 1047, Hills v. Gautreaux. Mr. Solicitor General," everything changed. As Bork strode to the podium and prepared to speak, I leaned forward to catch his every word. The movie set had vanished.

Bork quickly stated the facts. Then he launched into his argument with rhetorical flourish—we wanted twelve local housing authorities in more than 300 cities, villages, and townships to be "swept into this case, and put under judicial supervision . . . to remedy an act of segregation that occurred entirely within the City of Chicago." Were this to be done, HUD would be required to impose obligations on communities that were without fault, all for the purpose of "chasing demographic shifts" and attacking "de facto living patterns," which was clearly not a proper remedial function of courts.

As for our housing market area answer to Milliken, that was fallacious because any metropolitan remedy, even if directed only against HUD in a legal sense, would "actually destroy the autonomy and some of the political processes of the cities and housing authorities who have no connection with the violation in Chicago, forcing them to have public housing they didn't want." Even as to Section 8, though HUD could contract directly with private developers, communities that had committed no constitutional violation "are going to have to provide the services: the police protection, the fire protection, the additional schooling for families with children—to benefit citizens of Chicago." Finally—Bork's carefully prepared rhetorical finale—we were arguing for an "extraordinary legal principle" that would expand the traditional powers of a federal court and make it "a metropolitan-wide land use and social planning agency."

Most of the questions to Bork were about the facts and didn't reveal what the justices were thinking. There was, however, one disheartening exception. Rehnquist asked, "Mr. Solicitor General, what if there had been . . . a hearing . . . after a complaint in which all the outlying authorities had been joined, and . . . a finding . . . of interdistrict violations on the part of all? Wouldn't that put the case in a somewhat different posture?" That softball pitch certainly made it appear that Rehnquist had Milliken's interdistrict violation approach very much in mind.

Finally, it was my turn. Bork had been good, but there were no surprises. I quickly made the first of the seven "affirmative" points we had decided upon—that an order confined to HUD, but extending throughout the housing market area, would not be an interdistrict order under Milliken. Then I slipped in a "rebuttal" point I felt we needed, that Bork's "parade of horrors" description of any metropolitan remedial plan was inaccurate. But I had no chance to explain why, for Rehnquist interrupted with a question that terminated the planned presentation. What effect would the order I was talking about have on local housing authorities? It might have none, I said, having in mind but not specifying our Section 8 "level five." Before I could explain Rehnquist interrupted again, "Well, but might it have some?"

It might have an indirect effect, in two ways, I responded, shifting in my mind to public housing at level four. Both would be conditions imposed by HUD on housing authorities applying to HUD for funds to build public housing: first, that they build in predominantly white areas, a condition already essentially contained in HUD regulations; and, second, that a portion of the new housing be made available to members of the Gautreaux class.

"But how," Rehnquist responded, "can you justify the imposition of that second condition as against outlying authorities who have never had an opportunity to litigate any of these questions?"

"We don't," I shot back, adding that before Austin embarked on a consideration of metropolitan relief he should add the outlying authorities, just as we had asked, and only then "proceed to consider a metropolitan plan."

And if hearts can jump (novelists tell us they do), mine did with Rehnquist's next question: "Does this argument suggest that it is premature for us to grapple with the issues involved there? Because what you've been saying, I gather, is that there is no order yet. None of us knows what the contours will be. None of us knows the impact on the outlying municipalities, indeed even the impact on HUD."

"That's exactly correct," I announced soberly, striving to conceal my glee. Here we were at level one! Or if not that, maybe level four, for Rehnquist's question about "opportunity to litigate" could be taken to mean litigate about the "contours" of a metropolitan remedy, not about whether the suburbs had violated any law.

"Yet," Rehnquist continued, "don't you have to say that the court of appeals then, too, was premature in saying that there should be a metropolitan remedy?"

"I do," I agreed, exactly as we had determined in our moot courts to answer this question. "I am not here defending that opinion. I think the result is sound. But I think the language is overly broad . . . A remand to the district court would be in compliance with whatever this Court said . . . not with what the court of appeals said."

Then Chief Justice Burger cut in: "Isn't this case in very much the same posture that the Milliken case was when it came here?" "Not at all, Your Honor," I replied and then proceeded to explain how different we were from Milliken, emphasizing that the order in Milliken ran against local school districts and required them to do something. Not here, I urged.

"My very first point, in answer to Mr. Justice Rehnquist's early question, was that one envisionable form of relief in this case is a decree confined to HUD that does not run against anybody else." With visions of level one or level four dancing in my head, I pronounced emphatically that HUD administered housing funds on an area-wide basis, "not an area-wide multidistrict basis as in *Milliken*."

But that was the high point. There was more back and forth with Burger, about an order requiring HUD to condition funds it gave to housing authorities on making some of their housing available to Gautreaux families. Then Burger said, "but your theory in the district court . . . was that HUD's violations [were in Chicago]. Now it seems to me that when you get outside of the City of Chicago, you would have to make some sort of a new showing that HUD engaged in similar violations [there]."

My heart sank. (Novelists tell us that hearts do that, too.) Burger was stuck on political boundaries. Where had he been all during the housing market area discussion? "I think not," I said. "It's important to distinguish between what's necessary to demonstrate at the liability stage of the case and what's appropriate . . . to consider at the remedial stage of the case." And I went again through the market area analysis, concluding, "It is true that the nature of the wrong determines the scope of the remedy. But the nature of the wrong in this case is not a schools wrong, it is a housing wrong [where] we deal with market areas, we don't deal with identifiable . . . geographic units called school districts."

Burger interrupted: "It wasn't that the school districts were geographic units, they were political units . . . and here, too, you have political units." I tried one last time just as the red light came on: "And the political unit that's relevant," I said, "was HUD, which had chosen the market area for administrative purposes," and an order confined to HUD, affecting the conditions it placed on *voluntary* applicants for HUD money, would not compel any other political unit to do anything.

I sat down feeling like a punctured balloon. From the euphoria of the early Rehnquist questioning to Burger's fixation on political units had been an emotional trajectory, but the end point was ground zero—the focus was on the "innocent" housing authorities as political units.

In his reply, Bork immediately turned to the Rehnquist colloquy about a new hearing—local communities would be subjected to a hearing about a possible remedy, he objected, "when they have committed no violation." Immediately Rehnquist said, "Well, my question suggested not a hearing about a remedy but a question about whether there had been an initial wrong." So much for level four and dreams of a metropolitan public housing plan.

And then Bork took out after level five:

> Now, this talk about ordering HUD alone—and this not being inter-district as to HUD—is a semantic game . . . There will be an enormous practical impact on innocent communities who have to bear the burden of the housing, who will have to house a plaintiff class from Chicago, which they wronged in no way . . . There is no way that this is not an interdistrict remedy even though you use HUD as the conduit.

Finally, Marshall and White entered the fray and sparred with Bork a little. Marshall suggested HUD "wiped out" political lines when it chose the housing market area, and Bork disagreed. White wondered why HUD couldn't be subjected to some kind of order in its own market area. Bork didn't see the "predicate" for an order covering the whole market area because HUD "did something wrong in Chicago." Whereupon Burger jumped in, "Wouldn't that kind of order presuppose . . . someone is beating his wife and therefore stop beating your wife?" Replied Bork, "I think it would, Mr. Chief Justice," and any air still remaining in my collapsed balloon oozed out. Mercifully, Burger announced, "Thank you, gentlemen. The case is submitted."

My feelings were a jumble. We had not talked at all about confining Milliken to schools or suburban discrimination, levels two and three. Rehnquist and Burger seemed dead set against us on level four, and probably level five as well. Stewart, the key vote in Milliken, had asked nary a question. Neither had Powell, Blackmun, or Brennan. So it was difficult, I consoled myself, to know what to think.

Though I remained pessimistic about the outcome, I had a visceral feeling that I had not done too badly. It wasn't just Barbara's kiss implanted during the crush of optimistic congratulations from well-wishers in the outside corridor. I believed I had made a respectable presentation in a difficult situation. I had not been swept away by a volley of hostile fire. Bork threaded his way through the corridor crowd and offered a handshake with the comment that it had been a good argument. Positive news came from Daniel's scorecard: I had made all seven affirmative points.

After the intensity of preparing for the oral argument and the climax of the argument itself, February and March were down time. There was, about everything, a sense of treading water, marking time, waiting. The decision was bound to come before the end of the Supreme Court term in June, but there was no way of telling when. Decision-making in the Supreme Court was a well-kept secret.

When the call did come, therefore, although awaited and expected, it was a surprise that this particular telephone ring on this particular day would bring the news. A reporter was calling. Did I care to comment on the Supreme Court's decision? I might, I said, if he would first tell me what it was. Then, was I hearing correctly? Unanimous? Stunned, I repeated, "Unanimous? Gautreaux? For us?" The shock of joy, mingled with persisting disbelief, has blotted out any memory of what I then said to the unfortunate reporter, who was looking for a printable quotation and no doubt got gibberish instead.

I began wandering around the office, telling people what I'd heard and making phone calls—all with deliberate restraint because until I'd had some confirmation and actually seen the opinion, understood what it said and on exactly which of levels two through five it rested, a part of me remained unbelieving. Later, I learned that someone else had called Rubinowitz and asked him what he thought about the unanimous Supreme Court decision in Gautreaux. "You mean we didn't get a single vote?" he had groaned.

When we did get the opinion, it was immediately apparent that we had engaged in little more than damage control. We were firmly ensconced on level five; Milliken v. Bradley was alive and well. The opinion, by Justice Stewart, said straightaway that although Milliken had discussed the many practical problems of school district consolidation, the Court's decision was actually based on limitations on the remedial powers of federal courts "to restructure the operation of local and state governmental entities." So much for level two and confining Milliken to schools.

And with equal directness, noting that we had offered our suburban exhibit for limited purposes, not to show discrimination by suburbs or their housing authorities, the opinion said the court of appeals was "mistaken" in supposing that the exhibit amounted to evidence of suburban discrimination. So much for level three.

Then came the good, if limited, part. We had won on housing market area, but at level five, not four. "The relevant geographic area . . . is the Chicago housing market, not the Chicago city limits." But over and over again Stewart warned against "impermissibly" interfering with local governments and housing authorities, against "displacing" the rights and powers they possessed under either federal or state law, and against "coercing uninvolved governmental units." That could be avoided in this case, Stewart wrote, because under the new Section 8 statute HUD could contract directly with private owners and developers without local governmental approval, and because an order directed solely to HUD would not force unwilling localities to apply for federal housing assistance but merely reinforce HUD's determinations of which among competing applications to fund. We should return to the district court for further proceedings consistent with the Court's opinion. Marshall, Brennan, and White wrote a paragraph joining Stewart's opinion except "insofar as it appears to reaffirm the decision in *Milliken*."

But even the good, if limited, part of the opinion was qualified. "Our determination that the District Court has the authority to direct HUD to engage in remedial efforts in the metropolitan area outside the limits of the City of Chicago should not be interpreted as requiring a metropolitan area order." The nature and scope of any order to be entered against HUD was a "matter for the District Court in the exercise of its equitable discretion." On the issue of involving the suburbs, and maybe thereby letting the CHA off the hook, we had already been given more than a taste of Austin's "equitable discretion."

So we could possibly get a form of metropolitan relief, limited to Section 8, if we could persuade Austin that the circumstances demanded it. Regardless of success or failure in that endeavor, visions of suburban public housing for Chicago families went glimmering. The holy grail of a public housing program, in which the middle-class and affluent white neighborhoods of suburbia would have to accept a fair share of the region's public housing poor, was now unattainable. Under the circumstances, celebrations were muted. It was a great "victory." Yet it was also a devastating defeat. Milliken, in all its perniciousness, was now a fundamental principle of federal jurisprudence, not limited to schools.

Much of the newspaper comment missed the point. An extravagant *Baltimore Sun* article called Hills v. Gautreaux the most important decision since Brown. A cartoon showed two suburbanites gazing in disbelief at a sign announcing a public housing project over a caption that read, "There goes the neighborhood . . ." Patrick Buchanan, erstwhile Nixon speechwriter, railed in his syndicated column against the "tyranny" that had given federal courts "the authority to order [HUD] to scatter public housing for poor and black throughout the suburbs of Middle America." The *New York Times* also got it wrong. Its front page story began, "The Supreme Court ruled today that Federal courts can order the creation of low-cost public housing for minorities in a city's white suburbs to relieve racial segregation in housing within the city," failing to note the distinction between government-owned public housing and privately owned Section 8 housing. It would take some time for reporters to understand that public housing for city folk was not coming to suburbia.

Inevitably, second thoughts set in. What if I had said this or that? What if I had come on strongly, not been so polite? "The government is badly mistaken. Milliken has nothing to do with this case. There is one guilty defendant, HUD, which administers its housing programs throughout a single housing market area. Of course the federal courts can tell that guilty defendant to use its powers to remedy wrongs it committed within that self-same area. To repeat for emphasis, Milliken is plainly irrelevant."

Or, "Milliken is a school case. All nine justices made that clear. Under your own decisions Milliken's language about limitations on the remedial powers of federal courts is not to be read abstractly as announcing a general rule but is to be limited to the school facts then before the Court. In this housing case we start fresh, looking at the housing facts of HUD's programs. Milliken's overbroad language does not speak to those specifics."

Another kind of "what if" was: What if we had done things differently? What if we had faced the need for metropolitan relief at the outset and sued the suburban housing authorities as well as the CHA and HUD?

Probably that wouldn't have made sense. Apart from enlarging greatly an already large case, plausible explanations for the location of suburban public housing developments could have bogged us down.

Well, then, what if we had brought the suburban authorities in as soon as HUD's liability was determined in 1971? For relief purposes only, of course, not attempting to prove discrimination any more than we had in the city council case. That would have forced Austin to rule on our set-aside approach much earlier. Perhaps then we would have reached the Supreme Court before Milliken. Then everything might have been different. Without the bugaboo of busing the Court would have faced the interdistrict issue for the first time in the vastly more favorable context of HUD's housing market area.

There was still a third kind of what if, the absurd kind. What if Humphrey had gotten one more percentage point? What if Fortas hadn't resigned? Happily, present imperatives blotted out these delusionary musings. Having emerged alive from the Supreme Court coliseum—the lions had wounded us badly but we had not been devoured—now we had to focus on next steps. While joyous about being alive, though licking our wounds, the challenge of returning to the district court and figuring out how to write something intelligible on the tabula rasa of a metropolitan Section 8 program now had to be faced.

14

By 1974 in the case against the CHA, and now in 1976 in the case against HUD, we had finally hacked our way through the legal jungle. Emerging on the other side, we should now be able to get some unsegregated housing for Gautreaux families—scattered sites from the CHA and, if we could figure out how to do it, Section 8 housing from HUD.

The time the tortuous trek had consumed was depressing. Our children were now grown—Deborah and Daniel were adults of twenty-one and nineteen, off at college, and even our youngest, Joanie, was now fifteen. I had a new career at BPI, where we had fought successfully against Mayor Daley's proposal to build an airport in Lake Michigan ("Don't do it in the Lake!" was our slogan), unsuccessfully against political spying by the U.S. Army, and were attempting to combat both Lake Michigan pollution and the many nuclear power plants Commonwealth Edison Company was building in the Chicago area. Vietnam and the Nixon presidency were over. (It felt as if two abscessed teeth had been pulled, but the pain lingered and reconstruction loomed.)

In two ways we had been hurt seriously. The first was losing the quest for the metropolitan public housing grail. The second was time lost. From 1969, when the CHA had been found guilty, to 1974, when the Supreme Court refused to hear the city-CHA appeal from the city council veto power decision, five years had elapsed. In some of those years, public housing funding by historic standards had been exceptionally high. The production time and funding levels lost were irretrievable. So was the rapid loss of vacant land in white Chicago neighborhoods. With the best of will and ability on the CHA's part, the prospects for what could be achieved in a Chicago scattered-site program that didn't begin until the mid-1970s were poor compared to what would have been the case half a decade earlier. Though we had hacked our way through the jungle, the landscape we now faced hardly resembled Eden. The dreams of the civil rights revolution seemed distant indeed, the bright hopes for litigation as a social change lever naive.

Something—masochism?—led me to reread a talk I had given at a conference in Madison, Wisconsin, in February 1970. Madison was then a hotbed of antiwar radicalism. The title of the student-sponsored conference was, "Survival: 14 Years to 1984." My talk, "Urban Change through the System," had a theme not likely to be particularly appealing to the typical University of Wisconsin student.

At a time when the country was tearing itself to pieces over Vietnam, I thought Gautreaux held a relevant message. After a quick review of public housing segregation in Chicago, I described—in the wake of Austin's final order of the previous July—the prospect for "an affirmative desegregation plan covering the whole of a major metropolitan area." I acknowledged the scope of the nation's problems—the war, our dual criminal justice system (one for the rich, one for the poor), millions of impoverished families in the planet's richest nation. I also acknowledged doubt that real change in the system could be achieved without some force from "outside," that there never would have been an effective peace movement if it had remained entirely law-abiding and had not spilled blood on draft board files.

I was concerned, however, that the manner of curing societal evils not lead to a breakdown of the rule of law. Back from Communist Eastern Europe, Tom Wicker had found government there "faceless and unreachable," the system arbitrary, the individual reduced to a "whispered conversation in the bathroom with the water running." He had added that, for all its faults, what was best to come back to in this country was that it had not yet deprived its most impudent and troublesome of their right to be free, that its courts could still tell government that justice and law did not change with administrations, that its populace could still mass peacefully and march militantly. "It is that kind of freedom," Wicker had said, "above all, and at whatever cost, that must be preserved in America." I told the Wisconsin students that I agreed with Wicker, and felt that there were enough good people around so that the formula for change needn't and shouldn't imperil the rule of law.

My talk closed on that theme: "I believe . . . that it *is* possible to effect meaningful change *of* the system *through* the system. I believe further that if our tactical mix is wrong—too rich in blood and too lean in law—we will all surely wind up in an Orwellian nightmare. And I don't like having to talk in whispers with the water running."

What would I say now, should the Wisconsin students invite me back? That thought was immediately followed by the disturbing realization that "they" weren't there any more. The students—the country—had changed. Yes, in a sense the rule of law had prevailed. The miscreant in the White House had been forced out. But what havoc he had wrought before his departure.

In our housing corner of national policy, the years of Nixon rule had begun with the nation's recognition, in the Kerner, Kaiser, and Douglas reports, and John Gardner's affirmative administration prescription, that government policy had created a two-societies plague on America. It was imperative that the plague be eradicated. Yet in a few short years the country had been moved to a sanctimonious acceptance of it and an intellectually indefensible closure of the judicial route to change. Maybe it had been inevitable. Maybe George Wallace had laid bare the truth about America's soul, and there was little Nixon could have done but swim with the tide to stay afloat. But not in my book. I felt that Arthur Chotin had got it right. The president's job was to lead the nation toward the future, not back to a dark and miserable past. At least to try.

Tom Wicker had said, and I had believed, that America's courts could still tell government that justice and law did not change with administrations. It now seemed to me that Richard Nixon, though banished in disgrace, had changed all that.

✤   ✤   ✤   ✤   ✤

With the jungle, and Nixon, behind us, what lay ahead for Gautreaux? Mercifully, perhaps, I had no clear idea of the tales the next three chapters tell. Chapter 4 describes the bogs we slogged through on the scattered-site trail, chapter 5 our adventures with Section 8 and metropolitanization. In the 1990s a new remedial path opened up—public housing "transformation"—which involves us still, as chapter 6 recounts. Finally, chapter 7 considers what the whole Gautreaux journey—now nearly forty years of it—can tell us about America.

PART TWO

CHAPTER FOUR

MORASSES, QUAGMIRES, AND BOGS

Look at this muckheap!

—Estragon (*Waiting for Godot*)

1

It was an unseasonably warm evening in late fall. Glowing yellow in the twilight, streetlights revealed not a single parking place in the block that housed the church. Circling the unfamiliar streets, Barbara and I finally found a space three blocks away, then began walking past the solid lines of neat brick bungalows and two-flats. Clumps of people moved along the sidewalks toward the church like iron filings drawn by a magnet.

The church's dark-oak double doors were propped open. In the vestibule a square, black-and-white lettered poster board on a tripod announced, CHA MEETING DOWNSTAIRS. At the bottom of the stairs the hallway opened into a large meeting room. A stage at the far end faced twenty or twenty-five rows of folding chairs, arranged with a middle aisle and one on either side along windowless, mustard-yellow walls. Two chairs were stationed on each side of a center-stage podium; at stage right an American flag rested in its stand. In the three aisles and in the open area behind the rows of seats people were milling about, talking. Half the seats were already filled. The noise level under the low ceiling was like an assault.

Barbara and I stood there for only a moment before a tall woman in a red-flowered dress approached, smiling. "Are you Mr. Polikoff? I

159

thought so. Thank you so much for coming." After introductions she led us to the front row. "Why don't you sit here," she said. "We're about to begin."

Which they were. The 150 or so people in the room were asked to take their seats by a gray-haired, bespectacled man who firmly clutched both sides of the podium. He wore a suit and tie, unlike most of the men who were in open-necked sport shirts. The noise ebbed. I looked around but did not see a familiar face. Where was the CHA? They were supposed to be on the program.

I had accepted the invitation to speak, telling myself I shouldn't be inaccessible. And maybe there would be a new point of view, a different insight. Persuade someone? Not likely. After Sam Lucchese had finally opened his briefcase, the CHA sites remained on the front pages for days. Lois Weisberg had organized an "advisory panel" whose purpose was to persuade. Lois, Bernie's wife, was then the administrative director of BPI. Possessed of great energy and enormous creativity, she helped train a group of volunteers to go into the neighborhoods—homes, churches, meeting rooms—to explain why scattered, low-rise public housing would "work." The volunteers did not meet with success. "What I learned," Lois wrote later, "was that nice, ordinary people have preconceived ideas and feel threatened by people different from themselves."

The agenda for the evening was announced by our hostess in the red dress, who ascended the stage stairs and replaced the suit-and-tie man at the podium. There would first be some brief organizational business. The CHA had at the last minute sent its apologies, but Mr. Polikoff was here and would speak for fifteen or twenty minutes about the background of the case and then answer questions. Wasn't it nice to have such a pleasant evening and a good turnout? Afterward there would be coffee in the adjacent room. Everyone was invited.

The organizational business was indeed brief, after which our hostess motioned me to take one of the stage chairs, next to Mr. Suit and Tie, and then introduced me succinctly. She was accurate about my law school, where I had worked, and my present position, except that she said Business and Professional People in—not for—the Public Interest, a common mistake.

After light applause lasting microseconds, I launched into my stock speech—a brief description of the case, the overwhelming evidence of the CHA's wrongdoing, the important principle in our society that established wrongs should be remedied. Then came my main message, how careful Judge Austin had been (attributing everything to him) in crafting the remedy, the small number of apartments in any one area, the low-rise, low-density buildings that would fit right into the neighborhood. Nothing like the huge "projects" most people thought of when they heard "public housing." Next came strong CHA tenant-screening requirements to ensure that the families moving in would be good neighbors. Finally, my rhetorical capstone. Half the apartments would be reserved for families already living in the neighborhood, their own neighbors, not public housing families or others from outside. The only requirement was low income.

As soon as I had finished—the initial applause was not repeated—Ms. Red Dress rose from her chair to remind the audience that I had kindly consented to answer questions. They came like a flood. Some were shouted. Many were followed by bursts of applause. What about property values? Weren't we picking on working-class neighborhoods? What about Sauganash (one of Chicago's wealthiest, all-white neighborhoods)—why didn't it have any scattered sites? How could I be serious about CHA screening procedures? Why didn't the community have a role in site selection? Soon the questions became more personal. Who had chosen me to work on this case? Where did I live? How much public housing was there in my neighborhood?

I remained polite, trying not to sound too argumentative. Stick to the facts. Don't lose your cool. Be honest. It was all pretty familiar, and this meeting was not as rancorous as some. When the questioning began to get too repetitious, Ms. Red Dress called a halt and—so I thought—was ready to end the proceedings. Instead she announced, "We have one more matter before we adjourn—a presentation to Mr. Polikoff." Laughter rippled through the audience.

Mr. Suit and Tie quickly walked off stage and just as quickly returned, carrying an object of golden hue, about a yard long, which at first I didn't recognize. He strode briskly to the podium, waved what he was holding aloft for all to see, turned, and with both hands thrust it toward me. "Mr. Polikoff," he said, raising his voice so that the audience would be sure to hear, "we are pleased to present you with this gold-plated pooper-scooper, which you can use to clean up all the shit you're bringing to our neighborhood." Cheers, laughing, clapping, by far the most enthusiastic applause of the evening.

I hesitated briefly, for this was a moment without precedent. Then, feigning amusement, I said I accepted their "gift" in the spirit of levity with which it had been offered. After which I made my way quickly down the stage steps to Barbara's front-row seat, awkwardly holding the thing at my side. I considered leaving it there but decided not to. They would only pursue me to restore the "forgotten" gift. With Barbara, stone-faced, at my side, I made my way up the aisle and out into the night. How we disposed of the gold-plated object neither of us remembers.

The pooper-scooper incident was unique, but the views it symbolized were pervasive. They were articulated less metaphorically by another neighborhood organization, created in direct response to Austin's 1969 order. Its name—Nucleus of Chicago Homeowners Association—generated an acronym that made the organization's purpose abundantly clear.

In 1972 Nucleus sued to enjoin the CHA's first proposed group of scattered sites, asserting that the project violated the National Environmental Policy Act (NEPA) because HUD had not prepared an Environmental Impact Statement. NEPA mandated an EIS, a detailed statement assessing environmental consequences, for all major federal actions "significantly affecting the quality of the human environment." Nucleus charged that HUD's shortcut "finding of inapplicability" did not satisfy this requirement. Because HUD dollars would pay for the CHA's scattered sites, a "major federal action" was unquestionably involved.

The anticipated significant effect on the quality of the human environment was clearly spelled out in the Nucleus complaint. No beating around the bush. Public housing tenants as a group, compared to the "social class" of the Nucleus neighborhood residents, had a higher propensity toward crime, a lower commitment toward hard work, and a disregard for property maintenance. The social class of the residents emphasized work, respect for law, and property maintenance and improvement. Placing CHA units in the Nucleus neighborhood would therefore have an adverse effect on the safety of the residents and on the economic and aesthetic quality of their lives, in other words, on the community "environment."

The case was assigned to Judge Julius Hoffman, who had presided over the infamous "Conspiracy Seven" trial of Tom Hayden, Bobby Seale, and other leaders of the '60s counterculture. Reporters gleefully termed the Nucleus suit the "people pollution" case, especially when several social scientists, expert witnesses for Nucleus, testified that, statistically speaking, public housing tenants included a high proportion of unemployed, welfare, and multiproblem families. The CHA's scattered-site tenants, they concluded, were therefore likely to engage in antisocial acts.

Since the Nucleus case was technically unrelated to the Gautreaux litigation, we had to consider whether to attempt to enter it. We finally decided not to, for fear that joining the case would turn it into even more of a media event. And the Justice Department would probably mount a good defense for HUD. The trial lasted six weeks, and included the Reverend Andrew Greeley—later to become well known as a novelist—testifying for Nucleus that scattered-site public housing might speed up white flight to the suburbs. At the end Hoffman ruled that "although human beings may be polluters, they are not themselves pollution." Environmental impact within the meaning of NEPA did not include a group of human beings.

⟍

Pooper-scoopers and people pollution allegations did not exhaust the repertoire of scattered-site opponents. On the beastly hot evening of July 28, 1983, Barbara, Joanie, and I were attempting to keep cool in the recreation room—three feet below ground level—of our unairconditioned home. Suddenly one of us noticed a large crowd in the driveway, spilling onto the front lawn. Nonplussed, Barbara and I walked outside (I in bathing trunks) and into the milling throng. Joanie soon followed with our Siberian husky on a leash, for protection she later explained.

Two young men, spokespersons for the group, immediately confronted me. They were members of the Northwest Neighborhood Federation (NNF). Because, they said loudly and belligerently, I had refused to meet with them, they had come to me. By then I saw that most of the people standing around were white haired and perspiring, straining to hear what was said. Even though there were a lot of them, they looked more uncomfortable than hostile. (With a picture of me in my bathing trunks, suggesting that I had been interrupted while cooling off in my nonexistent swimming pool, the *Sun-Times* reported the next morning that two busloads of over a hundred NNF members had made the journey.)

We soon cleared up the matter of the supposed refusal to meet. Because of a schedule conflict I had declined an invitation to attend a community meeting but had written that I would meet with them at any mutually convenient time. "How about right now?" I offered. Hesitation and whispered consultation. Then the two leaders, maintaining their belligerent tone, rejected my offer. The meeting, they insisted, must be in the community. We quickly agreed on an evening the following week, and the assembled throng seemed satisfied with this denouement. Barbara overheard one of the women say, "Why did we come? He seems like a nice man."

While these "negotiations" were under way, some of the group were busy placing flyers in mailboxes up and down the block. Addressed to "Neighbors of Alexander Polikoff," they explained that NNF was visiting our "fine neighborhood" to arrange for me to explain what I planned to do "to correct the unfair distribution of public housing sites in our area." I had built my reputation, the flyer went on, as a White Knight (BPI's logo) crusading for justice. But in reality I had "proven to be a sham" because I had failed to ensure fair implementation of the scattered-site program—politically well-connected neighborhoods were not getting their fair share of scattered sites. "It seems," the flyer concluded, "Mr. Polikoff is more concerned with his own personal fame than the future of Chicago's neighborhoods."

The following week I met with about seventy-five NNF members in a local school. An hour of heated discussion achieved little. It satisfied no one to explain that I had no power over site selection as long as the CHA's sites complied with the black and white area ratios in Austin's order. Or that the reasons some neighborhoods received fewer scattered sites than others might have something to do with the availability and price of land and buildings. At the end, by a voice vote, it was decided to "visit" BPI directors at their homes.

Over the next several weeks a half dozen or so BPI directors were called upon by delegations of NNF members who, as in their visit to my home, used mailbox flyers to apprise the directors' neighbors of their concerns. "Help Put the White Knight Back on Its Horse," read the flyer headline. BPI had fallen off its white steed by failing to ensure that the scattered-site program was implemented fairly. Residents were urged to call their neighbor—the BPI director whose name, address, and phone number were supplied—to encourage him to "wake up BPI."

It was indeed true that the CHA had acquired no sites in some of the whitest, wealthiest neighborhoods of the city, which I lamented. And while the CHA would undoubtedly explain its site selection on price and availability grounds, in "clout city" it would be surprising if politics were entirely absent from the CHA's decision-making. It was also true, however, that in the NNF's neighborhoods the number of scattered-site apartments was 0.05 percent, 44 (in ten scattered buildings) compared to 84,759 occupied units. I suspected that what angered the NNF as much as perceived unfairness was my refusal at the school meeting to agree to a court order telling the CHA not to use three more buildings it had purchased in the NNF's area for scattered sites.

Some weeks later I was to receive an award from a foundation whose offices were in a Near North Side neighborhood. As I climbed out of my cab in front of the foundation's imposing edifice, I was surprised to see pickets marching back and forth along the sidewalk, carrying placards and passing out flyers. The surprise disappeared when I examined one of the flyers. It was from my old friends at the NNF and their colleagues of the Southwest Parish and Neighborhood Federation. There was my picture, alongside the headline, "Does This Man *Really* Deserve an Award?? He Thinks So . . . Do You???" The text noted that I was being given the award because I represented "the highest commitment to the public good." It continued, "We have a different perspective on Mr. Polikoff's activity," repeated the earlier NNF charges about unfairness, and ended with a clarion call about not standing for my hypocrisy.

The following year one of our BPI directors, Charles Hill, gentle, soft-spoken, an officer of the Federal Home Loan Bank Board, was phoned by a representative of the Southwest Parish and Neighborhood Federation. Hill was asked to attend a neighborhood meeting to discuss the CHA's proposed scattered-site acquisition in a Southwest Side neighborhood. The caller was concerned, he said, "about what kind of people the CHA would put in their neighborhood."

Hill asked what kind of people the caller was talking about. "Colored people," was the answer. To the question why colored people were objected to, the further answer was that letting the colored in would result in "all kinds of crime, rape, robberies." Hill then informed his caller that he was black and mused, "I guess you wouldn't want me to live in your neighborhood either." After only a moment's hesitation, the caller said, "That's right." To Hill's final question, did the caller think all colored people acted the same way, the answer was, "Yes, or at least 85 percent of them," adding that keeping all of them out was "our only way of protecting ourselves from the overwhelming majority who rape, kill, and throw babies from third floor apartments." At that point, Hill's memorandum says, "I decided to terminate the conversation."

In 1996 it was disclosed that a three-flat building in Hiawatha Park, a white working-class neighborhood on the Northwest Side at a considerable remove from the nearest black community, was about to be purchased for the scattered-site program. As if by spontaneous combustion a huge protest quickly materialized—more than 600 residents overflowed the local alderman's office and demonstrated in the street outside. The reaction would have been the same, said one observer, if a nuclear power plant had been proposed.

Before the incident ran its course there were countless impassioned public meetings, demands (rejected) to meet with the Gautreaux judge, calls for a congressional investigation (enthusiastically supported by the local congressman), insistence that Gautreaux court orders be modified, and even a statement by Republican presidential candidate Bob Dole about changing the way public housing was administered. The issue, as numerous spokespersons for the neighbors explained, was not race but property values. Chicago's mayor, Richard M. Daley, son of the "original" Richard J. Daley, weighed in on the side of the neighbors:

> Most of those people don't have stock portfolios. The only thing they have is their bungalow. They just want to know can they hold their value.

That the three-flat represented a tiny fraction of 1 percent of the neighborhood's housing stock, that at least one of the three apartments would go not to a CHA family but to a family already living in the community, that studies showed that scattered sites had not caused property values to drop in other neighborhoods which, like Hiawatha Park, were distant from the ghetto—none of this made a difference. Charles Hill's caller represented an extreme view. Mayor Daley did not. It was 1996, not 1966, but on the question of black families moving into white neighborhoods, time seemed to have stood still.

Yet it was superficial to dismiss all scattered-site opponents as racists. Kathleen Augustine, vice chairman of the Southwest Parish and Neighborhood Federation, in a 1983 letter to the *Tribune*, wrote:

> Because of our proximity to West Englewood, one of our city's most impoverished, deteriorated and crime-ridden black communities, Marquette Park and its adjoining neighborhoods have experienced a frightening increase in violent crime, an unprecedented wave of real estate solicitation, redlining, the seemingly irreversible deterioration of our primary commercial strip, and the serious decline of academic standards in our public schools.
>
> If we appear insensitive to the poor, it is because we have been fighting for years against enormous and almost unbeatable odds to ensure our middle-income community's stability, viability, and safety . . . facing the serious social and economic problems which are threatening to tear our beloved community apart.

When a black family chooses not to be the first "pioneer" in an all-white neighborhood, we do not attribute that decision to prejudice, although some black families are prejudiced. Instead, we acknowledge the serious risks of hostility and isolation that black families who make such moves may encounter. We accept a family's decision not to run such risks as an understandable human decision made in regrettable circumstances. Current events as well as history justify such decisions.

Current events and history also evidence the persistence of what I will call the "resegregation syndrome"—the probability Augustine's letter contemplated that once blacks enter a white neighborhood near the ghetto, transition to predominantly black will quickly ensue. The causes are multiple and complex. They include: residential segregation that closes many neighborhoods to blacks, leading to pent-up housing demand wherever blacks succeed in gaining entry outside the ghetto; the inclination of black families to move to areas where they feel they will be welcomed, as shown by the presence of other blacks; pervasive racial steering by real estate brokers and salesmen; and, sometimes, the deliberately manipulative preying on white fears by unscrupulous members of the real estate industry that is called "blockbusting." Whatever the causes, the probability is high that the transition to predominantly black will occur.

So also, in neighborhoods near the black ghetto, is the probability that adverse consequences will ensue. In 1979 Justice Lewis Powell wrote for the Supreme Court that the "harms" flowing from a racially changing neighborhood could be "profound." They amounted, the NAACP's Roy Wilkins said, to "hideous social disintegration," where murder was the leading cause of death among black males from ages fifteen through twenty-four, and where law-abiding families led "lives of sheer terror." The images we see each day on television, and in our newspapers and magazines, lead us to associate black skin color, especially in young black men, with the awesomely bad circumstances of the black ghetto. Augustine's letter reflected the fear that the resegregation syndrome would inexorably follow any movement of blacks into a white neighborhood near the ghetto, and would bring with it the changing neighborhood harms of which Justice Powell and Roy Wilkins spoke.

Thirty years earlier Hyde Park had confronted the identical fear. Would it, as historian Arnold Hirsch put it, "become the latest addition to the Black Belt"? The big difference between Marquette Park and Hyde Park was that the latter was the home of the University of Chicago. "It is not possible to operate and maintain a great university in a deteriorating or slum neighborhood," Chancellor Lawrence A. Kimpton declared. "The very life of the University is at stake."

Marshaling its money and power, the university was able to act in ways Augustine and the Southwest Parish and Neighborhood Federation could only dream of, from creating a potent local organization with direct access to the city's strongest levers of political and financial power, to changing state law to authorize redeveloping a community before rather than after it became a slum—"conservation" it was called. For the purpose, Hirsch says, of "control[ling] black migration into its immediate environment," and "preventing [Hyde Park's] annexation to the Black Belt," the university set out—in Kimpton's words—to "buy, control, and rebuild our neighborhood." This it did with considerable success.

Because of the university's money and power, Hyde Park was able to use redevelopment to achieve an economically upgraded, substantially white community. Lacking such resources, Marquette Park was reduced to using violence to the end of black exclusion. In each case the objective was the same—to avoid annexation to the Black Belt. The "serious social and economic problems which are threatening to tear our beloved community apart" were identical in both places.

✦

With the acquisition of lots and buildings in nonblack neighborhoods the Gautreaux scattered-site program was embarking on a deliberate crossing of Chicago's color line. Yet it was striking that the responses we were encountering—pooper-scoopers, lawsuits, mailbox flyers, picketing, protest meetings—were completely unlike white communities' previous reactions to blacks moving into their neighborhoods.

Putting aside as ancient history the violence of the pre–World War II period (Chicago's 1919 race riot had left 38 dead and 537 injured), Hirsch tells us that during the period from 1945 to 1950 Chicago experienced its most serious wave of racial disorders since the World War I era—some 357 "incidents" related directly to housing, 85 percent of them on the ghetto's borders, frequently involving arson and bombings.

The period also included a change in the CHA's role from wartime housing for factory workers to temporary housing for returning veterans. With funds from both Chicago and Washington, and twenty-two parcels of vacant land already owned by the city and other local governments, it was decided that the CHA would take on the temporary housing mission with trailers, Quonset huts, prefabricated homes, and plywood houses. Most of the twenty-two sites were in outlying neighborhoods. Since blacks made up 20 percent of the veterans needing housing, CHA officials decided to disregard the neighborhood composition rule and—carefully— to admit black veterans and their families to 20 percent of the temporary housing.

Given the CHA leadership of Robert Taylor and Elizabeth Wood, the CHA decision was not surprising. More surprising, on the surface, was the support of Mayor Edward Kelly. Yet supporting Taylor and Wood on temporary veterans' housing was part of a consistent Kelly strategy to bring blacks to the Democratic machine. (And Kelly did "suggest" an informal 10 percent black quota and the admission of blacks only to the larger of the temporary projects.)

Encouragingly, the first temporary project that included black veterans provoked no incident. The second was Airport Homes, a 185-unit development near Midway Airport. On the day in December 1946 when the first black families were scheduled to move in, a crowd estimated at between 1,500 and 3,000 gathered in front of the apartments. They battled about 400 policemen for two solid weeks, after which the black families, and Taylor and Wood, gave up. Airport Homes became and remained all white.

In mid-August 1947 Taylor and Wood tried again, at Fernwood Park Homes, also on the Southwest Side. The reaction this time was even more furious. Rioting continued for three successive nights. Crowds, ranging up to 5,000 persons, struggled with police in an unsuccessful effort to "take over" Fernwood Homes, then assaulted blacks in cars and streetcars and beat them in a fashion reminiscent, Hirsch says, of 1919. It took six months, but finally the black families were safely established.

While the veteran move-ins proceeded under the aegis of government, numerous "private" incidents were also occurring whenever, at the edges of the bulging ghetto, blacks sought more living room. In Englewood, for example, the sale of a single home to a black family so heightened tensions that a subsequent false rumor that other blacks were about to move in triggered a riot even bigger than the one at Fernwood Homes. At its peak the Englewood crowd was estimated at 10,000 persons.

Sometimes these violent reactions were successful in buying time for white neighborhoods near the ghetto, but not always. In the South Side's Park Manor, when the Seventy-first Street "border" was crossed by a black family's purchase of a two-flat building, the ensuing riot badly damaged the building. But two major Chicago lending institutions, concluding that Park Manor was "gone," began making loans to black purchasers. A resident reported, "All day real estate salesmen call us up and want to know if we would like to sell, and of course it is always to Negroes." Within four years Park Manor was nearly 80 percent black and most remaining whites were concentrated in a small enclave. Most of these, Hirsch says, reported they were moving.

Hirsch sums up two decades of Chicago racial violence, from the mid-1940s into the 1960s:

> The violence that gripped Chicago in the postwar years was an ordeal by fire as the spatial accommodation of the races underwent adjustment . . . The sheer force of numbers was compelling the alteration of heretofore rigid racial boundaries. It proved to be a painful procedure.

Why didn't our scattered-site program provoke comparable pain? Why did communities that threw gasoline bombs and beat blacks on streetcars in the 1940s, 1950s, and 1960s content themselves with pooper-scoopers, mailbox flyers, and peaceful protests in the 1970s, 1980s, and 1990s?

The answer has several parts. First, by the mid-1970s racial succession had already taken place in many white neighborhoods bordering the ghetto, relieving to a degree the overwhelming ghetto pressure and, to some whites, demonstrating the futility of violent resistance. Second, the civil rights revolution of the 1950s and early 1960s had modified the nation's mores. It was harder to pull blacks off streetcars and bomb blacks' homes after Birmingham and Selma, King's assassination, and civil rights laws. Third, no doubt the least of the factors, the design of the scattered-site program may have provided a modest degree of comfort to some — it was a citywide plan, not aimed at one or a few neighborhoods, involving small numbers of small units, with half indeed for white neighbors.

Whatever the calculus, once we had stripped the city council of its veto power, neighborhood opposition should no longer have been able to block the scattered-site program. The CHA could now buy real estate like any private purchaser. Angry, fearful neighbors could not prevent a landowner who wished to do so from selling his or her land or building. We also had a court order requiring the CHA to use its best efforts to develop scattered-site housing, and a separate order against HUD to use its best efforts to cooperate with the CHA. The full force of the law was directing two government agencies, whose business it was to develop housing, to do what they supposedly knew how to do, and by 1974 we had removed the legal obstacle that until then had blocked their way. January 14, 1974, the day the Supreme Court declined to review the city council bypass order, should have been the start of real scattered-site progress.

2

It was not. There were two obstacles, the CHA explained to the press, as soon as the Supreme Court order was announced. First, funding for most of the CHA's 1,500-unit scattered-site program remained frozen by Nixon's January 1973 moratorium on new public housing. Second, building the 267 units that had escaped the moratorium—on sites the city council had approved in June 1971—was stymied because construction bids exceeded HUD's cost limits.

Two days later we sent a letter to the CHA and HUD, copying Austin. "Either HUD's prototype costs for the Chicago area are unrealistically low or the CHA's proposed costs are unjustifiably high, or both," we wrote, and Austin should be told what HUD and the CHA were doing about the situation. When our letters went unanswered, we filed a motion asking Austin to schedule a hearing.

Three times, in recent years, when his order to develop scattered sites was proving ineffective, Austin had vigorously entered the fray. In 1970, he had directed the CHA to submit sites to the city council by a specific date. In 1971 he had ordered HUD to hold back Model Cities funding unless CHA sites were approved by the council. And in 1972 he had taken away the council's veto power. Surely, when in 1974 the two housing agencies were still producing excuses instead of housing, he would be vigorous once more. He was not. To our surprise and distress, Austin turned timid. Worse, he dealt the scattered-site program a grievous blow.

Instead of scheduling a hearing Austin ordered us to write briefs. Briefs on whether to hold a hearing! Then he accepted O'Brien's argument that if we wanted more information we should take depositions rather than waste the court's valuable time on a hearing. Forty-five days were allowed for depositions, after which still more briefs were to be filed. What on earth had happened to the little scrapper?

Dutifully we took depositions and uncovered what, in days gone by, would surely have aroused the meanest SOB in the valley. For most of its scattered-site reservation the CHA had submitted "development programs" to HUD—the next step in the process—the very morning of the first deposition. One could imagine the frantic, last-minute paperwork barely completed and the messenger pushed out the door minutes before deposition starting time.

Worse, most of the development programs lacked sites, even though HUD rules required them. HUD's witnesses had no idea when HUD would decide whether it could review siteless programs. The CHA, which had deliberately chosen to proceed without sites, had not bothered to first determine HUD's position. Nor had HUD yet approved the few development programs that did have sites (those approved by the city council three years earlier) for the astounding reason that it was awaiting comments—a courtesy it was not obligated to extend—from none other than that veteran opponent of scattered sites, the City of Chicago.

It was obvious that the bureaucratic processes weren't working. Yet the CHA and HUD were unabashed by the deposition disclosures. O'Brien's brief insisted that CHA was "striving energetically" to move ahead. HUD argued it wasn't taking too long to review development programs that had only just been submitted, and could not responsibly approve programs submitted without complete data (that is, sites). Both the CHA and HUD claimed their victory before Judge Hoffman in the *Nucleus* lawsuit showed how hard they were working.

In September 1974 Austin told us to prepare a draft order—a hopeful sign. Our suggested order proposed something new. Their bureaucratic game-playing had caused us to lose all hope that the CHA and HUD would move effectively. A recent decision of the Seventh Circuit Court of Appeals authorized the appointment of "commissioners" to prepare a desegregation plan when the school board had failed to do so. Arguing that our situation was similar, we asked Austin to appoint a commissioner to recommend next steps for the scattered-site program.

The CHA and HUD reacted like stuck pigs to our "newest stratagem." O'Brien wrote that we wanted a housing "czar" to "take over the most basic functions of both CHA and HUD." HUD said that a commissioner would usurp powers which belonged only to the secretary of HUD.

In November the new, timid Austin issued a proposed order—inviting written comment—under which he would refer the entire case to a magistrate to "pinpoint the responsibility for the fact that my orders in this case have been avoided and frustrated for over five years," and to recommend a plan of action. Magistrates were judicial officers who conducted hearings on issues judges referred to them and then made recommendations; they were not experts in housing. He was denying our motion for a commissioner, Austin wrote, because there was no evidence that the CHA and HUD had "directly contravened" his orders. To no avail we argued that Austin didn't need "direct contravention," and that the bureaucratic red tape that was strangling scattered sites could only be cut by someone who knew and understood government housing programs.

Though he was not moved, in his final order, entered on November 7, 1974, Austin gave us a crumb that turned out to be important. The order included language we had suggested—should he insist on rejecting a commissioner—that the magistrate be authorized to employ persons who possessed "specialized knowledge concerning federally subsidized housing programs."

Selected by lot from among the district court's several magistrates, Olga Jurco was assigned to conduct the inquiry Austin had ordered. Jurco had been appointed in 1971, the first woman to occupy a judicial position in the federal court in Chicago. She had begun her federal court career as secretary to a federal judge when, after graduating from law school in the depression year of 1938, she could not find a job as a lawyer. Later she had become her judge's law clerk and had remained in that position until her appointment as magistrate. Five and a half years after the CHA had been ordered to build scattered-site housing as rapidly as possible, with not one unit of housing yet built or even under construction, the unpromising next stage of Gautreaux was about to begin.

3

We met in a windowless auxiliary courtroom, equipped with a small judicial bench and a witness chair on a raised platform. Two tables squatted in front and below for the lawyers, before four rows of seats for spectators (we had none because Austin's order had said the proceedings were to be confidential). Engulfed in black robes, pencil poised at the ready, peering down from her bench through huge, dark-rimmed glasses, Jurco plunged into her task with apparent relish. I had the sinking feeling that this was a spicier dish than her usual fare and that she intended to savor it fully. She began with long speeches, encumbered with opaque passages. As nearly as I could determine we were in for a thorough canvassing of the near and distant scene. Not a single pebble would be left uninspected.

O'Brien and younger lawyers from his law firm, and Richard Flando, HUD's regional counsel, and his assistant, were only too willing to proffer an endless parade of the CHA and HUD functionaries who, to the faint whirring of the tape recorder (to save court reporter expenses), provided sententious renditions of the intricate details of HUD and CHA rules and procedures. It amounted, I thought, to a fatuous explanation of why, in Chicago at least, it was now impossible to build public housing.

Jurco set a leisurely schedule that suggested her hearings could crawl slowly forward toward an ever-receding horizon, eventually to consume the Gautreaux case not with a bang but a whimper. My efforts to cut through the bolts of bureaucratic fabric with which we were being strangled were summarily rebuffed.

Jurco's second report, in June 1976, confirmed my worst fears. Although she "could not conclude" that the CHA's initial target of 1,500 units "can be reached within the foreseeable future," she attributed this unhappy prospect to a variety of factors, particularly the apparent exhaustion of residentially zoned vacant land in white neighborhoods, that were not the fault of the CHA or HUD. As for Austin's charge to pinpoint responsibility for the lack of progress, the delay was not attributable "significantly" to deliberate actions of the CHA and HUD. Both agencies, she wrote, had been "using 'best efforts' to date to meet the Court's goal." No longer merely mired in a Jurco bog, we were now in danger of being sucked under.

How to persuade Austin to extricate us was a conundrum we pondered endlessly. He had, after all, chosen to consign us to this quagmire. Then, in February 1977, irrevocably ending all hope of appealing to him for help, Austin died.

The judge's addiction to cigarettes had been causing debilitating emphysema. That, we now realized, probably explained why he had handed off his responsibilities to Jurco in the first place. The unaccountably timid Austin, as we had viewed him, was in reality a seriously weakened Austin. He had accepted semiretirement with a reduced case load in November 1975, but even then had to be driven to work because he could no longer climb the stairs at his commuter train station. Finally, recognizing the inevitable, he had resigned. His death from congestive heart failure and emphysema came only days later. Unfortunately for Gautreaux, the little scrapper had lost his scrappiness prematurely.

The case was soon reassigned to John Powers Crowley, whom President Ford had appointed the year before. At thirty-nine, Crowley was one of the youngest persons ever to serve as a federal judge. Short, with a hint of pudginess, he had a rotund face that faintly suggested baby fat. He had been a prosecutor with the U.S. Attorney's Office in Chicago, then a highly successful criminal defense lawyer, and in his brief career had built a reputation as one of the best trial attorneys in Chicago. He was also said to be a thoroughly decent human being, a rumor which his polite, benign manner tended to confirm. Yet with all his positive qualities, as a new judge we feared he was not likely to rescue us from the bog into which his predecessor had chosen to dump us.

We bided our time as the magistrate hearings droned on. Carefully, because she was prickly on the matter of her authority, we nibbled away at Jurco, particularly on the theme that she needed expert assistance from someone who could pierce the bureaucratic veils. Finally, in the face of minimal progress on new housing (although with maximum explanations), in May 1977 we made a formal request that she employ the housing expert Austin's order had authorized. It took nearly another year, over the strident protests of the CHA and HUD, to whom Jurco gave generous time to file written objections. Then in her third report—by now it was April 1978—she finally agreed. "I believe that the expertise of a qualified person is desirable and recommend an expert be appointed."

Two days later we filed a motion before Crowley. After briefs, O'Brien objecting to this "noxious proceeding," in May Crowley signed an order authorizing Jurco to "employ and consult with a person having expert qualifications in urban housing matters." Our suggestion of Richard Babcock, a respected Chicago lawyer and past president of the American Society of Planning Officials, was also accepted. It took several more months to work out an order approving the details, but on September 5, 1978, Crowley signed a follow-up order and our long-sought expert was at last on board.

Babcock set to work with the crisp efficiency of the pin-striped senior attorney he was. With help from younger lawyers in his office he interviewed some thirty people, including Swibel, G. M. Master, the CHA's then executive director, Calvin Hall, the CHA's general counsel (Kula by now having succumbed to cancer), and HUD officials both in Chicago and Washington. Although his focus was principally upon the CHA, not HUD, when he issued his report in March 1979 he had done in six months what we had not been able to get Jurco to do in almost four years. The bureaucratic excuses were exposed as cant.

Crowley's order (which we had drafted) asked five questions. The first—had the CHA taken all practical steps to identify land suitable for the scattered-site program?—Babcock answered with a resounding no. The CHA claimed to be hamstrung by a lack of suitable sites, but its real estate work was being handled by one person in its engineering department, and it did not retain brokers or even consult multiple listing services.

The second question—whether the CHA had taken all practical steps to acquire the suitable land it did identify—produced another strong negative. The same engineering department person was also responsible for land acquisition. It was "disgraceful," Babcock wrote, "that an agency under court order to use its 'best efforts' to increase the supply of dwelling units 'as rapidly as possible' has assigned one employee, part-time, to such a crucial role."

The third, fourth, and fifth questions, all dealing with other CHA procedures, also drew negative answers. In his summary Babcock said the CHA's attitude was that "if it makes efforts slightly above levels that would warrant contempt citations it is complying with the court order." Then, acknowledging that he might be going beyond his assignment, he supplied "additional comments." Their gist was that a receiver—an agent of the court—should be appointed to take over the scattered-site work.

> The present management of CHA is unwilling or unable to stick its neck out . . . What is required is someone with (1) a working knowledge of the real estate market, and (2) a commitment to providing low-rent housing in both General [white] and Limited [black] Areas as rapidly as possible.

Hallelujah! Four years after beginning our tramp through the Jurco bog, someone with independence and credibility had finally uttered the truth. The job should be taken away from the CHA and given to a court receiver. The next step was to persuade Jurco to go along. Given the strength and detail of the seventy-two-page Babcock report, that should have been doable.

At the end of August 1979, Jurco issued her final report. She adopted virtually all of Babcock's conclusions and recommendations, saying he had "expertly diagnosed" the CHA's efforts. She also acknowledged "not much greater tangible progress" than in the years preceding Austin's reference order, and she could not "equate the performance of CHA as that of a forceful and aggressive actor." But—

> I [do not] recommend that a receiver be appointed . . . CHA action . . . is not attributable to abdication of responsibility or to studied disobedience of Judge Austin's directive. CHA now has the meaningful critique of the [Babcock report] and has the recommendations now being made to the Court.

Another disaster! We thought the CHA's conduct amounted precisely to "abdication of responsibility" and "studied disobedience." But, to be fair, maybe this disaster was partly of our own making. It came about because of the end of the reign of our longtime nemesis, Richard J. Daley.

On December 20, 1976, just weeks before Austin himself succumbed, Daley had suffered a massive heart attack in his doctor's office, keeled over, and died. His funeral had been a national occasion, attended by— among countless other dignitaries—president-elect Jimmy Carter. Thousands lined Chicago's streets to view the body. Said a reporter, "To be in Chicago for Richard Daley's funeral is to understand, in a way, what it was like in China when Chairman Mao died."

Daley had been succeeded by Michael Bilandic, his floor leader in the city council. Bilandic's arrogance, particularly questionable given that his power was inherited, antagonized voters. In the winter of 1978 and early 1979 several Chicago blizzards badly snarled public transportation. For days neighborhood streets were impassible and residents were powerfully frustrated. During it all Bilandic kept telling television audiences that everything was under control. Then he insisted on forcing a resolution through the city council praising his administration for its snow removal efforts. That did it. In the February 1979 Democratic primary, Jane Byrne, the diminutive, spunky, fast-talking commissioner of consumer affairs in Daley's administration, narrowly defeated the intensely disliked Bilandic. In April she swamped the lackluster Republican candidate and became Chicago's only woman mayor.

There was considerable irony in the astonishing Byrne victory. Fifteen years earlier, for no persuasive reason that anyone, then or since, could offer, Daley had reached out to a young Sauganash-bred widow and offered her entry to his Democratic machine. "Janie," as Daley would always call her, first had to pay her dues by spending several years in a mundane job in the city's antipoverty agency. Then, in 1968, to everyone's amazement, Daley took her into his cabinet as commissioner of the Department of Consumer Sales, Weights and Measures, as it was then quaintly called. Daley's ascension to the mayor's office in 1955 had come after a bruising battle to oust the incumbent; his Democratic machine had reigned supreme ever since. A quarter of a century later, Daley's machine suffered its most devastating defeat in mayoral politics with the ouster of another incumbent at the hands of handpicked "Janie."

None other than the ubiquitous Charles Swibel turned up as a Byrne advisor. In a matter of days after Byrne's April 1979 election, Swibel called me once again. "Can't we get together, Al, and make some progress? Mayor Byrne really wants to move on public housing." Plodding through Jurco's bog, with no certainty that she could be persuaded to follow Babcock's recommendations, we decided that something was better than nothing. In short order I agreed with Swibel on the elements of a deal, which HUD's local director, Elmer Binford, eagerly endorsed.

Some 800 scattered-site units would be given "special proposal" treatment under Austin's order and split evenly between white and black neighborhoods. Elderly housing would be added to the development programs to help bring down unit costs. To prevent the CHA from dragging its feet on white area projects, neither black area nor elderly units could be started unless construction had begun on matching units in white neighborhoods. We would all work together to persuade HUD to raise its allowable costs, at least for this special proposal. (HUD's cost ceilings were in truth too low, and we thought the prospect of a Chicago "deal" might help get them raised.) Byrne would publicly put city hall behind the program and assure city cooperation.

On May 18, 1979, Crowley signed an agreed order. Two days later, at a Sunday city hall press conference, Byrne and Swibel unveiled the new plan. Byrne had "confidence"—she had "discussed this problem with

President Carter"—that within two weeks HUD would revise its cost ceilings. (Which it did, a dramatic upward revision of 51 percent, announced by Byrne on June 5.) To a reporter asking about white neighborhood acceptance of public housing, Byrne answered, "With the scattered-site approach, I really don't think that's a factor any more in many communities." Her aides emphasized the neighborhood priority for half the family units, making it likely "the racial impact of any of these new units will be relatively slight."

We were pleased—the unusual Sunday press conference, President Carter's involvement, Binford's enthusiasm, HUD's promise of higher cost ceilings. It all seemed to portend a breaking of the logjam. Over five years had passed since the Supreme Court in January 1974 had declined to review the city council veto power decision. It had been a decade since the best efforts order of July 1969. With some bitterness, in light of the litanies in the Babcock report, I told reporters that while I was happy with our agreement, it could and should have been achieved five years earlier.

To Jurco, however, the May order represented a new day of cooperation that militated against appointing a receiver. "All progress," she wrote in her final report in August 1979, "appears now to be coalesced into the May 1979 order" for which the CHA had "evinced enthusiasm." For that, maybe we couldn't blame her too much. If we were willing now to begin anew with the CHA and city hall, wasn't that a poor time to take the CHA off the playing field and send in a court receiver? Why on earth had we been willing to settle for the Byrne deal once we got the strong Babcock report?

Bad judgment? At least in hindsight. We had no assurance we could persuade Jurco to adopt Babcock's receivership recommendation. Jurco had been a pussyfooter throughout the hearings. And she clearly relished her job; we had no idea when she would be willing to end it. It seemed probable that she would give the CHA time, perhaps considerable time, to address Babcock's recommendations before considering a receivership.

If that was what she chose to do, what chance would we have to persuade Crowley to reject her recommendation? Appointing a receiver to take over functions of a government agency was an extraordinary step judges took only rarely and reluctantly. A contrary recommendation from a judicial officer who had steeped herself in the minutia of CHA activity for years would only increase that reluctance. And—though it would be no more than a subliminal factor—Crowley had been a childhood friend of Byrne's. He had in fact been selected by the mayor-elect to administer the oath of office at her April inauguration. In view of all this, the prospect of city hall support, promised and publicly proclaimed, was an enticement we chose not to resist.

Six months after the "new day" had dawned, the skies remained overcast: the CHA had not bought a single additional vacant lot or building in a white neighborhood. It hadn't even secured HUD approval of acquisitions that predated the Byrne order. Although the CHA began hiring some new people to run its scattered-site program, the pace was glacial.

Completely out of patience, in December 1979 we filed a motion asking Crowley to appoint a receiver, and spent the next several months in intense preparation for trial. Among other things we took depositions of the CHA executive director, G. M. Master, and Edward Norton, the new head of the CHA's scattered-site program, who had been hired at the end of the year and had now begun assembling a staff. But the wretched deal with Byrne, and Jurco's report, still plagued us. After a two-day trial in April, Crowley ruled against us.

It was clear, Crowley's opinion acknowledged, that the CHA's performance was "far from impressive." However, Jurco had noted that in addition to its own failings, the CHA's poor performance was partly attributable to factors not within its control (a reference, presumably, to the Nixon moratorium and HUD's cost limits and review procedures). And she had concluded that the CHA had "finally accepted the course of conduct it must follow" and not recommended a receiver.

Crowley also was impressed with the CHA's claim that the big increase in HUD cost limits meant that scattered sites would proceed more rapidly. And he emphasized that since the Byrne order in May, the CHA had "hired new people, set up a new functional office . . . and plans to hire additional staff in the near future." This constituted some progress. With its increased staff and the "benefits" of the Babcock recommendations, the CHA now had "every opportunity" to provide the long overdue relief to which the Gautreaux plaintiffs were entitled.

"With great reservation," therefore, our motion to appoint a receiver was denied "without prejudice" (meaning we were free to try again whenever we thought another attempt was justified). To salve our wounds Crowley gave us some rhetoric:

> CHA is directed to make an immediate and substantial start toward full compliance with the [Byrne] order within six months. Best efforts will no longer suffice; compliance will be measured by results, not intentions. Bureaucratic inefficiency will no longer be tolerated by the Court.

Strong words, but for at least six more months the CHA would remain in charge of the scattered-site mission.

4

The six months turned into seven frightful years that included multiple changes in the CHA leadership, another new judge for the Gautreaux case, and another startling change in the occupant of the mayor's chair in Chicago. Whenever the ground under our feet seemed to be getting firmer, one of these twists or turns would lead us back into the muck.

In the early aftermath of Crowley's "measure by results" order, the CHA performed well enough, chastened no doubt by Crowley's rhetoric, and anxious to avoid the ignominy and loss of control over multimillion-dollar contracts that a receivership would entail. Swibel saw to it that the scattered-site program was taken from the engineering department and placed in a new housing section. Norton was given a measure of independent authority. Vacant lots and buildings for 34 units were acquired in the first six months following Crowley's order, even while the housing section staff was being assembled. In the next six months that figure more than tripled to 115 units. Not earthshaking, but enough to deter us from returning to court.

Then, unexpectedly, in June 1981 Crowley resigned his judgeship. He loved being an advocate, he said. He felt lonely as a judge. "The nature of this position requires, in fact demands, that you stand alone. The old friendships can't be the same." He found that he missed "the active life of practice, as opposed to the more passive life of a judge." An additional rumored reason for the resignation was that Crowley couldn't afford to send his children to college on a judge's salary.

Whatever the motivation, for Gautreaux it meant another judge to bring up to speed. Marvin Aspen, to whom the case was promptly reassigned, had been appointed by President Carter two years earlier, in July 1979. He had been a Cook County judge for eight years, and a City of Chicago lawyer for eight years before that. But not all of the many lawyers hired by the corporation counsel's office had been interviewed for their jobs by the mayor himself. "If anybody asks you who your sponsor is," Daley had told the young Aspen, "you tell them it's me." When Daley was subpoenaed to testify in the Conspiracy Seven trial following the 1968 Democratic Convention, it was Aspen who had represented Daley before Judge Hoffman.

The cartoon on Austin's door had proclaimed him a mean SOB. Quite different sentiments were expressed in a card under the glass top of Aspen's desk. He was reminded to "speak softly" and not to lose his judicial temperament "under any circumstances." Perhaps to balance these sober admonitions another of Aspen's desktop cards read, "What a beautiful day. Now watch some bastard louse it up." Whether Aspen's inclination was to be sober or humorous, it did not fill us with cheer to have an ex–Richard J. Daley lawyer as our next Gautreaux judge.

Our cast of characters changed yet again when in the middle of 1981 Byrne appointed a new CHA executive director to replace the retiring Master. Andrew J. Mooney was a young academic who had been an idealistic "good government" volunteer in Byrne's mayoral campaign. He promptly imposed a temporary freeze on new site acquisitions while he "reevaluated" the scattered-site program. His goal, he assured us, was to "expedite" scattered-site work, not to block it. We decided to take Mooney at his word. First, we believed that new judge Aspen would be inclined to give new administrator Mooney some breathing room. Second, Mooney had a divinity degree. Didn't that mean something? Finally, Mooney had been appointed, after all, by a mayor who was on record as a supporter of scattered sites.

Sure enough, the CHA's quarterly report to the court that fall advised that the Mooney freeze had been ended on September 30. Changes had been made in the scattered-site program, Mooney said, that would speed its pace. And in our meetings with Mooney he assured us that, although the complicated scattered-site work was not free of difficulties, it was moving along pretty well.

Divinity degree notwithstanding, we eventually learned that Mooney's assurances cloaked a very different reality. Mooney had taken over an agency that was broke and very nearly dysfunctional. The CHA's deficit was more than $33 million. Swibel had traditionally "balanced" the CHA's budget with special grants from Washington. Now Ronald Reagan was in the White House and Swibel's calls weren't returned. In addition, CHA management was in such disarray that HUD was threatening a takeover. As a condition of releasing some HUD money Byrne and Swibel had agreed to a management study of the CHA. When the study was released in March 1982, it was so bad that HUD demanded Swibel's removal as the price for not taking over the CHA. The newspapers jumped on the bandwagon—the CHA chairman had long been a favorite whipping boy—and trumpeted calls for Swibel's ouster.

Byrne felt that the HUD study was unfair, but she would soon be in a reelection campaign and could not afford to fight for the unpopular Swibel. Instead, capitulating to HUD's demand, she worked out a face-saving deal. The chairman's post would be made a full-time, paid position. Swibel would announce that if that happened he would have to resign because his private business interests would preclude him from devoting full time to the CHA. So it was, and in the summer of 1982 Byrne appointed Mooney to the new chairman's position, making him the undisputed boss of the CHA. A Byrne aide from city hall, Elmer Beard, became the CHA executive director under Mooney. Swibel's nearly twenty-year rule had ended with an ignominious forced departure, masked by a transparent ploy.

Mooney's tour of duty—it turned out to be a brief two years—was a disaster for the scattered-site program. Although he regularly proffered explanations and assurances of better days to come, and HUD—skeptical as it had every right to be of anything the CHA proposed—was not making things easy, a year after the Mooney freeze had ended few new sites had been acquired. I met several times with Byrne herself, venting frustration. She called Mooney and some of her own staff into the meetings to ask, "Why can't we get Alex what he wants?" To her abrupt, direct questions there were all sorts of complicated answers that boiled down to, "We just can't."

We were forced to admit that we had been "had." Even if Byrne had been honest in entering into our May 1979 arrangement, she was intensely political and—particularly as her reelection campaign drew near —needed to preserve whatever Northwest and Southwest Side white ethnic support she could muster. In the political world, forcing hated scattered sites upon those very neighborhoods was not something she could attempt.

In the spring of 1983 we filed our motion for a receiver with Aspen and began to prepare for yet another hearing. Because Crowley's order had made "results" the measuring rod, we were able to agree with the CHA lawyers on exactly what the results—the scattered-site "production" facts—were. The lead CHA lawyer with whom we worked was no longer the irascible O'Brien but his replacement, Mark Jones. The reason for that change was another—amazing—change in Chicago politics. Twelve days before we filed our motion with Aspen, Chicago inaugurated a new mayor.

Byrne had two competitors in the February 1983 democratic primary: Richard M. Daley, son of the late mayor, and Harold Washington, a black congressman. Though Byrne was far ahead of both in the early polling, as the primary date approached Washington began to show surprising strength. Daley, the namesake of Chicago's now legendary ruler, was denying her a good part of the white ethnic vote. Sensing an opportunity to elect one of their own, blacks were registering to vote in unprecedented numbers. Byrne was caught in a vise.

Throughout the campaign Daley ran third in the polls, while Washington steadily narrowed what had earlier looked like an insurmountable gap. In a great outpouring of black votes on election day, he squeezed ahead of Byrne with 36 percent of the vote to her 34 percent. The April general election was marked by viciously racist campaigning, and the white Republican candidate received heavy support from Chicago's normally democratic-voting electorate. But when the balloting ended Chicago had elected its first black mayor by a count of 668,176 to 619,926. The CHA immediately hired Jones, an old friend of Washington's, to represent it before Aspen.

Jones was courteous, folksy, and wily, a marked change from O'Brien. Our hearing took place on July 13, 1983. It was our first significant appearance before Aspen, and we didn't know what to expect. His dark, curly hair and horn-rimmed glasses gave him, like his predecessor, Crowley, a schoolboy look. Yet in spite of his relative youth and city hall origins,

Aspen had built a judicial reputation as his own man. He listened intently as we put on several witnesses (Mooney, Beard, another CHA employee, and one from HUD), as did Jones. But the case really boiled down to the agreed acquisition and production facts, the CHA's explanation for its poor progress, and—crucially, as it turned out—the CHA's promises.

Mooney and other CHA witnesses essentially attributed the CHA's problems to finances. They had basically run out of cash—at one point they were only days away from a payless payday. Mooney had put scattered-site acquisitions on hold while he remedied the situation he had inherited. Now, however, the CHA was in good financial shape. Answering a question from Jones, Mooney estimated that the CHA would acquire all the remaining sites it needed to complete the Byrne program and a later additional HUD reservation—requiring a total of approximately 300 units in nonblack neighborhoods—in just six to nine more months.

My heart sank when I heard Mooney's estimate. Would Aspen give the CHA yet another chance because of this prediction? My heart dropped further when Aspen himself asked a question at the end of Mooney's testimony.

COURT: Mr. Mooney, let me make sure I understand another point you are making. You indicated that within six to nine months you anticipate you will be able to acquire the remaining 300-odd units, is that correct?

WITNESS: That is our estimate at this moment.

COURT: All right. That is six to nine months from today you are talking about, is that correct?

WITNESS: That is correct.

COURT: Okay.

In my final argument I tried hard to erase the handwriting on the wall. I pointed out that during the past six months, after the alleged financial problem had been solved, we had been assured repeatedly that sites had been selected and would be acquired, yet that had not happened. I also noted the disingenuousness of filing quarterly reports in which Mooney gave similar assurances without ever disclosing what was now, for the first time, acknowledged to be the real explanation. Nor had Jones produced any evidence at all to support Mooney's prediction. Against the sorry record of the CHA's optimistic quarterly reports, there was no basis for once more letting the CHA off the hook.

Then I took aim at what I feared was going on in Aspen's mind. It would be understandable, I said, "if you were to say, well, Mr. Mooney looks like a good guy and Mr. Beard looks like an earnest man, and they say they are going to do good things, and I really ought to give them a chance." But, I continued, my voice rising, after fifteen years, after the record we had made of the CHA's nonperformance (the facts showed they were "getting worse faster"), after the failure to support Mooney's naked prediction with any evidence, after the years of frustration suffered by Austin and Crowley, Gautreaux families should finally be given the receivership to which they were entitled.

During all this impassioned rhetoric Aspen asked me only one question, and it was a disturbing one. To what extent, he wanted to know, did I think CHA conduct "reflects the city administration." Not much, I answered, pointing out that Byrne had once stood at a podium with Swibel and me and said, "We shall have scattered-site housing." I described the city hall meetings in which Byrne had called in subordinates to learn why more progress wasn't being made. With all the earnestness I could muster I said there was no more reason now than during the Byrne administration to believe the CHA could get the job done. There was a lesson to be learned from history, I concluded. Without a court receiver, the CHA bureaucracy would fail this time too.

If we had been in a debate my answer might have scored points. But we were in a courtroom, and Aspen had been a city lawyer, Richard J. Daley's personal lawyer no less. He would be sensitive to the political awkwardness of a city administration appearing to be so inept that one of its responsibilities was being taken from it and turned over to a receiver. That would be an especially weighty factor given that Aspen, a white judge from the Daley era, would be taking such an extraordinary step just weeks after Chicago had elected its first black mayor.

Jones concluded his argument on exactly that note. To appoint a receiver would bring "shame" to the new Washington administration. The predictable headline, "Receiver Appointed to Run CHA," would import lack of confidence and respect in the city and the law. Jones's last ringing sentence was, "We intend to comply and to finish this job within six months."

By now it was after noon. Aspen surprised everyone by announcing, "If you all want to come back at 2:30, I will have a ruling at that time." Lunch was tense, with more talk than food. At the appointed 2:30 hour the courtroom was full (the news had traveled quickly that a Gautreaux ruling was in the offing). Aspen entered, took his seat behind the bench, and began speaking immediately, referring only occasionally to notes.

Prior administrations, he said, may have adopted the philosophy of doing as little as possible to comply with unpopular Gautreaux orders, but he suspected that the current CHA and city administrations did not share that philosophy. "I suspect that the current administrations are committed to implementing the scattered housing site orders." Adjudication by "suspicion," I thought, somewhat bitterly. In fact, the Washington administration's support for the scattered-site program could barely be described as tepid. Concerned about antagonizing any possible white support, Washington's issues paper on housing had mentioned scattered sites only once, and then in a deliberately ambiguous way:

> Monitoring CHA's implementation of federal court orders to spend remaining funds on scattered-site housing in ways that support overall neighborhood development.

Aspen did throw us a bone. The CHA had not done its job. "The excuses that I heard this morning just don't hold water." But, "we do have a new administration in the city, one which, in spite of what Mr. Polikoff has said, I believe will have in the real world an impact on how CHA is going to conduct its business. And I do not wish to foreclose the CHA from the opportunity to do what it has to do by itself." Since, however, "the merits of Mr. Polikoff's motion are well taken," Aspen would grant our motion and appoint a receiver, but his order would not go into effect until February 15, 1984, "which is approximately seven months from now, the six months that Mr. Jones requested, plus an extra month." If within six months the CHA could accomplish "what they have to accomplish," the order would be vacated before it became operative.

So once more, three years after Crowley's order, thanks evidently to Harold Washington's narrow election, the CHA—like the cat with multiple lives—had yet another chance to escape receivership.

5

Twelve days after Aspen's ruling still another change in our cast of characters occurred. Mooney had been in a power struggle with one of his CHA commissioners. Renault Robinson was the head of an African American policemen's organization whose lawsuit had forced the Chicago Police Department to hire more African Americans. As a result of his litigation Robinson had been made to suffer gross indignities—the police department trumped up misconduct charges and reassigned him to patrolling behind the police headquarters building. Robinson, handsome, youthful, had become something of a folk hero. As a gesture to blacks, Byrne had appointed him to the CHA board.

Robinson was close to Washington and had helped him get out the black vote. With Swibel gone and Washington in power, Robinson believed it was his destiny to head the CHA. Mooney, no favorite of Washington's, stood in his way, and Robinson soon succeeded in lining up enough votes on the seven-person CHA board to make Mooney's life miserable. Whereupon Mooney obligingly resigned. That paved the way for Washington to appoint Robinson as the CHA chairman and boss.

As head of the CHA Robinson fell midway between a disaster and a catastrophe. He fired Elmer Beard on the ground that he, as full-time chairman, didn't need an executive director. He brought elevator service to a standstill by firing elevator contractors for bilking the agency (which they were) without having substitute contractors in place. He purchased a fancy car for himself without requisite board authorization. In a short time the hero of the Afro-American Patrolmen's League became a managerial absurdity and laughingstock of the media. The CHA tumbled back toward dysfunctionality.

Meanwhile the clock was ticking on Aspen's receivership order. With Beard gone, little was being accomplished on scattered sites. Late in the fall Washington sent Erwin France, an able administrator from city hall, to take over day-to-day administration from Robinson. To save face Robinson would stay on as chairman at a reduced salary, a sore point with the press. But as interim executive director, France would have effective authority.

France set to work to repair the Robinson damage—and to avoid a scattered-site receivership. We tried through intermediaries to persuade Washington to let the receivership happen, but to no avail. The combination of further loss of face after the Robinson debacle and control over all those contracts left Washington unpersuaded by the good sense of our arguments.

France's immediate task was to acquire sites for approximately 300 scattered-site units in nonblack neighborhoods before January 13, 1984. He hired the world-renowned architectural firm of Skidmore, Owings & Merrill to examine buildings for acquisition, and the top-drawer law firm of Kirkland & Ellis to secure options to purchase. In the last weeks of 1983 the two firms labored mightily and performed what in scattered-site historical terms was a miracle. By January 13, 1984, the six-month anniversary of Aspen's ruling, the CHA had obtained options to acquire sites and buildings for nearly a thousand scattered-site units, at least half in predominantly white areas, more than enough to satisfy Aspen's order. France issued a triumphant press release, "CHA Meets Federal Court Order on Scattered Site Program."

On January 13, by arrangement with Mark Jones, we appeared in court. Though France had secured mostly options to purchase, we couldn't imagine arguing successfully to Aspen the technical difference between "option" and "acquire." I conceded that under the terms of Aspen's order the receivership appointment should be vacated, complimented France on his performance, and expressed hope for real scattered-site progress.

France, who had not wanted more than an interim appointment, was soon replaced by Zirl Smith, executive director of the Delaware Housing Authority. Washington announced that at his direction and after a nationwide search the CHA was hiring its very first qualified, professional executive director. Smith seemed competent and anxious to perform well, including on scattered sites. The scattered-site train, I let myself hope, might now, at last, begin to run smoothly.

Of course, I should have known better. After all the clouds, why should the sun come out now? Robinson soon began to plague Smith just as he had Mooney. The same person who didn't need an executive director created the job of "executive administrative assistant" for his brother-in-law. He also assembled a chairman's staff of five employees, even though the chairman's only formal responsibility was to preside at monthly board meetings. Eventually Robinson began pushing through resolutions giving the board increased authority over Smith and the chairman a greater role. With Washington permitting the spectacle to continue, the CHA was beset with internal dissension.

HUD was frustrating Smith too. Lower-echelon officials, whose anti-CHA attitudes had been acquired over many years, smothered him with paperwork requirements and pushed him into regulatory cul-de-sacs. They were making Smith take every step "by the book" (the "book" being thousands of pages of HUD requirements) rather than trying to help him along.

In March 1985, a year after Smith had taken over, we filed a motion for a conference with Aspen, hoping that a little "push" from the judge would help. For a while it did. Smith reported a somewhat more receptive HUD and began to tackle what had become a festering problem— unrehabilitated buildings. Back in the Jurco days we had forced a reluctant CHA into acquiring buildings needing rehabilitation rather than limiting its purchases to vacant lots for new construction. The CHA had begun buying buildings in the late 1970s and early 1980s. Then its to-be-rehabilitated inventory swelled enormously with the France-engineered acquisitions. But the CHA was having trouble getting the rehabilitation work done. Now scores of CHA-acquired buildings stood vacant, not just eyesores but gang hangouts as well.

Smith's efforts to deal with this problem led to one disappointment after another. HUD rejected high bids from rehabilitation contractors. Shoddy workmanship and contractor disputes were endemic. I told Smith the reasons didn't matter. Crowley's criterion was results. Without results we were going back to court.

Faced with that prospect, Smith decided to do the work with CHA-hired work crews; "force account" it was called in HUD's lexicon. Though the new method started slowly and only with HUD's reluctant and limited approval, it soon began to pick up steam and gave promise of working reasonably well. By the fall of 1986, Smith had sixteen force-account work crews—more than 250 craftsmen under 5 supervisors—and had completed rehabilitation of about 100 units. Another 100 were in the pipeline. At that rate the CHA's entire inventory of acquired buildings awaiting rehabilitation would be taken care of in another six months or so.

As always with scattered sites, things were not as they seemed. The surface signs of progress concealed rot underneath. Smith was working with scattered-site budgets HUD had approved years before. Current costs required increased HUD funding, which the anti-CHA people at HUD wouldn't approve. Feeling intense pressure from my threat to return to Aspen, Smith began to use CHA operating funds to keep the scattered-site work going. Eventually, he thought, HUD would have to reimburse.

Then the Robinson-Smith war came to climax. Fed up with the managerial snafus at the CHA, HUD had set a 1986 year-end deadline for use of a $7 million commitment for lobby improvements at Robert Taylor Homes. Smith rejected a bid which suspiciously came in at $6,999,999, whereupon Robinson talked the CHA board into letting him take over the lobby project. He promptly ordered Smith's plans redone. Smith warned that the new design would be a $10 million job, but Robinson insisted he knew better. When the lowest bid came in over $9 million, the year-end deadline was missed, and HUD withdrew its $7 million commitment.

The lost funding soon became an issue in the mayoral campaign then under way when one of Washington's opponents in the democratic primary called for Robinson's removal. Robinson issued a press release falsely blaming Smith. At the end of his rope with Robinson, Smith arranged a meeting with the mayor and told Washington, "It's me or him." Explaining that Robinson had helped get him elected, Washington replied that he guessed it would have to be Smith. Whereupon, although he had been formally exonerated by the CHA board, which knew the true story, Smith resigned.

A few days later a HUD letter, placing the responsibility for the lost funding on Robinson, was leaked to the press. It led to damaging political fire, and on January 16, 1987, Robinson announced that to avoid embarrassing the mayor's reelection bid he was submitting his resignation. Washington immediately appointed his deputy chief of staff, Brenda Gaines, as interim executive director, and his pastor, Reverend B. Herbert Martin, as chairman of the CHA.

During his successful reelection campaign the mayor's responsibility for CHA operations was a major issue. Washington trumpeted "immeasurable improvements," and received near-unanimous support from public housing residents. But Gaines and her staff were discovering that the CHA was in serious financial trouble, in large part because of the scattered-site program. The relationship with HUD was abysmal. Maybe, they told Washington, a scattered-site receivership wouldn't be such a bad idea after all. "Not on my watch," the electioneering mayor responded. "I need to show we can do this thing."

A week after Washington's reelection, the *Tribune* reported a striking development. Major suppliers and contractors had stopped deliveries to the CHA because millions of dollars of bills and invoices were unpaid. Soon Gaines publicly acknowledged that the CHA owed some $17 million it couldn't pay. A week later she presented a blockbuster report to an emergency meeting of the CHA board. Instead of describing "immeasurable improvements," the Gaines report said, "CHA's chronic operating budget deficits, coupled with lack of reimbursement of capital expenditures, has resulted in a severe cash-flow crisis [that] threatens the financial future of the authority." The headlines read, "CHA Admits Financial Crisis." Reverend Martin conceded, "We've sinned." The biggest sin of all was scattered sites.

"Lack of reimbursement of capital expenditures" was a fancy way of saying that HUD had not been paying the CHA for Smith's force-account work, some $30 million in total. The money had been coming from CHA operating funds, which were now nearly depleted. Reserves of over $50 million at the beginning of 1986 had dwindled to $9 million and were still dropping.

Why hadn't HUD reimbursed the CHA for its force-account work? The CHA and mayoral press offices worked overtime blaming—depending on which day's press release was quoted—Smith and HUD. Smith blamed HUD and Robinson. HUD blamed the CHA. "I'm not interested in any finger-pointing," intoned Washington. "I'm interested in trying to come up with workable solutions for the problem that has been going on at CHA for many, many years before I became mayor." Nobody could explain how, to the extent of tens of millions, two government agencies, supposedly working together, could allow such a hemorrhaging of the CHA's reserves to continue for over a year.

On May 4 an emergency CHA board meeting authorized CHA lawyers to ask Aspen to allow a halt in scattered-site work until reimbursement from HUD was received. Aspen was on vacation and so the following morning CHA's new lawyers—the CHA had now hired my old Schiff Hardin & Waite law firm—appeared before James B. Moran, the judge assigned to hear emergencies. The courtroom was packed. Moran, white-bearded, courteous, and precise, had read the CHA's plea to stop the hemorrhaging. Nearly 300 force-account workmen were sitting around, drinking coffee and drawing pay, with no work to do because unpaid suppliers weren't delivering materials to the CHA. It was an untenable situation, and it had to stop. The argument was made by Aaron Kramer, who had been a young associate in my Schiff days. I was beginning to feel caught in a time warp.

Moran turned to me. Acknowledging that he was reluctant to act in Aspen's absence, he wanted to know what I thought about those workmen without work, drawing pay from a public agency that was fast running out of funds. The best I could do was to say we needed more facts—for example, about the prospects for quick HUD reimbursement. We should take a few days to get them before halting a court-ordered program, laboriously put together over many years. Once the men were let go they would find other jobs. Trying to put the program back together later would be like trying to unscramble an egg.

It wasn't good enough. Especially after HUD's lawyer said there was no prospect that HUD could act promptly, for it too needed time to gather facts. Admonishing us to appear before Aspen as soon as he returned, Moran gave the CHA the permission it wanted to "furlough" its scattered-site craftsmen, stop its rehabilitation work, and board up the unfinished buildings. Wouldn't they be fine symbols of the Gautreaux scattered-site saga!

Immediately we prepared yet another motion for a receivership and presented it to Aspen the following week. He looked tanned and rested, but he was angry. Several times during our hearing it seemed to me that his desktop injunction not to lose his judicial temperament was at risk. Perhaps he felt that someone was lousing up his beautiful postvacation day.

Our short motion relied on baseball's three strikes rule. The first strike against the CHA was the 1980 Crowley hearing, the second the 1983 Aspen hearing. The third strike was the CHA's emergency motion asking to shut down the scattered-site program. What better example could be imagined of the "bureaucratic inefficiency" Crowley had said would no longer be tolerated?

Kramer's opposition to our motion was supported by two inches of paper. Using our baseball analogy he argued that a new team was being fielded—a reference to Brenda Gaines coming straight from Harold Washington's inner circle. It should be given a chance to show what it could do, especially since the CHA's financial troubles stemmed from an "excess of zeal" in trying to get scattered-site units built. And there were all those cases about how extraordinary the receivership remedy was, and why judges should be extremely reluctant to employ it.

Kramer's argument was not troublesome. Crowley had been taken in by the same argument during Byrne's administration, and Aspen himself had suffered a like fate with Washington. Aspen would have little patience with the "new team" point, and he quickly made this evident with his frequent, unsmiling interruptions. When Kramer argued that a receiver could not in any event be appointed until there had been a trial, Aspen shot back, "Do you want to start at two o'clock this afternoon?" No, said Kramer, he wanted an opportunity first to take depositions, mostly on why HUD was not reimbursing the CHA. Aspen interrupted. "The question really is how many years do we wait. We've repaired the clunker over the years. Maybe it's time to get a new model."

HUD's position was more troublesome. The CHA was in dire straits. HUD was recommending that the CHA hire a private management firm, approved by HUD, to run the entire agency. If the CHA accepted that recommendation—HUD was otherwise threatening a forced takeover—then the private management firm could run the scattered-site program too. That would be better than creating a two-headed agency.

I tried to persuade Aspen that only a direct line of authority to the court, not some private manager responsible to the HUD and CHA bureaucracies, could save the scattered-site program. We had had new, supposedly competent managers in the past, and the results spoke for themselves. When the lawyers finished, Aspen took over with a long, angry speech about the CHA's incompetence over the years. Then he spoke those long-sought words, "I am going to appoint a receiver." He would ask me to draft a "comprehensive order." To avoid any appearance of "judicial patronage," he would appoint a committee headed by Edward Marciniak of Loyola University to recommend names to him. But, he added, he would delay his appointment for sixty days to allow HUD and the CHA to talk about HUD's proposal for new management to take over the running of the CHA. "If that private person is the type of person who I feel can handle the scattered-site program, I certainly will vacate my receivership order." He set July 13 as the date to make his decision.

Another private manager, reporting to the same old bureaucracies! Couldn't Aspen see that that was a recipe for more failure? As we set about drafting yet another order, and the Marciniak committee interviewed potential receivers, an air of the academic hung over the process. It would be more time wasted if HUD and Mayor Washington (who was now publicly calling the CHA's signals) agreed on some private management firm Aspen liked. Once again I saw the receivership, now tantalizingly close, slipping away.

What followed was a gargantuan public relations battle over, of all things, local control of public housing. Washington had been at pains to distance himself from the CHA while his minions mismanaged it. Now he embraced "his" agency and defended the sacred prerogatives of local control as if he were raising a flag on Iwo Jima. Ironically, the Reagan administration, wielding a sharp knife to trim a supposedly bloated central government, committed to passing power down to local officials, was now threatening a federal government takeover of a local government agency.

Rallying CHA tenants to his side, Washington proclaimed, "I'm not going to sit here and let HUD or mud or anybody take over the CHA." Gaines issued a rebuttal of an earlier HUD report critical of CHA management, calling HUD unresponsive, miserly, myopic, and the "primary cause" of CHA's problems. In a special meeting the CHA board authorized Schiff to fight any HUD takeover attempt. HUD's chief negotiator said, "We will have control," and promised that HUD would not give more money to an agency with the CHA's record of mismanagement. A laboriously arranged meeting between Washington and HUD Secretary Samuel Pierce terminated abruptly after fifteen minutes when neither side would budge.

The impasse was reported to Aspen, but both sides declined to say the talks were at a dead end. Aspen delayed again. It's best to wait a few more days, he said, now specifying August 3 as the day upon which he would appoint a receiver unless there were an agreement between HUD and the CHA that he found acceptable. Again, after repeating his mantra about not wanting to be a public housing czar, he pronounced his dread view: "I don't think it's important that the private entity which will manage the CHA scattered-site housing program have the designation of Court receiver."

August 3 brought a big surprise. Early that morning the CHA board held another special meeting, reversed its position, and supported a scattered-site receiver! Washington's public explanation was, "If scattered sites are ever to be built, this is probably the best way to do it." In fact, however, the mayor was less concerned about scattered sites than about his battle with HUD. He reasoned that if a part of the CHA were placed under the control of a court-appointed receiver, HUD would be less likely to take over the entire agency.

Faced now with both a plaintiff and defendant asking for a receiver, Aspen rejected HUD's request for still further delay while it decided whether or not to take over. "Reluctantly," he took the fateful step:

> I have no desire to be the public housing czar of the City of Chicago. I am a firm believer in local government . . . but because of the lack of cooperation and history here, I have no choice.

And he named the receiver he had chosen—Daniel E. Levin and his firm, the Habitat Company (no relation to Habitat for Humanity with which Jimmy Carter is associated).

Habitat was one of the Marciniak committee recommendations, three of whom Aspen had interviewed before making his selection. It had been in the real estate development and management business for thirty years, had strong organizational and financial capacity, and among the thousands of residential units it had developed were some low-rent, government-assisted projects. Levin, who headed the company, was a soft-spoken but hardheaded businessman. He had a law degree though he had not practiced law. In fact, he and I had been in the same law school class but had had no contact since graduation. Now Levin's curly hair had turned gray, and a paunch was developing, though his face had retained its boyish look. He was perhaps best known for having built an enormously successful health and fitness club along a run-down section of the Chicago River—the East Bank Club, it was called—that sparked a redevelopment of the entire area. Perhaps looking for new challenges, Levin was intrigued by the scattered-site prospect. He later recalled that many of those mentioned as possible receivers had no interest in the job—"they didn't believe in it, thought it was too complicated, felt they wouldn't make enough money, and would be criticized for their pains." But, he believed, "there's got to be a way of doing this thing."

At a press conference following the court session Washington observed, "Clearly, Judge Aspen has breached HUD," a facetious reference to HUD's need to declare the CHA in "breach" of its HUD contract as the first step in a takeover. Pierce was "disappointed" that Aspen had declined further delay, but promised full cooperation.

The threatened HUD takeover did not happen. In mid-September the CHA hired a new "managing director," Jerome W. Van Gorkom, who had a good reputation as a business executive and had served as an undersecretary of state in the Reagan administration in 1982 and 1983. Van Gorkom made the difference, and only days after he was hired the CHA and HUD agreed on a compromise that preserved "local control" but gave HUD a strong "liaison office" within the CHA and an arbitration panel to resolve disputes should the liaison and Van Gorkom disagree.

Meanwhile it took several months to work out all the operational issues. But by December the receivership finally became effective and Habitat assumed all of the CHA's powers to develop scattered sites. Seven years after Crowley had first denied our receivership motion, we had finally achieved that objective. "Achieved," however, is too strong. The fact was that we had been the beneficiaries of a financial crisis at the CHA and of Washington's desire to forestall a HUD takeover. It was an inelegant way to prevail. Regardless, now at last we would see what an independent receiver, responsible directly to the court, could accomplish with scattered sites.

6

Philip Hickman was the man Levin recruited to head Habitat's scattered-site work, a former developer, teacher of college-level economics, and director of the Oak Park Housing Authority. Hickman said he took the scattered-site job because he liked challenges. He was also impressed, he said, with Levin's commitment, even though Levin acknowledged he couldn't be sure "where he was going" with the scattered-site program, and could only offer a one-year job.

Hickman was both personable and thin, each of which characteristics belied his bulldog tenacity. He was also a team player. Though he assembled and headed a sizable staff, which at its peak numbered nearly thirty, all major scattered-site program decisions were made jointly with Levin.

Hickman's first task, after hiring staff, was to sort through the grab bag of some seventy-four buildings Habitat had inherited from the CHA, purchased for rehabilitation but allowed to stand vacant, in some cases for years. Eventually Hickman rehabilitated about half, sold others that were unsuitable, and demolished the rest. There's not much left, he said dryly, when you allow a building in Chicago to stand abandoned even for a week.

More laborious was negotiating the development process with HUD. The long history of CHA mismanagement, and the open warfare with HUD during the Robinson and Gaines regimes, had implanted a profound skepticism for any CHA proposal among HUD staff both in Chicago and Washington. That attitude was transferred to Habitat and Hickman, who also represented an unwelcome departure from HUD's usual way of doing business. Hickman did manage to get the budget increases HUD had denied Smith. But when he sought to shift acquired land among development programs—to "package" programs in similar sizes for competitive bidding—HUD made Hickman's life miserable with bureaucratic regulation.

Soon two auditors from HUD's Office of Inspector General descended upon Hickman's offices and spent ten weeks examining every detail of Habitat's scattered-site work. Finally, in the middle of the last week, the auditors called Hickman into their office. Red-faced, they confessed that after nine weeks of looking they "hadn't found a damn thing." What were they looking for? Evidence, one of them said glumly. With all the property transfers among development programs, HUD suspected Hickman of manipulating the books to "steal" land. Hickman never got a copy of the inspector general's report, but HUD's attitude toward Habitat did become less hostile.

The improved relations did not affect HUD's application of its "Modest Design and Cost Containment" rules, which had begun to plague Hickman's life in a different way. Not wanting scattered-site buildings to look alike and be identifiable as public housing, Hickman selected nine architectural firms to do his designs. HUD griped about the number—two would suffice, they thought—and promptly began to reject the architects' designs. Roofs should be flat, not pitched. Bay windows (to give a building character) were unacceptable because straight-line foundations would cost less. Fences should be chain link, not wrought iron. Better still would be no fences at all.

The break point came over brick, considered too expensive. Hickman was told to use painted plywood instead. The usually unflappable Hickman exploded. "Plywood? When the other buildings on the block are brick? When the upkeep costs over time will far exceed the initial cost of the brick?" HUD's response was, "That's what we have 'modernization' money for."

After months of arguing with HUD's Chicago staff, Hickman and Levin flew to Washington to present their case to higher-ups. After more months of discussions and letter writing, HUD finally agreed to "relax" its rules for Chicago (without changing them elsewhere). Hickman got his pitched roofs, his wrought-iron fences, his brick exteriors, and even his bay windows (on the second floor, however, so foundations could remain straight) wherever he could show that "contextual" architecture—fitting scattered-site buildings unobtrusively into the surroundings—required it.

By now, however, buying land for scattered sites had become nearly impossible because practically no developable land remained in predominantly white neighborhoods that could be purchased within HUD cost limits. Hickman had his staff survey every census tract classified "general" (below 30 percent black) under Austin's order and mapped the results on the walls of his "war room." The maps showed that Habitat was about to run out of vacant land. And purchasing buildings for rehabilitation was no longer an alternative. With rare exceptions, the buildings Hickman could now afford to buy had been built in the days of asbestos and lead-based paint. Current HUD rules required these materials to be removed during rehabilitation, and that drove costs above HUD ceilings.

The 1990 census figures became available in April 1991. With the new data some twenty-two census tracts, previously classified as "limited" under Austin's order, dropped below the 30 percent black figure. The city wasn't getting white, of course; rather, the twenty-two tracts had acquired large numbers of Latino residents. Gautreaux had always been a black-white case. In 1969, when Austin's remedial order was entered, the Latino population had been negligible. Any census tract with less than 30 percent black population—regardless of the racial composition of the remaining 70 percent—was classified "general." Since land costs were not too high in the twenty-two tracts, it appeared that Habitat and the scattered-site program could continue after all.

With a sigh of relief Hickman assigned some of his staff to buy up as many vacant lots as they could find in the twenty-two tracts, subject only to Austin's rules against overconcentration. (No more than about thirty-two units per site or 15 percent of housing units in a tract, but in practice Hickman had long since determined to stay well below both limitations. His average units per site were running below three, and per census tract below 9 percent.) But Hickman soon ran into two other problems.

First, although Latino neighborhoods were "in bounds" under Austin's order, HUD officials in Chicago began using HUD rules against concentrating public housing in "minority" neighborhoods to reject Hickman's purchases. Levin and Hickman took another trip to Washington, and then prepared and sent a detailed "book" demonstrating that land for scattered sites was unavailable outside Latino neighborhoods. The data showed that enforcing HUD's minority neighborhoods rule would mean ending the scattered-site program. I added a hint that unless HUD relented, we and Habitat would present the issue to Aspen. Finally, at the end of 1992, HUD agreed to waive its regulations in Chicago on the ground of "overriding need."

The second problem was community opposition, backed by a political powerhouse of the Humboldt Park neighborhood, Congressman Luis Gutierrez. As a Chicago alderman, Gutierrez had been one of the few aldermanic supporters of scattered sites. He had even helped Habitat buy city-owned lots in his ward on the ground that low-income housing was badly needed and half the units would be for his own constituents. In an accident of timing, however, Hickman's most recent purchases became known to the community during a congressional primary campaign. Gutierrez was promptly attacked for his cooperative stance and accused of being in league with Habitat. The congressman loudly proclaimed his "innocence"—and his opposition to Habitat's current purchases.

After months of noisy community meetings and behind the scenes negotiations, a compromise was reached. There would be fewer units in some locations, fewer units overall, and a revision of the community preference so the first priority would go to residents of the local census tract rather than of the larger community area. Hickman could of course have purchased what he originally proposed regardless of the opposition, but he believed it wiser to proceed with community support (the "lost" units would be replaced in Latino areas outside the Gutierrez district). I had no objection to the community preference revision, which made this feature of the scattered-site program even more local.

Yet the "concentration" of scattered sites in Latino neighborhoods remained a persisting criticism of Habitat's performance. Although Hickman was eventually able to place at least a few scattered sites in most of the nonblack communities of the city, more than half the units Habitat finally developed were in Latino areas, mostly working class or relatively poor. Compared with the objectors' vision of the way Gautreaux was supposed to work—"every public housing unit is perfectly constructed and located by itself in a solidly middle-class block," as one reporter put it—Habitat was seen as violating at least the spirit of Gautreaux.

Hickman responded that the demographics and economics of Chicago in the 1990s made achievement of the "spirit of Gautreaux" impossible. He also disagreed that the scattered-site units harmed Latino areas. Scattered-site buildings were frequently the best on a block. In Humboldt Park, Habitat proposed to add 105 housing units to a community of more than 20,000 units. And half of those 105 would be occupied by current residents of the community, now of the immediate census tract. He also liked to refer to a photograph on his wall of two adjacent, similar-looking six-flat buildings in Uptown. The one on the right was a fully occupied scattered-site building. The one on the left, undergoing rehabilitation, had a big sign in front advertising luxury condominiums.

Yet the criticism did not abate. One night during the Humboldt Park controversy Hickman was having dinner in a suburban restaurant. He thought his waiter looked vaguely familiar, and struck up a conversation. It turned out that the waiter lived in Humboldt Park and had been a vociferous scattered-site opponent at a recent community meeting. He told

Hickman he was working more than sixty hours a week at multiple jobs. He believed passionately that even a few scattered sites threatened the value of his Humboldt Park home, the one asset upon which his family's well-being depended.

Hickman thought it was as much a class as a race issue. In a gentrifying neighborhood of black homeowners on the South Side, the Kenwood-Oakland area, resident opposition to proposed scattered sites was as vitriolic and uncivil as anything Hickman had encountered in white ethnic neighborhoods. It reminded him, he said, of an old saying about blacks and whites, linked together arm in arm against the poor.

By the mid-1990s Hickman was running out of land in his twenty-two census tracts. Desperately he searched for alternatives. Had he overlooked something in the predominantly white areas of the Northwest and Southwest Sides, or along the north lakefront? "I had interns drive by every single vacant lot in every white census tract," he said. "Then we did a zoning overlay. Then we had half a dozen residentially zoned lots appraised." The prices for single family lots ranged from $60,000 to $100,000. That compared with Hickman's average per unit land cost of $10,000. He bought a property zoned commercial, after persuading the local alderman to have it rezoned residential. Buried fuel oil tanks sent his costs sky-high, and HUD admonished him to stick to residentially zoned properties. He found a few buildings in several areas within his cost range constructed after the asbestos, lead-paint era—Hiawatha Park was one of them—but only a few.

Mercifully, perhaps, the remaining Latino area properties and the few commercial properties and latter-day buildings Hickman was able to acquire used up the remaining scattered-site money. For by now Congress had determined that "distressed" public housing high-rises should be closed and demolished, and all funding for new public housing was earmarked as "replacement" for the demolished units.

(Unlike scattered sites, which added to the existing supply, replacement units were just that and did not increase the total number of public housing units. The replacement program, which began in 1995, overlapping the winding down of the scattered-site program, formed a whole new chapter of the receivership story and Gautreaux. It is discussed in chapter 6.)

When the very last scattered-site unit was completed and turned over to the CHA in 2000, Hickman and Habitat had developed 1,813 units at a cost of some $187 million. Under the demographic, economic, bureaucratic, and political circumstances of the previous twelve years in Chicago, that number was a minor miracle. Miracle or not, I could not view the number except through nightmarish visions. Visions of a closed-minded Austin denying us metropolitan relief. Of a weakened Austin exiling us to the Jurco quagmire. Of Crowley and Aspen ruling not on the evidence but on what they hoped Byrne and Washington would do, of Robinson destroying any capacity for performance the CHA might have had, of a meat-grinder HUD making sausage of CHA and Habitat proposals. And through fantasies. Fantasies of what might have been had we reached the Supreme Court before Milliken v. Bradley. And of what Habitat and Hickman would have accomplished had they been able to begin a dozen years earlier when costs were more reasonable and land more plentiful.

7

I first met Sue Brady at a 1980 neighborhood meeting in Uptown. She was tall, smiled easily, and seemed relaxed and comfortable with herself. She spoke quietly, with a gentle assurance that only hinted at an underlying firmness.

She had grown up on the North Side of Chicago, a self-described "city girl." When Brady, her husband Tony, and their five children moved to suburban Evanston in 1972, the essential Sue Brady did not change. She joined the human relations commission, worked for the PTA and the League of Women Voters, volunteered in the congressional campaigns of Abner Mikva. Eventually she joined Mikva's Evanston staff, but her job ended in 1979 when President Carter appointed Mikva to the U.S. Court of Appeals in Washington, D.C.

That's when Brady got involved in housing. She was hired to direct an affiliate of the Jane Addams Hull House Association called the Housing Resource Center (HRC). The HRC's mission was to provide technical assistance to landlords of low-rent buildings in Chicago's Uptown neighborhood. The idea was to improve the lot of Uptown's poor by improving their housing. But Brady soon realized Uptown was gentrifying. There were fewer and fewer responsible landlords of low-rent buildings with whom the HRC could work.

Because she was winding down the HRC's landlord assistance program, Brady was looking for other ways to accomplish the HRC's mission. After only a brief conversation, we came up with an answer: the HRC should take over the management of the CHA's scattered sites in Uptown. I didn't trust the CHA to manage its scattered sites any more than I did to build them. The HRC and Brady seemed to offer a hopeful alternative. For her part, Brady felt that she needed control of their housing if she was to help improve tenants' lives.

Brady and I began to talk to G. M. Master, then the CHA's executive director, about contracting with the HRC to take over management of the CHA's Uptown scattered sites. We talked, and talked, and talked some more—for weeks, and months, and then into a second year. Master wouldn't say he opposed our idea, on an experimental basis, as he always insisted. He just wasn't exactly in favor of it either. Private management would be new for the CHA. Fearing for their jobs, the management staff was strongly opposed. What we had going for us was the good sense of our proposal. Used to centralized management of large projects, the CHA wasn't having an easy time managing the scattered sites it was reluctantly developing. Locally based private management, especially with the image of Jane Addams included in the mix, might help improve the CHA's reputation in the neighborhoods.

Our talks with Master droned on until his retirement, then droned on more with his successor, Mooney. Finally, just before Mooney's resignation in July 1983, the deed was done. For the first time since it had been established forty-five years earlier, the CHA would employ private firms to manage some of its public housing. Beginning August 1, the management of 132 North Side scattered-site apartments would be taken over by the HRC (in 29 buildings spread over 7 community areas), and 59 South Side apartments would be managed by a for-profit company, the Albert H. Johnson Realty Company, both selected after competitive bidding.

It was a great "victory" when Brady at last signed her management contract. Yet she had at that point never seen the insides of "her" 132 apartments, although she had insisted on a contract provision requiring the CHA to make "all necessary repairs and replacements" or to pay the

HRC for the work. For six days between June 30 and July 21, 1983, CHA personnel, accompanied by Brady and her new staff (a property manager, two janitors, and a part-time aide), inspected all 132 units. Brady later said:

> There were windows cracked and boarded up and missing, and it had been at least four months since they had been broken. We had refrigerators that weren't working and no one had ever replaced or repaired them. No one had screens. The screens fell out in 1975 and were never replaced. The CHA thought that once residents moved into scattered-site housing, they would become like homeowners. They didn't make any provision for janitorial services.

How to work with the CHA's bureaucracy to change all this? At the top, in the early days, was Renault Robinson battling Zirl Smith. Below the top were the staff who opposed the whole idea. Not to mention the CHA's pervasive incompetence. Because of poor record keeping the CHA regularly sent eviction notices to tenants whose rent was current. Brady finally had her tenants pay rent to the HRC, which then paid the CHA. There was also the matter of paying the HRC. Her contract called for monthly invoices to be paid within fifteen days, but for two years, Brady said, "I had to go downtown at five P.M. and say, 'It's the twenty-fifth of the month and I'm not leaving until I get my check.'"

And there was never enough money. Mooney's view was that the private management experiment would be useful only if the private managers spent roughly the same amount of money per unit the CHA was spending on management. But as Brady pointed out, none of the buildings had been well constructed in the first place. Many housed large families who were home a good deal of the time. CHA budgets provided nothing for structural upkeep, or increased maintenance due to extra wear and tear.

Three-quarters of Brady's families were headed by females, over 90 percent had extremely low incomes, and nearly 80 percent lacked an employed adult. (Half were black, a third Latino, the rest mostly white.) A fifth of the tenants, Brady said, "should be evicted and would never have been selected if they were now applicants." She added, "We do a lot more than collect the rent and unplug toilets. But I couldn't get CHA to fund a community organizer if I stood on my head and spit nickels."

Brady plunged into her task with the same zeal she had devoted to Mikva's campaigns. She began a "management aide" program that paid stipends to residents to inspect buildings and handle routine maintenance. She hired residents to do painting, and organized self-help painting and screen replacement programs for families willing to work on their own apartments. She evicted twelve families in two years and replaced them with rigorously screened new tenants—her screening process involved checking with the police, previous landlords, and schoolteachers and inspecting the housekeeping at an applicant's current apartment. She became acquainted with almost all residents by name. She began a monthly newsletter, and tried—eventually with some success—to organize a tenant advisory council of representatives from each of her buildings.

Herculean, sensitive, and successful though Brady's efforts appeared to be, Zirl Smith did not renew the HRC and Albert Johnson two-year contracts. Instead he extended them for six months while he conducted a cost study, comparing the HRC and Johnson costs to those of the CHA's own management of scattered sites. "The jury is still out on private management," he said. "We [CHA] know something about property management, and I'm not convinced just yet this is the most efficient way to do the job." He did promise a decision once he received an evaluation he had commissioned by the Institute of Real Estate Management (IREM), a respected national trade organization.

The fall 1985 IREM report was positive—the HRC and Johnson were lauded for "a more than adequate job." Brady, putting her Mikva training to work, organized aldermen, tenants, and community organizations to pressure Smith. At a meeting of the HRC's tenant advisory council in January 1986, Smith announced that the HRC's contract would be renewed. He even hinted that the CHA might expand private management into other neighborhoods.

We were prevented from exploring the hint immediately by the turmoil at the CHA—the period of heavy fighting in the Robinson-Smith war, followed by the CHA's financial meltdown and the threat of a HUD takeover. But with the HRC having demonstrated that scattered-site private management was a good idea, we continued to push for expansion, and eventually, with the aid of a "bribe," got the CHA to turn over all scattered sites to private managers.

On the day before Thanksgiving 1987, Harold Washington's second term ended abruptly when the mayor died at his desk from a heart attack. Washington's successor, Eugene Sawyer, turned out to be merely a caretaker, and was soon succeeded by Richard M. Daley, who has remained in office ever since. In June 1988, however, before Daley's election, Sawyer appointed Vincent Lane, a real estate developer, to head the CHA. Van Gorkom had resigned after only a few months, unable to manage the CHA the way he was accustomed to managing businesses, but he had served his purpose. The HUD takeover had been averted. Lane sincerely wanted to reform the CHA and improve public housing. In 1989 I was able to persuade him to expand private management by hiring the nonprofit Hispanic Housing Development Corporation to manage an additional seventy-three scattered-site units on the Northwest Side. The following year I made a deal with Lane. If he would turn over all scattered sites to private management, we would get a court order from Aspen permitting $9.5 million of what would otherwise have been new scattered-site construction money to be used instead to repair existing scattered-site buildings.

He did, and we did. In January 1992, four new private managers took over the remaining scattered sites, two nonprofits and two for-profit firms. Each was experienced in managing residential property. Private management of scattered sites was now a substantial institution in its own right. The HRC's portfolio had grown to 362 units in seventy buildings across seven North Side communities. Hispanic and the four new managers (one of whom took over Albert Johnson's units) had management responsibility for another 1,386 units, with more scheduled to come on line in 1993 and subsequent years.

The deal with Lane was not difficult to justify. With all of Smith's talk about the CHA knowing something about management, CHA management was terrible. It made little sense to keep building scattered-site units that would then be managed poorly and allowed to deteriorate physically. To obtain better management and make needed repairs in more than 1,700 units was well worth the "price" of funding 100 new units, as Habitat and Aspen promptly agreed.

Like an idea whose time has come, the private management concept, begun so tortuously with Master, Mooney, and Smith, swept through the CHA. Management of all CHA developments—tens of thousands of apartments—was eventually contracted out to private firms. It might be said that Sue Brady had started a quiet revolution.

_____

But of what significance? The ultimate judgment on scattered sites would not rest on whether or not they were privately managed, but on what living in them meant for families. In the summer of 2001, Brady having retired, I talked with Jerry Williams, Brady's successor, and Janice Byron, Williams's assistant director. The HRC then managed 618 scattered-site units in 204 buildings spread over fifteen of Chicago's community areas. The numbers did not include an additional 857 HRC-managed apartments for the elderly and disabled in six senior elevator buildings. HRC's territory stretched from Lake Michigan to O'Hare Field, and from Chicago's Evanston border on the north almost to the Loop. Its staff had grown to fifty-seven full-time persons, and included—mostly but not entirely because of the seniors—people with bilingual facility in Spanish, Russian, Lithuanian, Polish, Romanian, Serbian-Croatian, Korean, and Bulgarian. Nine of the staff were tenants. The buildings and apartments that had appalled Brady when she first inspected them were now in pretty good shape.

Tenant participation was still part of the HRC's operation. Building meetings were still being held regularly, eight to ten a month, led by one of the HRC's resident-service coordinators. Every summer the HRC ran a garden program, every winter a weatherization program, and throughout the year a painting program. In the first two programs the HRC supplied the materials, garden tools and seeds, weather stripping and plastic sheeting, and residents did the rest. In the painting program, five gallons of paint could be purchased for twenty dollars, and HRC supplied tools and instructional materials, all delivered to the resident's door. Some 100 families participated each year in the garden program, 150 in weatherization, and about 65 in painting.

Yet gardening, weatherization, and painting did not reveal what was happening in the lives of the families who lived in HRC-managed scattered sites. The Gautreaux scattered-site program was supposed to remedy racial discrimination in CHA site selection. In theory that could have been accomplished by constructing new enclaves of segregated buildings in white neighborhoods. Scattered sites, we had hoped, would do something more—provide the "uplift" or "betterment" that might come from living among neighbors, not separate from them, in better neighborhoods.

On this score, Williams and Byron acknowledged disappointment. Most scattered-site families were still not part of the larger community. (But how many of their non–public housing neighbors were?) Their interest in becoming part of their community in a social or organizational sense was "low." Social isolation persisted. In some degree, perhaps, that was because of negative neighbor attitudes toward "those" people. But mostly, Williams and Byron thought, it was that the scattered-site families lacked the desire or will to break out of their isolation.

There were of course exceptions. The nine tenants on staff were full-time wage earners whose lives were quite different from what they had been when they moved into scattered sites. Yet the anecdotes ran both ways. Byron "worked" intensively with one of the tenants, a highly motivated mother whose favorable prospects ended when the young woman was stabbed to death by her boyfriend. Byron counseled another woman on the brink of eviction for terrible housekeeping. "Do you realize you're going to lose an important asset, your low-rent housing, if you don't do better?" She tried to break the task into manageable pieces. "Let's start with the stove. Let's just clean up the stove and keep it clean." This to an intelligent mother of two young children whose stated goal was to return to school. But who also had a serious domestic violence problem with a man about to emerge from prison, and who ultimately couldn't keep the stove clean, nor the walls, nor the bathroom free of sanitation problems, and who finally was evicted.

Drugs were pervasive in many of the HRC's scattered-site neighborhoods, and therefore in the scattered sites themselves, far worse than when Brady had begun in 1983. "Easily fifty percent of our tenants are involved, one way or another," said Williams. One way or another didn't in every case mean the immediate scattered-site family members, but included the cousins, or the friends, particularly of the teenagers. "When a family moves in," Williams explained, "it's not just the family. It's the friends and relations who come to visit and hang around. If they're into drugs, you're involved. And in the gang stuff that goes along with it. I would have to say that drugs and gangs seem to be tolerated more by scattered-site residents than by the general community."

"How do you deal with it?" I asked. "We can't do much more than enforce the lease," said Williams. "Management trying to do social work is tough because we're conflicted. There are confidentiality issues. I take ninety minutes to go over the lease with every new resident. Try to make sure they understand it. Then about all I can do is enforce the lease."

The scattered sites are safer and better maintained than the projects, something the residents know and appreciate. But the "gratefulness," Byron said, "only lasts three to six months." A reflective person who had been with the HRC for two decades, Byron added, "There is some serious dysfunction in most of our families."

In 1989, in an article about HRC management of scattered sites, Byron had written, "Public housing can work and work well." The article closed on the hopeful note that private management of scattered sites would "change the way public housing is perceived in Chicago." Byron does not now retract those views but has some additional observations. "The explanation for the dysfunctionality is to be found in the larger society. Decent housing is a foundation; it is critical, but not by itself enough. If you ask whether living in our scattered sites has changed lives drastically for the better, my answer is that for most families it has some positive effect, but not enough to take them over the hump."

Brady's retrospection breaks scattered-site families into three groups. One-third, she says, will probably never be employable. The best that can be done is to offer them safe and decent housing and concentrate on the children. For another one-third, "You don't need to do much for them." Once they have decent housing, they "get on with their lives." The final one-third, the in-between group, is composed of the families for whom, given a base of decent housing, comprehensive social services might make a difference. Yet, Brady adds, scattered-site housing cannot be expected to provide that assistance. "Public housing was meant for families able to live independently. It was not meant to solve the problems of generational poverty or dysfunctional families."

I went on to meet with the other private managers who collectively managed more than 2,500 scattered-site units. They all echoed Byron: for most families, scattered sites alone were not enough to take them over the hump. The managers preferred to talk about their success stories — such as the daughter who had just graduated from Notre Dame with distinction — but, when pressed, acknowledged that a majority of families appeared unmotivated or unable to significantly change their life patterns.

One may hope that over the long run life trajectories for the children will be different than had they remained in the high-rises. (Most, of course, have improved statistical odds of having lives whose trajectories may be examined.) But this is a hope, not a demonstrated fact. Conducted for a purpose unrelated to scattered sites, a recent study of the CHA's current tenant population concludes that a significant proportion of CHA families have extremely low incomes and little formal education and skills, and that at least one immediate family member has a criminal record and is having to cope with substance abuse, domestic violence, serious illness, or disability problems. If families such as these are to undergo significant and lasting change for the better, something more than a scattered-site unit in the Chicago neighborhoods available to the scattered-site program would be required.

Something more? Meaning middle-class and affluent suburban neighborhoods? What if Milliken v. Bradley hadn't blocked us from a metropolitan public housing program? The Gautreaux Section 8 program, which did operate metropolitan-wide and is discussed in the next chapter, helps answer that question.

In May 1986, at BPI's annual fund-raising dinner, my speech was about Gautreaux. On a scale of one to ten, I said, "the scattered-site part of the Gautreaux remedy would have to be judged as falling somewhere below zero." That was eighteen months before Habitat took over as receiver. Where, on the same scale, do I rank the completed scattered-site program? I will accompany my answer with some rumination.

First, the numbers. We wound up with about 2,700 scattered-site units built under Gautreaux, some 1,800 by Habitat and 900 by the CHA before Habitat took over. In relation to the more than 30,000 Gautreaux families entitled to desegregated housing opportunities, 2,700 is an unhappily small number. Of course, not all Gautreaux families wanted to move to scattered sites (we don't know how many would have made that choice if all had been given the chance), many received a different form of relief (the Section 8 rent subsidy), and 2,700 units—enough to house 10,000 persons, counting only original occupants—is not a negligible number. Yet the number is small not only compared with the size of the Gautreaux class but also in relation to the effort and time—some thirty years from the 1969 judgment order against the CHA—it took to get there.

Second, the locations. Several hundred apartments were in poor black areas because, under the 1979 deal with Byrne, the CHA could "match" white neighborhood sites with black sites. (Even under the original 1969 order, 25 percent were permitted in black neighborhoods.) Many units, originally built in white neighborhoods, ended up in black areas because of changing demographics. Hundreds of units were built in relatively poor Latino neighborhoods, not the kind of result—according to critics—Gautreaux was supposed to provide. (Latinos were historically underserved by the predominantly black CHA system and scattered sites in their neighborhoods helped redress the imbalance. Yet harassment by Latino neighbors drove several black scattered-site families from their apartments.)

Nor did we ever get even one scattered-site unit in affluent Sauganash, or very many, relatively speaking, in many of the predominantly white Northwest and Southwest Side ethnic neighborhoods. Even though most people would acknowledge that almost every scattered-site building was better located than a place such as Robert Taylor Homes, few scattered sites were in solidly middle-class neighborhoods.

Third, the units themselves. Some, especially the "rehabs," were wonderful. But many, built by the CHA before Habitat took over, were poorly constructed. Even Habitat's units, thanks to modest design and cost containment, were pretty small. (Yet size is relative. Once, when I visited a new Habitat unit, ready for its first family, I was appalled at how small the interior looked. "Sue," I said to Brady, "I don't think you can fit a bed in that third bedroom." Brady responded that earlier in the day the woman whose family would shortly be moving in had sat down at the kitchen table and cried for joy.)

Finally, the CHA's management of scattered sites was poor. Although the private managers, when we finally got them, did better, they remained hamstrung by CHA oversight procedures and limited private management budgets.

As I consider my answer to the ranking question, I cannot help thinking of "might have beens." If Austin hadn't been severely weakened by illness he might have given us a receiver in 1974 when vacant lots and buildings and federal funding were far more plentiful than later. That would have meant not only more, but also better located, units, and perhaps that would have helped more families over the hump.

There is also a niggling self-criticism that will not go away. Did we push vigorously enough and soon enough on the CHA's miserable scattered-site performance? Or was I so distracted by other Gautreaux tasks, for example, the Section 8 arrangements that followed the Supreme Court's 1976 decision, not to mention the running of BPI, that the scattered-site program did not receive the focused attention it deserved? Maybe I should have found some pro bono lawyer to take over just the scattered-site part of the case. Maybe, with single-minded attention to that, she or he would have done better—got us out of the Jurco bog sooner, or moved more quickly than we did on the CHA's failure to promptly rehabilitate its acquired buildings. I cannot avoid the belief that we should have done better on scattered sites and were therefore partly to blame for how it came out. Perhaps that sense of personal failure grows out of the contrast with Section 8, where—as the next chapter will show—we did much better.

The "answer"? Thanks mostly to Levin and Hickman I think we did creep above zero. But—because of Habitat's late start—not by much. On the ten-point scale I rank Gautreaux scattered sites at somewhere between two and three.

I've frequently used "we" to refer to the other Gautreaux lawyers and myself—writing briefs, arguing motions, doing research, making decisions. Does "we" mean the original quintet, minus Chuck Markels after his death in 1972? It's time to explain the pronoun.

Merrill Freed was the first to move to the sidelines. He didn't formally withdraw, but allowed his name to remain on the court papers and even handled occasional research assignments. But after 1969, as he later told me, he had serious misgivings when we chose not to consult with the black community about the shape of Austin's 1969 final order. Here were five white guys negotiating on behalf of a black constituency, not even talking to their clients, lacking any organized support from the black community. Merrill didn't like it, but Merrill is by nature a soft-spoken gentleman and he didn't raise the matter to a confrontation. He simply began to distance himself.

The issue arose early in 1969 when, after Austin ruled that the CHA was liable, we went through the intense several months of negotiating the order finally signed on July 1, 1969. Since this would be the "relief" prescription for thousands of CHA tenants and applicants who were our clients, shouldn't we be getting their views on what the order should say?

Client consultation in a class action, at least with a class as large as ours, is a tricky matter. Should we have held a "town hall" for all who were interested? Should we have consulted with the half dozen plaintiffs named in the complaint as "class representatives"? And how in either case should differences of opinion among class members or representatives have been handled? Or was there a better way?

There isn't a great deal of law on the obligation of "class counsel" to consult with class members. The courts recognize that because the "client" in a class action consists of numerous class members in addition to the representatives, and because class members often differ among themselves about issues in "their" lawsuit, it may be impossible for the class attorney to do more than act in what she or he believes to be the best interests of the entire class. The attorney's duty runs to the class as a whole, not to individuals.

Merrill wasn't urging us to hold a town meeting or treat the views of the representatives as decisive. He did believe there was another way: we should bring some black organizations into our discussions. Create some linkage between the Gautreaux case and the black community. But there were problems with Merrill's approach. We couldn't meet with every black organization in the city, so we would have to be selective, choosing some and excluding others, a distasteful course. There was of course no reason to assume that any chosen group of organizations would fairly represent (whatever that meant) the views of the families who were our clients, or even agree with each other. And if we did solicit the views of selected black organizations and then disagreed with what they recommended, where would that leave us? Either we would anger the very persons whose views we had sought by ignoring their counsel, or because of the views of some outsider to the case we would disregard our own best judgment, which is what our clients were entitled to receive.

There was no happy solution. In the end, contrary to Merrill's views, we did not consult either our clients or surrogates for them. To this day Gautreaux remains a case brought on behalf of blacks by white lawyers in which—after the initial impetus from the West Side Federation and the Urban League—neither the black class members nor others in the black community have had a meaningful role in litigation decisions. Not the ideal posture for a public interest lawsuit supposed to vindicate community rights.

Another of our starting quintet left the case for a different reason. In 1980 President Carter appointed Milt Shadur to the federal district court in Chicago. Milt had been active throughout his years with Gautreaux. His absence was a loss I felt deeply. And Milt was truly lost to us. It would have been improper even to talk to him informally about Gautreaux once he took his seat on the very court in which the case was pending.

Bernie Weisberg left the case in 1985 for a reason similar to Milt's. After thirty-two years in private practice he indicated he would accept a magistrate's position, and the federal judges in Chicago, able—thanks to a new law—to add several sorely needed new magistrates, had the good sense to jump at Bernie's offer. A newspaper article, "One Magnificent Magistrate," referred among other things to Bernie's having been an editor of the *University of Chicago Law Review*, a U.S. Supreme Court clerk, and the winner of a seminal 1964 case in the Supreme Court that established the right of suspects undergoing police interrogation to consult a lawyer. He had also been described by a noted constitutional scholar as "our most brilliant civil rights lawyer." As with the loss of Milt, the loss of Bernie was a hard blow. It was followed eight years later by a worse one. In January 1994, after a battle both he and his doctor thought he could win, Bernie succumbed to lymphoma.

To whom then does the personal pronoun refer? The answer is a succession of BPI lawyers, and some volunteers from elsewhere, who—had they all been working at the same time—would have made up a fair-sized law firm. From BPI there were Julie Brown, Cecil Butler, Doug Cassel, John Hammell, Bob Jones, Betsy Lassar (my "second chair" in the Crowley and Aspen receivership hearings), Howard Learner, Patricia Logue, Bob Vollen, and Tim Wright, as well as an annual crop of law student summer interns who "entered" Gautreaux, put in their time, and then moved on.

It is little short of astonishing that I have been enabled to remain with Gautreaux since its inception in 1966. The case has not, of course, occupied me full time. During the early years, the case was a pro bono sideline for an otherwise fully engaged member of a large law firm. At BPI I had the responsibilities of organizational management as well as a satisfying, ever-changing array of challenging projects, many of them in the courtroom. They involved, among others, Lake Michigan pollution, nuclear power generation, and public education reform, as well as suits against the U.S. Army (for political spying), the Veterans Administration (for mortgage insurance practices leading to neighborhood racial turnover), and the National Association of Realtors (over race-conscious marketing of homes).

But across the decades, through all the changes that life brings—the passing of Dorothy Gautreaux, Chuck Markels, and Bernie Weisberg, the passage from Austin to Crowley to Aspen, the aging of the segregated high-rises built in the 1950s and 1960s, not to mention the aging of its lead counsel, Gautreaux has been a constant in my life, and in the organizational lives of the CHA and BPI.

CHAPTER FIVE

FROM CABRINI-GREEN TO WILLOW CREEK

What are you insinuating?
That we've come to the wrong place?

—Vladimir (*Waiting for Godot*)

1

In 1977 Barbara wrote an article, "Cabrini-Green to Willow Creek," for the June issue of *Chicago* magazine. Here is its opening scene:

Everyone arrives early in spite of a winter storm. They assemble around the long conference table, anxious, skeptical, expectant—22 black women, several with young children, a Puerto Rican woman, and a middle-aged black man. Strangers until today, they have all gathered at the Loop office of the Leadership Council for Metropolitan Open Communities in response to a letter offering them a chance to move into subsidized housing in the suburbs.

More than 200 families randomly selected from the 44,000 whose names were on the Chicago public-housing tenant and waiting lists have received the same letter this week. Since the beginning of the program, some 4,000 others had received similar letters. Many thought it was junk mail and threw it away unread; some decided the letter was a hoax (why would "they" want to be doing anything like that if there weren't a catch to it?); many saw "suburb" and read no further. Of those attending the meeting, only a handful are drawn by the prospect of living in the suburbs. Most are simply desperate to move out of the projects and willing to explore any possibility. One woman has been burned out of her home and the middle-aged man wants to get out of Cabrini-Green to a place where he "can sleep in peace at night," wherever that might be.

The black woman who welcomes them to the meeting is Carol Hendrix. One of the Leadership Council's four housing counselors, Carol moved to a predominantly white suburb with her husband and children some years before.

Carol begins the meeting as she always does by trying to allay the fear universal among her listeners that the program is a plot. The people in the room have lived too long in a city ruled by whites not to be skeptical of everything, especially a program that promises as much as this one . . . Carol talks about the 1966 open housing marches led by Martin Luther King, Jr., recalling that it was Dr. King, along with other civic leaders, who set up the Leadership Council to carry on the fight for freedom in housing. Then she tells them about a lesser-known heroine, Dorothy Gautreaux, a poor black woman who wanted to move from her ghetto apartment into public housing but who found that the Chicago Housing Authority offered her only the same black neighborhoods, blighted by the same deteriorated conditions she wanted to escape.

So Mrs. Gautreaux and five other black tenants, with the help of American Civil Liberties Union lawyers, sued the CHA for discrimination. The case lasted ten years. Dorothy Gautreaux didn't live long enough to see it finally won in the Supreme Court last April. She died seven years ago, still living in Altgeld Gardens. But because of her, you in CHA have the chance for a free choice in housing. It's what she fought for. "That's why you're called the Gautreaux people, because of Dorothy Gautreaux, a very determined black lady."

The room is quiet. Carol pauses for questions but the faces around the table remain impassive. A little girl starts to whimper and her mother gives her pencil and paper, cautioning her to behave.

The history over, Carol turns to the subject of the subsidy, explaining that Section 8 of the Housing and Community Development Act of 1974 provides rent subsidy payments for lower-income families in privately owned apartment buildings. Tenants pay 25 percent of their income for rent and the government pays the rest. ("Do you all know about Section 8?" Most nod yes. The little girl with the pencil nods too.)

The next subject is the big one—the suburbs. Although the Council has placed a few families in city apartments, Carol explains that this program is focused primarily on the suburbs, where housing that meets Section 8 requirements is found in large private developments. (CHA has its own Section 8 program for the city.) Christened with fairy-tale names like Willow Creek, Royal Meadows, and Rollinghill Manor, the suburban developments are usually equipped with tennis courts, a swimming pool, a recreation center, and occasionally an added nicety like a fishing pond. Some developments are built well, others more cheaply. Most are one or two stories; many of the first-floor apartments lead out to small patios, the second-floor apartments to balconies.

The Puerto Rican woman raises her hand. "How far from the city are these places?"

Carol steps aside so that everyone can see the map of the six-county Chicago metropolitan area taped to the blackboard. So far, she has helped 45 families move to homes in outlying DuPage, Cook, and Lake counties, all in communities at least 30 minutes from Chicago. The efforts of the Council to find housing in suburbs close to Chicago quickly proved futile; there are so few vacancies in inner-ring suburbs that real-estate agencies don't bother advertising them. When there are vacancies, the rentals are higher than those permitted under Section 8.

"DuPage County, Lake County . . ." To most of the people looking at the giant map, bristling with names they've never heard, DuPage County is a foreign land. One woman had never been to downtown Chicago before coming to the meeting that day.

Carol asks everyone to open their minds and consider this new idea: If they choose to move it's not that important how close to Chicago they are because Chicago won't be their home any longer.

"If you go out to a suburb, why are you going? Because you're tired of living in a high-rise and lugging your groceries up ten floors when the elevator breaks down. Here most of the buildings are one and two stories. You're moving because you want a better education for your children. Here there are good schools with bus service from the developments to the school—bus service, not busing. Here's where you can find jobs; most of the new factories are going up here.

"Now, I'm not telling you that the suburbs are *better*; they may not be better for you. They may just not be your cup of tea. That's for you to decide. But they are different. And if you want something different from what you have now we've got it."

A hand is raised. The woman speaks so softly that Carol has to strain to hear. "The lady over the phone, she said you need a car to move out . . ."

Another big issue—a car. When the first rental units turned up exclusively in locations lacking public transportation, the Council, not wanting to raise false hopes, was forced to add the requirement of a car in the invitational letters. Unfortunately, this is a harsh requirement. A person on public aid cannot have more than $150 in the bank, and aid money may not be used to pay off notes on a car. Sixty percent of CHA tenants are on public aid.

Of the 24 persons present, only four own cars. Most of the others want to move so badly that they have come to the meeting hoping that there might be a way to manage the move without a car. Carol explains why a car is necessary.

"Now, I know what you're thinking. 'Lady, are you crazy? I'm on public aid, how am I going to get a car?' I know some of you are on public aid. I also know three other ladies who didn't have a car two months ago, but after deciding that they wanted to get out of the projects they found a way to get one. I'm not talking about a Cadillac or a Toronado, just one that holds together enough to get you back and forth to the grocery or to the movies or to the doctor. And some of you have told me that you don't even know how to drive, and I say, well, learn. You can. My ladies did. They wanted to move badly enough, so they learned to drive. I'm not saying I'd be real happy to meet them on the highway . . ."

She laughs, dispelling tension, charging the atmosphere with a vitality that makes the outrageous seem possible . . . perhaps. One young woman asks, "How long will you have these apartments?" Carol responds, "You mean, how long do you have to get that car? Well, this program is funded for a year, but after that, I can't promise you anything. As soon as you get that car call me, and if you're ready, and the apartment is ready, then we can begin talking business." She pauses . . .

"Now, some of you may be thinking, My boyfriend has a car and he's kind of living with me so that's the same as me having a car, isn't it? The answer is no. If you like your boyfriend enough to marry him, OK, but otherwise, he stays back in Chicago. *Your* name is going on that lease with the landlord, and he doesn't expect anyone to be living there but you and your children. This isn't CHA, this is the real world. If you don't live up to the terms of the lease, you'll be evicted."

Carol makes this point deliberately. Although most of the women are either separated or divorced, many may be living with men who aren't listed on the CHA tenant roster. She and the other counselors are careful about becoming matchmakers; the lure of a suburban apartment might induce couples to marry who shouldn't. This hasn't happened yet, but it's a possibility . . .

The next question is asked by a woman who has a 13-year-old son. "Is there any race trouble in these places?" The accompanying murmur indicates that the question has been on everyone's mind.

"The Council has never knowingly settled any families where there has been racial tension," Carol says. "All of the families I've worked with have moved into developments that already had black people living in them. A lot of minority people have moved into northwestern Cook County because of the factory jobs, and O'Hare airport employs hundreds of minority people. That means that most of the schools already have black children. Your child may be the first black child in his class, but he probably won't be the first black child in the school.

"Now, this isn't to say that someone might not be nasty, but then everyone doesn't love you in the projects either."

The woman is still worried. "My boy, he's 13. I don't want to have to worry about him going out by himself, that some white boys will gang up on him."

Another woman across the table cuts in. "And tell me, you don't worry now, living in the projects? That's no way to live, with people all stacked up like you're in monasteries or jails. You let your children outside, up from the 12th floor, you can't tell them from anybody else's children . . ."

The questions become more prosaic, concerned with the realities of daily living in the suburbs. Can we use our food stamps? A few years ago, when food stamps were unknown in many of the big chain stores that serviced suburban communities, Carol's answer would have been different. But with the recession, a person on aid need no longer feel marked when he pays for his groceries by tearing off $20 worth of stamps.

Medical cards are a different story. They involve the private doctor in burdensome paperwork and some doctors simply refuse to deal with them. Others, upset by turning away poor people, charge only token amounts rather than fill out the forms and wait to be reimbursed by the government.

"Can we move to another apartment if we don't like the one we're in?" The question comes from a 23-year-old woman who works as a typist in a nearby hospital.

"You sign a lease for a year. After that time you're free to renew the lease or move."

The woman tells Carol that she is earning $8,000 a year and has one child. She wonders how much more rent she would have to pay than the $90 she's paying now. Carol puts the figures on the blackboard—25 percent of $8,000. "So you'll have to pay about $150 a month. Now that's for a two-bedroom apartment that's renting on the private market for about $285. But if you want to keep your job and have to pay transportation costs, the move may not be worth the extra cost. That's something you'll have to think about.

"And," Carol adds, "no one but the manager has to know you're on a subsidy. There are no red doors and green doors to tell who is on public aid. These are mixed-income developments that already have minority people living in them. You don't need the stereotype of the poor black on public aid working against you."

Summing up, Carol explains that she will be running a credit check so that she can be sure of her ground when she recommends her clients as reliable tenants. "'I also need an income-verification form, signed by your employer or your social workers, and two letters of reference from long-time acquaintances.

"Now . . . any other questions?"

There are a few scattered nos and then a slight shuffling of chairs. Carol reminds everyone to fill out the "intake sheets" passed around earlier. If the sheet shows a family is interested, has a car, and can fit into a one, two, or three-bedroom apartment, she will visit them in their current home. "Then you can ask me any questions that are bothering you, and I can get to know you better."

Chairs are pushed back, people begin to talk now, to each other, to Carol . . .

"If you want to go and open a credit account you tell them where you live and they ask, is that in the projects, nine times out of ten, you're going to be rejected. I don't know what it is about CHA that people reject."

"Everybody in CHA is stereotyped as being the same thing—nothing."

People hand Carol the intake sheets. The room begins to empty . . .

The little girl yanks impatiently at her mother, complaining that she's hungry. With a sigh, the woman turns away, dragging the little girl faster than her small feet can carry her. Carol notices and doesn't notice. She has learned she must block some things out if she is to remain functional.

2

The first "Gautreaux family" moved in November 1976. In a case not notable for speedy progress, how did it happen that six months after the Supreme Court's ruling in April we had a program ready to open its doors in November?

The Supreme Court opinion had left us facing the uncertainty of a long proceeding in which the "usual" legal and policy arguments of HUD's Arthur Gang would be marshaled to oppose any but the most limited order against HUD. The secretary in Washington, not a federal judge in Chicago, was supposed to set national housing policy. Even if HUD had committed a technical wrong, the secretary—not a judge—should decide how best to provide exactly what remedy, especially with a brand new program like Section 8. Judicial decisions as numerous as leaves on trees told judges not to interfere with an executive agency's broad discretion. At the very least, HUD should be given plenty of time to develop recommendations. Then, as the cases said, the court should pay great deference to the agency's expertise. With his established disinclination to involve the suburbs, that was a posture Austin was likely to find quite comfortable.

We searched for an alternative to this grim prospect of drawn-out courtroom wrangling. Couldn't we imagine a way, working with HUD rather than fighting against it, to play the new Section 8 game on a metropolitan board? Because it had not been tried before, nobody knew how to "do" a metropolitan Section 8 program. Even if Austin could be persuaded to give us metropolitan-wide Section 8 relief, the reality was that we didn't know what to ask for. An opportunity to experiment and learn seemed sensible.

Two steps already taken gave us a model of sorts with which to begin our learning. After enactment of the Section 8 program in August 1974, we had persuaded HUD that it couldn't ignore Gautreaux in dispensing Section 8 in Chicago. Section 8 was not public housing and HUD took the position that Austin's orders applied only to the latter. But, we argued, Section 8 was the functional equivalent of public housing, which it had now virtually replaced as the federal government's main subsidized housing program. It would make no sense to limit Gautreaux relief to moribund public housing while leaving the CHA free to do as it wished with what amounted to a new form of the same thing. Our threat to take the issue to court finally led to a deal HUD accepted. Signed on May 5, 1975, the order required half of nonelderly Section 8 in Chicago to go to Gautreaux families.

The second step involved the Illinois Housing Development Authority (IHDA), a state agency that loaned money at low interest rates to developers who would produce housing for poorer families. Since Austin's May order covered all Section 8 in Chicago, any IHDA allocation for use in the city would have a Gautreaux string tied to it. When HUD announced that the IHDA would be receiving some $9 million for a Section 8 project-based program in Chicago, I received a call from Irving Gerick, the IHDA's executive director. He had been thinking, he said, about telling developers that if they wanted favorable consideration for the IHDA's sought-after loans, they should include some Gautreaux families in their Section 8 apartments.

I suggested we talk with Kale Williams, now the widely respected director of the organization birthed by the 1966 Summit Meeting, the Leadership Council for Metropolitan Open Communities. The council, I told Gerick, could be funded by the IHDA to select and counsel Gautreaux families willing to make Section 8 "moves." It could also certify to developers that the counseled families were likely to be good tenants and could offer help with any postmove problems. That would provide some comfort to the developers the IHDA would be asking to take the unprecedented step of renting apartments to black, inner-city, public housing families.

Williams was receptive. By January 1976, a one-year contract between the IHDA and the Leadership Council had been worked out. The IHDA would see to it that half its nonelderly Section 8 apartments were located in white areas. For at least twenty-five days after they were ready for occupancy, these "Gautreaux apartments" would be held exclusively for Leadership Council families. The council was to get lists of families from the CHA, inform them of the IHDA opportunities, and offer counseling and other assistance. For these services the IHDA would pay the council $50,000. And Gerick was willing to apply these arrangements to suburban as well as Chicago developments, even though Austin's order covered only the city.

Williams assigned Henry Zuba of the Leadership Council staff half time to the IHDA program. "Hank," as he was universally called, had a rough-hewn face and ready smile. Solidly built, he looked as if he might have been a construction worker. In fact he was a former Catholic priest who had been deeply involved in social justice issues with parish gangs. Zuba and Williams promptly began to interview candidates for what they called a "housing counselor" position. They soon selected Carol Hendrix, an energetic, articulate black woman. With a half-time secretary assigned from regular Leadership Council staff, the IHDA program was ready to sail into uncharted seas with the equivalent of two full-time crew members.

Williams worked out arrangements with the CHA to get lists of families. Zuba and Hendrix designed a leaflet for an initial test mailing of 200. As "another way" of describing the council's new program, they included four stanzas from Gwendolyn Brooks's poem, "The Ballad of Rudolph Reed":

Rudolph Reed was oaken.
His wife was oaken too.
And his two good girls and his good little man
Oaken as they grew.

"I am not hungry for berries
I am not hungry for bread
But hungry hungry for a house
Where at night a man in bed

"May never hear the plaster
Stir as if in pain.
May never hear the roaches
Falling like fat rain.

"Oh my home may have its east or west
Or north or south behind it.
All I know is I shall know it,
And fight for it when I find it."

The choice was understandable but chancy because in a later stanza, not included in the leaflet, Reed steps outside, gun in hand, and loses his life fighting rock-throwing whites who don't want a black family moving into their neighborhood:

By the time he had hurt his fourth white man
Rudolph Reed was dead.
His neighbors gathered and kicked his corpse.
"Nigger—" his neighbors said.

She "just wanted" to include the poem, was Hendrix's explanation. "Maybe I wanted to challenge people."

From the mailing to 200 families, 46 response cards were received. Hendrix promptly set out to visit all 46, who however were soon reduced to 16. Some families needed more than three bedrooms (which the IHDA developments wouldn't have) or didn't want to move to the suburbs. Others didn't phone Hendrix back to make an appointment, or were too fearful to open the door when she arrived. Yet 16 families were definitely "interested," a start. (Zuba and Hendrix quickly abandoned the time-consuming initial home visits and substituted group "briefings" at the council's office.)

Hendrix was also busy familiarizing herself with the IHDA developments slated to provide apartments. The first group consisted of eight new suburban rental complexes with names like "Pebbleshire" and "Four Lakes," scattered north, west, and south of Chicago, and one thirty-five-story apartment tower, Elm Street Plaza, located on Chicago's fashionable Near North Side. Hendrix made specific arrangements with the on-site development managers, and learned about social service and employment resources in each area, as well as such matters as shopping, hospitals, and beauty salons (if any) where black women could get their hair done.

More mailings went out in succeeding weeks. In April Hendrix took nine families to Arrowhead Village in Palatine, a white, middle-income suburb in northwest Cook County, to see four apartments reserved for the Leadership Council. Four of the nine families applied and were accepted. The first two (both from Cabrini-Green) moved at the end of May. Also in May nine more apartments at Regency Terrace in Bloomingdale—another white suburb—were offered to the council. Though tiny, the IHDA program was beginning to look real.

And became so through the remainder of the year and into the next. In December the Leadership Council's contract with the IHDA was renewed for another year, to January 1978. By midyear 1977, some forty-four families had moved into ten developments, and eight more available apartments were in the council's "pipeline." Nearly 20,000 letters had been mailed, producing 2,243 responses. And Gerick's "persuasion" was working—most IHDA developers, eager for the IHDA's low-interest loans, were cooperating.

Some, however, more willingly than others. One manager who repeatedly turned down Gautreaux families eventually made a fatal error—he forgot to retrieve his notes from a file before returning it to the Leadership Council. The notes included the scribbled phrases, "not our cup of tea, *really* black, looks like a streetwalker." The council's lawyers sued and eventually settled the case for a sizable money payment and an apartment for the family, as well as additional apartments for other Gautreaux families.

The tally of mailings, responses, and moves does not of course disclose what was happening to the families. In his monthly statistical reports to the IHDA, Williams usually included a "follow-up" section. In August 1976 he reported on a "get-together" with three of the five families then at Arrowhead. There had been "relatively minor racial incidents," but the families "were very pleased with the development and their decision." Families and friends, initially skeptical, were frequent visitors and "are now looking for housing in the area."

In early 1977 Williams reported that one family at Grand Oaks in

Gurnee had "skipped." Follow-up meetings with families at Arrowhead and the Villas in Bolingbrook considered the "common problems" of a time lag in transferring public aid cases from Chicago to a suburban office, difficulty in finding physicians who would honor Medicaid cards, and major differences between the IHDA's utility allowances and actual utility bills. (The council was working on each of the problems.) On a happier note, reporting on meetings with managers at Arrowhead, Elm Street Plaza, and the Villas, Williams wrote that "all three complexes intended to offer to renew leases to all Council clients as their first year of tenancy is completed . . ."

Yet each new development was a new experience. On a Saturday afternoon Zuba and his wife Marge helped a Gautreaux mother and her ten-year-old daughter, the first blacks in their Elmwood Park complex, move their belongings. The janitor was surly. As boxes were carried up to the third floor, several corridor doors were loudly slammed. Returning from one trip to the ground level for more boxes, Marge found dead flowers outside the apartment door. It was nearly dark when the moving was completed. Zuba was apprehensive. He drove Marge home, then returned. Parking where he could watch the front door of the complex, he stayed at his "post" until dawn. All, however, remained quiet on the Elmwood Park front.

Soon after the Supreme Court's April 1976 ruling I began to talk with HUD's general counsel, Robert Elliott, the lawyer who had sat at the counsel table with Bork in the Supreme Court. Elliott agreed with the logic of working something out on an interim, "learn-by-doing" basis. I explained the IHDA program and we talked about a modification of it as a way we might experiment with metropolitan relief.

By now I was desperate to get tangible results. The scattered-site program seemed to be going nowhere. Whether the IHDA program would even be workable was unknown, but at best—given the small numbers of Section 8 units in the limited number of IHDA developments—it would produce only a minor supply of apartments. HUD, running a project-based program parallel to the IHDA's, was getting virtually no proposals for Chicago's white neighborhoods. In the CHA's tenant-based program few landlords in white neighborhoods were offering to rent to CHA families.

The key conversation with Elliott took place at dinner one night in Miller's Pub, a noisy restaurant with good food in Chicago's Loop. Amid the dining din, Elliott and I roughed out the elements of our gestating agreement on a big paper napkin. HUD would give the Leadership Council 400 Section 8 certificates—our target for first-year moves—for use throughout the metropolitan area. HUD would pay the cost of the council's work (a staff of about nine was contemplated) similar to what was being done with the IHDA, except that the council would have to find landlords willing to participate. HUD would not require developers to offer apartments to the Leadership Council as the IHDA was doing—an issue I lost in my bargaining with Elliott. Any further Section 8 authority to the IHDA would have a Gautreaux string—marketing arrangements "acceptable" to the plaintiffs. We settled on a one-year trial period.

On June 7, 1976, Elliott and I signed a letter agreement that fleshed out the napkin notes. In early August HUD signed a contract with the Leadership Council, agreeing to pay $178,000 for "a program to assist the members of the Gautreaux Plaintiff Class to find existing housing units and locate owners of housing willing to participate in the Chicago Section 8 Demonstration Program." The Council was to use its best efforts to help approximately 400 families move during the one-year contract period.

In regular Section 8 programs, certificates could be used only within the territory of the housing authority that issued them. A family with a certificate from the CHA could not use it to rent in the suburbs. Now Gautreaux certificates would be "portable" throughout the metropolitan area. We would at last have metropolitan relief, although in a form nobody had in mind back in 1969, five years before Section 8 was enacted.

What exactly could be accomplished with this new Gautreaux Program was terra incognita. Yes, the new program would be metropolitan, but everything depended on finding enough vacant apartments in non-black areas whose landlords would rent to Gautreaux families. Not to mention the uncertainties facing families who would be leaving the familiar cocoon of the CHA in Chicago to try to put their lives together in strange new communities. Except for the fledgling IHDA program, what we were calling "housing mobility" was nothing but an untested idea. Yet, after a decade of litigation, an untested idea that actually involved offering Gautreaux families opportunities to move to nonblack neighborhoods seemed preferable to more courtroom battling that—even if we should "win"—might result in little more than the experimental program we would now have with HUD's agreement.

3

The press applauded. "An important step in areawide desegregation," pronounced a *Sun-Times* editorial two days after Elliott and I signed the letter agreement. But "untested idea" was exactly right. Though the IHDA program was beginning to provide experience in counseling families, the IHDA was supplying the apartments. Now, in the vast Chicago metropolitan area—6 counties, more than 200 municipalities, 2.3 million housing units, nearly 7 million people in 3,690 square miles— the Leadership Council had to figure out how and where to find housing for Gautreaux families.

The HUD program was to be much bigger than the IHDA's. Because it used tenant- rather than project-based Section 8, it was also more complex. Arrangements had to be made with public housing authorities to administer the Section 8 contracts for Gautreaux families moving into their areas—paying rent to landlords, inspecting apartments, handling paperwork. Local government officials had to be notified about the Gautreaux Program because the law gave them a right to comment on proposed subsidized housing developments within their jurisdictions, including the right to object on grounds of "inconsistency" with their housing plans. (After much discussion about how to handle this sensitive matter—would mayors and city councils fight a program designed to bring in black, inner-city families?—carefully phrased letters were mailed and HUD finessed the half dozen or so responses by concluding that the "comments" did not amount to "objections.")

Apart from addressing these and other administrative matters, there were the basic tasks of hiring staff, contacting and counseling families, finding landlords. Williams assigned Zuba to the HUD program, adding it to his IHDA responsibilities. Williams and his deputy director, Harry Gottlieb (a former executive of a real estate and mortgage banking firm with good contacts in the real estate industry), both devoted much time and energy to getting the new program underway. Zuba interviewed seventeen people and hired four to start, including Mary Davis as a housing counselor and Mary Messer as a "real estate specialist"—a Sherlock Holmes to find landlords. Davis, a vivacious, personable young black woman, had herself grown up in Cabrini-Green. Messer was a seasoned professional (white) who had once run a small public housing authority. By January 1977 Zuba's staff had grown to seven full-time and two part-time persons, not counting Williams and Gottlieb, and in that month Hendrix began to divide her time between the IHDA and HUD programs.

Williams and Zuba hired a public relations firm to prepare materials for landlords—a manual about how Section 8 worked and a brochure about the Gautreaux Program that included reassurance about tenants:

> All families will undergo income verification and credit reports, and will be visited in their current homes before they are recommended ... These prospective tenants are families who are seeking a healthy environment, good schools and an opportunity to live in a safe and decent home.

The brochures were mailed to lists of landlords but the real work of landlord contact fell to Messer, who examined directories and newspaper listings and made countless telephone calls to verify published information. Then, brochures in hand, she personally visited owners and managers in selected areas, principally northwest Cook and DuPage counties where research had indicated most vacancies in job-rich, white areas might be found. In October Zuba's staff gave a presentation to some 160 property managers at a meeting of the Chicago chapter of the Institute of Real Estate Management, after which the chapter mailed the council's brochure with a cover letter to its 400 members.

All this activity produced some apartments, but hardly a flood. Years later Rubinowitz, by then a law professor at Northwestern University, teamed up with a sociology colleague, James Rosenbaum, to write a book about the Gautreaux Program. Their book listed the major challenges the untested idea had faced at the beginning. Finding available apartments was at the top.

There were at the time approximately 1.1 million rental units in the Chicago metropolitan area, a big figure in relation to the target of placing

400 families. To meet its goal it looked as if the Leadership Council needed less than 0.04 percent of Chicago area rental units. But that big figure was a deceptive illusion that was quickly cut down to size.

First, there were "fair market rents," known as FMRs. The FMR was Congress's way of handling two issues: (1) the tension between access for poor families to decent private housing and keeping the federal government's subsidy costs reasonable; and (2) concern that if poor families got better housing than middle-class families, fairness questions would undermine support for the entire Section 8 approach. The law therefore required HUD to set Section 8 ceiling rents—FMRs—by area and size of apartment. Any apartment whose rent exceeded its FMR simply could not be leased under Section 8. HUD generally set FMRs at 45 percent of what it determined to be average rents in the local area, so FMRs took a huge initial bite out of the supply of apartments theoretically available to the Leadership Council.

Second, many rental apartments were in precisely the segregated, high-poverty places from which the Gautreaux Program was supposed to enable families to escape. Nor did the council want to risk "tipping" racially integrated communities through Gautreaux placements. So the council ruled out large parts of Chicago (eventually Chicago was excluded entirely), "satellite" cities such as Waukegan and Joliet, and even south Cook County suburbs where the black population was already large and growing.

Third, even if an apartment in a nonblack area had a low enough rent, its availability depended on the voluntary decision of the landlord to lease it to a CHA family. Messer encountered multiple reasons why landlords declined, but race and class seemed to come first. As Rubinowitz and Rosenbaum put it in their book:

> Most landlords in predominantly white suburban areas were accustomed to renting to white middle-class families . . . The Gautreaux program was a drastic departure . . . because it meant accepting low-income Blacks, many of them female-headed, single-parent families who lived in public housing . . . The combination of . . . race, class, gender, family composition, and inner-city origins tapped into landlords' stereotyped fears that gangs, drugs, and violence would accompany them.

Some landlords were philosophically opposed to getting involved in the red tape of any government program. One absentee owner, a New York insurance company, actually fired its local management firm for merely inquiring about whether it would be all right to participate in the Gautreaux Program. Section 8 provided particular red tape reasons for nonparticipation. The HUD-required form of lease was unfamiliar. HUD-mandated eviction procedures raised the specter of inability to evict bad tenants promptly. Public housing authorities were sometimes late with monthly rent checks. Even landlords willing to participate had virtually no three-bedroom or larger apartments. Big Gautreaux families—of whom there were many—were simply out of luck.

Miraculously, by mid-October 1976 the council was ready to hold its first briefing session, followed by home visits, and—for those who "passed"—escorted trips to apartments Messer had found. At the briefing sessions many families made it clear they didn't want to move to the strange land called "the suburbs," even though mailed materials had clearly identified their likely destinations as suburban. "Are you crazy?" one Gautreaux mother exclaimed.

Half the families "failed" or declined to proceed after the home visit that followed the briefing session—some were too large for available apartments or were unwilling to move to where the apartments were located. Others lacked funds for a security deposit or their housekeeping was poor. There was fallout too among those who did proceed. Many families, encountering the suburbs for the first time, were deeply skeptical. One woman, whom Davis was driving to DuPage County to inspect an apartment, changed her mind and insisted that Davis turn the car around when a traffic jam clogged their route. Well before encountering traffic jams many Gautreaux families, whether they gave Davis their reasons or not, had concerns about racial harassment or discrimination, feared the loss of support institutions and friends or of racial and cultural identity, or felt an ideological commitment to remaining in a black community. A survey later showed that only 12 percent of families who did not respond to the Leadership Council's invitation were willing to consider a move to the suburbs.

There was fallout too among families who succeeded in moving. The first Gautreaux family to enter a spanking new development in Orland

Park turned out to have a drug problem, badly damaged its apartment, and was soon evicted. "It broke my heart," said Davis. "I learned very early that everyone wasn't going to work."

The multiple problems on both the landlord and tenant sides of his equation led Zuba to call an evaluation meeting in mid-December 1976. Everyone was there, including Williams, Gottlieb, Davis, Hendrix, Messer, Rubinowitz, Barbara (then starting work on her *Chicago* magazine article), and me. Zuba was close to despondent. Instead of sporting its usual smile his mouth was clamped shut for most of the meeting. Six weeks had passed since the first family in the HUD program had moved on November 1. In that time there had been only nine more moves. Making the most optimistic assumptions he could about the future course of the program, Zuba could project no more than 210 moves by the end of the program year. Perhaps Elliott should be called with the bad news.

Wiser heads prevailed. Zuba was reminded that no one had known what rate of placement to expect. The 400 figure was only a target, set deliberately high so the council would not run out of Section 8 certificates. The practical outcome of Zuba's meeting was an agreement to stop inviting larger families to briefings and to put them instead on a separate list for special handling when the rare larger apartment turned up. In fact, Zuba's projection turned out to be optimistic. At the end of the first program year placements stood at 168.

Yet we did in effect follow Zuba's suggestion, though Elliott was soon gone in the wake of Jimmy Carter's election in November 1976. The new HUD general counsel was Ruth Prokop. In a series of phone calls to Carter's HUD team, now installed in Washington, I said that without badly needed new arrangements we would go to court for a metropolitan order when the program year ended. The phone calls led to a meeting in Washington on May 4, 1977. Prokop was there, along with a phalanx of HUD lawyers, including her deputy, Ed Norton, and our nonfriend, Arthur Gang. Our group consisted of Milt Shadur, Kale Williams, and myself.

Our position was simple. The Gautreaux Program was unsatisfactory in its present form; if it couldn't be radically improved we would return to court. Our three demands for improvement were (1) higher FMRs; (2) reserving some portion of all newly constructed "hard," project-based units for Gautreaux families (the issue I had lost with Elliott a year earlier); and (3) more subsidies to the Chicago area so more new hard units could be built.

"I don't think returning to court should be necessary," Prokop responded. "This is a new administration which shares your goals." The next day Norton called with the news that Prokop had formed a "task force" of himself and one of HUD's Chicago lawyers to work with us. Over the ensuing weeks, as usual in such bargaining situations, we "won" some and "lost" some. The upshot was that on July 29, 1977, Prokop and I signed another Gautreaux agreement, but only after last-minute letters had extended the program, week by week, from June 30 to July 29, while negotiations dragged past the original June 30 expiration date. The Prokop homily about shared goals had not transmuted easily into program agreements.

The new arrangement we finally hammered out continued the Gautreaux Program for a year and a half, through December 1978, and increased target placements to 500. In addition, HUD would provide at least 500 more units by attaching a Gautreaux string to all hard unit funding in the Chicago area. The string—marketing arrangements on each project satisfactory to the council—would remain tied until we had received 500 hard units in addition to our 500 certificates. On FMRs HUD granted special increases of up to 20 percent for Cook and DuPage counties.

These agreements represented a substantial ratcheting up of HUD's commitment, yet we were plagued by doubts. Shouldn't we be getting more? Here we were, "victors" in a unanimous Supreme Court decision on behalf of tens of thousands of families, playing around with a relief program for only a thousand of them. Yet HUD's arguments for not doing more had some merit. Stronger "Gautreaux conditions" would risk deterring new construction and rehabilitation; black developers were already complaining about the dampening effect Gautreaux was having on new housing in black neighborhoods. Legitimate as were the concerns of the Gautreaux plaintiffs, HUD's funding obligations to the rest of the country had to be balanced against Gautreaux needs. As the federal government's expert housing agency, HUD was doing a responsible balancing job that a court should not second-guess. We believed that it would be a long shot to persuade Crowley—now the Gautreaux judge in the wake of Austin's death in February 1977—to do that second-guessing.

Nor were we clear what the second-guess should be. We and the

Leadership Council were still sailing uncharted seas. We had no surefire, magic-bullet way of providing instant relief for thousands of Gautreaux families. In the end, we decided to continue on the bargained terms rather than try to obtain something better in court. Subject to tinkering designed mostly to produce more apartments, the still hardly tested idea of the Gautreaux Program was becoming our primary litigation remedy.

4

Our decision did not mean clear sailing. By March 1978 I was writing Prokop and Norton "out of frustration." In a number of ways, laid out in no fewer than nine numbered paragraphs, I said HUD was part of the problem, not the solution. A "drastic change" in HUD's attitude was required. Yet kicking over the traces and trying for something fundamentally different would have meant exchanging complete uncertainty for arrangements that were in fact providing some relief. We negotiated further extensions with HUD through 1979 and into 1980. By October 31, 1979, exactly three years after the first Gautreaux family had moved, the Leadership Council reported 611 "placements."

Meanwhile, two reports were written about these early Gautreaux Program years. With Ford Foundation funds the Leadership Council hired Rubinowitz for a study that focused mostly on the council's procedures and the FMR and landlord and tenant participation problems. Rubinowitz reported that of some 270 families whose files he had reviewed, a considerable number had experienced difficulties of one sort or another, including high utility bills, unexpected school fees, local physicians declining to accept Medicaid cards, and inadequate public transportation. He concluded, however, that most participating landlords were "pleased" with their Gautreaux tenants, and that the moves "seem to have been generally successful."

In October 1979 HUD released a study of its own, based on interviews with 330 families. HUD's overall conclusion was:

> Most Gautreaux families were satisfied with their move and felt the quality of their life had improved . . . Two-thirds of them said they wanted to remain in the suburbs . . . Poor public transportation . . . was the main

reason given for wanting to move by one-third who preferred to live in the city.

Our 1977 negotiations with HUD had also begun to include conversations about "ultimate disposition" of the litigation. From the moment of the Supreme Court's ruling in April 1976, HUD's concern had been how to make precise its open-ended obligation to Gautreaux families. Like investors, public agencies abhor uncertainty. HUD wanted a court order— a "consent decree"—that would give it certainty and a terminal date.

The process was tortuous. As late as the fall of 1980 it was unclear whether we would reach accord. Apart from endless telephone conversations and countless written drafts, Gottlieb (who was helping me in the negotiations) and I, as well as HUD's team—Jane McGrew had now replaced Ruth Prokop as HUD's general counsel—shuttled back and forth between Washington and Chicago for a number of "crucial" meetings. At the end of November we finally did agree and advised Crowley, who would have to approve our proposal.

Ronald Reagan's November 1980 election was the precipitating factor. With Reagan's victory we knew that McGrew would be replaced by someone totally new to Gautreaux. We also feared that trying to craft Gautreaux relief would be problematic under the conservative Republican administration soon to take over HUD. With a large "investment" in our negotiations and a strong desire to gain for HUD the certainty that a consent decree would provide, McGrew was likewise eager for closure.

(We were dead right about the anticipated Reagan atmosphere. A few Carter administration programs designed to promote "regionalism" in housing were promptly dismantled by the Reagan people as wasteful social engineering. Why "social engineering" became an epithet in a country that had settled the frontier with land grants, fought the Great Depression with social security and unemployment benefits, and fostered post–World War II suburbia with FHA mortgage insurance, is something of a mystery.)

In addition to continuing the flow of Section 8 certificates and funding to the Leadership Council, HUD agreed to give the Chicago area enough extra Section 8 project-based funding to pay for 350 new units each year. It would also require developers to set aside 6 to 12 percent of each project's units for Gautreaux families (the precise number to be arranged with the council). These provisions would remain in effect until 7,100 "occupancies" had been provided to Gautreaux families, counting from the date Crowley approved the consent decree. When the 7,100 figure was reached our lawsuit against HUD, and HUD's obligations to Gautreaux families, would end. Finally, there were detailed provisions about such matters as how to handle disagreements, requiring a minimum percentage of larger apartments in new developments, and creating a revolving fund of $3 million to help finance new Section 8 developments.

Some of these agreements were easily arrived at while others were hasty, postelection compromises. The basic idea of continuing the Gautreaux Program was in the former category (but the most we could get on FMRs was HUD's agreement to review them in consultation with the Leadership Council), and so was extra funding for hard unit development, although the 350 units per year figure was the subject of considerable haggling. The 7,100 occupancies figure—an arbitrary, compromise number—was virtually the last item to be buttoned down. Coupled with previous CHA (scattered-site and tenant-based Section 8) and HUD and IHDA program placements, it meant that we were settling for a "relief" figure of about one-fifth the number of our Gautreaux families (8,000 as against 40,000).

If Carter had been reelected, the bargaining would have continued longer. As it was, both sides felt a compulsion to "wrap up." On December 18, 1980, barely a month after the election, Crowley reviewed our proposed decree and set a "fairness hearing" for January 14, 1981. Notices were mailed to the thousands of Gautreaux families, and the hearing was held on several days in January and February. The strongest objector was the IHDA, which felt that the required "set-asides" of apartments for Gautreaux families and restrictions on the size and location of Section 8 projects were unwise and beyond HUD's authority. Several Chicago neighborhood groups also objected because they feared a new "revitalizing area" concept, appearing for the first time in the consent decree, threatened their fragile neighborhoods. At HUD's insistence, because of the intense pressure to allow more development in black neighborhoods, revitalizing areas permitted new Section 8 housing to be developed in selected black neighborhoods if sufficient redevelopment were taking place to permit a forecast of community "revitalization." Selection of the designated areas was itself a subject of hard bargaining.

In a packed courtroom the fairness hearing was surprisingly intense. Then Crowley didn't rule for almost four months. Finally, on June 16, 1981, he issued an opinion endorsing the consent decree. The IHDA and the neighborhood groups appealed, but the consent decree was upheld by a unanimous panel of the court of appeals on September 30, 1982. At that point the framework was in place for the remainder of the Section 8 relief in the HUD case and—some sixteen years after it had been filed— for eventually ending our suit against HUD.

Our acceptance of the revitalizing area concept was a reluctant concession to frustrated black developers, strongly backed by HUD. The West Side district of Congresswoman Cardiss Collins, then head of the Congressional Black Caucus, included many black neighborhoods that badly needed housing and had plenty of vacant land "left over" from the riots of the 1960s. Collins had actually proposed a law to "exempt" project-based Section 8 from Gautreaux. When her legislative proposal foundered because HUD declined to support it (she had personally met with Carter in an unsuccessful effort to enlist HUD), Collins exerted more pressure by scheduling a committee hearing on "The Gautreaux Decision and Its Effect on Subsidized Housing."

Held in a federal building in Chicago's Loop on September 22, 1978, the all-day proceeding was marked by impassioned rhetoric. Two black developers testified that Gautreaux was having a "devastating" effect on black neighborhoods desperately in need of new housing. Worse, Gautreaux was "insidious," and had become an "inverted restrictive covenant, strangling the mortal remains of a large segment of black Chicago neighborhoods." Neighborhood residents testified about how badly they needed new housing. HUD's local director provided data on the dearth of production in white neighborhoods, and the IHDA filed a statement attacking the Gautreaux orders.

There were defenders, too. John McDermott, a Freedom Movement representative at the Summit Meeting a dozen years earlier, now editor and publisher of a journal on race relations, testified that the political establishment in Chicago, not Gautreaux, was the villain.

The public housing policy of this city with its vast highrise projects has been a social disaster . . . We must not allow the same mistake to be made with the use of the Section 8 program.

Michael Meyers, assistant director of the NAACP, filed a strong statement:

The Gautreaux principle promises to give the black and the poor a chance to move outside the confines of the ghetto, and seek a status equal to that of whites . . . *Gautreaux* recognizes that the effect of gilding the ghetto is to deprive blacks of favorable, equal opportunities in housing.

At the end of a long day (the hearing began before 10 A.M. and didn't end until 7 P.M.), I got in my licks:

White neighborhoods don't want housing for the poor because many of the poor are black, and the political establishment acquiesces in this rejection and transforms private prejudice into public policy . . . There are really only two choices. One is to knuckle under . . . [and] permit all or nearly all subsidized and assisted housing to go into minority neighborhoods . . . The other course of action is . . . to join together to force . . . the city and CHA, and, I would add, the Department of Housing and Urban Development, to provide subsidized and assisted housing in white as well as black neighborhoods.

In what was supposed to be a dramatic gesture, I reported that we had filed a motion that afternoon to require HUD to impose conditions on Chicago's pending application for $112 million of community development block grant funding. The conditions would require "specific and enforceable steps" by the city to provide housing in white neighborhoods. (The city did not attend the hearing, and as a good Democrat Collins had not insisted.) The idea was that the city was receiving millions of community development dollars under a law that conditioned its right to those funds on progress in subsidized housing. HUD, which held the purse strings, should be required to see to it that there really was progress.

The Collins hearing produced no legislation but neither did our motion produce "specific and enforceable steps." In a huge expenditure of time and energy that rivaled the Jurco hearings for frustration, we spent four years trying to get HUD to prod the city into using its block grant money and power to foster subsidized housing development in white neighborhoods. First, after six months of courtroom warfare, Crowley denied our motion. In October 1979, after another six months, we persuaded him to change his mind, but it took almost another year, until September 1980, before we were able to get an order directing HUD to impose the conditions.

The order we finally secured from a reluctant Crowley—over the tenacious objections of both the city and HUD—was hardly earthshaking. It merely imposed oversight and reporting obligations on HUD with respect to steps the city was supposed to take to help Section 8 developers in white neighborhoods. HUD eventually concluded that the city was doing all right because the shortfalls in achieving its housing goals were due to factors beyond the city's control, primarily developer financing difficulties in a period of high inflation. In June 1982 Aspen concluded that the block grant conditions had resulted in "some tangible benefit."

Probably they had. HUD's mandated, detailed, project-by-project reports, with the implicit threat of losing future block grant money, perhaps helped bring to completion several hundred more hard Section 8 units in white neighborhoods than would otherwise have been the case. But now the Reagan administration was terminating any new Section 8 project-based funding. The stream had been "reduced to a mere trickle," Aspen said in one of his opinions in our largely unsuccessful effort to get HUD to give some financing relief to developers. Not unreasonably, he said we were stuck with our consent decree and had no right to receive more. Fortunately the decree provided that if the Section 8 project-based program dried up, our funding for 350 units each year could be shifted to other uses.

The net effect of all this activity was that hard, project-based Section 8 units never played the major role in housing Gautreaux families we had hoped they would. The principal source of Gautreaux relief continued to be the landlords whom the Leadership Council's tenant-based program—now directed by Mary Davis, Zuba having moved on—could persuade to participate.

5

It took an unexpectedly long seventeen years from Crowley's approval of the consent decree until the Gautreaux Program ended in 1998 when we reached the 7,100 figure. Yet the "stretch-out" had a benefit—it gave the Leadership Council ample time to fine-tune the program. The first of two notable changes began late Sunday evening, January 22, 1984, when about fifty people camped for the night in the corridor next to the council's offices on the twenty-first floor of a Chicago Loop building. About 4 A.M. the next morning a crowd began to gather on the sidewalk outside. The reason was that January 23 had been designated as registration day for the Gautreaux Program.

In the beginning, registration had been offered only to families on CHA-supplied lists. Later, other families who heard about the program and came to the council office were also permitted to apply. Eventually, the council selected a "Registration Day" in August 1983, when any eligible family could apply. Throughout the designated day families appeared in an orderly procession; no more than thirty or so were in the council offices at any one time. The process worked so well that Williams and Davis decided to repeat it at six-month intervals and chose Monday, January 23, 1984, as the second registration day. Under the new procedure, applications would be accepted only on registration days.

By the time the council's staff arrived for work early on January 23, the throng on the sidewalk numbered several thousand and had spilled into the street. Buses had to be rerouted. Mounted police had trouble keeping order. Davis and her harried crew tried to pass out application forms as rapidly as they could, but the police soon decided that the milling crowd was a danger and had to be dispersed. Using a bullhorn, Davis and her staff announced that the registration was canceled, but skeptical applicants refused to leave. Eventually the staff had to print and pass out cancellation notices. Even so, it was 1 P.M. before the last of the crowd would go.

Regrouping, the council decided to try a different system. A bank of phones would be installed in the council's offices. After public notice, the phones would be turned on for two days and calls would be received until the number of registrations desired for that year was reached. (The "ceiling" number was dictated by the council's inventory of certificates and the size of its staff.) On Wednesday, February 16, 1984, some twenty-five council telephones, all connected to a special number and staffed by volunteers with pencils and registration forms at the ready, began ringing at 9 A.M. At 1:40 P.M. about half the 1,750 calls the council had expected to receive over two days had already been accepted. Davis and Williams decided to turn off the phones so that those who had intended to call on Thursday would have a chance. The telephone company later reported that thousands of Gautreaux calls had jammed its equipment and for a time threatened to disrupt service for the entire city.

Gautreaux Program registration had suddenly become so popular, Davis explained, because the public housing grapevine was such an effective communication system. Over the preceding seven years Gautreaux families who had successfully relocated were regularly visited by relatives and friends. Many liked what they saw, submitted applications themselves, and told others. As the number of Gautreaux Program moves grew, so did the number of visitors and the number of "grapevine transmissions." By the time the council decided to limit registration to two days each year, demand far exceeded the number of annual registrations the council would accept. The stage had unknowingly been set for the "State Street fiasco."

The telephone "lottery" (so called because chance determined which incoming calls made it through the busy signals) became a fixture of the council's registration. In succeeding years it was generally held around Martin Luther King's birthday each January. Through the last registration in 1996, the lottery never failed to produce the 2,000 or so new registrants with which the council began each program year. Usually the phones were as busy as they had been in 1984. Because of circuit jams in dense public housing portions of the city, some callers began traveling elsewhere—even to the suburbs—to make their calls. That was a big change from the early days when only forty-six families responded to the first Zuba-Hendrix mailing.

Occasionally I served as a phone volunteer. One year I took a call about 11:30 A.M. that began with two solid minutes of laughter. When the caller was finally able to control her voice, she apologized. "I'm laughing for joy," she explained. "I've been dialing since eight this morning and I can't believe I finally got through."

The second notable change in the council's procedures had to do with finding apartments. From the beginning families had been encouraged to search for themselves, but most units came from Messer and her successors. Then Davis noticed that more families were actually finding units and presenting themselves—successfully—to landlords whose vacant apartments they had located on their own. From the stories she was hearing Davis sensed that some landlords were more willing to take a chance on personal contact with a human being than on the abstraction of a program.

A "tough love" and "you can do it" spirit began to characterize council briefings. The usual information about housekeeping, credit, and suburban services was still provided. But now the counselors added pep talks on self-esteem and more detailed information on housing search strategies and how families could present themselves favorably to landlords. Women who had already moved came to the briefing sessions to tell their stories. More explanation of the Section 8 program was offered so families could become knowledgeable "consumers," able to discuss program features with prospective landlords. Instead of deferring families for credit and housekeeping reasons, the counselors explained the expectations of landlords and offered referrals to agencies for help. Addresses of available units were still supplied, but there were not enough for all families conducting simultaneous searches.

The new strategy worked. By the early '90s many more apartments were being identified by the families themselves than by the council. In the single month of November 1992, when seventy Gautreaux families moved, sixty-eight of the apartments were located by the families themselves. "Empowerment" of families—to find available apartments and persuade landlords to rent to them—had become an important feature of the Gautreaux Program.

Another "longevity benefit" was that more subsidized housing funds were given to the Chicago area than would have been the case had the Gautreaux Program reached its goal sooner. By the time 7,100 occupancies were achieved in 1998, the 350-unit annual "set-asides" amounted to almost $40 million a year. The aggregate for the seventeen years was many hundreds of millions of dollars.

Of perhaps greatest importance, the longevity of the Gautreaux Program gave "housing mobility" a visible place on the housing policy landscape for over two decades. In 1987 Congress made Section 8 certificates "portable" across housing authority jurisdictional lines. In 1991, Congress authorized a ten-year, five-city housing mobility demonstration program to further explore the Gautreaux approach. In 1994 and 1998 conferences on housing mobility were held in Washington. By the time of the second conference some fifty-two mobility programs were operating around the country. About a dozen grew out of settlements of Gautreaux-type lawsuits against HUD, some were HUD programs that gave incentives to housing authorities to cooperate in regional Gautreaux-type arrangements, and a few were voluntary initiatives.

Ironically, however, housing mobility was orphaned in the city of its birth. In 1997 we asked Aspen to order the CHA to provide relief to Gautreaux families through Section 8. With scattered sites winding down, and with the Gautreaux Program soon to end as we reached 7,100 occupancies, our two streams of Gautreaux relief were about to run dry. The right thing to do, we argued, would be to continue the remedial flow with Section 8.

Aspen denied our motion. In an August 1997 opinion, he wrote that he would have to explore the link between persisting public housing segregation and the CHA's original wrongdoing before he could do what we asked, including taking a look at the CHA's remedial efforts, past, present, and even future. He also threw in "demographic shifts over the years" as part of the required exploration. He seemed to be saying that if the CHA couldn't do much to provide more scattered sites in white neighborhoods—because, for example, little developable land remained in predominantly white neighborhoods—that would be reason enough for barring Section 8 relief.

The opinion befuddled us. With thousands of Gautreaux families still living in segregated public housing, and the CHA possessed of a means—Section 8—for offering them relief (even though in a different form than scattered sites), didn't desegregation cases require the wrongdoer to use all available means to remedy its still persisting wrong?

We thought so, and got ready to try to walk through the door Aspen had left ajar by implying that further evidence—the "exploration"—might get us what we needed. Then the CHA asked us to negotiate before filing a new motion and—perhaps unwisely—we agreed. Interminable discussions followed, after which the CHA did enter into a contract with the Leadership Council for a small, two-year "Gautreaux II" Program, later somewhat enlarged and extended for another two years. It was not the comprehensive program we might have achieved had we filed a new motion and won. But given Aspen's unencouraging opinion, and the reality (which probably explained it) that the conservative Supreme Court was steadily undermining the earlier school desegregation decisions most helpful to us, we decided to accept the partial loaf.

The Gautreaux numbers themselves could be viewed as a glass half full or half empty. The glass was half full if the number of families assisted—about 6,500 in the Gautreaux Program, another 1,500 in IHDA developments—is multiplied by the average number of persons in a household (conservatively, three). This produces nearly 25,000 assisted persons, a nonnegligible number even though it took over two decades to get there. The glass was half empty if the 8,000 assisted families are compared with the initial 40,000 families in the Gautreaux class, although no one knows how many eligible families would have wanted to enter the programs and been able to succeed if all had been offered the opportunity.

I am reminded, however, of the adage that although some see the glass as half full, others as half empty, the glass may be the wrong size. We will never know what the results would have been had we done battle before Austin in 1976, or before Crowley in 1977 or 1980, instead of signing agreements with Elliott, Prokop, and McGrew.

My feelings fluctuated between pleasure, even pride, at what we had accomplished, and disappointment that we had not done much more, particularly in light of our failure—next to be discussed—to "go national" with the Gautreaux Program. I rank our housing mobility relief higher than our scattered-site program, but still not more than a six or seven on my ten-point scale.

6

The numbers do not reveal what effect their new homes and neighborhoods were having on the lives of Gautreaux families. As to that, neither the Rubinowitz nor HUD assessments claimed social science rigor, which demands that for a study to be taken seriously "selection bias" must be eliminated. If a family does well in its new neighborhood, the good results may be due as much to the family's motivation and personal characteristics as to its new location. The social science solution is to randomly assign two groups of families to new housing, an "experimental" group to better neighborhoods, defined, for example, by a low poverty rate, and a "control" group to high-poverty neighborhoods. This, social scientists believe, will enable them to separate neighborhood effects from family characteristics.

In 1982 sociologist James Rosenbaum, Rubinowitz's colleague at Northwestern University, joined initially by Rubinowitz, began studying the experiences of Gautreaux Program families. Rosenbaum knew he didn't have true "experimental" and "control" groups. But he believed he had an approximation. Before the Leadership Council began its motivational counseling, Gautreaux families had been offered the next unit from the council's supply, and virtually all had accepted their "assigned" units, whether in the city or the suburbs. This could be viewed as a kind of random assignment that created approximations of experimental and control groups.

There were still problems, Rosenbaum acknowledged. His sample sizes were small. In one study, for example, 114 families were interviewed in 1982. In follow-up interviews seven years later, Rosenbaum found himself down to 68 of the original 114.

Nor could Gautreaux families be viewed as representative of public housing residents generally, let alone the black inner-city population. The Leadership Council had screened out families with serious housekeeping and credit problems, and had virtually no units at all for families with five or more children. Only families with enough motivation to apply even entered the Gautreaux Program, and only about 20 percent of entrants actually moved.

On the other hand, Rosenbaum's statistics showed that the "suburban movers" and "city movers" had similar characteristics—income, employment, schooling, family composition, and so on. The big difference between the two groups was not in family characteristics but in the places to which they had moved. Surburban locations were mostly very low poverty, predominantly white, and far from high-poverty areas. City locations had higher poverty and black populations, and were much closer to high-poverty areas. Relying on his view that the council's assignment procedure gave him reasonably comparable groups, Rosenbaum used questionnaires, interviews, and some information from schools and welfare agencies to examine the experiences of suburban-moving and city-moving Gautreaux families.

The results were not only positive but in some respects spectacularly so, especially for children. A Rosenbaum study released in 1991 showed that the children of suburban movers were four times more likely than those of city movers to finish high school. Suburban movers' children were also twice as likely to attend college (54 percent versus 21 percent) and, for those who did not attend college, far more likely to find jobs (75 percent versus 41 percent). And mothers were more likely to be employed—50 percent more likely among those who had never had jobs before their moves. A social scientist in the audience at a University of Chicago presentation said that if, by moving to suburbia, poor, inner-city families could achieve the life-enhancing results Rosenbaum was reporting, then policymakers should drop all other initiatives and concentrate on Gautreaux-style programs.

Rosenbaum was "happily surprised" by his high school results. One of his earlier studies had shown that suburban movers' children were struggling to meet academic standards, and that 20 percent of them, compared with only 7 percent in city schools, had been put in special education classes. Yet by 1989 high school grades were virtually the same for both groups, implying greater achievement for suburban movers because of the higher standards they had to meet. "They had a lot of catching up to do," Rosenbaum said. "But they did it."

In their book, published in 2000, *Crossing the Class and Color Lines*, Rosenbaum and Rubinowitz summarized their studies. The most "striking and unexpected" finding was that families who moved to the suburbs were no less socially integrated than those who moved within the city. Although there were some serious incidents of racial harassment, they did not compare to city dangers. Of her own son one suburban mother said, "He would be on drugs, dead or in a gang." Moreover, the harassment incidents declined over time, and "the real story was the quiet general acceptance by the larger community." Compared with city movers, suburban movers were more likely to be "(1) in high school, (2) in a college track, (3) in a four-year college, (4) in a job, (5) in a job with benefits, and (6) not outside of the education and employment systems." Their studies showed, Rosenbaum and Rubinowitz concluded, that when poor black families were enabled to cross society's class and color lines, they were "capable of handling the difficulties that arise, and they experience many benefits from these moves."

One consequence of Rosenbaum's work, published in various journals, was to kindle public interest. Numerous stories, some in considerable detail, described the experiences of "successful" Gautreaux families. They appeared not only in Chicago newspapers and magazines but across the country. In 1992 *Newsweek* called the Rosenbaum figures "stunning," and the Gautreaux Program a simple idea "that renews one's faith in the struggle." In 1993 the *New York Times* ran a front-page article calling the Gautreaux Program a "modest variation on the Underground Railroad," and said it had reached "a kind of legendary stature." In 1995 the Gautreaux story jumped the Atlantic—Rosenbaum's figures on children's experiences in high school, college, and employment received a full page in the *Economist*.

There were even national television treatments—*60 Minutes, Good Morning America, The Phil Donahue Show,* and CNN's *Democracy in America,* among others. All were favorable. In 1992 Nat Hentoff, writing in the *Washington Post* about the CNN show, said the Gautreaux Program was "actual evidence that American Apartheid can be broken through." Instead of its usual exposé approach, *60 Minutes* provided virtually unadulterated praise in its Gautreaux segment, "Alice Doesn't Live Here Anymore," aired on December 19, 1993.

The "Here" of the title was a CHA project where, as interviewer Morley Safer puts it, "streets are paved with broken glass and drugs are as certain as death and taxes." The "Alice" was Alice Jackson, twenty-five, a black single mother who had been pregnant at fifteen, again at sixteen, and dropped out of school and into welfare. "You could see the rainbow, that just may be it," Jackson says of her move a few months earlier to a mostly white suburb. Safer describes Jackson's boys as "two project kids in a sea of towheads" who have their work cut out for them because suburban schools are way ahead. But, he goes on, if they catch up, and the statistics show they will, "they'll graduate from high school and probably go to college. They'll get better jobs and better benefits than their friends downtown. It will not be a perfect world, but it will be a world of choices."

The camera then shifts to Arletta Bronaugh, a Gautreaux mother who had moved in 1986, seven years before Jackson. A divorced mother on welfare, Bronaugh had found a job and was off welfare within a year. Her son Jason, eleven, an honor student, is interviewed by Safer who asks the traditional question, "What do you want to be when you grow up?" Sitting at a picnic table in a park, Jason hesitates thoughtfully before answering, "I really haven't made up my mind . . . construction worker, architect, anesthesiologist," pronouncing the last word perfectly. "Anesthesiologist," Safer repeats. "Mm-mm," says Jason, continuing his thoughtful demeanor.

The camera turns to Valencia Morris, a Gautreaux mother who had moved with her three daughters to Woodridge sixteen years earlier. All three girls excelled, Safer says, taking part in everything from cheerleading to debating to overseas exchanges, while their mother went back to school, got a nursing degree, and got off welfare. A few months earlier the Morris family had moved back to Chicago, to the integrated, middle-class neighborhood of Hyde Park, near the University of Chicago. "For the first time in her life," Safer says, "Kiah [the youngest Morris daughter] is going to a school not as a minority." She didn't fit, Kiah says. "I had white friends, but I wasn't really accepted by them . . . And then the black kids, they basically ignored me . . . I never really got a connection." Valencia Morris says she moved back to the city "with hopes that [Kiah] would find some relationship that she would feel comfortable with."

Safer asks, "Would you three ever live in a pretty much all-white suburb again?" Clara, the eldest sister, answers, "If that's where our opportunities were, yes." Safer asks, "Are you glad your mother did what she did?" Kiah says yes, and the middle sister, Jamillah, chimes in, "Oh yes. Yes. Because, you know, now we have a choice . . . we can choose, because we know." Safer asks a last question: "Has this opportunity meant the end of poverty for this family?" Valencia Morris answers, "Yes, it has meant the end of poverty."

Accompanying the Morris interviews is some footage with Dr. Bill Sampson, a black sociologist at Northwestern University, described by Safer as a critic of the Gautreaux Program. "That's assimilation," says Sampson. "I have to be just like you in order to function in this society . . . value the same music, wear the same clothes . . ." Safer asks what is the worst thing that a Gautreaux family faces when it moves. Sampson answers, "I think disruption from and potentially alienation from—from community and maybe self." When Safer refers to the melting pot Sampson says, "I'm against that." Safer says, "It's happened not just to blacks, but to Poles and Jews and Germans." Sampson replies, "It hasn't happened to blacks. It will not happen to blacks."

Dennis Byrne, a *Sun-Times* columnist, interviewed Sampson after his *60 Minutes* appearance. He concluded that Sampson's "giving up our blackness" meant adopting middle-class values. The values Byrne referred to related particularly to children—"to motivate and discipline" them, to provide material necessities "so that your children have a chance to better themselves." Byrne wrote that he couldn't accept the "nonsense" that middle-class values such as these were unknown to blacks. "Or that when you enrich your lives with these values, you somehow compromise your race."

In a series of articles Rosenbaum set out to explore why Gautreaux suburban movers were experiencing such positive results. He focused on "efficacy," a term social scientists use to refer to a person's sense of her or his ability to control what happens to them. One school of thought contended that efficacy was a relatively persistent, personal characteristic, formed early and unlikely to be much changed in later life. Books and articles about the so-called culture of poverty illustrated this view. Children are thought to absorb culture early in their socialization and carry it with them thereafter. For children raised in a culture of poverty, the fatalism prevalent in their poverty environments would be like an injection of low efficacy that would remain in their bloodstreams throughout later life, even in changed environments.

Others argued that environment not only influenced opportunities but might even, as one article said, "modify the innate and acquired characteristics of participants . . . [and their] ability to plan and sacrifice for the future."

Thus, Rosenbaum wrote, we have two opposing models:

> The culture of poverty model implies that low-income individuals who acquired a low sense of efficacy will retain it, regardless of subsequent events, while the geography of opportunity model implies that they will not retain it if they subsequently move to a place which offers more opportunities.

Rosenbaum began to explore which model better fit the experiences of Gautreaux families.

In one article, based on a survey of 655 Gautreaux participants, Rosenbaum found a "significant relationship" between neighborhood placement and the participants' later sense of efficacy. Then, through interviews with about 100 mothers and children, he explored *why* suburban movers reported a heightened sense of efficacy after their moves.

The explanations didn't sound like rocket science. For many, the housing projects had been virtual prisons. One suburban mover (a rare father among those interviewed) referred to his former Robert Taylor home as a "concentration camp." The interviews generally described a society in which gangs ruled, police were unresponsive, drugs and violence were endemic, retribution for opposition swift and sure. Residents felt unsafe, constantly threatened, "nervous and worried all the time," as one mother said. What we have learned about the psychology of Nazi concentration camp inmates is relevant in understanding the belief of public housing project families that they were not and could not be in control of their circumstances, that efforts to bring about change had no chance of success and would lead to certain and dire consequences.

By contrast, Rosenbaum wrote, the suburbs represented freedom. "Individuals reported that their attitudes changed as a direct result of experiences in their new neighborhood environments." What were those experiences? Rosenbaum asked, and received a variety of answers:

A new address. "Because they don't usually like to give you credit when you live in public housing."

Jobs. "Well, it [moving to a suburb] opened up quite a few opportunities for me and my children, too, because they were able to get jobs . . ."

Middle-class know-how. "[My son's friends were] into talking about college, not gangbangers . . . [My daughter is] the first person in my entire family that graduated from college, so I think it was the influence of kids . . . wanting a future . . . and knowing how to make it happen."

Manageable challenges. "Unlike the projects [Rosenbaum wrote], where participants did not call the police to report crimes because the police would not respond and because gangs would retaliate, in the suburbs, many participants did contact authorities and the police did respond."

It was only a small survey, not a scientific experiment, yet the conclusion had the ring of common sense about it. His cases illustrated, Rosenbaum wrote, how "a change in a person's life situation can alter what was once thought to be an inherent, unwavering individual characteristic."

In a later article, based on interviews with about 150 Gautreaux mothers (a "modest preliminary investigation"), Rosenbaum explored further. Simply moving to an affluent neighborhood, he wrote, was not a sufficient explanation of what was happening. Affluence would not necessarily benefit all residents.

> A superior public library, theater, summer camp, YMCA may charge entry fees and be unavailable by public transportation. If a camp or other activity has a limited number of positions, admission may be limited to people whose social networks provide early notification, or to people who have connections. Although a strong labor market means that jobs are available, employment is only possible for workers with the right skills and for those who have access to good child care and transportation.

Rosenbaum referred to another concept some social scientists called "social capital"—the accepted standards of conduct, and the people, institutions, and information channels upon which residents of a community can draw to help solve problems in their own lives. In this view, social capital gave people capabilities they would not have had in other social situations.

Social capital helped Rosenbaum understand what his 150 Gautreaux mothers were saying. Suburban standards of conduct, strange and constraining at first, turned out to be a form of protection leading to freedom. Suburbia's relative intolerance for drugs, gangs, and disruptive behavior gave rise to a liberating feeling of safety.

> In the summer, most of the families in the complex look out for each other. In my old neighborhood in the city, I would run from the front door to back door, fearful about my kids' safety . . . but not here.

Neighbors cared about each other.

> You can leave and rest assured that someone will watch your house. You can swap keys and neighbors will take care of your house.

"Many participants now feel," Rosenbaum wrote, "that their neighbors and police are watching out *for* them, not against them." He went on to describe numerous instances of mutual help (babysitting, assistance with cars, and so on) that "permitted Gautreaux mothers and children to have capabilities that they would not have had otherwise." A later Rosenbaum study showed that, fourteen years (on average) after their initial moves, some two-thirds of Gautreaux suburban movers were still living in suburbia.

Skeptics continued to point to the limitations of Rosenbaum's studies, and some of his later work was openly speculative and anecdotal. An article reviewing the "neighborhood effects" literature concluded that empirical research generally confirmed that "neighborhood environment has an influence on important outcomes for children and adults." But, it went on, neighborhood effects were usually much smaller than the effects of family characteristics such as income and educational attainment. Some studies had found "no independent neighborhood effects."

Yet the controversy over neighborhood effects seemed counterintuitive. A poll informs us that nearly three-quarters of Americans believe that a good neighborhood is more important than a good house. For most American ethnic and racial groups, says *American Apartheid,* a widely respected book on residential segregation, socioeconomic mobility is a cumulative process: economic advancement (a better job) is translated into residential progress (a neighborhood with better schools and services, social contacts, and so forth), which in turn leads to additional socioeconomic gains (children get better education and jobs).

One might expect that a journey along America's normal avenue to socioeconomic advancement would be especially important for children enabled, in their formative years, to escape neighborhoods where gangs rule and drugs and violence are the norm. It is impossible to believe that whether or not a child is raised in such an environment will make no difference in later life. Studs Terkel once interviewed a ten-year-old girl skipping rope outside Robert Taylor Homes. When Terkel asked her the same question Morley Safer had asked Jason Bronaugh, he received a quite different answer: "I might not live to be grown up. My life wasn't promised to me."

One might also expect that the journey would work for the poor as well as for the nonpoor. Indeed, the history of most American immigrant groups, begun in poverty, is precisely one of such a journey. In fact, most poor *white* Americans do live in nonpoor neighborhoods. A central theme of *American Apartheid* is that residential discrimination bars most blacks from taking the entry ramp to America's normal avenue of socio-economic advancement.

The other side of the socioeconomic mobility coin is what William Julius Wilson calls the "concentration effects" of concentrated poverty. (Beginning in the 1980s, Wilson's books and articles made the study of urban poverty respectable again after a long hiatus following Daniel Patrick Moynihan's famous "benign neglect" memorandum in the 1960s.) Based upon extensive research in poverty neighborhoods, Wilson emphasized that in a neighborhood without working- and middle-class residents, children seldom interacted on a sustained basis with people who were employed or with families that included steady breadwinners. This lack of contact adversely affected the development of job-related skills, and even school experiences. "Teachers become frustrated and do not teach and children do not learn. A vicious cycle is perpetuated through the family, through the community, and through the schools." Sustaining basic institutions becomes difficult. "And as the basic institutions declined," Wilson wrote, "the social organization of inner-city neighborhoods (including . . . explicit norms and sanctions against aberrant behavior) likewise declined."

Sociology professor Mary Pattillo-McCoy, one of Rosenbaum's colleagues at Northwestern, argued that the "long reach of the ghetto" extends into black middle-class neighborhoods. Author of a thoughtful book on the black middle class, *Black Picket Fences,* Pattillo-McCoy also wrote an article discussing large disparities in school test scores between middle-class black and white students. Pattillo-McCoy contended that an important part of the explanation was that over the years the black students had had higher percentages of classmates from nearby, low-performing ghetto schools than had the whites. She referred to a study showing that nearly four out of five black middle-class Chicago households (compared to only 36 percent of white middle-class households) lived within four blocks of census tracts where a third or more of the population was poor. The proximity meant, Pattillo-McCoy explained, that youth in black middle-class neighborhoods had not been distanced as had white middle-class youth from the concentrated poverty of the ghettos. The title of Pattillo-McCoy's article was "It's the Neighborhoods, Silly."

The neighborhood effects debate persisted. But against the background of analyses by Wilson and other scholars of the harm concentrated poverty neighborhoods wreaked upon their residents, Rosenbaum's later articles seemed to offer an understandable explanation for why Gautreaux families, who had moved out of such neighborhoods, were experiencing significant life changes for the better.

7

Beyond generating public interest, Rosenbaum's work caused policymakers to take note. In fact, they led directly to a demonstration program that became one of the largest research efforts ever undertaken by HUD.

On February 8, 1989, the *New York Times* ran a four-column story about the secretary of HUD under newly elected President George Bush—former pro football star and congressman Jack F. Kemp. The new secretary intended, he said, to push for "bold, radical and experimental programs" in the fight against inner-city problems. This, I thought, was a virtual invitation to try to move the Gautreaux Program to the national stage.

I wrote to Kemp, telling him I had a suggestion for him, even though it was no longer experimental, and perhaps no longer bold or radical either. But, I said, according to studies by Northwestern University and HUD itself, it had the great virtue of demonstrated workability. It was also, at a one-time cost per family of under $1,500, cost-effective. "Compared to the societal costs of the alternative for these families (remaining in their—frequently pathological—environments), this may be one of the biggest bargains around."

With my letter I enclosed a *New York Times* story of February 3 about the Gautreaux Program, "Some Chicagoans Are Moved out of Projects into a Future," and a *Times* editorial of the previous November, "Chicago's Housing Pioneers." The editorial compared Gautreaux families to the pioneers "who climbed aboard Conestoga wagons and settled the frontier." Though cautioning that not every ghetto family could benefit from such a program, the editorial concluded, "For those who can cross this frontier, the rewards for the next generation are great."

On March 10, an answering letter from an acting deputy assistant secretary said HUD agreed that "some of the successes of the Gautreaux Program can be attained in other cities," and encouraged all housing authorities to foster housing mobility under their Section 8 programs. I was also thanked for my suggestion "concerning this important issue."

I decided that cordiality was the right responsive tone. Cordially, I wrote that a key element of the Gautreaux Program was the funding of an agency to "outreach" to landlords and to screen, counsel, and escort families, and that experience in the regular Section 8 program had shown that without that key element, mobility prospects for many inner-city families were poor. I also said I would be interested to learn what specific steps the new administration was considering to achieve some of the Gautreaux Program successes in other cities.

Three weeks later another, shorter letter from my correspondent advised that regulations concerning the portability provisions of the 1987 law were soon to be issued. I was further informed,

> We have found that the existing opportunities for mobility amongst very low income families is [sic] sufficient. We see no need to create or support a "special council" or agency to further the efforts of mobility for very low income households.

Again I was thanked for my thoughts.

Striving to maintain my cordial tone, I wrote back that HUD's own 1979 Gautreaux study pointed to the program's success in enabling families to move out of heavily minority and high-poverty areas, and expressed doubt that families in regular Section 8 programs were really making such moves. I asked for HUD's data on that.

A long silence ensued. Then, after six months, I received a surprising answer. With unusual candor the letter acknowledged, "There does not seem to be any evidence of a pattern of movement from segregated to integrated census tracts." I was advised, however, that it was not HUD policy to sponsor race-specific counseling, although such counseling could be conducted through local agencies.

I jettisoned cordiality. My petulant reply questioned whether a re-assessment of HUD policy on race-specific counseling might be in order given that residential integration was viewed as one of the goals of the Fair Housing Act of 1968, which HUD was responsible for administering.

It was now clear, I thought, that my exchanges with Kemp's staff were going nowhere. Another letter to the boss could hardly worsen the al-ready dim prospects. Enclosing the aimless correspondence of the past ten months, I mailed Kemp two brief paragraphs:

> Earlier this year I heard Deputy Undersecretary Kenneth Blackwell say, "When we find things that work, we should see to it that HUD doesn't drop the ball."
>
> I think HUD is dropping the Gautreaux ball, as the enclosed corre-spondence indicates. May I talk to you about it? I'll call in a couple of days to see if that can be arranged. Thank you.

My call produced an inconclusive conversation with a "scheduling sec-retary," after which—was I now engaged in mindless perseverance?—I sent Kemp yet another letter. This one quoted a new Rosenbaum study calculated to have special appeal to Kemp because it dealt with his fa-vorite subject of employment. Rosenbaum's latest conclusion was that helping low-income black women move to areas with better employment prospects "greatly increases their ability to find work, even for people with no previous employment experience."

Silence ensued, but this time for only two months. Then came a let-ter from Assistant Secretary John C. Weicher, responding, he said, to my two most recent letters to Kemp, and suggesting that in the employment context HUD might be willing to encourage housing authorities to es-tablish Gautreaux-type counseling programs. (Had Rosenbaum's refer-ence to women getting jobs hit home with Kemp?) Three surprising sen-tences followed:

> Thomas Humbert, the Deputy Assistant Secretary for Policy Develop-ment, and Lawrence Goldberger, the Director of the Office of Elderly and Assisted Housing . . . would be pleased to meet with you to explore these issues further. We would be particularly interested in hearing your

ideas on the specific types of activities that should be included in such a counseling initiative . . . Please let us know if you are interested in having such a meeting.

Interested? I was amazed. Encouraging HUD to encourage housing authorities to replicate the Gautreaux Program was exactly what I had been seeking in a year of pointless letter writing. Now, when I least expected it, HUD was suddenly inviting me to "explore these issues further" and wanting to hear my ideas.

The upshot, however, was not exactly the dialogue I had hoped for. What happened—it was now June 1991—was a brief, standing-outside-his-office, somewhat peremptory conversation with a very busy Humbert, a young, fair-haired man who had not been with HUD very long. Humbert quickly made it clear than HUD would not "sponsor" race-specific counseling. Indeed, because HUD's budget for the forthcoming fiscal year (FY1992, running from October 1, 1991, to September 30, 1992) had already been prepared, it was too late for HUD to sponsor any type of Gautreaux initiative. However, if a Gautreaux-type demonstration program—based solely on poverty, not race—were to be developed under other auspices, HUD would not oppose it. That was as far as the department was willing or able to go. And it had been nice talking to me.

Concealing my disappointment, I honed in on the "concession," if one could call it that. For Humbert was talking about a demonstration program, not a new HUD policy, poverty rather than race, and about somebody else's legislative initiative. What, I asked Humbert, did "non-opposition" mean? If I were able to get legislation introduced (having not the faintest idea whether I could), would HUD really stick to a position of nonopposition? Or would there be subtle undermining? Humbert assured me that he had stated the departmental position. In fact, I could work on the legislation with Jill Khadduri of his office, to make certain the specifics would be acceptable to HUD. Admonishing myself to keep in mind the value of half loaves, I hunted up Khadduri, who said she would indeed work with me.

What happened over the next several weeks was like a syllabus page for a high school course in legislation. I called Robert Embry, a foundation executive in Baltimore, and explained what was going on. Embry had been at HUD in the Carter administration and was a Gautreaux supporter. He also knew Maryland senator Barbara Mikulski, head of the Senate committee that handled HUD appropriations. Embry soon called back. I should get my "proposal" into the hands of Kevin Kelly, an aide to Mikulski who ran the committee. There were no promises, but Kelly would see what could be done.

I called Kelly immediately. He told me he needed two pieces of paper—legislative language creating a demonstration program for insertion in an appropriations bill the committee was then considering, and "report language" for inclusion in the committee report that would explain why the demonstration was a good idea. He also told me that the demonstration should be operated in five cities by housing authorities using nonprofits for counseling, and gave me the eligibility criteria, designed, no doubt, so that Baltimore would qualify—cities with populations exceeding 400,000 in metropolitan areas with populations exceeding 1.5 million. Leave a blank, Kelly said, for the committee to fill in the amount of the appropriation. And do everything quickly, because the HUD appropriations bill was even then on its way through the committee.

I did some quick drafting with Khadduri—who made it clear that the proposal was to be short and sweet, leaving it to HUD to work out details. We soon got to Kelly what he needed—ten lines of legislative language and four paragraphs for the committee report. Together they described a five-city, metropolitan-wide demonstration program "designed to assist families with children to move out of areas with high concentrations of persons living in poverty." As Humbert had specified, it was a demonstration program only, and it had only a poverty, not a racial, criterion.

With the "hurry-up" part of the job completed, the "waiting" part naturally followed. For weeks I could learn nothing from Kelly. My phone messages elicited no response from him personally, and from people in his office only the unilluminating information that the appropriations bill was still under consideration by the committee.

September 26, 1991, found me in Washington for a conference. During the lunch hour I went to Kelly's office. He was out, so on his chair I left a handwritten plea for information. In Chicago the next morning my desk bore a note from a colleague about a phone message that had come in the night before: "Kevin Kelly from the Appropriations Committee called, $20 million is the amount, language you wanted is in."

I now understood that Kelly had been away from his office during the lunch hour on the previous day because the committee was finally meeting to pass the HUD appropriations bill. A month later, on October 28, 1991, the bill was signed into law by President Bush. And presto—we had congressional authority for a Gautreaux-type experiment in five metropolitan areas.

Kemp, or someone on his staff, had evidently become a believer in housing mobility. By coincidence I was in HUD's Washington building on the very day in January 1992 that HUD unveiled its proposed fiscal year 1993 budget. In the cafeteria I wrote a memorandum for Kale Williams and Jim Rosenbaum to give them the good news that a second year of demonstration program funding had been included—an additional $50 million for 1,500 more certificates, along with $1.5 million for housing counseling. Five pages of HUD's press package described Moving to Opportunity (MTO)—HUD's chosen name—in a glowing narrative. There truly was a glow because one page depicted Rosenbaum's figures on school dropouts, college attendance, and employment in a brilliant, multicolored bar chart. One sentence especially gladdened Rosenbaum's heart:

> Research findings on the Gautreaux Demonstration appear to demonstrate for the first time that living outside of an area of poverty by itself has positive effects for high risk families.

The following October HUD's proposed budget was enacted into law with MTO now fleshed out from the ten lines of the previous year's appropriations bill. Fifty million dollars was approved for fiscal year 1993, with the instruction that $52.1 million was to be added in fiscal year 1994. The population requirement for eligible cities was reduced to 350,000, which added seven cities to the pool of twenty-one eligible at the 400,000 level. The families to participate in the demonstration were to be very low-income public housing residents. (HUD had initially intended to use

Section 8 waiting lists, but I had no objection to public housing families.) Details aside, we now had $70 million plus some counseling money, with hope for more to come. It was time for HUD to get the MTO show on the road.

That, however, would be done by a different HUD. A week after HUD's budget was signed into law by President Bush, William Jefferson Clinton became president-elect. The new Democratic administration would be responsible for implementing MTO. Clinton's HUD secretary would be Henry Cisneros, a rising Hispanic star in the Democratic Party firmament. Cisneros had hardly been sworn in before he was saying that one of HUD's top priorities would be to attack the "extreme spatial segregation" by race, class, and income of American communities. And the people he put in charge of MTO, his chief of staff, Bruce Katz, and a deputy assistant secretary for research, Margery Turner, both strongly supported the MTO idea.

It took many months for HUD to develop the specifics. High-poverty areas were defined as census tracts with poverty populations of 40 percent or more, low-poverty areas those with less than 10 percent. Participating families would be divided into three groups. An "experimental" group would receive mobility counseling from a nonprofit organization and Section 8 certificates to move to low-poverty areas. A "regular Section 8" group would receive certificates too, but only "regular" housing authority counseling. Unlike the experimental group, they would not be required to move to low-poverty areas. The "control" group would receive no certificates and would remain in public housing.

Families who enrolled in the program would be volunteers and would be assigned randomly to one of the three groups. All families, whether they moved or not, agreed to be "tracked" for the ten-year life of the demonstration. They would be interviewed at start-up, after five years, and after ten years, about employment, income, children's schooling, housing and neighborhood conditions, attitudes about neighborhood and future prospects, and overall social well-being. The purpose was "to definitively measure the impacts of a change in neighborhood on the employment, income, educational achievement, and social well-being of poor families."

HUD's MTO notice was finally published in August 1993, after which applications were received from fourteen big-city housing authorities and their "partner" nonprofits. In due course five were selected—Baltimore, Boston, Chicago, Los Angeles, and New York. MTO was finally about to begin, some five years after my initial letter to Kemp about an idea no longer bold, radical, or experimental.

An unforeseen roadblock lurked ahead—the "Baltimore Debacle" it could be called. In the spring of 1994, a government employee who lived in the eastern part of Baltimore County walked into HUD's Washington headquarters. He was looking for a copy of the Baltimore Housing Authority's MTO application. He told the HUD official with whom he spoke that the MTO demonstration appeared to be secret because no one in the county knew much about it. Was Baltimore County being targeted as the destination for residents to be moved out of Baltimore city's public housing projects? He was concerned, he said, for the quality of his neighborhood, and that his young daughters might date black persons.

Like many metropolitan areas, Baltimore had by the 1990s become black and poor compared to its surrounding county. While the county as a whole was flourishing, the economic indicators were strongest in its outer rings. Inner-ring, blue-collar suburbs, including one called Essex, were beginning to experience some of the problems of the central cities. In many places industrial employers were downsizing. Some had closed down. Unemployment in Essex in 1990 was double the rate for the rest of the county. Minority population in the county had increased by 60 percent in the 1980s, but the increase in Essex was over 90 percent. At about the same time, plans were being laid to tear down much of Baltimore city's public housing. Where would its 18,000 families go? And—of surpassing importance—1994 was an election year.

In March 1994 some Baltimore County residents formed the Eastern Political Association (EPA). The EPA's purpose was to oppose MTO. The headline of an early EPA poster read, "Hear Us Shout." It continued:

> People living in drug- and crime-infested Lafayette homes and Murphy homes [public housing projects in Baltimore City] could be moving to Essex. The Moving to Opportunity program could affect our neighborhoods, our schools, and the number of families receiving county social services.

Public meetings and rhetoric heated up. Residents viewed the information that Baltimore's MTO would move only 145 public housing families
as a smokescreen to cover plans for moving 18,000 families.

A meeting was scheduled on June 21, 1994, at Chesapeake High
School in Baltimore County. HUD and Baltimore housing officials were
there to set the record straight. Hecklers and angry questioners made that
impossible by interrupting the planned presentations only minutes after
they had begun. A "noisy, racially tinged free-for-all" was how the *Baltimore Sun* described the meeting. "It was a lynching," said a HUD official.
For those with long enough memories, it was a throwback to George Romney's "lynching" in Warren, Michigan's Fitzgerald High School in 1970.

In election campaigning in Baltimore County that summer and fall,
it was nearly impossible to find a candidate who did not lambast MTO.
Fears about where Baltimore's 18,000 public housing families might go
were rampant. "They might send out people who have to be taught how
to bathe, how not to steal, and how not to smoke pot," said one local candidate. (He added, however, "I'm not discussing race or poverty.") The
"fairness" argument was also widely employed. One version was offered
by a local professor: "If people are paid by the government to act as if they
have achieved economic success, why should they bother to achieve the
real thing?" Another came from the Essex resident who had first sought
out Baltimore's MTO application:

> People here moved from Baltimore city, and they worked for that move.
> Now somebody could move in down the street, not have a job, get a
> 100 percent rent subsidy, send their kids to the same school I'm sending
> my kids to. And that's not fair.

Mikulski, long a supporter of federal housing programs, felt she
had no choice but to join in the condemnation. The program had been
"bungled," she announced. There hadn't been enough consultation with
the community "out there," and as a result discontent had been exacerbated to the point "that it would be only a hollow opportunity for the poor
people in the program." Only Cisneros's intervention saved MTO from
complete demise. The compromise Cisneros brokered killed off additional MTO funding, leaving it with only the original $70 million from
fiscal years 1992 and 1993.

Then, as soon as the November 1994 elections were over, "organized community panic" (as one observer called it) ended. The campaign against MTO expired as abruptly as if a spigot had been turned off. Although HUD would now be fighting for its life against Newt Gingrich and the conservative Republicans to whom the election results had turned over Congress, MTO was still alive, trimmer than had been planned but weighty enough to carry out its mission.

Emboldened perhaps by the Baltimore Debacle, two journalists seized the moment and attacked not only Gautreaux and MTO, but the Section 8 program itself. Spreading over three columns of the *Wall Street Journal,* an article appeared on August 9, 1994, titled, "Clinton's Wrecking Ball for the Suburbs." The author was James Bovard, who hailed from a right-wing Washington think tank called the Competitive Enterprise Institute. The gist of Bovard's article was that Section 8 was "sowing chaos" in the suburbs, rewarding dependence, and alienating middle-class Americans. "Taxpayers are paying for welfare recipients to live in apartments they themselves could not afford."

The next month Bovard followed up with an article in the monthly review the *American Spectator,* with another arresting title: "Not in My Neighborhood—But Yours." The subtitle was, "James Bovard on Henry Cisneros's Schemes and Scams." A cartoon on the magazine's cover showed a smiling, self-satisfied Cisneros. Behind him crouched a sleazy character—who looked for all the world like Dickens's Bill Sikes—waving a Section 8 certificate. "Section 8," the article warned, "is the flagship of the Clinton administration's effort to impose racial and economic housing quotas on American suburbs."

In December the *Wall Street Journal* was at it again, this time with an article about a "Trojan Horse." Written by Howard Husock, from Harvard's Kennedy School of Government, the Trojan horse argument was that Section 8 would "undermine the working poor and lead to controversy and resentment." In the spring Husock followed with a magazine article, "A Critique of Mixed Income Housing: The Problems with 'Gatreaux' [*sic*]," elaborating his Trojan horse views.

The three main Bovard-Husock arguments were that Section 8 wasn't a good idea for the families who moved to the suburbs, that it wasn't fair to working families who had had to earn their way to suburbia, and that housing mobility on a scale large enough to be meaningful would undermine the stability of "receiving" communities. Bovard mounted his charges with breathtaking journalistic irresponsibility—he didn't even mention the Gautreaux Program or Rosenbaum's studies. Husock at least acknowledged the existence of the Gautreaux Program, but for the purpose of pointing to its "folly"—the "greatest tragedy" of such programs was "not so much the problems they pose for the middle and upper classes, but the long-term harm such programs will inflict on their hoped-for beneficiaries."

The rejoinders to Bovard-Husock did not of course command equal time. Two weeks after its wrecking ball article the *Journal* printed Cisneros's answering letter under the defensive-sounding caption, "HUD Program Not Wrecking Suburbs." My letter to the *Journal*, criticizing Bovard's piece as diatribe, went unpublished and unacknowledged.

I had an opportunity to respond when I wrote the introduction to the papers from the October 1994 conference on housing mobility. To the "it's not good for them argument," after pointing to the contrary evidence of the Rosenbaum studies, I referred to a column in the *New York Times* about "butchery," especially of children, on our inner-city streets. "Who are 'we,'" I asked, "to withhold an available, escape-the-ghetto opportunity from 'them' on the ground that we know better than they what is in their interest?"

The fairness argument, I wrote, proceeded from a faulty premise— "that suburban homeowners had 'earned' their way to their communities without government assistance." In fact, buying suburban homes was made possible for millions of post–World War II homeowners by FHA insurance, federal highway and sewer money, and homeowner tax deductions.

As to the third argument, that receiving communities would be undermined, my introduction pointed out that in the entire country only about 1.8 million poor families lived in extreme urban poverty areas. If, through housing mobility programs, one-third (say) were enabled to escape their ghettos over a ten-year period, that would in a single decade put a substantial dent in our urban poverty concentration. Based on the Gautreaux experience of families moving to more than 100 different suburban communities, the one-third goal could be reached using only 50 suburbs in each of our 100 largest metropolitan areas at a rate of a mere twelve families per year per suburb. That was hardly enough to "undermine" communities.

Bovard and Husock had also made two subsidiary points which—it pained me to acknowledge—were not without merit. The first was that Section 8 rents were sometimes too high, though both Bovard and Husock carefully omitted the qualifying "sometimes." Making them sound like typical Section 8 rents, Bovard and Husock had misleadingly (without disclosure) based their charge on rents for four-bedroom apartments in a few high-rent areas. Yet it would have made sense for HUD to better enforce its "rent reasonableness" rule (regardless of FMRs, rents had to be reasonable in relation to local market rents) which was supposed to prevent exactly such extreme cases as those Bovard and Husock made so much of.

The remaining point was that Section 8 families were "clustering" in a few communities, risking the creation of new ghettos. This accusation, also based on a few exceptional situations, could have been addressed by importing into Section 8 the Gautreaux Program requirement of placing families in a "dispersed" manner. But HUD stubbornly refused to address the clustering issue, thereby unnecessarily handing Bovard and Husock their only valid (albeit limited) argument.

As time went on Bovard and Husock continued their attacks—each wrote more articles but without additional arguments. Unlike the Baltimore Debacle, however, their concerted campaign did not beget tangible consequences. Section 8 encountered no serious challenge, in or out of Congress, and MTO was launched with more than 4,000 participating families. Trimmed down though it was, it appeared that MTO would eventually provide useful evidence about housing mobility and neighborhood effects.

8

Cisneros was more than a breath of fresh air; at the very least he was a gust. The first Hispanic mayor of a large American city (San Antonio, from 1981 to 1989), he was literally—as they used to say in the movies—tall, dark, and handsome. Harvard educated and an excellent speaker, he was perhaps the most visible Hispanic politician in the country. Frequently mentioned as a possible governor of Texas, he had resigned his seat on the board of the Dallas Federal Reserve Bank to campaign for Clinton. Within months of his confirmation as HUD secretary, he was saying that racism was the "great Achilles' heel of our nation's future." He was intent, said the *New York Times*, on reducing the concentration of subsidized housing in central cities and making it "more prevalent in white suburbs."

By early June 1994, David Broder wrote in his nationally syndicated column that Cisneros was on a "mission to remake the face of urban America . . . to break up the concentration of crime- and drug-ridden public housing by dispersing residents from the projects throughout the metropolitan area." He had found a "working model" for his plans in the Gautreaux Program, which was to be conducted on a "vastly larger national scale." Cisneros was asking Congress to shift funding from rehabilitating places like Robert Taylor to tearing down some of the high-rises and moving tenants "through Gautreaux-like programs" into the metropolitan area.

Cisneros had actually spent several nights in Robert Taylor. Afterward he said,

> In these enclaves of poverty, people have been literally cut off from the rest of society . . . with low-wage or no jobs . . . living where gangs and drug dealers control the stairwells, where children can't go outside to play, where mothers put their infants to bed in bathtubs.

Cisneros, Broder wrote, had become the Clinton administration's "passionate crusader against racial and economic segregation."

In September 1994 a HUD policy paper, "Residential Mobility Programs," described housing mobility as a key part of a larger strategy to deal with concentrated urban poverty. The Gautreaux Program, it said, was the "first and best known attempt to facilitate the movement of low-income African Americans from inner-city neighborhoods to predominantly white suburbs." Under Cisneros, HUD would make "promot[ing] the geographic mobility of low-income households" a priority. But even under Cisneros, HUD was unwilling to bite the racial bullet; as in MTO, poverty, not race, would be the criterion. Yet the "high correlation between race and concentrated poverty" made it likely that both the participating families and the places to which they moved "will turn out to be substantially the same [as if a racial criterion had been used]." The central feature of the new strategy would be "grants that allow the key component of the Gautreaux Program—comprehensive housing counseling services—to be extended to the entire Section 8 program."

In October, Cisneros's message to the first conference on housing mobility said the mobility discussion "cuts directly to the heart of who we are as a nation." He went on:

> There are millions of families in America today who want to lift themselves out of poverty, but who have no real options where they live. For them, poverty has become as much a matter of geography as personal circumstance.

It was beginning to look as if we had another George Romney back at HUD, but this time with a supportive president, and a program—Section 8—more likely than scattered-site public housing to make its way through the shoals of suburban opposition (because there was no need to subordinate local zoning powers, the Section 8 law having in effect done precisely that for Section 8 certificates).

But there was a giant fly in the Gautreaux ointment HUD was spreading around. A Gautreaux certificate was usable only in nonblack areas. It passed to another family if the initial family failed to find a properly located unit. Some 80 percent did in fact fail; over the years only 20 percent of the families who entered the Gautreaux Program succeeded in making mobility moves. Meanwhile, in the very city in which Gautreaux was operating successfully, more than 80 percent of the CHA's Section 8 families were winding up in heavily black areas of Chicago. Unless, in Gautreaux fashion, HUD's proposed program earmarked certificates for use solely in low-poverty areas, one could expect that most certificates would be used in high-poverty areas. The Gautreaux 20 percent "success rate" was being achieved when families knew they had to find a nonblack area or lose their certificate. If families who failed to find a low-poverty unit could still use their certificates to move to high-poverty locations, Cisneros's vaunted crusade would turn out to be a dud.

Desperately, I wrote to Cisneros and Katz, five times in fact from November 1994 to January 1995, making a pest of myself. Half of all available certificates should be earmarked for low-poverty areas only, I urged. The other half could be "regular" certificates, usable anywhere, thus preserving plenty of "choice" for families who didn't want to or couldn't move to low-poverty areas. I closed one of my letters with a reminder about Cisneros's message that poverty was as much a matter of geography as personal circumstance: "We will not change that situation with a certificate program over 80 percent of whose users do not change their geography."

The upshot was that I was offered a meeting with Joseph Shuldiner, the assistant secretary in charge of public housing. Once again—I was no stranger to this experience—good arguments didn't necessarily make acceptable politics. Between Cisneros's summer plans to remake the face of urban America and my earmarking pleas in late fall and winter came the "Gingrich revolution" of November 1994. HUD was now fighting for its life against calls for its demise from the new conservative Republican majorities in Congress. HUD's mind was not on earmarking, a choice-inhibiting proposal (as it would be described) that would be social engineering grist for the conservative Republican mill. Shuldiner didn't even discuss the merits of my arguments. He opened our meeting by telling me flatly that, although my views were appreciated, the earmarking proposal simply could not be adopted as HUD policy at that time. And that was that. The November 1994 Republican takeover had led to such an intense congressional focus on HUD that there was "no room to maneuver." In that charged environment, my earmarking proposal was dead on arrival.

With a great deal of fancy footwork—Cisneros "reinvented" HUD, simplified its programs, cut back on its red tape—HUD managed to survive the Republican effort to slay it. But the moment of opportunity to turn Section 8 into a Gautreaux-like mobility program went up in the smoke of the electoral revolution of November 1994. Gautreaux had birthed an MTO research program, not a remaking of the face of urban America.

9

The three-quarter-inch-thick, midterm MTO report—prepared for HUD by a team of three contractors and called the "Interim Impacts Evaluation"—appeared in 2003. "Interim" meant that it was roughly the halfway point in the ten-year life of MTO. There is supposed to be a final evaluation after the last family has completed its tenth year in the program.

Families entered MTO between 1994 and 1998. Each of the 4,248 "sample families" (those assigned through December 31, 1997) had agreed to be "tracked" for ten years, and had been randomly assigned to one of three groups. The "experimental group" of 1,729 families received Section 8 vouchers (as certificates are now called) usable only in low-poverty—below 10 percent—areas, plus special counseling to help them find and lease units. A "Section 8 group" of 1,209 families also received vouchers, but could use them to rent anywhere they chose and received no special assistance. A "control group" of 1,310 families living in public housing received no vouchers at all. After one year in its new location, any family in the two "treatment groups" could move wherever it wished. Control group families didn't have to wait a year to move.

By tracking the families over ten years, and comparing the experiences of each treatment group with the control group, MTO was supposed to help answer the question, What were the effects for poor families of moving from high- to low-poverty neighborhoods? However, as with many of mankind's endeavors, what was conceived did not match exactly what emerged.

The idea of contrasting the experiences of families moving to high- and low-poverty neighborhoods was compromised at the outset. Poverty rates were measured by the census, but the 1990 census data were several years old by the time MTO got under way in the mid-'90s. As a result, some experimental group families moved to census tracts that had less than 10 percent poverty in 1990 but more than that at the time of the moves. The interim evaluation estimated that "only about half of [moving families'] destinations had poverty rates below 10 percent at the time of the move."

Other experimental group families moved to neighborhoods whose poverty rates, though below 10 percent at the time of the move, were rising, and still others made a second move into higher-poverty neighborhoods after their first year in the program. The result was that at the time of evaluation many moving families had spent some—even all—of their MTO time in tracts with more than 10 percent poverty. Indeed, the report says that at evaluation time only 13.3 percent of experimental group families who had initially leased under MTO were living in census tracts with less than 10 percent poverty as measured by the 2000 census. This was a substantial watering down of the original concept that experimental group families would move from high- to low-poverty areas.

In addition, although HUD's refusal to "sponsor" race-conscious counseling left MTO without a racial criterion, there was a hope (if not an expectation) that 10 percent poverty tracts would turn out to be mostly white, or at least integrated. That wasn't the case. The report said that 60 percent of experimental group families who had moved were in "heavily minority areas," and that three quarters of all moving families were in census tracts more than 80 percent minority. MTO was as far from achieving the scattered-site vision of a public housing family moving to a white or integrated middle-class environment as were Gautreaux scattered sites themselves.

The evaluation examined six aspects of families' experiences, but emphasized that while some effects might be expected to occur in the short or middle term (one to three, or five to six years), others would not be likely to appear until more time had passed. In the not-expected category were education, employment, and—as measured by receipt of welfare—economic self-sufficiency. In accord with expectations, the evaluation disclosed only small effects on education, and none on employment or welfare receipt.

The small education effects were largely confined to lower percentages of poor, minority, and limited English proficiency children in schools attended by sample children; there were virtually no effects on educational performance. This was not surprising, the report said, since nearly three-quarters of experimental group children whose families had leased under MTO were attending schools in the same district as they had previously. Some children had not even changed schools. In addition, as Rosenbaum observed, five years is "fairly early" for gains to appear in school scores; his studies of Gautreaux families had produced "unimpressive" education results in that time frame.

Adult employment more than doubled (from around 25 to 52 percent), presumably because of the economic boom during the 1990s and welfare reform, but the pattern for all groups was about the same. There was also no significant effect on youth employment, although girls in the experimental and Section 8 groups perceived their chances of going to college and getting a good job as much higher than their counterparts in the control group, and the "idleness rate" (neither in school nor working) was substantially reduced for girls—no change for boys—among experimental group moving families. Rosenbaum speculated that the strong labor market and welfare reforms of the late 1990s distorted results by leading to employment gains for control group families who remained in public housing. That "fluke of history," he said, probably wiped out employment benefits from moving.

As for self-sufficiency, the final, no-change-expected category, the proportion of families on welfare dropped, and average incomes increased, but the pattern here too was similar for all three MTO groups, presumably also because of the improved economy and tougher welfare rules.

Assessing these "no significant effect" results, the report suggested that over time more effects might be observed. It recalled Rosenbaum's finding that one to six years after families moved to the suburbs many children were "still struggling to catch up," but that seven years later Rosenbaum had found substantial effects on eight of nine education- and employment-related outcomes for the same children.

Short- to midterm results were expected, however, for the other three aspects of families' experiences—delinquency and risky behavior, health, and neighborhood conditions (including safety and housing). Delinquency meant behavior problems at home or school, gun or gang involvement, property crimes, and violent behavior or arrests; risky behavior meant drug usage and sexual activity.

For most of the behavioral factors there were no significant differences among youths in the three groups. Differences however did appear in four factors: reduced risky behavior for experimental group girls; reduced arrests, especially for violent crime, for Section 8 girls; more self-reported behavior problems (mostly smoking) for experimental and Section 8 group boys; and more property crime arrests for experimental group boys. The report speculated that the increase in arrests might reflect more stringent policing in new locations rather than more criminal behavior, and there was some evidence that the relatively higher rate of property crime arrests did not persist after the first four years. The report couldn't explain why boys and girls appeared to react differently to the challenges of moving to a new neighborhood.

Among health factors the evaluation found a large reduction of obesity among adults in both experimental and Section 8 groups, and mental health improvements among experimental family adults, but no significant effects on other health measures for adults. Among children, there were reductions in distress and anxiety for girls (not boys) in families moving with MTO vouchers.

As to neighborhood conditions, adults described substantial increases in their perceptions of safety, plus large reductions in being victims of, or even observing, crime. They also reported less difficulty in getting police to respond to their calls; large reductions in litter, trash, graffiti, abandoned buildings, people "hanging around," and public drinking; and, for families who moved with MTO vouchers, substantial improvement in the quality of housing. The gains in all these areas were greater for the experimental families than for the Section 8 group, but substantial for both.

What to make of the MTO evaluation? The most significant effects were in the neighborhood conditions category. "MTO substantially improved the quality of housing [for] families who moved with program vouchers," and "substantially" increased perceptions of safety, with large reductions in being victimized by—or even witnessing—crime. So too with the quality of the physical and social environments—large reductions in litter, people "hanging around," and so on, and a much higher sense of satisfaction with the new neighborhoods. Families who moved with MTO vouchers lived in neighborhoods "with higher adult employment rates, a substantially higher proportion of two-parent families and high school graduates, and nearly twice as many homeowners."

All of these differences were significant for both experimental and Section 8 families, although the gains were about twice as large for the experimental group. Yet, unlike the startling effects Rosenbaum had found for Gautreaux movers, these neighborhood differences did not lead to observed effects in education, employment, and so on. How come?

Apart from the "fluke of history" and five-year time-frame points, part of the explanation may be that many experimental group families did not move to areas that were far from high-poverty areas, but to areas that were and remained low-poverty. The finding that only 13.3 percent of experimental group families were living in less than 10 percent census tracts in 2000 means that many of these families lived some part of their MTO time in neighborhoods with more than 10 percent poverty. The evaluation did not separate the families who moved to and stayed in census tracts that remained below 10 percent poverty from those who spent MTO time in higher-poverty census tracts. Instead its analysis blended the experiences of both groups.

The high percent (60) of experimental family movers who, at evaluation time, were living in "heavily minority areas" is probably also important. In her book, *Black Picket Fences*, Mary Pattillo-McCoy writes, "The black middle class overall remains as segregated from whites as the black poor," in neighborhoods "often located next to predominantly black areas with much higher poverty rates." Though it strives hard to leave poor neighborhoods behind, it has "never been able to get very far." As if written to support Pattillo-McCoy's point, a *Chicago Tribune* study of 2000 census data shows that 78 percent of black middle-class areas in Chicago (compared to fewer than a quarter of white middle-class areas) lay within half a mile of neighborhoods in which at least one-third of the residents lived in poverty.

In short, as Pattillo-McCoy explains, geographic proximity to the ghetto leaves the black middle class engaged in a constant struggle against ghetto ills subversively insinuating themselves, through children and teenagers, into the middle-class lifestyle it strives to maintain. It is quite likely, therefore, that regardless of the poverty rate of their new census tracts many experimental group families living in "heavily minority areas" were living near the ghetto or other high-poverty areas. The MTO analyses likewise blended the experiences of these families with the experiences of those who had moved far from high-poverty neighborhoods.

Perhaps, then, it is not surprising that, except for neighborhood improvements, the interim evaluation revealed fewer significant effects than had been expected. By contrast, the Gautreaux families Rosenbaum studied did not have the good fortune to encounter a "fluke of history," and Rosenbaum's work eventually spanned longer time frames than did the interim evaluation. Unlike many MTO experimental families, most of Rosenbaum's suburban movers went to middle-class, white, or integrated communities, far from black ghettos. Even though they were not controlled experiments, Rosenbaum's studies are probably the best information we have so far on what happens to black families who move from ghettos to very low-poverty, white or integrated communities distant from the ghetto residents they have left behind. The implications of that for national policy is a matter I discuss in the final chapter.

CHAPTER SIX

STARTING OVER

We could start all over again perhaps.

—Vladimir (*Waiting for Godot*)

1

When Harrison Salisbury was appalled by the public housing he observed in 1958, his focus was on the physical—broken windows, pilfered hardware, sagging doors, playground seas of muddy clay, the gigantic masses of brick and concrete. Perhaps he could have imagined, but he did not then witness, the human debasement that such places would foster. The gangs, the guns, and the drugs attained their awful maturity later.

In *The Promised Land: The Great Black Migration and How It Changed America,* Nicholas Lemann tells the story of one family in Robert Taylor Homes. Ruby Haynes moved into Apartment 902 in the sixteen-story Taylor building at 5135 South Federal Street in October 1962. Taylor had only recently opened; at the dedication ceremony the huge welcome banner read: "Building Good Homes, Good Citizens."

Moving into Taylor was an "emblem of possibility" for Haynes, who had emigrated from Clarksdale, Mississippi, in 1949, and struggled to find her way in her pre-Taylor Chicago life. The emblem soon frayed. During her sixteen and a half years in Apartment 902, one of Haynes's six sons barely managed to survive beatings by rival gang members, a second was sent back to Clarksdale to live with a childless relative, a third went as a "gift child" to a friend in Ohio, and George, the eldest, either committed suicide or was murdered. By the time George's naked body washed up on the Lake Michigan shore, the hope Haynes had invested in Chicago and Taylor had long since died. She "hated the city, and hated Robert Taylor Homes." On the first anniversary of George's wake, April 5, 1979, Haynes moved back to Clarksdale, to a two-story scattered-site public housing building in a middle-class neighborhood.

Haynes's only daughter, Juanita, then moved into Apartment 902. Juanita was twenty years old, on welfare, a prison widow, and a single mother. Soon she had a second child, then became addicted to cocaine. Deeply in debt to her dope man, she began to beg and steal, and she became pregnant again. In the mid-1980s she sent her two oldest children to Clarksdale to live with her mother. Then, after a cocaine session, she went into cardiac arrest but was revived in a hospital. Terrified, Juanita packed her things and with her remaining child took a bus to Clarksdale. They too moved in with her mother.

Apartment 902 passed to Juanita's brother, Johnnie, who invited a male friend to share it. The two began dealing cocaine out of the apartment, cheating not only their customers but each other by skimming the pouches they sold. Before long a fight ensued, which ended with the friend setting the apartment on fire. That terminated the fight, and also the quarter-century Taylor tenancies of Haynes and her children.

But not the family saga in Taylor. Connie Henry, a former daughter-in-law (Johnnie's ex-wife), lived three floors below in Apartment 610. Miraculously, by her "formidable force of will," as Lemann puts it, Henry managed to put her five children on an achievement track. At the time Lemann was writing, in 1990, Henry's four daughters had finished high school, one had gone on to college, and her youngest child, a son, had begun high school outside the "perilous" Taylor neighborhood.

There is a considerable literature about heroes, such as Connie Henry, who manage to survive—and see to it that their children survive—in the concentrated poverty, high-rise environment. Occasionally a writer will not only praise the courage, resilience, and ingenuity of individuals, but the "community" of high-rise environments as well. This is a little like praising the "community" described in Kenneth Clark's *Dark Ghetto* because some of its victims managed to help each other survive its horrors with a semblance of human dignity. Henry's own "strategy" for dealing with Taylor was to avoid contact, to "tune it out." Despite her success, after living there for nearly two decades Henry felt "weary and depressed." For years she had been on the CHA's Section 8 waiting list. What she wanted, "more than anything," was to get out.

Not everybody wants out. Some, for understandable reasons—family, friends, institutional ties, fear, age—do not wish to move. Once, after I had finished a talk about the Gautreaux Program at Cabrini, an aged woman hobbled over to me. "You keep doin' what you're doin'," she said, waving her arthritic finger in my face. "It's right for my grandson. He's seven. But not for me. I've lived here a long time, and here's where I'm goin' to die."

Lemann thought the building at 5135 South Federal was "quite possibly the worst place in the country to raise a family." Its census tract was the third poorest in the United States. The poorest, immediately to the north, was also wholly within Robert Taylor. Yet the social disorder of the project was worse than the poverty. Many places had low per-capita income, but few could compare with Taylor in infant mortality, life expectancy, crime, and family disunity.

Three decades later, Lemann equals Salisbury's physical description:

> The entrances to . . . Taylor Homes are bleak and forbidding. Most of the time they are littered with empty bottles and piles of uncollected garbage. Gang symbols are spray-painted all over the lobbies . . . All the access points to the buildings—the elevator cabs, the stairwells and the hallways—reek of urine and cheap wine.

It is Lemann's description of social disorder and crime that surpasses Salisbury—gang recruitment at ages eight and nine, drugs everywhere, pervasive crime and violence.

> Minor crime never stops, and major crime is no rarity. In the course of one year, 1988, according to building residents, a girl who lived on the ninth floor at 5135 was taken to a vacant apartment and shot by a group of young men; in 5201, a boy was killed on one of the breezeways . . . by a shot to the head from a .357 Magnum; in 5001, a boy was shot in the head and left to die on a breezeway, twin girls were shot but survived and a boy was shot and killed in one of the elevators. Quite often those who commit murder in the Taylor Homes are never brought to justice, in

large part because witnesses are afraid that if they cooperate with the police, the gangs will kill them later.

Taylor is not atypical. Alex Kotlowitz's acclaimed *There Are No Children Here* is about another of the CHA's high-rise complexes, Henry Horner Homes. The book recounts what life is like for two young brothers, Lafeyette and Pharoah, in a Horner where violence is a "constant," where the surrounding neighborhood is a "black hole" with an infant mortality rate higher than in a number of Third World countries, where eleven-year-old Pharoah "sat on his bed one day and cried because he worried that he might never get out of the projects," where a friend of Lafeyette's, who was able to move out, "knelt at his bedside before he went to sleep and prayed that God would not make him move back to Horner."

The Hidden War is a book about three CHA developments: Horner, Rockwell Gardens, and Harold Ickes Homes. Over a period of several years in the 1990s, Susan Popkin, a senior researcher at the Urban Institute in Washington, and her coauthors, interviewed many residents. Too few adults, says *The Hidden War,* were capable of enforcing standards of acceptable behavior; there was not enough trust or cohesion to allow them to address their common problems. The gangs had created a social order and an economy that enmeshed most residents.

Many children had been "permanently damaged"—injured in gang wars, broken elevators, or darkened stairwells, burned by unprotected radiators, poisoned by lead paint. Many others hadn't survived, slain by gangs or fallen out of high-rise windows with no screens or window guards. Still more, *The Hidden War* continues, are

> victims of the overwhelming social disorganization, abused or neglected by drug-addicted parents, . . . arrested or incarcerated for their involvement in the drug trade, or permanently traumatized by the stress of coping with the constant violence and disorder.

Surely, by the 1990s, the images of George and Juanita Haynes, of Pharoah and Lafeyette's friend, of the stairwell killings, the infant mortality figures, the life-expectancy statistics, the appalling human suffering and human waste, would have motivated Chicago to do *something* about its public housing high-rise disasters.

2

In 1969, at the end of the CHA's postwar building spree, Judge Austin's order ruled out more CHA high-rises for families with children. At about the same time Congress did likewise for the whole country, unless there were "no practical alternative." The reason, in the understated prose of a congressional report, was that "high-rise, elevator structures provide an undesirable environment for family living." Building family high-rises, it seemed, was effectively outlawed.

But what about *rebuilding*? The high-rises at Taylor, Horner, and elsewhere had gone up in the 1950s and 1960s. By the late 1980s they were physically wearing out. It was clear that the infamous structures either had to be fixed up or torn down. Incredibly, Chicago seemed to be opting for fix-up. The headline of an August 1991 *Washington Post* article captured the moment: "Chicago's Not About to Give Up on a Bad Idea." The article described the CHA's plans for high-rise rehabilitation, with an overall price tag of $1 billion. Some of the money was for desperately needed repair and maintenance. But much of it was for rebuilding, at costs—equivalent to those for new construction—of up to $80,000 per apartment, designed to extend the "useful" lives of the family high-rises by twenty to thirty years.

Why, knowing what life was like in its high-rises, would the CHA propose to rebuild them? Why, if it were going to spend $80,000 per apartment—enough to build single-family townhomes or pay for Section 8 private market housing—would the CHA not jump at the chance to replace its high-rises with low-rise construction or Section 8 certificates? The answer lay with Congress and HUD; for once, the CHA's incompetence was not to blame.

HUD's public housing funding had never provided a reserve for capital replacement. In 1968 HUD began to remedy the omission with a "modernization" program. During the 1970s modernization money funded roof repairs, boiler replacements, and other major building work. In 1980 Congress sought to rationalize this piecemeal activity by directing public housing authorities to develop overall plans to maintain and upgrade their buildings. Beginning with fiscal year 1992, authorities were required to plan "modernization" needs five years in advance.

By then, modernization had become a big-ticket item, $5 billion between 1980 and 1985 alone. Even so, needs outpaced expenditures. In 1989 HUD examined backlogged modernization needs and estimated that up to $9.2 billion was needed just to meet HUD standards for health, safety, and building integrity. The estimate did not include "improv[ing] quality" or enhancing "long-term viability," especially needed in family high-rises that frequently lacked such "amenities" as sufficient elevators. Nor did it include funding to avoid a recurrence of backlogs.

Given this financial picture, one would have expected HUD not to throw good money after bad by permitting deteriorated family high-rises to be rebuilt for another twenty to thirty years. The expectation would have been wrong. Gertrude Jordan, HUD's top official in Chicago at the time (1991), announced—if she did not fully explain—Secretary Kemp's position:

> We [HUD] feel, and I personally feel, committed to rehabbing those [CHA high-rise] developments . . . HUD Secretary Jack Kemp has often spoken of the fact that he wants to get those buildings rehabbed and get people back in. He does not want to be known as the secretary of demolition for public housing.

The reasons for HUD's position went beyond Kemp's concern about his public image. Congress had first addressed public housing demolition in 1974, and over succeeding years its prescriptions evolved. By 1987, the law said HUD could not approve demolition unless units were replaced by new construction or Section 8 subsidies committed for fifteen years. Nor could modernization money be used to pay for replacement housing. For that public housing authorities had to turn to funding expressly appropriated for new housing or rent subsidies.

In the latter part of the 1980s, following the lead of the Reagan and first Bush administrations, Congress cut appropriations for new public housing steadily and severely. Section 8 funding was also in short supply, and the diminishing amounts were committed for fewer than fifteen years. The result—virtually a Catch-22—was that it made little sense for public housing authorities to propose to demolish their high-rises when, with funding for replacement housing unavailable, HUD would not approve their applications.

The situation was described by Vince Lane, who had been appointed the CHA's boss after Jerome Van Gorkom's resignation. As quoted in the *Washington Post* article, Lane said:

> If I had the dollars to build low-rise, scattered-site housing, I'd be the first one out there with a sledgehammer, knocking [the high-rises] down . . . But I don't have the resources. And therefore I'm looking to how I can begin to at least make these places livable.

Lane was tall, handsome, well-dressed, almost debonair-looking. His appearance belied his birth to dirt-poor parents in small-town Mississippi, where his mother grew vegetables and raised chickens to make ends meet. Later the family moved to a cold-water flat above a grocery store in Chicago, where his father worked for thirty-five dollars a week at a copper-smelting plant. Lane's parents insisted that he get an education, and he earned a business degree from Roosevelt University and, in 1973, an MBA at night school (while holding down daytime jobs) from the University of Chicago. Then he went to work for a nonprofit housing development group and soon started his own housing management and development firm, concentrating on federally subsidized housing. Within a decade he was a millionaire.

Van Gorkom's resignation had left the CHA in dire need of a top management blood transfusion. A civic group laboriously put together a plan that involved former Illinois governor Richard Olgivie as chairman and Lane as executive director. Just when the pieces were finally in place, on May 10, 1988, Olgivie died of a heart attack. That night Lane flew back from New York City for a what-to-do-now meeting. He would take over the CHA, he said, but only if he could be both chairman and executive director, with a voice in the selection of a new board. Lane got his way, and became head of the CHA in June 1988.

Before long Lane was making miracles. During the period of Renault Robinson's mismanagement, the CHA's modernization funding had dwindled to around $20 million a year. Lane rebuilt the CHA's relationship with HUD, partly by agency reforms, partly by highly publicized police "sweeps" of high-rises to clear out gang members and drug dealers, partly by exercising his charm on HUD with his vision of an economic mix among public housing tenants, and of using modernization money not to "build housing for poor people [but] housing that poor people can live in." Soon Mayor Daley was saying of Lane, "He has brought life back to CHA." Soon, also, Lane became a Kemp favorite—the politician Kemp enthused, "He transcends politics." One result of Lane's hard work was a sharp rise in CHA modernization funding to $91 million for 1990.

In the spring of 1991 Lane filed two more modernization applications. The first, for the year 1991, requested the breathtaking sum of $218 million. The second, the CHA's five-year plan for 1992 through 1997, sought $680 million. "CHA Unveils Billion-Dollar Repair Plan," blared the front page *Sun-Times* headline on June 12, 1991. (A projected $180 million for 1997 pushed the grand total over the one billion figure.) After all those years of CHA mismanagement, Vince Lane seemed finally to be doing something right. On the cover of the *Chicago Tribune Magazine,* Lane was pictured astride the roof of a Cabrini-Green high-rise. He was wearing a navy blue pin-striped suit, a white shirt, and a patterned red tie. His hands were placed confidently on his hips. In huge letters, the magazine cover asked, "Can This Man Save the CHA?" The article, titled "High Hopes," strongly implied an affirmative answer.

However, from a Gautreaux perspective Lane's success with modernization funding created a problem. Of the $218 million for 1991, nearly half was for rebuilding high-rises. Of the $680 million for the next five years, over a third was for the same purpose. Here was the CHA's savior proposing to spend hundreds of millions of dollars, real money in those days, to rebuild the illegally located CHA high-rises in their still segregated neighborhoods, extending for twenty to thirty years the life span of the most visible symbols of the wrong that had given rise to Austin's Gautreaux decision. Unlike the CHA's usual irrational justifications for its mindless conduct, Lane also had good reason for what he was proposing. He could not demolish without replacement, and there was no replacement money; if he did not rebuild, the modernization money would go elsewhere.

3

What we should do was not obvious. Any effort to thwart the immensely popular Lane would be viewed like rain on a parade. The judgment order against the CHA called for building new public housing; it contained not a word about fixing up what already existed. Our distinction between "rehabilitation" and "rebuilding"—the latter defined as spending about as much for fix-up as the cost of building new—was clear in our minds but did not exist anywhere else. Above all, with more than 150 high-rises in Chicago needing modernization, and the CHA and HUD ready to spend hundreds of millions to do the work, did we imagine that Aspen—who at every opportunity had reminded the world that he did not aspire to be Chicago's public housing czar—would for a moment consider an expansive reading of Gautreaux orders that seemed designed to place him in precisely that position?

Our response to Lane's modernization proposals developed haltingly, and did not lead to our finest hour. It first took shape in North Kenwood–Oakland, on Chicago's lakefront just north of the Hyde Park home of the University of Chicago. In 1949 this had been an attractive neighborhood with a thriving commercial street and old stone residences that looked like architectural ornaments. Beginning in the 1950s, as the postwar exodus to suburbia accelerated, North Kenwood–Oakland plummeted to become one of Chicago's badly depressed areas. By 1980 its median household income had dropped to $5,317, only a third of Chicago's then median. Many of its grand old buildings had been abandoned or demolished. By the end of the 1980s, its stores were gone and 40 percent of its land area was vacant. Much of North Kenwood–Oakland looked like a battlefield after the battle, dotted with ugly board-ups and only an occasional still lived-in, elegant-looking residence to recall better days.

In the 1950s the CHA had built two high-rises in North Kenwood–Oakland, fifteen-story Y-shaped brick buildings near South Lake Shore Drive and the lakefront park. Residents in upper stories had lake views. (The land was one of the vacant inner-city sites approved by the Chicago City Council in its 1950 "compromise.") In 1962 and 1963 the CHA built four more high-rises a few hundred feet further south—concrete monoliths, sixteen stories tall, of the Taylor Homes design. Each of the six buildings housed some 150 apartments.

The "Lakefront Properties," as the six buildings were called, soon went the way of the CHA's other high-rises. By the mid-1980s they were so deteriorated that the CHA vacated all six, promising to rehabilitate them and offering a priority to former tenants to return. Several years passed with the CHA's corporate mind on other things—the years of the Robinson-Smith wars and the HUD takeover threat. Modernization funding was applied for and HUD responded with a $14 million allocation, but the rehabilitation didn't happen. Vacant and boarded up, the fifteen- and sixteen-story hulks remained giant, brooding presences overlooking Chicago's south lakefront to the east and the remains of North Kenwood–Oakland to the west.

One of Lane's earliest steps after his arrival in June 1988 had been to obtain HUD's permission to devote the entire $14 million to the two brick buildings on the north. Then Lane proceeded in an inventive way. With his reputation rapidly becoming national—in 1989 he was appointed cochair of a national commission to study "severely distressed public housing"—Lane successfully lobbied Congress to try out the mixed-income part of his public housing vision.

The legislation was called MINCS, for Mixed Income New Communities Strategy. It authorized renting half the apartments in a public housing building to families whose incomes ranged up to 80 percent of the area's median, still within public housing eligibility limits but well above typical resident incomes and high enough to include working families. Private housing was to be developed in tandem, a quarter of it rented to public housing families. For the first MINCS project in the nation, Lane was going to begin with the two Lakefront Properties brick buildings, renamed "Lake Parc Place."

MINCS made sense, promising a hopeful new kind of public housing. Lake Parc Place's sleek marketing literature, designed to attract working families, didn't even mention CHA ownership. The 282 refurbished apartments would have ceiling fans, wood cabinets, and stainless steel kitchen sinks. There also would be restrooms on the ground floors and twenty-four-hour security. The additional 564 privately developed units Lane promised (141 of which would be rented to "regular" public housing families to replace the Lake Parc Place apartments going to higher-income families) would be a step toward a revitalized North Kenwood–Oakland.

By usual CHA standards, Lake Parc Place happened so quickly—rehabilitation began in 1989 and was completed in mid-1991—that it never appeared on our radar screen. Yes, it amounted to rebuilding segregated high-rises in a black neighborhood, but in a new and promising way. As the first MINCS project in the nation, it was supported by the direct authority of Congress. In the face of the formidable array of good things Lake Parc Place had going for it, it is doubtful that we would have tried to raise a Gautreaux question about its rebuilding even had we given it thought.

But the other four buildings were another matter. In 1988 a community planning effort had begun in North Kenwood–Oakland. Approved in the spring of 1989, the plan called for demolition of the four concrete eyesores and their replacement with 600 scattered-site units. The city council soon designated the neighborhood a "conservation area," giving the plan quasi-official status. Yet Lane ignored the community and went ahead with his plans to rehabilitate the four high-rises. HUD soon supplied an allocation for the first of them, with work to begin in February 1992. Funding for the other three was included in the CHA's five-year modernization proposal.

Lane talked as if the additional rehabilitation would be an extension of MINCS, but it wasn't so. In fact, the promised private housing portion of Lake Parc Place never materialized, and—except for the working family rentals in the two brick buildings—MINCS was stillborn. Of the first Taylor-type high-rise scheduled for rebuilding, the CHA's own consultant said its two-elevator system was inadequate, that its exposed common areas were a "building maintenance and aesthetic failure," and that its building design "seriously limit[ed] quality of life for occupants." If Lane's plan to impose 600 of these units on North Kenwood–Oakland were carried out, the prospective revitalization of the community would be frustrated, and with it the prospect for 600 scattered-site units.

Nor were we comfortable sitting idly by and letting a modernization precedent be set that would surely apply to scores of other high-rises. Gautreaux was already a quarter century old, yet here was the CHA proposing to continue for another quarter century the very condition found to have offended the U.S. Constitution.

⟋

In November 1990, after considerable cogitation, we filed a motion for "further relief" against the CHA and HUD. The motion asked Aspen to hold off rehabilitation of the Taylor-type buildings for a reasonable time during which the CHA would be directed to work with the community to see if 600 scattered sites could be developed instead.

Our brief didn't mount a frontal assault on the CHA's right to rebuild; it argued only that the proposed rebuilding would frustrate a major scattered-site opportunity, violating the CHA's duty to use its best efforts to develop as many scattered sites as it could. Deathly afraid of Aspen's reluctance to play czar, we were sure that asking him to take on the citywide rebuilding issue would look as if we were proffering him precisely that role. Impassioned HUD and CHA responses pointed out that what was really at stake was exactly what we hadn't wanted to talk about—"This Court should decline plaintiffs' invitation to control which public housing in the City is to be rehabilitated, and which demolished." Correctly, they argued that the CHA and HUD orders addressed only new development, not rehabilitation. The CHA's brief even included pictures of how nice the rehabilitated Lake Parc Place looked. We were really after demolition, they said, and demolition was impossible because there was no replacement housing money.

Oral argument on March 1, 1991, added heat but not light. On April 2, Aspen denied our motion in a two-page written opinion. He was "not unsympathetic," he acknowledged. But, he pointed out, rehabilitation was not scheduled to begin until February 1992, and the timing on the remaining three buildings was uncertain. That was "ample time," he wrote, for alternatives to be explored.

Yet Aspen's opinion also said that we were seeking relief "beyond the scope" of the court's orders, implying—he gave no reasons—agreement with the CHA and HUD that Gautreaux rulings didn't cover rebuilding. That language made the future look unpromising, if not downright bleak. In retrospect I faulted us for including HUD in our motion. As a first step it would have sufficed had we just gone after the CHA. We didn't need all those additional pages of HUD arguments, placing the weight of the federal government on the scales against us. The realization that we had done something really dumb didn't make Aspen's "beyond the scope" language easier to swallow. We badly needed a "Plan B."

4

Plan B had two parts: litigation and negotiation. The idea was to create a litigation atmosphere within which negotiations would be seen as desirable. The first step was to develop a credible legal theory, which we now fashioned out of the CHA's duty to disestablish segregation—a duty long ago embodied in Austin's 1969 order which directed the CHA to

> affirmatively administer its public housing system in every respect . . . to the end of disestablishing the segregated public housing system which has resulted from CHA's unconstitutional site selection and tenant assignment procedures.

We had referred to "disestablishment" in our previous, losing effort, but had linked it to the duty to develop scattered sites. Now our sole point was that the CHA's modernization applications paid no attention to disestablishment. Their language was all architecture and costs. We argued that the CHA could not base its modernization plans exclusively on technical grounds, giving no consideration to disestablishment.

The cases, mostly involving schools, seemed helpful. A court's basic duty in a desegregation case was to eliminate segregation. Remedial powers were not limited to enforcement of the original order. One Louisiana case especially gladdened our hearts.

> The failure sufficiently to satisfy this [constitutional obligation to eradicate segregation] continues the constitutional violation . . . A court must continually be willing to redraft the order . . . to insure that the decree accomplishes its intended result.

We even found a case, an outgrowth of the 1954 Brown decision, holding that a judge could give additional relief thirty-five years after a lawsuit had begun if what had been done so far was inadequate.

Yet we carefully limited what we would ask Aspen to do. We would seek only amended modernization applications and not specify what the amendments should be. Our metaphor was to send the CHA back to the drawing board, not to tell it what to draw. Aspen should only direct the CHA to "consider" desegregation. The "how" would be entirely up to the CHA. We hoped that such a narrow order would not make Aspen look like a czar.

⟡

The negotiation part of Plan B included the city because CHA commissioners were mayoral appointees, and because HUD's new five-year plan requirements called for a sign-off from the mayor, making the city a formal party to the CHA's five-year modernization proposal.

In June 1991, therefore, I called David Mosena, Mayor Daley's chief of staff. A big issue was at stake, I told Mosena, the shape of Chicago's high-rise public housing for the next generation. The mayor was going to be involved because he had to endorse the CHA's five-year modernization plan. We were going to court, and the issue would be all over the papers. Wouldn't it be better to talk privately together rather than publicly in court?

Mosena wanted something in writing, so I sent him a list of the CHA's 167 family high-rise buildings. I also said I would share with him as soon as it was finished an argument about why the CHA wasn't faced with "use it or lose it." I was convinced, I said, that a credible case could be made the other way (referring to our search for a "loophole" in the modernization statute that would allow the money to be used for replacement housing), but should I turn out to be wrong, the correct course would be to amend the law, not to spend hundreds of millions to remake past mistakes.

With time running out (we had learned that HUD's local office would be acting on—presumably approving—the CHA's 1991 modernization application on August 9), a break appeared to come when HUD lawyers agreed to meet with me on July 31 in Washington. The meeting was not a happy one. Four HUD lawyers were adamant that we were wrong about everything. First, modernization funding could not be used for replacement housing. Even if the statute were ambiguous, the history of the modernization legislation and HUD's practice over the years showed how the ambiguity had to be resolved. Regretfully I came to the conclusion that HUD had the better of this argument, and that we would lose if we tried to make it before Aspen.

Second, the HUD modernization program did not require considering desegregation. HUD had never taken such a position in all its years of administering modernization. A contrary view would mean that HUD had been violating the law, and HUD would resist that strongly. Also, since so much public housing was in segregated neighborhoods, our view would mean more demolition, something Secretary Kemp, as we knew, did not favor.

On the meaning of Gautreaux orders, the HUD lawyers said that in the many years the CHA had been receiving modernization funding we had never taken the position that Gautreaux orders applied, and now it was too late to change our position. Finally, even if we filed our motion only against the CHA (as we planned), HUD would enter the case and oppose us because if we prevailed against the CHA, HUD's duty to co-operate with the CHA would be implicated.

There was absolutely no "give" in any of what HUD was saying. As if to emphasize how firm it was, four lawyers were saying it. I took careful notes at the meeting, which was easy to do since they were doing all the talking. The last line of my notes read, "HUD hard line means we should file."

I was disappointed but not surprised. Although HUD was probably right that modernization money couldn't be used for replacement housing, I believed that its "interpretation" over many years that modernization plans did not have to consider desegregation would be weighty but not determinative. And I was unimpressed with its "too late" argument because, before North Kenwood–Oakland, the CHA had not proposed modernization costs high enough to amount to "rebuilding."

The real break came just as I returned to Chicago. Mosena called with news that the mayor was willing to play a limited role—he would invite Lane and me to his office and urge us to talk and avoid litigation. Lane might be agreeable because the mayoral request would give him an "excuse" with HUD for slowing down his modernization timetable. Under those circumstances HUD might go along with some delay.

The sticking point was that Mosena assumed that under his proposed scenario we wouldn't file our motion. I was reluctant about that because I felt we had to be on record before August 9. Finally, with Mosena seeming to acquiesce by not saying no, I suggested that we could file our motion and then—if Lane said yes to the mayor's request—immediately continue the motion until further notice. Nothing would then happen in court until one side or the other took some further action.

We filed our motion on August 5, 1991, scheduling a court presentation for August 9. Through Mosena I received a telephone "summons" to appear in the mayor's office on August 6. At about 3 P.M. on that day, Lane and I, who had had no personal conversation about what had now apparently been worked out, met in the mayor's reception room. We small-talked until Mosena appeared to usher us into the mayor's large office. Daley promptly came out from behind his desk and extended his hand for two shakes along with cordial "Hello, Vince" and "Hello, Alex" greetings. He motioned us to chairs in front of the desk, where he and Mosena took seats also.

Sitting in a circle the four of us chatted briefly, after which Mosena gently slid into the reason for our being there—"Mr. Mayor, we have this matter of the CHA buildings in North Kenwood–Oakland." Daley quickly said, "You know, it would really be better to work this thing out without going to court, don't you think?" Lane said that he had some problems with HUD but if that was what the mayor wanted he was certainly willing to try. I agreed that the plaintiffs were also willing to try. "Good," said Daley, enthusiastically, "that's the best way to go," adding, as he rose to signal the end of the meeting, that he would ask Mosena to handle the discussions. After handshakes with smiles all around, the three of us exited. The entire meeting hadn't taken much more than ten minutes. Mosena, the consummate administrator, had done his work well.

Much later I realized that the date we had selected to present our now-continued motion to Aspen was, to the very day, twenty-five years after the filing of the Gautreaux complaints on August 9, 1966.

5

Now that we had some breathing space, what came next? After an initial meeting among Mosena, Lane, and myself, Mosena handed off his North Kenwood–Oakland responsibilities to a deputy, Valerie Jarrett, who—astoundingly—was Robert Taylor's granddaughter. But Jarrett also had other qualifications for the job of fending off the rebuilding of the segregated high-rises, twenty-eight of which had been named—like a bad joke—after her forebear. She had an undergraduate degree from Stanford, a law degree from Michigan, and had served for four years in the corporation counsel's office. In a matter of a few weeks she was to take over as head of Daley's Planning Department, the appropriate place for North Kenwood–Oakland's revival to be shaped. Relatively young, Jarrett was smart, polite, a good listener, seemingly gentle, yet firm. She was also no stranger to the issues — on Mosena's staff she had participated in the meetings about heading off a "court blow-up."

Lane had agreed to talk, but he still wanted rehabilitation and carefully kept his modernization applications to HUD alive. With increasing urgency he was also seeking sites for the private housing part of Lake Parc Place. Yet the community planning council, composed mostly of black homeowners, was dead set against rehabilitation. In spite of its initial nod toward scattered-site housing, it now also opposed scattered sites, and MINCS as well, viewing the latter as just another form of public housing. Several thousand CHA units with a dozen high-rises lined North Kenwood–Oakland's northern boundary in three huge, contiguous projects: Ida B. Wells Homes, Clarence Darrow Homes, and Madden Park Homes. Additional scores of public housing units, including another high-rise, sat directly within the community. Passionately, the homeowners believed that they already had more than their fair share.

Toni Preckwinkle, alderman of the Fourth Ward, which included North Kenwood–Oakland, took the side of her homeowner constituents. "I want a diverse economic community," she wrote in an article.

> Vince Lane and the CHA . . . want not only to rehab all six of the lakefront property buildings there but to build a substantial number of low-rise units . . . I think you're going to have a hard time getting the private market to invest in a community where it's perceived that CHA-eligible individuals predominate.

Much of the North Kenwood–Oakland vacant land Lane was eyeing for his MINCS sites was owned by the city. Under the city council's "aldermanic courtesy" practice, the council would not approve disposition of any city-owned land if the local alderman objected. So Preckwinkle could hold Lane's hoped-for MINCS sites hostage to the homeowners' views. If under these circumstances a frustrated Lane went ahead with rebuilding the lakefront high-rises, we would of course proceed with our motion in court. But that would delay the whole planning and neighborhood revival process and precipitate the very "court blow-up" Mosena and his staff had wanted to forestall.

Through this maze the Jarrett meetings sought to find a path. The basic thrust was to keep talking while enlarging the group with people who might help in the path-seeking. The first of the new additions was Allison Davis, a well-connected lawyer friend of both Lane and Jarrett. Next came Jonathan Kleinbard, vice president for community relations of the University of Chicago. Then came Paula Wolf, a former aide to Illinois governor James Thompson and now chancellor of Governor State University in the south suburbs, and George Ranney, another well-connected lawyer and a resident of Kenwood, who was also a director of the MacArthur Foundation.

Eventually the Jarrett meetings acquired a focus. The idea was to concentrate on a revitalization plan for North Kenwood–Oakland that would emphasize homeownership, but might later include some public housing, in effect submerging present discussion of the high-rise issue within the challenge of developing a broader community plan. To spearhead the planning, an entity and someone to head it were needed. Davis came up with an ideal candidate, Bishop Arthur Brazier, the seventy-one-year-old pastor of the 9,000 member Apostolic Church of God, located in Woodlawn, just south of Hyde Park. Brazier was a good choice because he had Lane's confidence (at Lane's request he was serving on the CHA board), and also had sufficient stature to unite contentious factions behind a community redevelopment vision.

Because Brazier would serve only if the mayor gave his personal support, another of the orchestrated mayoral meetings was arranged at which the mayor asked Brazier to take on the task and Brazier agreed. In August 1992, the Fund for Community Redevelopment and Revitalization was formed with a group of directors carefully selected by Brazier to represent all community factions, and with an experienced development hand, personally chosen by Brazier, as executive director. Ranney was then able to persuade the MacArthur Foundation to make a $1.2 million initial grant to the Fund.

Yet all this community redevelopment talk was not getting Lane what he wanted, on either the Lakefront Properties or MINCS sites. On September 2, 1992, the *Hyde Park Herald* reported that the "CHA had been given the green light" to solicit architectural contracts for work on the first of the lakefront high-rises, and that funding would be allocated within thirty days. Lane announced that the renovation would be "just as nice, if not nicer" than Lake Parc Place. Soon Kleinbard reported on a dinner he'd had with Lane and a meeting with Preckwinkle. The report was not encouraging. Lane was "going ahead" with rehabilitation. If he did so, said Preckwinkle, she was ready to "go to war." All our careful strategizing seemed about to take us nowhere.

Then the fates took charge. In October 1992, seven-year-old Cabrini resident Dantrell Davis, walking to school on the project grounds, holding his mother's hand, was fatally shot by a single bullet from a sniper's rifle. For whatever reason the slaying touched a nerve that countless others, including two of Dantrell's schoolmates the previous summer, had not. Perhaps it was the image of Dantrell *holding his mother's hand.*

The killing was front-page news for a week. It had "shaken the city," the *New York Times* said. The *Tribune* soon editorially commanded, "Tear down the CHA high-rises." Do it now, it said, while the memory of Dantrell Davis "burns our civic memory." Six days after Dantrell's death Lane held a press conference in Mayor Daley's city hall office. Mixed-income, he said, was what was needed for public housing. "We've got to get working people in our developments." And he closed and sealed the four largely vacant high-rises among which Dantrell had been walking. In no more than the time it took to pull a trigger, Lane found he could begin to talk about what had until then been off limits—demolition.

October developments in Washington were equally profound, if less dramatic. Gautreaux lawyers had not been the only persons in the country who believed rebuilding the high-rises was ridiculous. In March 1992 the trade association of large public housing agencies had proposed more permission to demolish and more flexibility and money for replacement housing. In April HUD itself had formally proposed a more flexible replacement policy to Congress.

During the summer, congressional committees worked on the Catch-22 of no demolition without replacement, yet little replacement funding. The previous year, I had written an article about the problem (borrowing—with credit given—the *Washington Post*'s catchy title about not giving up on a bad idea). The article had led to a small conference at the Urban Institute. Bruce Katz, a key staff member of a key congressional committee, attended the conference and then labored mightily in committee deliberations to bring about change. The upshot was that in October two significant pieces of legislation passed Congress, and shortly before the November election President George Bush signed them.

The first new law, slipped into a HUD appropriations bill by Maryland senator Barbara Mikulski, created an Urban Revitalization Demonstration Program (URD) with $300 million in funding to be allocated equally among six housing authority projects selected by HUD through competitive proposals. What was to be revitalized was "severely distressed" public housing; demolition was authorized and program funding could be used for replacement housing. Although it was only a demonstration program, URD—the program's unlovely acronym—clearly marked a turn away from Kemp's abhorrence of demolition.

A second October law was a new housing bill, an outgrowth of the national commission Lane had cochaired. The bill provided greater flexibility both by increasing replacement housing funding and by permitting Section 8 certificates with only five- rather than fifteen-year commitments to be counted toward replacement. It spoke even more plainly than URD of the growing congressional sentiment against rebuilding the high-rises.

The effect of the Dantrell Davis slaying, followed by the new legislation, was then quickly amplified by the election of Bill Clinton and his choice of Henry Cisneros as HUD secretary. With his openly stated view that attacking "extreme spatial segregation" would be a top priority for HUD, Cisneros was signaling that Kemp's bias against demolition would no longer drive national housing policy.

The result of this spate of activity was that within a few short months following the sniper shot that snuffed out the life of Dantrell Davis, the political and legal environment within which we had all been operating in Chicago was radically changed.

6

Lane's first steps in the new circumstances were taken at Cabrini. Two days before Christmas 1992, Lane told the *Sun-Times* he would apply for a $50 million URD grant to begin "overhaul" at Cabrini. Some buildings would be "torn down," and private developers might be allowed to build replacement apartments. Lane's vision was an economic mix of welfare, blue collar, and middle-income families. "Neighborhoods used to work," he said, "when you had architects and lawyers and bus drivers and people on welfare living together. They had problems, but they aren't the problems we have now." He hoped Cabrini could be a blueprint for the country. "I think Dantrell Davis . . . will probably be a milestone."

In February Lane outlined his plans. He had recently "admitted," said the *Sun-Times*, that demolition was an option. Now, at a meeting of residents, he forthrightly announced, "We will have to demolish some of the buildings." Some Cabrini land would be leased to private developers, but the number of occupied units would be maintained and no residents would be displaced.

Residents charged that a "white land grab" was underway. A tenant leader vowed that if residents opposed demolition, "those buildings won't be torn down, believe me." But Lane negotiated this shoal successfully, placating resident leadership by adding social service promises to his no-displacement assurance, and filed his URD application in May. To everyone's surprise, Cabrini was passed over in the first round of URD funding because Lane failed to touch base with two key congressmen. But he soon remedied that problem, and in December 1993, wearing a broad smile, Lane announced that in URD's second round of funding the CHA would receive a $50 million Cabrini award.

The following month Lane made his first public statement that he would consider alternatives to rehabilitating the Lakefront high-rises. It was now almost two and a half years since we had gained breathing space through the meeting with the mayor and Mosena. Although there was still more talk than action in North Kenwood–Oakland, talk without the action of rehabilitation was exactly what our strategy had called for. In retrospect, our ten-minute meeting in the mayor's office had held off high-rise rebuilding at a key moment.

Instead of plunging promptly into Cabrini redevelopment, Lane spent a year fashioning a complicated financing plan under which the CHA would issue nearly a hundred million dollars of bonds. In May 1995

HUD's assistant secretary for public housing, Joseph Shuldiner, sent Lane a thirteen-page, single-spaced letter, the gist of which was, "no." HUD didn't like Lane's financing proposal—simpler approaches, Shuldiner wrote, involved lower costs and fees. A *Tribune* article speculated that what HUD really didn't like was Lane's naming of politically connected law firms and developers to various profitable roles, circumventing by a technicality HUD rules that required competitive bidding for those juicy positions.

HUD also was concerned that under Lane's plan only 167 of 685 new and rehabbed public housing units would be reserved for the poorest families who made up the great majority of Cabrini's residents. HUD funding, wrote Shuldiner, was for "revitalizing communities, not displacing and replacing them."

While this treading water was going on at Cabrini, the death knell for North Kenwood–Oakland high-rises was finally pronounced. Still seeking city-owned sites for MINCS, in March 1995 Lane wrote the head of the neighborhood's community planning group that if he could get those sites, "we will demolish the four (4) vacant high-rises." They were, he said, "in severe disrepair, making rehabilitation financially unfeasible." Hallelujah!

Meanwhile, the focus of interest had suddenly shifted to a third CHA development—Henry Horner Homes. Built in stages in the 1950s and 1960s on the Near West Side, Horner's nineteen high- and mid-rise buildings dominated the skyline a few blocks north of the Chicago Stadium, venerable home of the Chicago Blackhawks and then of the Chicago Bulls as well. Horner was another of the CHA's failed high-rise complexes, with vacancy rates approaching 50 percent. Its residents were in despair. In 1991 a group of them had sued the CHA and HUD, contending that Horner was literally uninhabitable. What the CHA was doing, they said, amounted to demolition without complying with HUD demolition requirements.

Events on the national stage soon gave the Horner lawsuit special importance. The Chicago Stadium was torn down and replaced with a gleaming new edifice, the United Center, to serve as the skyboxed home for Michael Jordan and his Chicago Bulls championship teams. The Democrats selected the new center for their 1996 National Convention, the first to be held in Chicago since the riotous one in 1968 that had so blackened the city's name. Determined that this convention, unlike the one hosted by his father, would show Chicago to advantage, Daley began to fix up the United Center's environs—new streets, curbs, and sidewalks, tree plantings, a new park, a new branch public library. Adjacent to the library, the prosperous Bulls planned the James Jordan Boys and Girls Club, dedicated to Michael Jordan's murdered father. A community organization, helped by the Bulls, facilitated rehabilitation of nearby housing. In record-breaking time the neighborhood surrounding the United Center was being transformed.

But there was one jarring blight on the transforming scene. In plain sight, just a few short blocks north of the United Center, Horner's grim buildings, with their boarded-up windows and surrounding expanses of mud and rusted playground equipment, were a gross violation of the resurgent West Side image being so carefully constructed.

It was no surprise then that the Horner suit was settled. In the fall of 1994 HUD put $30 million on the table and a deal was cut: two Horner high-rises would be demolished and replaced with low-rise buildings, three mid-rises would be rehabilitated, and some new units would be built. A few of the new units could actually be under construction when convention delegates arrived. With building under way and the story of the settlement to tell, the visual eyesore could be transformed into a tale of progress.

Unaccountably, however, perhaps because they were already before a federal judge, it wasn't until the eleventh hour that the CHA and HUD "remembered" that they couldn't simply build new public housing in the black Horner neighborhood. An order from Aspen would be required, and Habitat, not the CHA, had to be the builder. A call came from CHA lawyers, asking for a Gautreaux "sign-off" on the great victory for the public interest the settlement was said to represent. And we were requested to act quickly, lest HUD withdraw its generous $30 million offer.

Months of acrimonious negotiations ensued. If we were going to recommend Aspen approval for Horner, we wanted a mixed-income development, not a mid-rise and low-rise version of concentrated poverty. Horner would perhaps be benefited by all the good things that were happening around the United Center, but it was still at a remove of several blocks. Cabrini showed that the concentrated poverty of a public housing ghetto could exist in virtual isolation from a nearby affluent neighborhood, and the Horner neighborhood was not affluent but marginal.

Like Lane's vision for the URD at Cabrini, we insisted that Horner had to have a mixed-income occupancy. It would be a challenge to attract working families to the Horner area. Too many units for the very poor would prejudice that prospect. And all of Horner's awful buildings had to go. Rehabilitation of the three mid-rises—strongly desired by Horner residents—could remedy the most visible deficiencies. But we feared there would be little chance of attracting higher income families to the very institutional-looking buildings that were among the CHA's worst.

Meeting our demands required more new units and therefore more money, because the Horner lawyers insisted on enough new units to house all the tenants—mostly very poor—who wished to remain. And demolishing the mid-rises and starting "fresh" was more costly than the mixture of new construction and rehabilitation the Horner settlement had contemplated. In the end we got our way, but only through sweetening the pot by adding $20 million of Gautreaux dollars (if Aspen would agree) to HUD's $30 million. Gautreaux money was available because we still had about $40 million left—not yet obligated to any specific use— from HUD's annual, 350 unit set-asides under the HUD consent decree.

With the Gautreaux money added, we could pay for enough new construction to satisfy both the Horner tenants' demand to house all families who wished to remain and ours for an income mix. The mix would be accomplished by reserving half the new units for public housing families whose incomes were between 50 and 80 percent of the Chicago area median. At that income level—over $50,000 for a family of four—families were likely to be working, which would break the Horner pattern of unemployed, impoverished tenants. It wasn't the equivalent of Lane's Cabrini vision, where nearby affluence made it possible to attract unsubsidized families. But for Horner it would be a big step in the right direction. With economic "spillover" from the United Center, and all the convention-related neighborhood improvements, once the concentrated poverty of Horner was eliminated one might hope for genuine neighborhood betterment.

When agreement was finally reached in March 1995, we took it to Aspen with a detailed presentation about the horrors of Horner and what might be done to remedy them, pointing out that the proposed demolition and mixed-income replacement might even lead to eventual racial integration. "The ultimate goal is racial integration," Lane told Aspen. I chimed in that nobody could guarantee that that would happen, but the prospect was not a chimera.

Aspen went along, enthusiastically. He praised the Horner plan as "a twenty-first century view of Chicago and its housing problems." He volunteered that although the plan did not deal directly with racial integration, it did so indirectly "in the broad sense of impacting the conditions of the ghettos of Chicago." Then he signed the order we had drafted, designating the original part of Horner (excluding a later stage left for future redevelopment) a "revitalizing area," and authorized Habitat and the CHA to proceed, subject to specifics to be spelled out in a further order if the settlement were approved by the Horner judge.

When that was done in August 1995, Aspen signed a second order supplying the specifics. In the formal language we had drafted the order said that, although the principal "remedial purpose" of the case was to provide Gautreaux families with desegregated housing opportunities, the court had sometimes permitted public housing to be built in racially segregated areas upon a sufficient showing of "revitalizing" circumstances "such that a responsible forecast of economic integration, with a longer term possibility of racial desegregation, could be made." That forecast could be made about Horner "if the terms and conditions of this order are met."

We had used the revitalizing rubric before with small developments, mostly of the Section 8 project-based sort. But this was the first application of it to a large public housing redevelopment proposal, and it marked a watershed. In the important redevelopment context, our racial desegregation case had now been transmuted, with the judge's blessing, into a mixed-income, economic integration vehicle.

Whether or not this was cause for celebration is a good question. Using income as a proxy for race can be a dubious proposition. Yet insisting on immediate racial integration as the price for allowing Horner redevelopment would indeed have been viewed as chimerical. And, had we stood in their way, the powerful national and local political forces bent on prettying up the United Center environs for the Democratic Convention could well have swept Gautreaux away, ending any role at all for the case in public housing redevelopment.

For once, all the talk and court orders produced prompt action. "CHA officials don't entirely dispute," said the *Tribune*, "that the Democratic Convention has juiced the Horner process." On a steamy day in August 1995, on the crumbling surface of what had been a Horner basketball court, bleachers were speedily erected to seat dozens of dignitaries, including Daley, Cisneros, and Mamie Bone, longtime Horner tenant leader. Positioned off to the side, ready to go into action as soon as the talking ended, stood fire-engine red "Big Mama," the National Wrecking Company's 100-ton crane, complete with a 160-foot boom and 4-ton steel-cast wrecking ball.

Horner's revitalization, said Daley, speaking from a podium in front of the bleachers, was an essential part of the city's vision for the Near West Side. Applause. When his turn came, Cisneros added, "Chicago stands as a symbol for the country [of] what we're going to be able to do in public housing. As goes public housing in Chicago, so will go public housing for America." More applause. Wiping her brow with her handkerchief, Bone then concluded the speechmaking: "I can't say that I'm overjoyed, but I do feel that this is a road open for progress." Final applause.

The script now called for Big Mama to begin her work. Instead, several members of the Revolutionary Communist Party immediately raced toward her, leaped aboard, and clasped their arms and legs around her railings. During the speeches they had distributed "Stop the Wrecking Ball" flyers among the crowd, demanding that the buildings be fixed up, not torn down, and concluding, "HUD's Plan for Urban Renewal = Black People Removal." A superior force of CHA security guards quickly hauled off the objectors. Then Big Mama rumbled, her boom began to move and her steel wrecking ball swung, smashing against the topmost southeast corner of the fourteen-story high-rise known as 2145 W. Lake Street. A cheer accompanied the sound of bricks crashing to earth. As the dust cloud rose, a new era for Chicago public housing was beginning.

7

Sandwiched between the March and August Horner presentations to Aspen, an earthquake dramatically altered the public housing landscape in Chicago—and swallowed up Vince Lane. Though there had been earlier tremors, it was at the end of May 1995 that the ground beneath the CHA split open.

In a special meeting on Friday, May 26, 1995, all the CHA commissioners, succumbing to a demand from HUD, agreed to submit their resignations to HUD's Shuldiner. Day-to-day-control over operations, along with all of the CHA's power and authority, would pass to Shuldiner or his designee on May 30. Shortly after that date HUD dispatched Shuldiner to Chicago to take over and run the CHA.

What had happened? Why was the luminary, the savior, the man who was said to be bringing life back to the CHA, now suddenly, ignominiously, gone? The answer, like Gaul, is divided into three parts: security (the lack and cost of it), management (the failures of it), and Vince Lane, the imperfect human being.

Security—the gangs, drugs, and violence that plagued so many of the CHA's projects and their residents—had become Lane's obsession. In 1988 he initiated "sweeps," surprise police raids to catch gang members and drug dealers on their own turf. He hired private security guards and created his own CHA police force. He intensified tenant patrols and started drug treatment clinics at CHA developments. His first "Operation Clean Sweep" soon became the CHA's "Anti-Drug Initiative," intended to be a national model for crime prevention in public housing.

By early 1993 Lane was ready to proclaim a "turning point" in his battle against crime and drugs. At a news conference, staged at a police station, Lane proudly recited statistics showing that violent crime on CHA property had dropped during the previous year. Flanking the triumphant Lane before the cameras were Chicago's police superintendent as well as representatives from key law enforcement agencies, both federal and state—the FBI, the U.S. Attorney, the federal Drug Enforcement Bureau, the federal Bureau of Alcohol, Tobacco, and Firearms, the Illinois State Police, and the Cook County State's Attorney.

The celebratory announcement was premature, the hopeful statistics nothing more than that. Though enormously costly, draining huge sums from the CHA's other operations, the sweeps weren't effective over the long run. In late summer 1993, when several children fell to their deaths from unprotected Taylor Homes windows, crews sent to install window guards had to stop work because gang members began firing guns at them. Attacks by the ACLU brought curtailing court orders. Eventually Lane himself had to acknowledge, "Every building is controlled by a gang."

With Lane so focused on crime, the CHA's day-to-day management began to deteriorate badly. A securities scam cost the CHA's employee pension fund some $20 million. Millions more disappeared into swollen procurement budgets—an internal investigation disclosed that CHA employees were helping to rig bids. Security firms were routinely billing for work not done—another investigation showed that every one of the CHA's six security contractors was doing it. HUD denied the CHA's request for money to expand its Section 8 program because of "chronic mismanagement and understaffing," and soon began its own investigation into bribery allegations. HUD was becoming concerned that the CHA was spinning out of control.

There was, finally, the personal factor, the imperfect human being. When, with considerable fanfare, Lane announced his plans for redeveloping Cabrini, Daley's chief of staff learned about it from reporters and had to call the CHA to find out what was going on. At a housing conference in London, Lane was all the rage, expounding to the press on his vision for public housing. Shuldiner, America's top public housing official, cooled his heels, largely ignored, including by Lane. Not the best way to make friends in important places in Chicago and Washington.

Then Lane's private business corporation acquired a distressed company with a large portfolio of subsidized housing. Worried about possible conflicts of interest, HUD insisted that Lane give up control of the CHA's day-to-day operations and confine himself to policy matters as head of the CHA's board. Appearing to comply, Lane hired Graham Grady, Daley's commissioner of zoning. But he gave Grady the title of chief operating—not chief executive—officer, and effectively continued to run the show himself. Grady had been on the job for barely nine months when, to HUD's distress, Lane peremptorily fired him.

A specific conflict of interest concern also arose. In May 1994 Lane had hired the New Life Self-Development Company to manage and provide security for two CHA developments. New Life was affiliated with the Nation of Islam; its boss was the Nation's chief of staff, Leonard Farrakhan, who was Louis Farrakhan's son-in-law. In May 1995 HUD revealed it was investigating a possible conflict of interest involving New Life and Lane. Details emerged in a *Tribune* story on May 17. Lane, it was said, had made a deal with the Nation of Islam: in exchange for the management and security contracts, the Nation would lease space for a grocery in a shopping mall Lane had developed. The grocery lease, as he later acknowledged, helped rescue Lane from "personal financial disaster"—with the signed lease in hand he had been able to restructure the shopping mall's debt and fend off threatened foreclosure. Though denying they were linked, Lane admitted discussing both the grocery lease and the security contracts in a single meeting with Leonard Farrakhan.

Soon after the May 30 HUD takeover, a "memorandum of agreement" between HUD and a no longer independent CHA set out reasons for HUD's action. The CHA was a "profoundly troubled" agency that, after numerous recent federal investigations, was still contending with chronic drug activity, violent crime, and "deplorable housing and living conditions." The firing of Grady, followed by the resignation of its entire board, had left the CHA without leadership. By implication, HUD had had no choice but to take over.

In an article entitled "Graft and Mortar," the *Economist* put it less formally. Vince Lane was a man of "bold ideas" who wanted to tackle ghetto crime, break up concentrations of poverty, and build new communities that would mix current tenants with ordinary working families. "Nevertheless, as Mr. Lane touted his visionary ideas in Washington, graft and corruption flourished at home."

Graft, corruption, the failure of Lane's expensive anticrime program, bad management even by historic CHA standards, allowing personal business to appear to be entangled with CHA contracts—all contributed to Lane's downfall. There was, however, one more factor. Had Lane actually succeeded in turning the CHA around, he would have been popular enough to pose a political threat to Richard M. Daley. Not many years earlier, when HUD had threatened to take over the CHA during Harold Washington's administration, the mayor had fought HUD tooth and nail. This time the scenario was markedly different.

Shortly before the CHA's special May 26 meeting, Cisneros visited

Daley in Chicago. He emerged from the mayoral office with a go-ahead for the HUD takeover. "I think the mayor is frustrated at the slow [CHA] progress," said the HUD Secretary. It does not require cryptography to decode that statement: Daley wanted Lane gone.

Then Cisneros met with Lane in Washington. The talk was candid. The brutal realities were that HUD had live ammunition and it was prepared to shoot. This time, far from opposing a federal takeover, the mayor was eager for it. Lane quickly concluded that the realities were indeed brutal and that he ought to bow to them. He told Cisneros he would go along. After seven years as head of the CHA, he added, he had planned to step down anyway.

Within days arrangements were made. Marilyn Johnson, the CHA's in-house lawyer who had been designated acting executive director in the wake of Grady's departure, had a long telephone conversation with Shuldiner. At the special board meeting she related what Shuldiner had told her. HUD would take over the CHA. To supply the legal authority it would formally declare that the CHA had violated its basic contract with HUD, which it would have no trouble proving in court if necessary. But a "voluntary, consensual and collaborative approach" would be preferred, and Johnson read to the commissioners the "consensual" resolution language she had prepared.

Lane, who "attended" the meeting by telephone hookup from Philadelphia, was unusually quiet. He sounded "resigned," one of the commissioners recalled. Repeatedly Bishop Brazier asked, "Do we have a choice or not?" Other commissioners nodded, as if they too wanted that question answered. Johnson responded that one way or another, it looked as if HUD were going to take over. Then Bob Whitfield, a former aide to Lane who was no longer on salary but had stayed on as a paid consultant to help Johnson, spoke in his quiet, uncommonly low-pitched voice. "Y'all bein' fired," he said with a smile.

Abruptly, the atmosphere changed. Bluster evaporated. If Lane were going along, as he seemed to be, why should the others resist? One of the commissioners, who had put in countless volunteer hours on CHA business, felt relieved. We assumed, he later reflected, that it was what the mayor wanted, and we were his appointees. If the mayor were supporting Lane, wouldn't Lane have resisted the HUD takeover?

In short order, the commissioners agreed that Johnson's consensual resolution "would be the way to go." And that, with Johnson wrapping up the formalities, was the way they went.

8

Though he was now gone from the scene, Lane's bold ideas—except for sweeps—prevailed. Radical-sounding notions that had tripped easily from his tongue—mixed-income, working families, housing that poor people could live in rather than housing for poor people—became the new conventional wisdom. Having added momentum with his talk of "spatial deconcentration," Cisneros was now more explicit. In a policy paper entitled, "Public Housing Transformation," he wrote: "Old, deteriorated, high-rise public housing [will] come down . . . New housing will be built to smaller, more humane scale . . . to look like any other housing."

Soon HUD came up with a "viability" test—would rehabilitation cost more than the combined cost of Section 8 relocation and demolition?—and in 1996 demolition was mandated for buildings that didn't pass. More than 18,000 CHA apartments failed the test, including fifty-one high-rises and the entirety of places such as Robert Taylor Homes. Shuldiner was now not only free to demolish, but was required to. A Herculean physical development and human relocation job was his reward, or punishment, for taking the CHA job.

Shuldiner's task was not made easier by the mess he inherited. The CHA's books were a "nightmare." After three months of trying to untangle them a $52 million deficit was announced, much of it because of security costs and contractor overbilling. Crime and drugs continued to dominate CHA high-rises. Although their living conditions were horrible, residents were fearful and distrustful of all this talk of demolition of the only homes many of them had ever known. A tenant lawsuit blocked Shuldiner's attempt to restart the stalled Cabrini process.

Frustrated also by the need to work with Habitat, whose receivership powers appeared to give it, not the CHA, the power to develop the new public housing that was to be part of the mixed-income replacement communities, Shuldiner started a suit of his own. He hired a former federal judge to argue to Aspen that Habitat should have no role in the new context because replacement public housing was a new ball game, different from the old scattered sites. He lost before Aspen, and lost his appeal too, and Gautreaux revitalizing orders and power-sharing with Habitat remained a part of the CHA's redevelopment process.

Yet the HOPE VI program—the new name for a beefed-up URD, redesigned to pour big money into the redevelopment of neighborhoods dominated by "severely distressed" public housing—was now in high gear and was supplying the means to destroy many of the redoubts sheltering gang members and drug dealers. The acronym stood for "Housing Opportunities for People Everywhere." (The VI reflected the evolutionary history of the program, which had gone through several iterations.) It soon became, as a research report described it, "one of the most ambitious urban redevelopment efforts in the nation's history." Before Congress began to cut back on appropriations in 2004, some 446 grants for planning, demolition, and redevelopment had been awarded in 166 cities at a total cost of $5 billion. Because HOPE VI dollars were supposed to, and did, leverage other public, private, and philanthropic investment, the total spent on HOPE VI redevelopment projects far exceeded the HOPE VI dollars themselves.

With one of its own at the helm, it was not surprising that HUD quickly made the CHA a big HOPE VI grant recipient. Over the next several years it gave the CHA nearly $200 million in HOPE VI grants for four developments (one of which—at Cisneros's insistence—was Robert Taylor Homes), a total that did not include either the $50 million award for Cabrini or the $50 million from HUD and Gautreaux for Horner. To change the face of the CHA Shuldiner faced a monumental task, but he had significant resources with which to begin.

The Shuldiner reign lasted four years, until June 1999. At that point HUD returned the CHA to local control, a process that was not without friction. In August 1998, HUD secretary Andrew Cuomo—former New York governor Mario Cuomo's son, who had served under Cisneros and taken over when his boss retired after the first Clinton administration— announced that he was removing the CHA from HUD's "troubled" list and—surprise!—would soon hand it over to Mayor Daley. Chicago mayors appointed CHA commissioners, but they had generally maintained considerable public distance between city hall and the "independent"

CHA agency. Now, as he had done in 1995 with Chicago schools, Daley planned to take open responsibility for public housing, although an adviser warned that that would be tantamount to "political suicide."

If he were going to risk self-destruction, Daley wanted freedom from HUD's countless three-ring binders of micromanaging rules. But reaching agreement on new arrangements turned out to be flinty and wasn't accomplished by the already scheduled turnback date. Announcing his new CHA leadership team, Daley was cautious: it would take "several more months" to shape up the ground rules.

It did. Daley's team, headed by his own chief of staff, Julia Stasch, herself a former federal bureaucrat, kept working over the specifics with HUD for the "several more months" and then some. Daley insisted on flexibility, so that HUD wouldn't have to approve every diced carrot that went into the CHA's stew; an assured funding stream, so that a multiyear task would not be placed on the guillotine with each annual congressional appropriation; and so on.

But HUD's bureaucratic fingers didn't unclasp easily. Though numerous editorials admonished HUD to give Chicago what it wanted, for weeks it looked as if HUD and Daley/Stasch might never agree. Even BPI issued a public statement supporting the CHA's goals and, conditional upon effective relocation, urged HUD to play the "partner" role it had promised six months earlier. Yet the acrimonious negotiations dragged on past the new millennium.

In frustration, Daley lobbied the White House—HUD was, after all, part of a Democratic administration. With the Republicans controlling Congress, Daley also got in touch with Rick Lazio, the Long Islander who headed the congressional committee handling HUD appropriations. An obliging Lazio scheduled hearings and, on January 20, 2000, invited Daley to testify about how HUD was blocking his reform efforts.

The Lazio-threatened hearings may or may not have made the difference. HUD of course denied it. But suddenly, before the scheduled hearing date, the logjam broke. On Saturday morning, February 5, 2000, Cuomo and several aides flew into Chicago to meet Daley and his Chicago entourage for a signing ceremony and press conference. With the cameras popping and assorted dignitaries looking on, a smiling Cuomo and a beaming Daley signed what was called the CHA's "Plan for Transformation."

It had taken time, not to mention bruised relationships, but Daley got much of what he wanted. Over a decade, from 2000 to 2010, it was a $1.5 billion deal. Subject to annual appropriations from Congress, the CHA could count on some $150 million a year from HUD and—of considerable importance—could borrow money in the private market against that funding stream. There were numerous "waivers" of HUD rules that meant the CHA could indeed select the ingredients for its stew without HUD approving each one.

With the promised dollars the CHA would demolish some 18,000 "obsolete" public housing units and would build or rehabilitate about 25,000—enough to house all "lease compliant" tenants. That would entail a net loss of some 13,000 units, most of them vacant. The loss was "concerning," as the Transformation Plan described it, but "there was no alternative."

The $1.5 billion figure looked impressive, but it wasn't enough to do all that was planned. The CHA's "capital needs" were "in excess of $3 billion," and the gap was to be filled with a wing and a prayer from other federal, city, and private sector sources, including developers who could make a profit from market housing built on CHA land. The new and rehabilitated housing would be built "to a standard of quality sufficient to attract a mix of incomes so that public housing does not again become home to extreme concentrations of poverty." Still, thousands of families—tens of thousands of human beings—would have to be relocated.

Truly, it was an enormous undertaking—relocating families, demolishing buildings, preparing the infrastructure for new developments, and planning, designing, building, and marketing new mixed-income communities on an unprecedented scale. *Newsweek* ("Razing the Vertical Ghettos") said that while eighty cities across the land had leveled at least some of their worst public housing, "none has attempted such a complete overhaul."

"CHA to Be Torn Up, Rebuilt," was the *Tribune* headline. From Cuomo came the homily, "You can no longer put a Band-Aid on a bullet wound." It was a demolition plan, he acknowledged, but it was also "a tenant-protection plan." Daley went further. The Transformation Plan would not only replace buildings, it would "rebuild lives."

9

That was the way it was supposed to be—a three-part prescription for a "complete overhaul" that would "rebuild lives." First, the Taylors and Horners would be eradicated. Second, where those awful places had festered new communities would rise that would include but wouldn't *be* public housing—where, as Vince Lane had envisioned, neighborhoods worked because "you had architects and lawyers and bus drivers and people on welfare living together."

Third, lives would be rebuilt. Maybe not every life, but many, and everyone would have a chance. Some would move into the new communities with architects and lawyers. Some would move via Section 8, following the path into better life circumstances taken by the Gautreaux families Rosenbaum had studied. And the rest?—for there wouldn't be enough public housing in the new communities for everyone, nor could all the remaining families be expected to make a Gautreaux-type success of Section 8. The rest would move either to other CHA developments, low-rise (mid-rise at most), admittedly 100 percent public housing but fixed up to be decent, or to Section 8 apartments in neighborhoods that were far from ideal but better than Taylor and Horner.

The first step, tearing down, was the easiest. Some residents, of course, objected. A "Coalition to Protect Public Housing" was formed that staged rallies, issued press statements. The Cabrini lawsuit, eventually settled, slowed what otherwise might have been the pace of Cabrini demolition. But the Big Mamas of the Transformation Plan steadily swung their wrecking balls. By 2005 only two of Taylor's twenty-eight buildings remained standing. Madden Park's six and Darrow's four were entirely gone, as were six of Stateway's eight. The four Lakefront Properties were imploded with dynamite, and on a cloudless morning all crumbled to the ground in minutes. Some high-rises still remained at Cabrini and elsewhere, but it would be only a matter of time before they too came down. Chicago's public housing high-rise cityscape, erected in the 1950s and 1960s with high hopes for "Building Good Homes, Good Citizens" (while keeping poor blacks out of white neighborhoods), will—after fifty years—have been reduced to rubble.

The second step, the construction, is going more slowly, partly because land must be cleared before it can be built upon, partly because construction always takes longer than demolition. Mostly, however, because what is to be built is uncommonly challenging. Vince Lane's recollection was rooted in history. But architects and lawyers lived in the neighborhoods Lane recalled because they had no other choice; being black, they could not move outside the ghetto. When they got the chance to move out, after housing discrimination was made illegal in 1968, they took it. The challenge now was to build communities in which architects and lawyers, including whites, would *choose* to live near black bus drivers and welfare families. And pay prices that would enable private developers of the new mixed-income communities to turn a profit. Does it not sound like a fool's mission?

And yet . . . A block of old urban renewal land on North Larrabee Street was cheek by jowl with Cabrini on its northeast side. With some of Cabrini coming down and the expectation that the rest would follow, and with a new high school, police station, supermarket, and other upscale development nearby, developers believed the time had come for the long-awaited redevelopment of the Cabrini area's prime real estate. The North Larrabee block looked like a ripe plum waiting to be picked. Not quite so fast, said Daley. If you want our urban renewal land, take some Cabrini families. And that—with Lane's old friend, Allison Davis, as one of the developers—became the deal.

Today Mohawk North, as the development is called, is eighty units of townhomes and three-flats. Sixteen of them, spread among and indistinguishable from the rest, are public housing—leased to the CHA for forty years to house sixteen Cabrini families. The sixteen units are managed by a Davis-selected firm, which had the final word on the qualifications of the Cabrini families and screened out those with serious problems. The same firm received an eighteen-month contract from the CHA to assist the selected Cabrini families with job training and placement, day care, and the like. Though buyers were of course told that 20 percent of the residents would be public housing families, the sixty-four privately owned units sold out within days of the offering.

Now, nearly half a dozen years later, the manager reports "nothing spectacular." Early problems (loud music, harsh words) were "worked through." Management is still "labor intensive," but the condominium owners have "worked out their relationships" with the ex-Cabrini families living in the same buildings or next door. They aren't friends, but they coexist peacefully. Most of the Cabrini families have jobs. Except for living in safe, excellent housing, they have not, says the manager, undergone a discernible life transformation. The market prices of Mohawk North units are now double what they were at the beginning.

Another mixed-income community went up on the west side of Cabrini on Halsted Street. Called North Town Village, it was larger and more complicated than Mohawk North. On seven acres, with 261 rental and for-sale apartments, condominiums, and townhomes, North Town Village's 30 percent public housing ratio was half again as much as Mohawk North's.

North Town Village has problems. First, the adjacent Cabrini highrises haven't yet come down; depending on the time of day, some North Town Village units are literally in their shadows. Second, most of the public housing families have children, and many of the other families do not. North Town Village is adjacent to a park, but the park adjoins the highrises and is felt to be dangerous. Most of North Town Village's children, mostly black, hang out in the community's interior space—access areas with bushes and small trees, not designed for play. Even though CHA families had to pass drug tests and tough screening to get in, the impression a visitor (or prospective purchaser) might get is not of a mixed-income community but of a predominantly black development overrun with children.

Peter Holsten, North Town Village's developer, acknowledges the problem. He had hoped the high-rises would have been gone by now. When they are, and the park "opens up," he believes the play space problem will be resolved, and with it the off-putting first impression.

North Town Village had the good fortune to be offered in a superheated real estate market. The sale units went like hotcakes, at prices of more than $300,000, though the buyers knew that 30 percent of the units would be occupied by public housing families. Today, partly because of the market downturn and partly because of the still standing high-rises and play space problems, some of the owners aren't happy campers. (Some are not "campers" at all. Mohawk North buyers had to agree to live in their units for two years, but many North Town Village units were sold to investors.)

Still, Holsten is optimistic. The high-rises will eventually go, and with them the play space problem. The nearby area boasts solid, upscale development. What North Town Village has shown, Holsten believes, is that—even in the shadow of CHA high-rises—in some circumstances, at least, some whites will pay for good housing values knowing that three of every ten fellow residents will be from a public housing family.

It turned out that at Mohawk North and North Town Village some rich whites were willing, after all, to live next door to public housing families. Would that prove to be true elsewhere than in the affluent Cabrini environs? And on the grand scale of the CHA's Transformation Plan? More than 11,000 mixed-income dwellings are planned for Henry Horner, Lakefront, Madden Wells, Rockwell Gardens, and others, plus Robert Taylor Homes and its next-door neighbor, Stateway Gardens, on the infamous State Street corridor. Not one of these public housing neighborhoods boasts the affluence of the Cabrini area. Some, like Rockwell, Taylor, and Stateway, have been among the roughest of Chicago's ghetto neighborhoods. As *Newsweek* had said, no other city had attempted such a complete overhaul. What chance was there that such a grandiose plan would be "transformed" into reality?

Because of the immense scale of Chicago's Transformation Plan, there is no "comparable" in another city. But each individual redevelopment project, with its own development team and its own neighborhood characteristics, is in many ways independent of the others and will succeed or fail on its own. At the scale of individual developments, comparables can be found.

Centennial Place in Atlanta, one of the earliest HOPE VI developments, is a success so far. Beginning in 1995, nearly 1,200 units of terrible public housing, probably as bad as Chicago's archetypes, were transformed into 758 two- and three-story garden and town houses, some 42 percent of them public housing. By completion in 2000, Centennial Place had become an attractive, well-working community, with rentals for market units comparable to those in Atlanta's good neighborhoods.

In fact Centennial Place had itself become a "good neighborhood," with low crime levels, a good school, and the other characteristics "good neighborhood" connotes. True enough, Centennial Place abuts Georgia Tech, is close to downtown, and was mightily helped by Atlanta's selection as the site for the 1996 Summer Olympic Games. Still, it was quite a success story, and now even has some white residents in what had been a nearly 100 percent black neighborhood.

Similar developments elsewhere, for example, Park DuValle in Louisville and Murphy Park in St. Louis, though not yet completed, are well under way. With initial phases constructed and occupied, rentals in the market rate units have increased modestly (up to 12 percent) since original leasing. At both places, studies report neighborhood-wide physical improvements, reductions in crime, and the like.

Apart from precedents in other cities, there were favorable signs in Chicago. During the economic downturn of the early Transformation Plan years residential construction in Chicago remained strong. Developers like Davis and Holsten were interested in CHA plans, even in neighborhoods other than Cabrini, and were willing to take financial risks to participate. Once the high-rises started coming down, the atmosphere in some places changed palpably. With most of Taylor's buildings gone but a few still standing, and with on-site construction not yet begun, signs of residential rehabilitation, even of modest new construction, appeared in adjacent areas where for decades nothing had been rehabilitated or built.

It seems premature therefore to write off the mixed-income communities objective as a "fool's mission." If the economy or something else doesn't abort the plans, it is just possible that the Transformation Plan will accomplish what its name promises. In any event, measured at least by demolition, replacement plans, and developer interest, the plan's second step of building mixed-income communities to replace the downed high-rises is clearly under way.

The third step, rebuilding lives, was at once the most ambitious and the most problematic. It was also the step the CHA performed least well. Relocation was the threshold task. Where would the families go who had to be moved out before the wrecking balls could swing?

The answer was soon apparent. Most were going from one black-segregated neighborhood to another, either to other public housing developments not slated for "transformation" or, via Section 8, to other black (mostly high-poverty) neighborhoods on the South and West Sides. Based on the CHA's own data, the documentation on the Section 8 families came from a study by a Lake Forest College professor, Paul Fischer, hired for the purpose by a Chicago public interest group. The Fischer study showed that from 1995 to 2002 virtually all of the 3,265 families moved via Section 8 wound up in heavily black census tracts—the exact figure was that 86.3 percent of the Section 8 families moved to census tracts that were 80 to 100 percent black. Only 4.7 percent were moved to tracts with less than the Gautreaux ceiling of 30 percent black population.

Why was the Fischer-documented resegregation occurring? The main reason was that the CHA was failing to provide effective mobility counseling—the Leadership Council's Gautreaux-type assistance. In the early relocation years the CHA furnished virtually no counseling at all. When it finally hired relocation contractors, it didn't require them to do the job right. Instead, the counselors were permitted to follow the path of least resistance—to funnel displaced families as rapidly as possible into other parts of Chicago's black ghetto, not infrequently into shoddy apartments.

Because of a requirement in the Transformation Plan's tenant protection package, and our threat to go to Aspen, the CHA finally hired a former U.S. Attorney, Tom Sullivan, to conduct an "independent audit" of the relocation process. After months of careful investigation, at the end of 2002 Sullivan reported on what was happening to the Section 8 families:

> The result has been that the vertical ghettos from which the families are being moved are being replaced with horizontal ghettos, located in well defined, highly segregated neighborhoods on the West and South Sides of Chicago.

It was true that the relocation task was not easy. For many CHA families good mobility counseling wouldn't have been enough without simultaneously addressing their multiple social problems with quality social services. But the CHA's pretense of offering services—when the CHA finally got around to it—was as flawed as its housing counseling. Sullivan's report said that the CHA's services program was "grossly underfunded, and . . . grossly understaffed, with the result that it was only marginally effective in assisting a relatively few residents." (Yet even with good counseling and good services, many families would remain fearful about leaving familiar environments.)

Talking to the CHA proved fruitless. Finally, with BPI's help, public interest groups crafted a relocation plan of their own and urged it upon the CHA, threatening litigation as the alternative. This failed too, and in January 2003 suit was filed. The complaint asserted that the way the CHA was handling relocation violated federal law as well as the CHA's Transformation Plan agreement with HUD. The experiences of the first-named plaintiff illustrate the relocation challenges many moving families faced. In 1997, burst sewage pipes forced Diane Wallace and her two children out of their CHA apartment in the Robert Brooks Homes. On an emergency basis the CHA moved Wallace with a Section 8 voucher to a South Side apartment that turned out to be beset on the inside with rats, roaches, and a broken bathtub, and on the outside with rampant drug activity. The nearby public school failed to diagnose Wallace's daughter's learning disability, stemming from lead poisoning in the Brooks Homes, and soon expelled her.

For four years Wallace complained to no avail, the CHA contending that her apartment met "housing quality standards." Finally, in 2001, the CHA moved Wallace to a different neighborhood. Though somewhat better than the first, the new apartment had roaches, leaking faucets, poor insulation, and inadequate heat. Like its predecessor, it too was in an all-black neighborhood.

Together with pressure from others, particularly the MacArthur Foundation, which has been a strong backer of the Transformation Plan, the lawsuit led to improvements in the CHA's relocation arrangements, at least on paper. Relocation contractors were told to try to avoid moving families to heavily black neighborhoods, and a video portraying the benefits of moving to "opportunity" areas was prepared. The CHA has announced that it will double its services money, enabling it to reduce case manager loads from as high as 300 to 1 down to 55 to 1. "On paper," however, is an important qualification. After the reported improvements were supposedly put in place, Sullivan and an independent Columbia University researcher both reported that relocation in 2003 was still badly flawed and not much better than in 2002. Then, in early 2005, the lawsuit was settled; the CHA agreed to modify its relocation procedures for families yet to be moved and to "retrofit" relocation for families already moved by offering them enhanced mobility counseling.

10

Some of the Transformation Plan difficulties (but not the relocation failures) could be chalked up to the size and complexity of the plan task.

When had such a huge undertaking ever been carried out flawlessly? Yet some critics seriously questioned the premises of the whole enterprise. Their three major objections were that mixed-income communities were overrated, that few of the displaced public housing families would ever get into them, and that in any event the cost of creating mixed-income communities—particularly the reduction of the public housing stock at a time when poor families were facing an affordable housing crisis—was too high.

The objections were not frivolous. There is little "hard" evidence about how successful mixed-income communities will be over the long run, partly of course because they are so new. One study of eight HOPE VI developments finds that they have "experienced considerable improvement" and that their economic conditions "are now generally better than those in other high-poverty neighborhoods," though below city averages on important indicators. Another study says preliminary evidence indicates that "mixed-income, public housing communities can work," although the most comprehensive examination of HOPE VI projects to date concludes that their long-term viability "remains an important unanswered question."

HOPE VI redevelopment may of course benefit the surrounding community too. One study speaks of "remarkably positive impacts," leading it to conclude that the economic and related payoffs from HOPE VI can be substantial. Yet viability and benefits to the surrounding community also characterized the urban renewal program of the 1950s and 1960s, which "succeeded" at the expense of displaced, mostly black residents. Whether HOPE VI redevelopments will rebuild the lives of the public housing families fortunate enough to return to them must be part of the calculus. Much depends on what is meant by "rebuild lives." The critics point to anecdotal but growing evidence that there is little social interaction between displaced families who return and their more affluent neighbors.

But that may not be the right criterion for mothers and children who have been enabled to escape from an environment such as Taylor's. Isn't it too much to expect adults and teenagers who have lived much of their lives in places like Chicago's public housing high-rises to be quickly transformed into solid, wage-earning citizens who enjoy social intercourse with affluent neighbors? Aren't safer, more humane environments an important first step, particularly for young children? Perhaps the lives to be rebuilt are those of the next generation, who will be enabled to live their formative years in circumstances less damaging than public housing high-rises. Only time will tell to what extent a move to a mixed-income community can lead to modified patterns of behavior for longtime CHA residents.

There is hard evidence to support the second objection—that few of the displaced public housing families will get the chance to move into the new communities. An article by Susan Popkin, on what she called the "Gautreaux legacy" of deconcentration, persuasively argued that the only beneficiaries of the CHA's plan would be the least troubled families. The larger population of "vulnerable families," Popkin wrote, could not be expected to survive screening by the private managers of the replacement mixed-income communities. HUD's figures for the first HOPE VI decade, covering more than 150 projects in nearly 100 cities, show that only 11.4 percent of the families who had lived in HOPE VI demolished buildings had been able, or were even expected, to return to the replacement mixed-income communities.

Again, however, the implicit criterion—in this case the percentage of public housing "returnees"—may not be the right one. Reducing the on-site public housing stock is a predicate of the mixed-income approach. Lessening the concentration of impoverished families is as essential to developing a mixed-income community as demolishing the high-rises. Criticizing mixed-income developments because most former public housing residents can't return is a little like criticizing scrambled eggs because the eggs are broken.

Nor would returning necessarily be the best or preferred course for everyone. I talked with a consultant to a number of HOPE VI projects who spoke of families being "released from the captivity of public housing." She also reported that many families who had moved out with temporary Section 8 vouchers chose not to return to the new public housing when it was ready for them, preferring to remain in their private market circumstances. The consultant's anecdotal impressions are supported by a number of surveys of residents displaced by HOPE VI.

A better criterion would be what is happening to all displaced families, including those who don't return as well as those who do. This is a segue to the critics' third objection that the nation's affordable housing crisis makes this the wrong time to reduce the country's public housing stock. A recent report discloses that in the Chicago area a worker earning the minimum wage would have to work three and a half full-time jobs to afford a typical two-bedroom apartment. HUD acknowledged that only forty units of affordable housing were available for every hundred extremely poor families. Scores of thousands of poor families were paying half and more of their income for rent, forcing many to choose whether, as the saying goes, "to heat or eat."

In the 1970s there were almost a million more cheap apartments in the country than there were poor families. In a *New York Times Magazine* article Jason DeParle, a longtime reporter for the *New York Times* and the author of a recent book on welfare, described what then happened. Renewal (read, bulldozing) knocked many of the cheap units down, gentrification (read, higher rents) fixed others up, and rising rents outstripped inflation. Meanwhile, as affordable housing was disappearing, the number of housing-needy families exploded during decades of steady wage erosion.

On top of all this, housing subsidies plummeted. In the mid-1970s HUD was subsidizing about 400,000 new apartments a year. By the early 1990s that number had dropped to around 36,000. In 1996 President Clinton signed a housing bill that reduced the number still further—to zero. That was the nadir, but the average number of new units subsidized each year has failed to keep pace with the continuing downward pressure of bulldozing, gentrification, rising rents, and wage stagnation. Today, millions of families are on Section 8 waiting lists; in larger cities the wait can be eight to ten years. Given the huge and still growing deficit of housing for poor families in America, how can one justify destroying all those public housing apartments, reducing still further the supply of shelter the very poor *can* afford?

The answer takes us back to Ruby Haynes and her children. If, to avoid losing public housing units, we were to rebuild the high-rises, some version of the Haynes story would almost certainly be the lot of succeeding generations. The Haynes saga is not an exaggeration of the failures of public housing high-rise communities, as Popkin's *Hidden War* description of the problems faced by a "significant proportion" of CHA families shows:

It is very difficult for young men in CHA housing to avoid being recruited by gangs . . . It is not at all unusual to have someone who has been
arrested or has served jail time in the household . . . CHA residents
also . . . cope with substance abuse, domestic violence, serious illness and
disability . . . , the sudden death of family members and friends . . . and
other mental problems.

In her foreword to *The Hidden War*, Rebecca Blank, an economics
professor specializing in poverty issues, says the projects Popkin and her
coauthors describe have become "synonyms for lost lives." Arnold
Hirsch's book review in the *Tribune* says the tale is one of a "humanitarian disaster." Another study reports that many HOPE VI families waiting
to relocate have physical and mental health problems, histories of domestic violence and substance abuse, criminal records, and poor credit.
More than a third of adults reported chronic illness or health problems,
and young children suffered from asthma at more than three times the
national average.

It is true that it wasn't always that way. Nostalgic accounts tell us that
in the beginning the high-rises were places of hope. Couldn't those days
be recaptured? In a critique of the HOPE VI program entitled "False
Hope," a respected housing advocacy organization urges a return to the
one-for-one replacement requirement. Given the challenge—read im-
possibility—of building scattered-site public housing on a significant scale
in decent neighborhoods, as exemplified by the Gautreaux scattered-site
experience, this amounts to a rebuild-the-high-rises prescription.

But there is every reason to believe we can't go home again. Vince
Lane tried as hard as one can imagine anyone trying to make the high-
rises livable again. *The Hidden War* is a poignant account of millions of
dollars worth of trying that bankrupted an agency, destroyed a visionary,
and ended in failure. The good old high-rise days predated the gangs and
drugs. We can no more restore the high-rises of that era than we can restore the frontier to cowboys and Indians.

"False Hope" suggests restoration not just through physical rebuilding but through better services as well. By raising the incomes of the very
poor with job training and child care, accompanied by substance abuse,
domestic violence, and credit counseling, mixed income would be ac-

complished "from within," that is, "by assisting current residents to secure new or better-paying employment, rather than [by] simply forcing residents out." Self-sufficiency would be achieved not through higher-income neighbors but "by providing jobs—and training, childcare, and other services to allow residents to take these jobs."

This is a pipe dream. History gives us exactly zero examples of the successful redevelopment of a concentrated poverty high-rise through improved social services. It is impossible to imagine Ruby Haynes and her children, and the other Taylor residents from 1962 to 1979 (let alone in the years following Haynes's departure when conditions greatly worsened), brought to "self-sufficiency" through improved social services in and around even a fixed-up Taylor.

Lewis Spence, a respected figure in recent public housing history, who served as a court-appointed receiver for the Boston Housing Authority, succinctly explains why. Given the devastation we have wrought, Spence writes, only a program that integrates nonworking with working families could hope to foster the circumstances "out of which hope and opportunity grow." Spence refers in this context to William Julius Wilson, who however goes further (in his book *The Truly Disadvantaged*) and writes of the importance to a neighborhood of a sufficient number of working- and middle-class professional families. It is not merely that such families provide mainstream role models to reinforce mainstream values. Far more important, Wilson writes, is the institutional stability these families are able to provide because of their economic and educational resources.

"Institutional stability" includes stores, good schools, recreational facilities, and the like—the fabric with which we weave what we call "community." That fabric has long since been torn away from most public housing high-rise communities. Restoring it would require much more than fixing up the buildings and offering services to a population beset with a dizzying array of serious problems.

If, from a compassionate instinct amid an affordable housing crisis, we rebuilt Robert Taylor for its present occupants, we would be rebuilding their failed lives. We would be condemning them, and their children, and their children's children, to an appallingly high statistical likelihood of early death from violence, drugs, or chronic disease, or, for those who escaped these fates, to the ravages of ghetto schooling and the lives of impotence and irrelevance long ago described by DuBois.

Better to be rid of those awful places, and work at improving counseling and social services for those families who have a Gautreaux-type possibility of moving to decent neighborhoods, where institutional stability *is* in place because working poor and professional families already live there. The responsibly administered Section 8 program sought by the new relocation lawsuit is far more likely than a rebuilt Robert Taylor, even with improved social services, to foster the kind of integration of which Spence and Wilson write, and which they correctly see as essential to family betterment for the population described in *The Hidden War*.

———

But what happens to the "vulnerable" families whose problems are so severe that they cannot be helped to move to the mixed-income communities, or via Section 8 to other decent neighborhoods—the "tenants nobody wants," as they are sometimes called? Regardless of "vulnerability," this group will include large families whose multibedroom needs are often impossible to satisfy elsewhere than in public housing.

There are three possibilities. First, some will be rehoused in other public housing—low- or mid-rise developments, smaller and likely to be somewhat better, certainly no worse, than the Taylors. Second, like Diane Wallace, some will move into terrible Section 8 apartments and neighborhoods. Unhappy though their situations, these families too will not be worse off than they were at the Taylors and Horners (if the relocation lawsuit succeeds most will be better off). A nationwide study reports that the average census tract poverty rate for Section 8 voucher recipients in HOPE VI projects dropped from 61 to 27 percent.

The final possibility is that some families will be forced out of the subsidized housing system entirely—into unsubsidized private rentals (including "doubling up" with family or friends) or homelessness. Homelessness is of course the worst-case scenario. It is understandable that, contemplating it, some advocates argue that the loss of public housing units is to be avoided at almost any cost.

Society should not be forced to choose between Taylor and homelessness for any family. But of the two, a rebuilt Taylor seems the poorer option. Most of Ruby Haynes's progeny were doomed to dismal lives. One can at least imagine possibilities for the progeny of homeless parents that are less dismal than the certain horrors of Taylor.

Some time ago I gave a talk at Northwestern University along these lines. I was criticized by three professors for exaggerating the not-worse-than-Taylor thesis. For some families, they argued, the alternatives *could* be worse. Due to severance from family, friends, and institutional supports, disruption of schooling for children, and the like, a forced move to a strange neighborhood that is no better than the old, or into homelessness, may in fact be a "net loss." A recent book likens it to "root shock"—plants yanked from the soil frequently droop, sometimes die. I thought the professors were right, and I changed my text to acknowledge their point.

My revised text argued that even if the number of net losses is not negligible, two reasons persuaded me that the course we are on is the right one. The first is the improvement in life circumstances for those families who do manage to return to the replacement mixed-income communities, or who make it to good Section 8 locations. In a recent study of "neighborhood outcomes" for relocated families at five HOPE VI developments in five different cities, nearly three-quarters of relocated families reported that their new neighborhoods were safer, and one-third were in neighborhoods with poverty rates below 20 percent. Not surprisingly, all were in places with lower poverty rates than they had been before. In addition, of course, adjacent neighborhoods and the larger society benefit from eliminating the festering high-rise sores.

This is not to say that ghettos, terrible ones, don't exist outside public housing high-rises. They do, and Diane Wallace was forced to move into one of them. It is to say that society's opportunities for remedial action, and individual families' self-help options, are greater in the spread-out ghettos of a sizable neighborhood than in the gang-controlled redoubts of the high-rises.

The second reason is the possibility that the "net loss" will be short-term, that over the long run life will be better even for those families who suffer the net losses. Each such family has been enabled to escape from the "humanitarian disaster" of a Taylor environment. In the new environment there is likely to be greater opportunity to improve the circumstances of individual families than was possible in Vince Lane's hidden war at Rockwell, Horner, and Ickes.

"Winning" in the high-rises, as *The Hidden War* showed, was like trying to win in the jungles of Vietnam. Winning with dispersed Section 8 families, with families in low- or mid-rise public housing, or even with families in homeless shelters, is more imaginable. Postmove counseling is the key.

The very problems—health, skill and education deficits, drug addiction, poor credit, criminal records—that make it difficult for many families to negotiate Section 8 moves at all create a risk that they will not survive even in their less than optimal Section 8 apartments should they manage to get there. Eviction may be the prospect for many. To address these problems, for a period of time, say two years after the move, skilled social services agencies should offer such families "intensive care"—individualized, case-managed, one-on-one counseling designed to help move families to housing stability. Indeed, the CHA's resident protection package calls for "postmove counseling" and—either because it has seen the light or as a result of litigation pressure—the CHA is beginning to take this obligation more seriously. Such counseling is likely to be more effective outside the gang-controlled high-rises than within them.

A second move, even a third and fourth, remains a possibility for families who have made a disastrous initial Section 8 move. The CHA's "Second Mover" program offers assistance to families who, when their leases come up for renewal, think about—or can be persuaded to think about—moving again. The traumas of moving must be balanced against the advantages of better neighborhoods. But moving to better neighborhoods is, after all, a familiar route to betterment for many American families. Once a family has been weaned from the "captivity" of public housing and becomes accustomed to dealing with a private landlord, it may be more receptive to moving "farther out" to a better neighborhood. Similar postmove help can be offered to those whose first relocation moves are to other public housing developments.

For the hardest cases—Popkin says "some residents are so damaged that they will never make a successful transition"—Popkin's prescription is "supportive housing," specialized transitional housing providing a range of intensive, on-site social services, an approach that she says has been used successfully to help the homeless. Supportive housing, too, seems more feasible outside gang-dominated high-rises than within them.

In short, even for the "worst-case" families who suffer "net losses" from involuntary relocation, I conclude that—quite apart from the societal benefits—we would be doing them no favor by preserving the high-rise shelter they now have. That would be a different kind of "false hope."

In 1999 BPI decided not to fight but to support the CHA Transformation Plan, while resolving to try to make relocation as compassionate as possible. In effect, we supported the trade-off of reducing the public housing stock in exchange for getting rid of cancerous high-rises, to be replaced with mixed-income communities and housing mobility. It is true that the CHA has botched housing mobility. But even bad Section 8 housing in bad neighborhoods is, for most families, no worse than were the Taylors and Horners, and the relocation lawsuit is striving for improvement. In retrospect, in spite of the CHA's botching, the trade-off looks sound. If relocation is improved for families yet to be moved, and quality postmove counseling—better late than never—is offered those already relocated, it will look even sounder.

We are driven to such choices by insufficient public subsidies for affordable housing, and by society's refusal to permit what is developed to go into decent neighborhoods. A reordering of national priorities will be required to get more housing subsidies. Optimists, indeed, see signs that affordable housing may at last be creeping up on the national agenda. That is likely to happen eventually if only because the affordable housing crisis gets so severe that politicians can no longer safely ignore it. As for the location problem, the relocation lawsuit could ameliorate that problem for the CHA's relocated families. For other ghetto-trapped families? That is the subject of the next, and final, chapter.

PART THREE

CHAPTER SEVEN

"THE MOST FORMIDABLE EVIL"

Mr. Godot told me to tell you he won't
come this evening but surely to-morrow.

—Boy (*Waiting for Godot*)

1

It is January 2005 as I write this. Unbelievably, thirty-nine years have elapsed since Chuck Markels and I had pizza at Edwardo's with Hal Baron and Zoe Mikva. My hair, now thoroughly gray, is lamentably thin. Deborah, Daniel, and Joan are married, living their separate lives, and Barbara and I, grandparents of five, have celebrated our golden wedding anniversary. In September 1999, after twenty-nine years on the job, I stepped aside as executive director of BPI; now I work four days a week as a BPI staff lawyer, still handling Gautreaux.

"Still handling Gautreaux" means (mostly) Transformation Plan work. The scattered-site program is over. So is the Gautreaux Program. What remains, rising from the rubble of the demolished Henry Horners and Robert Taylors, is the public housing part of the plan's mixed-income communities. This replacement housing can't be built without approval orders from Judge Aspen, and the leverage of the required orders helps us to insure that the CHA conforms to the "spirit of Gautreaux."

That phrase has come to mean maximizing the amount and dispersal of public housing in the new developments, consistent with not preju-dicing the chances of persuading unsubsidized families to rent and buy there, successful persuasion being an essential ingredient of the mixed-income recipe. This is Aspen's "twenty-first century view" (as he said of the Horner revitalizing order)—an economic mix in the short run may bring racial integration in the long run.

So the time has come to reflect on what Gautreaux has meant for me personally and on what it may signify for the larger story of black Americans.

The personal side is easy. I grew up on Chicago's North Side; perforce, I was a Cubs fan. Being a Cubs fan means suffering with a permanent viral infection. No matter how dismal their prospects, how inevitable their failures, how absurd their stratagems (such as three coaches instead of a manager), the Cubs were my team. Like the color of my eyes, it was a given; it came from within. In the Schiff Hardin days we represented Bill Veeck in his purchase of the White Sox, and that exciting year the Sox went to the World Series under the tutelage of Veeck and Hank Greenberg (who treated Barbara and me to Fritzel's strawberry cheesecake to celebrate our wedding anniversary). Yet when I opened to the sports pages each evening, it was not the Sox box score but the Cubs to which I invariably turned first.

That's how Gautreaux has been for me. The failed high-rises, with their incalculable damage to both their residents and society, and the ever-present challenge to do something about them (because after Edwardo's I was the one who had the Gautreaux bear by the tail), are with me always. Not always at the surface of my mind, any more than the Cubs are always at the surface. But I can no more rid myself of the Gautreaux "virus" than I can of the virus of the Wrigleys.

For the larger story of black Americans, the question is what learning can be gleaned from all the years devoted to scattered sites, then to housing mobility, and now to mixed-income replacement for the demolished high-rises? I've already described each of these Gautreaux remedial streams. But isn't there a bigger story here?

My reflections have brought me to Alexis de Tocqueville who, some 170 years ago, called racial inequality the "most formidable evil threatening the future of the United States." He went on to prophesy that the evil of racial inequality would not be resolved, and that it would eventually bring America to disaster.

Today we might insert "domestic" before "evil." But with that insertion made, I believe that Tocqueville's observation remains accurate, and that his prophecy is given current urgency by today's black ghettos—that the black ghetto is a wellspring of our racial inequality evil that, if we are to avoid the fate Tocqueville prophesied, must be dismantled. A further conclusion is that Gautreaux tells us how best to go about the dismantling. My remaining purpose is to explain these reflections.

Completing the tale of America's twentieth-century racial conflicts, which chapter 1 related only up to 1966 when Gautreaux was filed, will be a good way to begin. Once the law could no longer be used to keep blacks in the South from getting too high, what ensued? And what happened outside the South, following the culmination of the struggle that Garry Wills believed was one of the nation's proudest moments?

The answer to the first question is that the South "adjusted" by adopting the strategy of the rest of the country to keep blacks from getting too close. The answer to the second is that after 1966, the conflict outside the South went on much as before; the proud moment had little effect on the battlefields.

The adjustment in the South had actually begun earlier as rural blacks moved into ever more defined black residential areas in southern cities. Ironically, writes Stephen Grant Meyer, southerners were "catching up to the rest of the United States in the way they maintained racial distance."

Outside the South, battling over space continued from coast to coast. Portraying "almost continuous racial conflict over housing in the twentieth century," Meyer writes that a "thousand examples" show threats and intimidation even when bombs do not actually fly. From reports of the Southern Poverty Law Center and others, he and Rubinowitz-Perry describe "move-in crimes" just like those of the earlier period. Illustrative acts in the last three decades of the century include:

Torching a black-owned home on Long Island.

Firebombing a Boston apartment building after three black families moved in.

Throwing a tire iron through the living-room window of an apartment rented by a black family in Chicago. Beer bottles, bricks, and shouted racial slurs continued through the night.

Burning a garage and crosses and throwing bricks through windows of blacks' homes in Dubuque, Iowa.

Breaking into a house in North Bend, Washington, severing its telephone lines, and strewing its yard with eggs thrown from passing cars.

Firebombing a black's home in Brooklyn.

Firebombing a black's home in a Louisville suburb. (The home was only damaged, but two months later it was destroyed by an arson fire.)

Bombing a public housing town house under construction in a white neighborhood in Yonkers.

Spreading excrement on the mailbox, piling feces on the welcome mat, and leaving a misspelled "Nigers go Home" note at a black's home in Ridgewood, New Jersey.

Shooting at black families moving into apartments in Boston and damaging their cars (broken windshields, tire slashings, and the like).

Hanging a noose from a tree in the yard of an interracial couple in DeWitt, Iowa.

Firebombing a black's home in Cleveland.

Nor did move-in crimes end with the new millennium. After all the calendars and computers were changed, crosses continued to be burned, windows to be broken, and swastikas and "KKK" to be spray painted on homes and cars from sea to shining sea.

A ray of hope in all this bleakness was that the move-in crimes of the last third of the century were characterized by fewer mobs and riots. After the 1960s, Meyer writes, entire communities no longer took part in violent resistance. White flight was a major reason. The millions of whites who moved to the suburbs after World War II did not decamp solely to escape pressure from black ghettos; many were also reaching for the postwar dream of green grass and a small town lifestyle. Yet for some it was flight from blacks as well, or from the threat of them. Countless families who might otherwise have remained to repel the "invasion" of their neighborhoods chose flight over fight. One effect was that housing adjacent to ghettos opened up, and ghettos were able to expand a little at their edges with less bloodshed than earlier.

The suburban dream of course resonated for some blacks too, especially since government programs made it financially feasible. No matter; the way for blacks was barred. William Levitt, head of Levitt and Sons, one of the biggest suburban builders, explained that if he sold to blacks, then 90 to 95 percent of his white customers would not buy. Martin Sloane's testimony in our metropolitan hearing before Austin showed how effective the FHA had been in keeping blacks from joining the exodus to suburbia.

If blacks did manage to find their way to the new subdivisions, they met with familiar forms of resistance. When William Myers, a black veteran, moved into a ranch-style home in Levittown, Pennsylvania, in 1957, a crowd of white neighbors gathered. Soon they began lobbing rocks through the windows. Local police tried to restore order but state troopers had to be called. The disturbance lasted a week. The crowd, sometimes growing to 400, pelted police with stones, burned a cross, and smeared "KKK" on the home of a white neighbor thought to have been overly friendly to Myers. Only after a court injunction did the protest die out. Seven protesters were convicted of minor crimes, such as disturbing the peace.

Yet some blacks did begin to make inroads into suburbia. Where that happened most whites declined to move in, and many already there departed. Predominantly, even entirely, black suburbs began to appear in some metropolitan areas, usually older, close-in suburbs with big debts, poor services, and declining tax bases. In many ways these suburbs replicated inner-city problems.

Change in the law was a second factor mitigating the intensity of move-in violence. The price paid to Republicans and southern Democrats for enacting the 1968 Fair Housing Act had been to strip the bill of its enforcement provisions—the act was "a beautiful bird without wings to fly," as one political scientist put it. The Meyer and Rubinowitz-Perry accounts make clear that the stripped-down law did not guarantee against move-in violence. Still, the legal environment had changed.

Then, in 1988, the Fair Housing Act's enforcement provisions were strengthened—the bird was at last given wings. Penalties for discriminating were increased, the Justice Department role was enlarged, and HUD was permitted to file cases based on its own investigations. More than in the earlier era, the law enforcement system would on occasion enforce the law. Though whites were still resistant to blacks entering their neighborhoods, their willingness to resort to violence was dampened by the knowledge that the law might sometimes be enforced. Sanction and impunity were not entirely things of the past, but no longer could they be taken for granted.

Record-keeping is poor, and no one can say for sure by how much move-in violence has diminished. About 8,000 hate crimes are reported to the FBI annually, but the voluntary reporting system is full of holes. The Southern Poverty Law Center estimates that if all states reported at the same per capita rate as New Jersey, which has a relatively low hate-crime rate and a good reporting system, there would be about 25,000 reported hate crimes annually, not all against blacks, of course, and not all move-in crimes. (Limited data indicate that move-in cases may be about three-quarters of all federally prosecuted racial violence cases.) In the absence of better information, one might guess, or hope, that Meyer's thousands of examples are getting down into the low thousands each year.

2

If the war to keep blacks from getting too close has moderated, are blacks actually now getting close? Is black residential segregation diminishing? Are the ghetto icebergs breaking up and dissolving into the great surrounding seas? The answers are a modest yes on residential segregation, but an unhappy no on ghettos.

Turning first to the good news, black-white segregation—though still very high—decreased modestly from 1970 to 2000. To measure segregation, Douglas S. Massey and Nancy A. Denton, the authors of *American Apartheid,* use an index of black-white "dissimilarity"—the percentage of blacks who would have to move if each census tract were to mirror the racial composition of its metropolitan area. At a score of 100 blacks and whites share no neighborhood at all; at zero blacks and whites are evenly distributed. Scores over 60 are considered "high," those above 70 "extreme." What Massey and Denton found was that scores outside the South averaged 84.5 in 1970, and that by 1980 they had declined to 80.1.

No area outside the South had a dissimilarity index under 70, a level well above the highest ever recorded for European ethnic groups. In the South, with its history of lesser residential segregation, the index moved from 75.3 to 68.3.

To put their 1980 figures in perspective, Massey and Denton compared them to the experiences of Hispanics and Asians. In the thirty metropolitan areas with the largest Hispanic and Asian populations, the dissimilarity figure for Hispanics was 49 and for Asians 34. For blacks it was 75.

Massey and Denton also examined indices of black suburbanization, of "isolation," and of "hypersegregation." None of these alternate statistical approaches changed the segregation picture very much. The suburbanization numbers showed only slightly less extreme segregation. No other group came close to the level of black isolation. And neither Hispanics nor Asians were hypersegregated in any metropolitan area, while blacks were in sixteen of the thirty metropolitan areas containing the largest black populations.

The *American Apartheid* conclusion was that during the 1970s whites continued to avoid neighborhoods near black areas, and to be "highly sensitive" to the number of black residents in their own neighborhoods. In metropolitan areas where most blacks lived, segregation persisted at "extremely high levels that far surpass the experience of other racial or ethnic minorities."

The drift toward lower levels of segregation, begun in the 1970s, continued throughout the remainder of the century. By 2000, the Census Bureau reported that the average nationwide level of black-white residential segregation was down to sixty-four, still in the high range but below figures that averaged in the seventies in earlier decades. True, the encouraging drop masked some less encouraging realities. Black-white segregation indices remained "extreme" in the nation's largest urban black communities, and roughly a third of all black Americans still lived in hypersegregated conditions. The Census Bureau said that most of the decline in black-white segregation from 1980 to 2000 took place in the West and South, and that the large metropolitan areas that had been the most segregated in 1980 remained "at or near the top of the list." Half the metropolitan area black population lived in census tracts that were 50 percent or more black (14.5 of 29 million). The modest good news was indeed modest.

Even that characterization may be optimistic. In a study of the Chicago metropolitan area, comparing 1990 and 2000 census data, Harvard's Civil Rights Project came to the sobering conclusion that the color line was being "redrawn" in the suburbs, and that suburban blacks were beginning to experience segregation "equivalent" to that in the inner city. Without strong public policy interventions, the report said, "the suburbs will experience the same dynamic of segregation and resegregation in the 21st Century as the city experienced in the 20th Century."

For the bad ghetto news I turn to the 2000 census data and Paul A. Jargowsky, a professor of political economy at the University of Texas, Dallas. In his 1997 book, *Poverty and Place,* Jargowsky analyzed the census data from 1970 through 1990, and in a later paper examined the 2000 figures. Jargowsky's analyses show that from 1970 to 2000 extreme-poverty metropolitan area census tracts (40 percent or more poverty) doubled from 1,117 to 2,251, and that the black population of these tracts increased 12 percent from just under 2.5 to just over 2.8 million (2,447,455 to 2,801,655). About half the black families in the tracts had incomes below the poverty line (1,247,299 in 1970 and 1,371,783 in 2000). In other words, comparing 2000 with 1970, extreme-poverty metropolitan census tracts covered more geography, and had more blacks and more poor blacks living in them.

The figures did not move in a straight line. They rose sharply between 1970 and 1990 and then, thanks to the economic boom of the 1990s, dropped by 2000. If the trend of the century's last decade had continued, one might be hopeful that, over time, our black ghettos would contract. But today's picture is worse than it was at census time. The 2000 census figures are a "snapshot," taken in April 2000, just at the end of an economic boom. The ensuing years have seen a serious downturn, notable for job hemorrhaging and wage stagnation; the Census Bureau reports that the nation's poverty rate grew each year from 2001 through 2003. In population at least, our black ghettos have undoubtedly grown since 2000.

Three conclusions may be drawn from all the numbers. First, over the last three decades of the twentieth century, slowly, very slowly, the residential segregation of nonpoor blacks has lessened, though it is still very high. Second, because the total metropolitan black population grew considerably from 1970 to 2000 (16,999,633 became 29,003,818), the *proportion* of the metropolitan black population living in extreme poverty areas decreased. But third, even in the face of the sustained good times of the 1990s, these extreme poverty areas have spread over a wider area, and the absolute numbers of blacks and of poor blacks living within them has increased.

This gloomy picture of persisting black ghettos is not gloomy enough. The truly gloomy fact is that the ghetto population is now not only bigger than it was when *Dark Ghetto* and the Kerner Report were written in the 1960s, but that today's black ghettos are qualitatively worse than they were then. The two major reasons—jobs, and crime and drugs—are related.

When European immigrants arrived on American shores early in the twentieth century, the demand for unskilled labor was strong. Work was available nearly everywhere. In this respect, the really big emigration of blacks from the South, beginning in the early 1940s and continuing through the 1960s, came at a terrible time. These migrants had the colossal misfortune to arrive just when the demand for unskilled labor in central cities would soon begin to dry up.

For a description of what happened we may turn to William Julius Wilson, who writes that in the 1940s, 1950s, and in some places as late as the 1960s, most black adults were working, even in ghettos. Then two incipient developments gathered such steam that, in less than a generation, the low-skill jobs that had been the ghetto dwellers' mainstay largely disappeared from the cities to which the migrants had journeyed.

The first development was an exodus of low-skill jobs to the suburbs, later to overseas as well. The early trickle soon became a stream, then a flood. Factories, wholesale and retail businesses, even corporate headquarters, picked themselves up, lock, stock, and barrel, and removed from the central city to the suburbs and exurbs. A study on the "redistribution" of American jobs shows that for the entire ten-year period from 1975 to 1985, *essentially all* the growth in entry-level and low-skill jobs was in the suburbs and nonmetropolitan areas.

In 1993, Mark Alan Hughes, a thoughtful student of urban affairs, described what was happening this way:

In many metros, outer areas are gaining jobs three times as fast as residents . . . [The suburbs] are increasingly the engines of metropolitan employment growth . . . The inner city was once accessible to employment. The ghetto was a part of an urban machine that created opportunity. Now that machine is broken for many poor and black people, with its parts spread across the vast metropolitan landscapes.

In a 1994 lecture, Wilson told how Chicago's Bronzeville neighborhood had been a reasonably well-working community as late as the 1950s. When the jobs moved to the suburbs, and housing discrimination (among other factors) prevented Bronzeville's black workers from following them, Bronzeville quickly became an impoverished, severely distressed community. "Economic restructuring has broken the figurative back of the black working population," said Wilson.

Compounding this exodus of jobs to suburbia was the accelerating internationalization of trade, including the outsourcing of manufacture to countries with large populations of low-skill, low-wage workers. Half the world's workers leave school at age sixteen or earlier, Wilson writes. As these workers are brought into the global economic competition, "the consequences are unlikely to be positive for low-skilled workers in developed countries."

The other development, also incipient during the Great Migration, was technology—the increasing complexity of jobs due to robotics, computerization, and the like. The workplace was revolutionized by these technological changes, and education and training became prerequisites for most good jobs. Educated workers benefited, while those without college degrees found it increasingly difficult to meet job qualifications. One study of 3,000 employers in Atlanta, Boston, and Los Angeles found that only 5 to 10 percent of central city jobs were open to applicants without college degrees. Most employers, Wilson's research showed, began to insist on high school degrees, specific work experience, and job references. The effect of the technology revolution on many workers is neatly captured by the drawing that accompanied the *New York Times* review of Wilson's 1996 book, *When Work Disappears*. A drowning man's hand breaks the surface of the water, and a would-be rescuer reaches to offer him—not a life preserver but a craftsman's heavy metal wrench.

The unsurprising, almost tautological, consequence of this loss of low-skill jobs was accelerating joblessness among black ghetto residents, particularly young males. As early as the 1970s, the great majority of ghetto adults became unemployed. From the late 1960s to the 1990s, unemployment for central city black males doubled to quadrupled, depending on the region of the country. Wilson worried that many blacks were being "permanently locked out of the mainstream of the American occupational system."

Two factors exacerbated the effect on the ghetto of this loss of low-skill jobs. First, the end of legal housing discrimination allowed more working- and middle-class blacks to leave inner-city ghettos (though frequently for communities that were, or soon would be, predominantly black). The result was to weaken institutions and strip the ghetto of mainstream role models. In the 1940s, 1950s, and 1960s, says Wilson, working- and middle-class blacks in ghetto communities provided stability and reinforced mainstream behavior patterns. Their departure left behind higher concentrations of the most disadvantaged, and removed an important "social buffer" that had helped keep alive the perception that education was meaningful, employment a viable alternative to welfare, and family stability the norm, not the exception.

The second exacerbating factor was that just when inner cities were losing dramatically large numbers of blue-collar and low-skill jobs during the 1970s and 1980s, the ghettos were experiencing great increases in their populations of young blacks with no education beyond high school. These were the children of the migrants who had arrived in the 1950s and 1960s, when decent jobs requiring only limited education and skills were still available in the inner city.

The result was to strand ever-growing numbers of unemployed, increasingly unemployable, young blacks in job-poor, inner-city ghettos from which working- and middle-class adults were departing. Poor neighborhoods without work, Wilson wrote, led directly to communities characterized not only by joblessness but by single-parent families (men without work are not marriageable), teenage pregnancies, out-of-wedlock births, and serious crime. By 1980, said Wilson, who is not given to hyperbole, the impact of these developments was "catastrophic."

For a discussion of crime and drugs, the other major reason ghetto conditions have worsened, I turn first to Elliott Currie, who teaches criminology and sociology and has written several books on America's criminal justice system. In *Crime and Punishment in America*, Currie examines the relationship between violent crime and chronic joblessness or underemployment (that is, jobs without decent pay and the prospect of advancement).

A number of studies, Currie explains, indicate that stable, rewarding work tends to reduce violent crime by supporting the material and emotional infrastructure healthy families need, by enabling families to provide positive nurturing for children, and by making it more likely that youth will successfully complete the transition to responsible adulthood. Chronic un- or underemployment, on the other hand, hinders the formation of stable families, undermines family functioning, and makes illegitimate activities more appealing.

In one of the studies to which Currie refers, rates of violence among white youths were not very different than those among black youths until the two groups moved past adolescence. As white youths entered the job market their rates of serious crime dropped. Rates for the black youths, unable to move into satisfactory jobs and locked into a kind of "perpetual adolescence," did not. In another study, mostly of whites who had been seriously delinquent in adolescence, two turning points had the greatest influence on whether the adolescent delinquents stopped committing crimes as they entered adulthood—getting a stable job and getting married.

A third study traced the substantial drop in wage rates from 1973 to 1993 for male high school dropouts and for male high school graduates without college degrees. Plotting this drop against changes in violent crime in urban areas across the country, the researchers found a "strong and consistent relationship" between the wage changes and increases in murder and assault. Though the study could not pinpoint the reasons for the correlation, it suggested a plausible explanation: young men, faced with steadily declining wages, often substituted criminal activity for legitimate work.

None of this is surprising. Currie calls it the "common-sense view" that people trapped in idleness and bleak futures at the margins of the legitimate economy are more likely than those within the economy to commit violent crimes. Another study sums up the common-sense view, describing a cascading series of changes in community life that followed the loss of blue collar jobs in U.S. cities in the 1980s:

> As the more capable men moved out of the community in search of work . . . "collective supervision of youths suffered" and "informal social controls weakened" . . . Drug markets flourished, overwhelming the fragile social controls that remained in these communities and flooding the neighborhood with guns . . . What began as an economic change, in short, quickly rippled through virtually every institution, public and private, in the inner cities, radically transforming the culture of poor communities and precipitating a rise in violent crime.

Poverty, another aspect of the relationship between joblessness and crime, is so obvious it is likely to be overlooked. From a number of studies Currie summarizes the evidence showing that the links between extreme poverty and delinquency/violence are strong, consistent, and compelling. "There is little question," he writes, "that growing up in extreme poverty exerts powerful pressures toward crime." The phrase "growing up in" refers to neighborhood as well as family. In a study of crime levels in Columbus, Ohio, neighborhoods were divided into those with low, high, and extreme levels of poverty ("extreme" meaning that 40 percent or more of the residents were poor). Violent crime generally increased as the percentage of poor residents increased, but jumped sharply once a neighborhood's poverty rate rose above 40 percent. Poverty, not race, appeared to be the linking factor, for in another study the poorest white neighborhoods suffered almost twice the violent crime rate of low-poverty black neighborhoods.

Knowing that there is a powerful connection between poverty and crime doesn't explain how the connection operates. It can't be an individual's lack of money alone, Currie wryly observes, for if that were the case graduate students would be dangerous people. Rather, acknowledging that we don't know all we would like to know, Currie says a large body of research points to two effects of extreme deprivation that cumulatively wear away at the psychological and communal conditions that sustain healthy human development in a family or neighborhood: (1) diminishing adults' capacity to supervise the young and parents' ability to raise children effectively; and (2) stunting children's intellectual and emotional growth and increasing the risks of child abuse and neglect. Extreme poverty, Currie concludes, "creates neighborhoods that are both dangerous and bereft of legitimate opportunities and role models, makes forming and maintaining families more difficult, and makes illicit activities far more alluring to teenagers and adults."

In *American Apartheid,* Massey and Denton explain the linkage between neighborhood poverty and black ghettos. Even though blacks are generally poorer than whites, if blacks and whites live together in the same neighborhood without residential segregation, they will experience the same degree of neighborhood poverty; all neighborhoods will have the same mix of (black and white) poverty. When racial segregation is introduced, however, the poverty level of black neighborhoods increases while that of white neighborhoods drops.

With four diagrams, simple yet elegant, Massey and Denton show why. In a hypothetical city in which 20 percent of blacks and 10 percent of whites have incomes below the federal poverty line, the first diagram assumes no racial segregation. Whites and blacks therefore live in neighborhoods with identical poverty rates. The second diagram adds some racial segregation, the third even more. In each, the poverty rate in black neighborhoods increases while the rate in white neighborhoods drops. When the final diagram—complete segregation—is reached, the black part of the city has twice the poverty rate of the now entirely separate white part, 20 percent versus 10 percent.

⌐

There is a final aspect to the crime picture whose importance cannot be overstated. In the early 1980s crack cocaine arrived in black ghettos, bringing with it a way for jobless black men to make desperately needed money. Already subjected to the catastrophic consequences of the loss of low-skill jobs, the black ghetto was now to be hit by two more catastrophes.

The first was the devastation wrought by the powerful, highly addictive drug itself—the ravages visited upon Juanita and Johnnie Haynes writ community-wide. In *The Hidden War*, Susan Popkin and colleagues give us the harrowing words of residents of three CHA communities—of once strong women wasting away because of crack addiction, of friends barred from apartments for fear they would steal whatever they could to support their habit, of men pressuring girlfriends to become users to get their welfare money for drug purchases, of children neglected and abused (a five-year-old taking care of a four-month-old, a twelve-year-old shooting at other children), of drug trafficking so pervasive it was like "going in and out of a gas station," of the hopelessness of trying to control it, and— above all—of the constant violence. For the adults, *The Hidden War* summarizes, the problems of living in this "inherently destructive" culture are "overwhelming," while the children suffer the psychological trauma that comes from "living in guerrilla war zones like Cambodia or Mozambique."

The second catastrophe was the official response to the crack cocaine ghetto scourge, called the War on Drugs. In his 1980 election campaign Ronald Reagan paid lots of attention to "crime in the streets," and vowed to increase the federal government role in combating it. After the election he directed the attorney general to establish a task force to explore how; focus on drugs was the answer.

The FBI promptly made drugs a high priority; from 1980 to 1984, FBI antidrug monies increased from $8 to $95 million. Antidrug funds for the Defense Department more than doubled, from $33 to $79 million. The Drug Enforcement Administration budget grew from $215 to $321 million. Simultaneously, however, funds for drug treatment, prevention, and education were cut. For example, the budget of the National Institute on Drug Abuse was reduced from $274 to $57 million.

The president put his mouth where his money was going. In speech after speech he trumpeted the theme that government's function was to "protect society from the criminal, not the other way around." Crime did not result from poverty but from a conscious choice to exploit others. The crime threat was "a cumulative result of too much emphasis on . . . the rights of the accused and too little concern for . . . [protecting] the lives, homes, and rights of our law-abiding citizens."

With the Democrats dashing to catch the political train, tough new antidrug legislation became grist for the congressional mill—including severe penalties for possession of even small amounts of crack cocaine, mandatory minimum sentences for many drug offenses, permission to use illegally obtained evidence in drug trials, and the death penalty for some drug-related crimes. The War on Drugs moved into high gear.

In his book *Race, Crime, and the Law,* Harvard law professor Randall Kennedy reminds critics that a legitimate purpose of the expensive, high-profile War on Drugs was to help black ghetto residents—the principal victims of drug trafficking and drug violence—by imprisoning those who would otherwise prey upon them. The trouble was, as *The Hidden War* and other accounts make clear, the War on Drugs was a failure. Dealers were not cleared from the streets. Prices did not rise. Crack cocaine did not become harder to find and buy. Drug violence persisted, largely unaffected by the massive law-enforcement effort. The huge amounts of money to be made in the "business" meant that an eager new recruit immediately took the place of every slain foot soldier. The preying continued, virtually unabated.

In September 2001 the retiring U.S. Attorney in Chicago, Scott Lassar, said in his valedictory that a decade of effort had "proved conclusively" that long prison sentences were not deterring others from entering the drug business, that there was "no hope" of preventing drugs from reaching the market, that despite increases in seizures "the price [of cocaine and heroin] remains steady while the purity has increased dramatically." He concluded that we had to find a way to reduce demand by treatment and education. "We are," he said, "making no impact on the market," a conclusion supported by the current (2004) facts that drugs are cheaper and more plentiful than ever.

But while failing to achieve its drug reduction and crime control objectives, the War on Drugs had a disastrous effect on young black males in black ghettos. Most objective analysts of our criminal justice system agree that blacks commit proportionately more crimes than whites, and that that fact, not racial bias in the law enforcement system (though bias is there too), is the principal reason greater proportions of blacks than whites get entangled in the system. The elephant in the living room, writes author Shelby Steele, is that blacks commit crimes "vastly out of proportion to our numbers in society."

Yet crime by blacks was not getting worse when Ronald Reagan beat Jimmy Carter in 1980. If anything, the trend for black crimes—except for homicide rates—was slightly down. Still, disproportionate punishment of blacks began to get worse, much worse. (Murder being a relatively rare crime, homicide rates do not explain incarceration rates.) Since 1980, the number of blacks in prison has tripled. By 1990, nearly one in every four young black males in the United States was under the control of the criminal justice system, one way or another. The figures in major cities were staggeringly higher—more than 40 percent in Washington, D.C., more than 50 percent in Baltimore.

In his book *Malign Neglect,* Michael Tonry, a professor who teaches law, criminology, and social policy, writes that the rising levels of black incarceration did not just happen.

> Anyone with knowledge of drug-trafficking patterns and of police arrest policies and incentives could have foreseen that the enemy troops in the War on Drugs would consist largely of young, inner-city minority males.

One might summarize by saying that, having locked the black poor into ghettos from which gainful employment opportunities then largely departed, with predictable consequences on crime levels, for the last twenty "crack cocaine years" we have been systematically sending in our police to arrest the young, jobless men, typically for drug-related violations, after which we cart them off to the prisons and jails we are fast building to hold them all. What is disturbing about this oversimplification is how much basic reality it captures. As Tonry puts it, the blackening of America's prison population (by 1998 over half of all prisoners were black) is the product of "malign neglect" of the foreseeable effect on black Americans of our War on Drugs.

The ghetto riots of the 1960s were rage and fury, lashing out at the symbols—police and white-owned property—of what DuBois called confinement to impotence. What has happened since the 1960s is even more disturbing. Instead of rage and fury, there is self-destruction through drugs and violence, a life cycle—death cycle?—that is epitomized by the saga of the Haynes family, and that is abetted by the dual policies of maintaining black ghettos while dealing with the crime they inevitably generate through an ineffective War on Drugs coupled with a policy of mass incarceration.

Is this depressing picture exaggerated? Can't a case be made that black Americans are really on the road to progress? After all, the bird of the Fair Housing Act was at last given wings. Large judgments have been rendered in court cases against housing discriminators. The underlying myth of racial inferiority did not survive the Holocaust and the Cold War, at least in respectable discourse. Little Black Sambo and Aunt Jemima have long since been replaced by Bill Cosby and Colin Powell. We now have a black middle class that dwarfs the one of the 1960s.

It is true that the iconography of black Americans has undergone an astounding change. In an airline safety video a black American occupies the pilot seat. Mainstream advertising now courts the black middle class. Black Americans can today be found in virtually every aspect of American life, not just sports and the arts and government, but business and the professions and science. Nor are their positions all token. Black Americans have headed the nation's largest foundation, and its armed forces. A black American has been elected governor of Virginia. A *Newsweek* cover features three black Americans who have become CEOs of three enormous business corporations, among America's largest and most powerful. In 2003 more than a quarter of black households (28.6 percent) earned the equivalent of at least $50,000 a year, a figure that was only 14.2 percent in 1970.

It boggles the mind to recall that 150 years ago most black Americans were slaves, that 100 years ago the president of the United States—voicing a widely held opinion—spoke of them as a biologically "stupid race," and that 50 years ago our laws permitted them to be sent to the back of the bus and required their children to attend separate schools. Surely the glass of racial progress may be said to be at least half full?

The trouble with the metaphor is that it employs only one glass. Describing the situation of black Americans requires two—one for the middle class and a second for the poor, especially the ghetto poor. The glass may indeed be half full for the middle class. ("May be" because, in spite of all those black consumers courted by mainstream advertisers, the black middle class—as I pointed out in chapter 5—is very fragile indeed.) But not so the glass for the black poor.

The unemployment rate for blacks is double the rate for whites. So is the infant mortality rate. Black babies are more than twice as likely as white babies to be born with low birth weight, and 2.5 times more likely to die before reaching their first birthday. These are figures for the entire population; those for the poor are far worse. Measured by the federal government's poverty definition (which is well below a real-life poverty line), in 2000 some 21.6 percent of all blacks lived in poverty, compared with 5.1 percent of whites. For families with children the black figure was also four times that for whites.

Focusing on children is particularly sobering. A recent report from a national foundation says that for black children, "the concentration of child poverty in severely distressed neighborhoods is truly staggering"— 44.7 percent of all poor black children lived in a severely distressed neighborhood, nearly nine times the 5.1 percent figure for non-Hispanic white children, and double the 22.9 percent figure for Latino children. The 2000 census figures, said the foundation, reflected an "enormous gap" between mainstream society and a significant segment of the minority community.

Helen Epstein, a journalist who specializes in public health, writes, "Something is killing America's urban poor," and she is not referring to drugs or gunshot wounds but to diabetes, stroke, certain kinds of cancer, high blood pressure, and other killing diseases. "Poor urban blacks," she continues, "have the worst health of any ethnic group in America, with the possible exception of Native Americans." In 1990, Epstein reports, two doctors found that so many poor blacks in Harlem were dying young from heart disease, cancer, and cirrhosis of the liver that men there were less likely to reach age sixty-five than men in Bangladesh.

Why? No one can say for sure, but the two main theories, stress and the multiple deprivations associated with extreme poverty, are each directly related to neighborhood conditions—the black ghetto conditions of inner cities. "Neighborhoods could be destroying people's health," writes Epstein; the "something" that is causing all that chronic disease among ghetto dwellers "may come down to geography." Epstein was "stunned" by the health improvements reported by families she interviewed who, via Section 8, had been enabled to move out. ("If moving out of southwest Yonkers were a drug, I would bottle it, patent it and go on cable TV and sell it.")

Though the glass for the black middle class may look half full, the glass for the black poor, especially the ghetto poor, looks pretty close to empty. But now the metaphor must be discarded as inadequate. For once we add to the poverty figures the loss of jobs, then add the "something" that is killing black ghetto dwellers, then add the ravages of crack cocaine and the mass incarceration of young ghetto blacks, the descriptive powers of Kenneth Clark or W. E. B. DuBois are required. Yet it is impossible to imagine how even they would describe today's black ghettos. How could Clark exceed his description of human debasement in his pitiless rendition of institutionalized pathology, or DuBois find a more powerful metaphor than the hysterical screaming of entombed souls behind his invisible wall? Perhaps all that can be said is that not only has the black ghetto population grown since the 1960s, but that today's black ghettos have become indescribably terrible places.

3

There are reasons not to have expected growth in black ghettoization and worsening of ghetto conditions after the 1960s. The Holocaust horror had eliminated racism from responsible public discourse. A bloody conflict had finally ended Jim Crow. In the aftermath of the civil rights movement and the Fair Housing Act, discrimination against blacks in many areas of public life had lessened. The struggle against black penetration of white neighborhoods was moderated by a reduction of communal violence. The black middle class grew and a nascent affluent one appeared. In the 1990s we enjoyed one of the most sustained periods of economic growth in our history.

The explanations do not assuage the disappointment. First, the Fair Housing Act was passed only after government policies had, as Arnold Hirsch puts it, "frozen the [black-white residential separation] pattern in concrete." In the 1930s and 1940s the federal government had mandated residential segregation. Through the 1950s and much of the 1960s it had fostered segregation. Housing discrimination was finally outlawed in 1968 only after a twenty-year postwar building boom that, in Hirsch's words, was "a federally supported centrifuge [FHA insurance, public housing segregation, urban renewal, interstate highways, homeowner tax deductions] that separated an outer layer of whites from a dense black core."

Second, the new law did not end housing discrimination. Resources for enforcement were always puny. Even after enforcement powers were strengthened in 1988, the political will to use the new powers was very much a sometime thing. Increasingly conservative judges planted land mines in the litigation road. And, as Hirsch points out, there are fewer centralized levers or buttons to push than in education and employment, where the actions of school boards and large employers can be closely scrutinized. Much of the housing market remains in the hands of un-counted decisionmakers, "thousands of real estate agents, lenders, buy-ers and sellers."

To say that the new law did not end housing discrimination is like say-ing that the League of Nations did not end war. The enormity of the un-derstatement is explained by John Yinger, a professor of economics and public administration at Syracuse University, in his book *Closed Doors, Opportunities Lost*. From a 1989 nationwide study done for HUD, Yin-ger summarized the "overwhelming" evidence of persisting discrimina-tion by real estate agents. Some 25 percent fewer homes and apartments were shown to blacks than to equally qualified whites. In 5 to 10 percent of the test cases, black homeseekers weren't even told about available housing, were offered far less information and assistance than whites, and were often steered to black neighborhoods.

Yinger's book also summarized lending studies showing that a sober-ing 60 percent of the time blacks were more likely than equally qualified whites to be turned down for a mortgage loan, were given less favorable terms when they did receive loans, got less information about available mortgages, less help in preparing their applications, and had more trouble buying homeowners' insurance.

A decade later, HUD-funded studies concluded that both housing and lending discrimination persisted at significant levels. Although the measured incidence of housing discrimination against blacks had moder-ated somewhat, one of the lead researchers pointed to troubling indica-tions that geographic steering was on the rise. The studies find, she said, that blacks searching for housing or inquiring about mortgages in 2000 "are still being denied the information and the opportunities that whites take for granted."

As we move into the first decade of the new century that unhappy state of affairs persists. HUD research showed that in 2004 some 80 per-cent of persons experiencing housing discrimination failed to report it. In the same year a study by an advocacy group, the National Fair Housing Alliance, reported over a million race-based housing discrimination violations annually. In all of 2003 the federal government filed a grand total of ten cases against such discrimination, prompting the alliance to charge that widespread housing discrimination was going "virtually unchallenged."

To housing discrimination must be added ubiquitous "exclusionary zoning" by suburban cities and towns—requiring large lot sizes, banning multifamily housing, and the like. Although discrimination against blacks is rarely acknowledged as one of the motives, the effect of such zoning is to prevent poorer families—disproportionately black—from even having a chance to rent or buy in large portions of cities and towns from coast to coast.

Yinger then adds the vital point that discrimination in housing and lending is more than what it may appear to be, more than a painful but discrete and isolated incident in a person's life. Whether in the form of a firebomb or a polite denial of a mortgage loan, housing discrimination is the fount of a discriminatory "system"—an octopus whose tentacles reach out to injure or destroy its victims' quality of life. Residential segregation leads to school segregation, and for blacks that means poorer schools and poorer educational outcomes. Poorer educational outcomes in turn feed directly into the job market; dozens of studies show that educational attainment is a key determinant of employment status and earnings. And poor school and work performances increase the likelihood of poverty.

Indeed, john powell, a professor at Ohio State University who is a student of racial issues (and who does not capitalize his name), suggests that we would do well to speak of "opportunity-based" rather than "desegregated" housing, thereby to focus on the consequences of racial residential segregation. To illustrate his approach, powell and Myron Orfield, a former Minnesota legislator now teaching at the University of Minnesota, are engaged in a classification of Chicago-area municipalities based on "opportunity" factors—jobs, school quality, community health, transportation, public services, and tax capacity. Although the work is still in progress, a preliminary finding is that an astonishing 95 percent of blacks in the Chicago metropolitan area (compared to 55 percent of whites) live in "low-opportunity" communities. Just 4 percent of the households in the "highest opportunity" group are black. Massey and Denton likewise conclude that residential segregation "systematically undermines the so-cial and economic well-being of blacks in the United States."

In the early decades of the Great Migration, as *American Apartheid* explains, middle-class whites were repelled by what they saw as the "un-couth manners, unclean habits, slothful appearance, and illicit behavior of poorly educated, poverty-stricken migrants who had only recently been sharecroppers." Working-class whites feared for their jobs (blacks were frequently hired as strikebreakers). Scorned themselves by native whites, immigrants "reaffirmed their own 'whiteness' by oppressing a people that were even lower in the racial hierarchy."

Yet uncouth manners and job security were not the whole of the ex-planation, even in the early days, and certainly not today. Way back in 1925, the first blacks to move onto a white, middle-class block in Detroit were Dr. and Mrs. Ossian A. Sweet. Dr. Sweet had studied medicine, both in this country and abroad, and had practiced his profession for two years. His wife was a graduate of Detroit Teachers College. Yet the Sweets' move-in was met by a stone-throwing crowd of more than 1,000.

In 1948, Nat King Cole purchased an estate in a fashionable Los An-geles neighborhood. After the local homeowner association tried unsuc-cessfully to persuade Cole to sell, a "Nigger Heaven" sign appeared in his yard, and later the first word on the sign was burned into his lawn. In 1957, when the great San Francisco Giants outfielder Willie Mays moved into a white section of San Francisco, his front window was smashed with a rock.

These anecdotes illustrate the point that black segregation does not correlate with affluence. "Rising economic status had little or no effect on the level of [black] segregation," say Massey and Denton. By contrast, they note, Hispanic and Asian segregation generally begins at a relatively modest level among the poor and falls as income rises. The patterns are similar when segregation is examined by education and occupation. The persistence of black segregation in America, they conclude, is a matter of race, not class.

The point may be emphasized by noting where poor whites live. There are almost twice as many poor whites as poor blacks in the country as a whole, but nearly six times as many black poor as white poor live in high-poverty census tracts in metropolitan areas. In other words, by and large, poor white families live among the nonpoor. By and large, poor black families live mostly with other poor blacks. David Rusk, an economist and urban policy analyst who has authored several important books on urban issues and is a former mayor of Albuquerque, writes that a major reason white poverty rates are so much lower than rates for blacks is the "mainstreaming of most poorer white households in middle-class communities."

Yinger also makes an additional point that is critical to understanding what lies beneath these unhappy segregation facts: disparities in housing, schooling, and jobs all feed stereotypes that underlie prejudice against blacks. Yes, they are a cause of discrimination, by real estate agents, lenders, and others, but they are also a cause of the prejudice—the persisting, pervasive negative attitudes about black Americans—that underlie the entire discriminatory system. Wayne State urban economist George Galster describes a self-reinforcing "ghettoizing cycle" in which ghettoization induces "behavioral adaptations" by ghetto dwellers. Widely reported by the media, ghetto behavior is then seen by whites as validating and legitimizing their prejudicial attitudes. The prejudices, Galster writes, lead to withdrawal from blacks, and to discriminatory conduct in housing, zoning, employment, and institutional arrangements of all sorts, which result in more ghettoization.

The Yinger and Galster observations are not new insights. Sixty years ago Gunnar Myrdal, in his monumental study of race relations, *An American Dilemma*, wrote,

> White prejudice and discrimination keep the Negro low in standards of living, health, education, manners and morals. This, in its turn, gives support to white prejudice.

Forty years later sociologist Elijah Anderson, in a well-known, fourteen-year study of a black ghetto and an adjacent racially mixed, middle- to upper-middle-class gentrifying neighborhood, concluded that the "vicious circle" described by Myrdal was alive and well. More recently Glenn Loury, in his widely discussed book *The Anatomy of Racial Equality*, called the black ghetto a leading example of racial stigma at work. While ghetto residents, Loury wrote, are a people apart, experiencing an internalized sense of despair, their purported characteristics make them objects of public derision and subject them to "symbolic degradation."

A story about a sleepy commuter suburb south of Chicago is illustrative. In the 1970s, Matteson's 12,000 residents were virtually all white. By the mid-1990s half were black, and black homeseekers outnumbered whites twenty-five to one. To try to maintain a racially balanced community, the village council decided to spend taxpayer money to recruit white homebuyers. A year later NBC's Tom Brokaw reported that only a few whites had moved in while several dozen more had left.

Brokaw's reporters tried to find out why. After scores of interviews with current and former white residents, three explanations emerged: rising crime, declining schools, and falling home values. When NBC checked the facts, it turned out that these were perceptions only. Matteson's crime rate had been pretty stable, at the high school there had been no change in student achievement, and there was no evidence that Matteson home prices had fluctuated any more or less than those of most other Chicago suburbs. (From 1990 to 1995, Matteson home prices had increased 32 percent.)

Sallie, an upper-middle-class white woman who had recently moved from Matteson, told Brokaw that she and her husband had encountered no problems there. Nor was she surprised when Brokaw said Matteson's crime rate, school performance, and housing values all had been stable. She had just been "uncomfortable" at the shopping mall where the majority of shoppers were black. "A lot of people just . . . keep moving away from it . . . move somewhere else where it's not going to happen for a few more years," she said.

Musing about the NBC show, David Rusk asked what was the "it" to which Sallie had referred. Was it just having black neighbors today? To Rusk that didn't seem to be the whole story. Many of the whites who had been interviewed were concerned about "what might happen tomorrow." Many conceded that rising crime, declining schools, and falling home values might not be happening in Matteson *yet*. But, Rusk emphasized, "that was the current reality in many black neighborhoods in Chicago itself or suburbs closer in." It had been the reality where many of Matteson's white residents or their parents had once lived, and from which they had escaped because crime rates *had* risen, school scores *had* fallen, and—thanks frequently to blockbusting real estate agents—home values *had* tumbled.

Rusk concluded that the unspoken motivation of many of Matteson's current movers was, "Get out of Matteson while the getting's still good." Like an image that persists on the retina after the seen object has moved, images of the ghetto persist in the mind's eye, revivified daily in television crime reporting and in the other electronic and print media. Studies show that while 71 percent of the nation's poor are nonblack, 62 percent of media stories about poverty are accompanied by pictures of blacks.

Echoing Myrdal's vicious circle and foretelling the fears of Matteson's whites, Anderson found that whites in the adjacent middle-class neighborhood he studied relied on race as their key to avoiding danger. "The public awareness is color-coded," Anderson wrote. "White skin denotes civility, law-abidingness, and trustworthiness, while black skin is strongly associated with poverty, crime, incivility, and distrust." Whites in American society at large act in the same way—their public awareness is also color-coded, and they therefore steer clear of poor blacks and keep them in their ghettos. Predictable ghetto behavior then intensifies whites' sense of danger, validates their color-coding, and drives their conduct.

By feeding prejudice against blacks the vicious circle helps to explain the continuing growth of black ghettos in the face of reasons to have expected the contrary, but why is the prejudice there in the first place? Historian George M. Fredrickson tells us that although medieval Arabs and Moors had white slaves as well as black, they generally assigned blacks the menial and degrading tasks. In southern Iberia, the most conspicuous Moorish slaves were black Africans, and Christians as well as Muslims "began to associate sub-Saharan African ancestry with lifetime servitude." Well before Columbus made his first landfall, when Portuguese navigators were offering West African slaves for sale in the port cities of Christian Iberia, "the identification of black skins with servile status was complete." "Race," writes Thomas Sowell, author of *Race and Culture,* "is one of the ways of collectivizing people in our minds." Yet, as Sowell also writes, race isn't needed for collectivizing—religion, nationality, language, caste, tribe, and other characteristics can serve as well. In some societies, Sowell points out, people who are physically indistinguishable from the surrounding population have faced humiliation, oppression, even genocide. The Burakumin of Japan, who are ethnically "pure" Japanese, are a case in point.

Treated as outcasts or "lowly people" centuries ago because their occupations—tanning, pottery, gardening, peddling, and others—were viewed as lowly or dirty, the lowly people were forced to live together in areas apart from the rest of society, "ghettoized" we would say today. From their own experience, Americans not versed in Japanese history could easily predict the consequences: disproportionate poverty, bad housing, poor education, welfare dependency, single motherhood, high crime.

Reform efforts followed feudal Japan's entry into the modern world. An "Emancipation Declaration" was promulgated soon after ours (1871). Japan's 1946 "American Constitution" prescribed equality for all, and "liberal" legislation ensued. But old habits of discriminatory thought die hard, no less with ethnically invisible Burakumin than with color-identifiable black Americans. As late as the mid-1990s, Burakumin were on the welfare rolls at seven times the national average. They continue today to suffer from disproportionately high unemployment. Some of Japan's largest companies, such as Toyota and Nissan, have been purchasers of "*buraku* lists"—book-length compilations of Burakumin used to screen job seekers. With ethnic Koreans, Burakumin dominate organized crime. Persisting Japanese discrimination against Burakumin was on the agenda at the 2001 United Nations World Conference Against Racism and Discrimination.

Yet discrimination against Burakumin is lessening. In spite of continuing opposition and the use of private detectives to research the background of potential spouses, intermarriage is increasing. In a recent book about a Burakumin "abolitionist," one young person reports hopefully, "These days you hardly ever hear of [parents] committing suicide because of it [intermarriage]." No doubt the situation of the Burakumin is slowly improving. But the adverb should be emphasized, for in the year 2000 there were 300 *reported* incidents of discrimination against Burakumin in Osaka alone, ranging from graffiti and anti-Burakumin Web sites to abuse in the workplace.

In his classic study, *The Nature of Prejudice*, Gordon W. Allport writes that it is a serious error to ascribe prejudice to any single taproot, whether of economic exploitation, social structure, mores, fear, aggression, sex conflict, or "any other favored soil." A few years ago an academic conference addressed three competing theoretical perspectives on why

American whites resist policies designed to increase racial equality—one deriving from "social-psychological theories of prejudice," one from "theories about structural inequalities in society," and one from theories about "conventional partisan politics." Needless to say, the conference failed to reconcile the competing theories.

Yet Allport says the historical context of each case is unquestionably important. So America's history of slavery is a shaping factor. So too is the notion of a single pan-European or "white" race that began to develop in the eighteenth century, thanks in part to the science of the Enlightenment. Races were classified and ranked as to intelligence, beauty, and other characteristics. Jefferson believed blacks to be the equals of whites in morals, was uncertain about their intellectual inferiority, but did not doubt that they were the uglier race. Ironically, Fredrickson notes, the Enlightenment made racism based on science thinkable just when its doctrine that all men were created equal called into question the justice of black slavery.

Americans proved equal to this intellectual challenge and developed all manner of supports for the ideology of inherent black inferiority. God had placed a curse on the black descendants of Ham. Slavery had existed in biblical times, was never condemned by Christ, and was therefore not sinful. Blacks had degenerated from the original race of white Adamites, and the deviation had become irreversible. The "types" of mankind were created separate and unequal. Racial Darwinism explained black inferiority. And so on. It would take World War II, the Holocaust, and the Cold War to discredit the ideology that blacks were an immutably inferior race.

Yet attitudes associated with the discredited ideology persisted, even in the top echelons of American government. John Ehrlichman, in his memoir *Witness to Power*, recounts Nixon explaining that "America's blacks could only marginally benefit from Federal programs because blacks were *genetically* inferior to whites." Thirty years later Trent Lott, majority leader of the U.S. Senate, lost his job for musing aloud that the country "wouldn't have had all these problems over all these years" if it had followed Mississippi's lead and voted for arch-segregationist Strom Thurmond for president in 1948.

The persistence of related attitudes in ordinary folk is captured in Studs Terkel's interview with Diane Romano, a devout Catholic, mother of six, who in the 1960s was a strong supporter of civil rights and wanted her children to see that "these people [blacks] are no different from any other people." A quarter of a century later, now in a law enforcement job, Romano has "mixed feelings":

> For the ten black people that I know who are very sweet and very good, a pleasure for anybody to know, I've got a hundred that are just the opposite . . . Because the majority of them are not the decent type of person that I would like to meet.

In surveys about American whites' attitudes toward blacks, a starting point for the last thirty years or so is a much-cited 1976 study conducted in the Detroit area. Published under the catchy title "Chocolate City, Vanilla Suburbs," the study found that once a neighborhood reached 20 percent black, half the surveyed whites would refuse to move in, and that when it reached about one-third black, the white refuse-to-enter figure rose to nearly three-quarters (73 percent). At the one-third point, over 40 percent of resident whites would actually try to leave. Surveys in other cities—Milwaukee, Omaha, Cincinnati, Kansas City, Los Angeles—all showed that while blacks preferred an even division of whites and blacks in a neighborhood, most whites would leave if that happened. Given these white attitudes, the preference of blacks for integrated neighborhoods is irrelevant. Integrated living patterns will be impossible to achieve as long as white attitudes about living in neighborhoods with blacks do not change.

Other surveys help to explain the attitudes. Blacks are viewed as more likely than whites to cheat, steal, and commit sex crimes, and less likely to take care of their homes. Hence, having blacks as neighbors brings crime and undermines property values. These are not local, idiosyncratic views. In a nationwide survey conducted by the National Opinion Research Center of the University of Chicago, over half the respondents thought blacks more prone to violence, less intelligent, and lazier than other groups.

Yet fears about crime and property values are not the whole of the attitudinal explanation. After all, Dr. Sweet, Nat King Cole, and Willie Mays were not themselves expected to commit crimes, or by their single move-ins to bring down property values. What lies behind the attitudes is fear of numbers—the floodgates opening. Once blacks, *any* blacks, begin to move in, it is feared that others will follow in numbers that will overwhelm the neighborhood and within a short time turn it predominantly or entirely black. Engendering this fear is the dual housing market and residential segregation. Poor blacks remain confined to ghettos with bad housing and terrible conditions. If a better neighborhood suddenly "opens" to blacks, as shown by a black family actually moving in and not getting firebombed out, others—many others—will surely follow. The white residents do not fear Willie Mays. They fear the influx of black families who will follow him.

Of course, the fear is not solely about numbers. As long as poor blacks are confined to the institutionalized pathology described by Kenneth Clark, there will be fear—Diane Romano's fear—of the sort of person produced by that pathology. But both fears—of inundation and of antisocial conduct—are fed by the existence, the *fact*, of the black ghetto.

The case of the Burakumin suggests that we may never achieve a complete understanding of negative white attitudes toward black Americans, for it teaches not only that prejudice can arise without race as its correlative but that societies, as if possessed by an instinctive need to stigmatize, may invent a correlative where an "objective" one is lacking. The story of the Burakumin also illustrates how difficult it is for societies to rid themselves of stigmatic thinking, even when the historical basis for the stigma has atrophied. How much more difficult is the task likely to be when a new correlative—in our case the black ghetto—is substituted. Yet even though we may never entirely understand Americans' negative attitude toward blacks—any more than the Japanese will ever fully understand their attitude toward Burakumin—the historical roots of the American attitude, and the ghetto as the modern objective correlative of black stigma keeping the vicious circle going, are clear.

Should we sit back and allow "nature to take its course," as Warren's mayor Ted Bates argued to George Romney? Will the black middle class continue to grow and eventually, somehow, counteract or overcome the stigma and break the vicious circle? Not likely. To hope that the black middle class will solve the ghetto problem is to ignore the reality described in *Black Picket Fences*, Mary Pattillo-McCoy's book to which I referred earlier.

Clustered in the sales and clerical fields, it should really be called the "lower middle class," writes Pattillo-McCoy. The black middle class is grievously lacking in wealth—even college-educated blacks average less than a third the net worth of college-educated whites. Homeownership plays a key role in accumulating wealth in America, but historic and current housing discrimination contribute to a 20 percent lower homeownership rate for blacks than for whites. The homes black do own, mostly in segregated areas, have less value than comparable homes outside segregated areas. Living mostly near high-poverty areas, as Pattillo-McCoy points out, struggling to keep ghetto evils at bay, the black middle class is a most unlikely instrumentality for resolving ghetto ills. Probably the best we can do for most middle-class black Americans is to dismantle the ghetto. Until that is done, much of their energy will understandably be devoted to the daily struggle Pattillo-McCoy depicts to keep the ghetto tide from washing over them.

Massey and Denton conclude that until the black ghetto is dismantled, "progress ameliorating racial inequality in other arenas will be slow, fitful, and incomplete." More forcefully, I would say that it is just about impossible to foresee much amelioration so long as black ghettos, with their stigmatizing feedback constantly circling back into the larger community, persist as the modern successor to black slavery and Jim Crow.

Indeed, there appears to be nothing to prevent the vicious circle from spiraling us into more color-coding and more ghettoization. In 1980 there were over three times as many black men in college and university as in prison and jail, 463,700 as against 143,000. Twenty years later the number of black men in college and university was actually fewer than the number behind bars, 603,032 compared with 791,600. If Currie and the "large and impressively consistent body of research" to which he refers are correct, what lies in store for black Americans who are poor? What will the college/university and prison/jail numbers look like twenty years from now, and twenty after that? And what will America look like then? What is happening to America's black poor today can be seen as the canary in our coal mine, a warning about Tocqueville's "most formidable evil threatening the future of the United States."

4

Does "threatening our future" sound alarmist? After all, the black ghetto population is a small fraction of America's total population—only

2.8 million black Americans out of a total population a hundred times larger. But we should take little comfort from small numbers; only a few American Communists led us to the havoc of McCarthyism. Jason DeParle makes an analogous point about the small ghetto population.

> The poverty and disorder of the inner cities lacerate a larger civic fabric, drawing people from shared institutions like subways, buses, parks, schools and even cities themselves . . . Perhaps most damaging of all is the effect that urban poverty has on race relations. It is like a poison in the national groundwater that is producing a thousand deformed fruits.

What deformed fruits? I will offer three examples, but the reader will have no trouble adding more.

My first example is nothing less than the break-up of the coalition that birthed the New Deal and the civil rights movement, a political sea change that began in the World War II years, gathered strength over the next two decades, then led to Richard Nixon's election in 1968, followed in 1980 by the triumph of Ronald Reagan and the final dissolution of the New Deal coalition with its reigning creed of consensus liberalism.

Powered by the trauma of the Great Depression, America was becoming a nation concerned with social justice. New Deal measures were of course partly driven by social justice ideals. In 1944 FDR called on Congress to enact a "second" Bill of Rights, this one to be devoted to social and economic, rather than civil and political, "rights." He even vetoed a revenue bill because it failed to tax "unreasonable" wartime profits and provided relief "not for the needy but for the greedy." To be sure, the veto was overridden. Yet the Fair Deal moved "fairness" to center stage, and Truman initiated desegregation of the armed forces in its name. Johnson's Great Society was to be great precisely because it elevated social and economic justice to explicit national policy. Though far from having carried the day, social justice was clearly "in play" in the American psyche for the three decades from the onset of the New Deal through the cresting of the civil rights movement in 1965.

In November 1968 that psyche underwent fundamental change. From a nation concerned with fairness we became a nation that under Richard Nixon slammed the doors on school and housing desegregation. After a brief interlude of "trusting" Jimmy Carter, our changed character

reemerged with traits deepened and intensified. Under Reagan we became a thoroughly uncaring nation, obsessed with the "free" market and
with crafting rules to foster still more personal acquisition by the most favored. The animating visions of the New Deal, the Fair Deal, and the
Great Society—"Government by organized money is just as dangerous as
Government by organized mob," FDR once said—had become as irrelevant as ancient relics.

There is no single explanation for America's character change. But a
major factor was disaffection by the blue-collar workers and white ethnics
who had been core elements of the New Deal coalition. Disaffection over
what? The answer is the one concern that, for them, trumped all others—
fear of blacks from ghettos trying to "invade" their neighborhoods.

Focusing on Detroit, Professor Thomas Sugrue's study, "Crabgrass-
Roots Politics," illustrates what happened at the local level. Detroit had
long been a New Deal bastion. For years, blue-collar whites and white
ethnics had voted overwhelmingly for Franklin Delano Roosevelt. But in
Detroit, as elsewhere, blacks were seeking housing outside the ghetto. In
Detroit, as elsewhere, whites were pushing back. For the twenty years
and more following World War II, as Sugrue relates, the push out and
push back was the predominant issue in local Detroit politics.

Democrats were seen as the party trying to improve the condition of
black Americans, from Truman's desegregation order to the espousal of
civil rights by Johnson and Humphrey. Inevitably, that meant identification with the black struggle for housing. Inevitably, in turn, that meant
disaffection on the part of blue-collar workers and white ethnics in Detroit, all interested—*above all*—in protecting their neighborhoods, their
homes, and their children from blacks seen as invaders. By 1972 George
Wallace would not only win the Michigan Democratic Primary, but in the
process would sweep every predominantly white ward in Detroit.

At the national level, the story of the political sea change originates
with southerners attacking the civil rights movement with law and order
rhetoric, deliberately coupling blacks and lawbreakers. Even before Johnson's crushing 1964 victory over Barry Goldwater, Theodore H. White
wrote a prescient analysis for *Life* magazine about white resistance to integration. Backlash, he wrote, is "as invisible, yet as real, as air pollution."
Division over race was an obvious peril for the Democrats. The Republicans had to choose between designing a program of social harmony or be-

coming "the white man's party." The issue, White said, would outlast the election. If the need for constructive answers were ignored—here he echoed Tocqueville's language exactly—"disaster lies ahead."

Instead of answering with a program for social harmony, Republicans seized the racial moment. Angling for the 1968 Republican nomination, Nixon was soon playing the law and order theme regularly and loudly. A 1966 issue of *U.S. News and World Report* featured a Nixon article, "If Mob Rule Takes Hold in the U.S.," that blamed crime and violence on civil rights leaders. Not more money for a war on poverty but more money for "more convictions," Nixon argued.

The racial subtext of Nixon's anticrime message was clear. Kevin Phillips, whose position papers for the Nixon campaign were the blueprint for Nixon's strategy (they were restated in his 1969 book, *The Emerging Republican Majority*), frankly argued that a long-term political realignment in America was possible on the basis of the race issue. He suggested—as one study puts it—"coded anti-Black campaign rhetoric." Nixon understood. "That subliminal appeal to the anti-black voter was always present in Nixon's statements and speeches," wrote John Ehrlichman.

In his retrospective on the 1968 election, White observes that 28 percent of the Americans who voted for Johnson in 1964 repudiated him four years later, "a repudiation greater than that suffered by any President except Herbert Hoover." Not even in 1932, White says, had a major party vote shrunk so dramatically. The shrinkage cannot of course be attributed solely to what White calls the "primordial" issue of race. Vietnam was an obvious factor (although neither Nixon nor Humphrey had a clear Vietnam message), as well as the violent protests it spawned. So was a conservative campaign against "soft-on-crime" and welfare policies that blamed crime and poverty on bad people making bad choices, not on bad housing, bad schools, unemployment, and other matters for which society was largely responsible.

But race was explicit in Nixon's "southern strategy" for bringing the historically Democratic South into the Republican column, and it was "subliminal" in the crime and welfare debates. Overall it was a key factor in Nixon's win against Humphrey, which was closer than many remember—the winner wasn't known until the early morning hours, and in the popular vote Nixon's percentage was 43.40 to Humphrey's 42.72. Once in office, Nixon paid back the South on school busing and—by deep-sixing George Romney's plans—the "backlashers" on housing.

After Watergate, crime issues largely disappeared from national political discourse and remained off the agenda for the rest of the decade. For obvious reasons Gerald Ford was disinclined to emphasize crime fighting, and Jimmy Carter did not do so either—his administration initially advocated decriminalizing marijuana.

However, in his 1980 campaign, Reagan's speeches on crime and welfare were a virtual rerun of Nixon's themes of twelve years earlier. Although other issues were of course involved, such as the economy and the Iranian hostage crisis, Reagan not only played the crime issue with its racial subtext exactly as had Nixon, but stood as had Nixon with the now-emerged Republican majority that had replaced the race-sundered New Deal coalition. It was a majority built on the "ruination" of the Great Society, says Patrick Buchanan, and "Nixon was its architect." In their thoughtful book, *The Politics of Injustice: Crime and Punishment in America,* professors Katherine Beckett and Theodore Sasson succinctly sum up Buchanan's "ruination" point: race had eclipsed class as the "organizing principle of American politics."

My second example of a deformed fruit is the War on Drugs, targeted on black ghettos. When Reagan beat Carter most Americans did not attribute crime to coddling criminals. A 1982 ABC poll found that 58 percent of Americans believed that unemployment and poverty were the most important causes of crime. Only 12 percent thought "lenient courts" were the main cause. It was the politicians, led by Reagan but supported by Democrats afraid to appear "soft," who made crime the hot-button issue it became after 1980. (By the mid-1990s, with the rate of violent crime remaining steady, television and newspaper coverage of crime increased some 400 percent; for the decade of the 1990s, crime was the leading nationwide television news topic.) It was politicians also who chose drugs, as they had a dozen years earlier, for the federal government's point of entry into what, in earlier periods, had been primarily a state and local government issue. Concludes Tonry, the War on Drugs and its harsh crime-control policies—focused as we have seen on ghettos—"were launched to achieve political, not policy objectives."

Even though the evidence shows virtually no correlation between patterns of incarceration and patterns of crime, since Ronald Reagan took office we have built more than 1,000 new jails and prisons, many crowded beyond capacity and spawning prison violence, while reducing what we spend on prisoner education and vocational training. Our sentencing practices are draconian. Using a heartless baseball analogy, we have enacted "three strikes" laws that impose mandatory, long-term prison sentences for a third conviction, even for nonviolent offenses. In 2003 the Supreme Court ruled that it did not violate the Constitution to sentence a thirty-seven-year-old heroin addict to virtual life imprisonment (fifty years without parole) for shoplifting some $150 worth of videotapes to feed his addiction. California has meted out a twenty-five-year sentence for the "third strike" theft of a slice of pizza, and another for the pilfering of some chocolate-chip cookies. Thirteen-year-olds have been given mandatory, life-without-parole sentences. *Time* magazine asks, "Should we make 11-year-olds eligible for life behind bars? Nine-year-olds? Seven-year-olds?"

Heartless sentencing may not be the worst of it. Beckett and Sasson point out that, like Prohibition, the War on Drugs is directly responsible for the black market and for the crime it breeds, fueling some of the very ills that are among the root causes of crime and diverting money from education and social initiatives. Between 1980 and 1995 the proportion of California's budget devoted to prisons grew from 2 percent to 9.7 percent, while the higher education proportion dropped below prisons, from over 12 to 9.5 percent.

In short, driven by a color-coded fear of black—particularly ghetto—crime, as a nation we are doggedly pursuing a mass incarceration policy that is both mindless and destructive of traditional American values. It is mindless because at enormous cost we insist on pursuing a policy (imprisoning people at fourteen times the rate in Japan, eight times the rate in France, six times the rate in Canada) that is having no demonstrable effect on drug availability, drug crime rates, or crime rates generally. It is destructive of values because it has driven us to extremities that no fair-minded person can defend. "The United States is transforming itself," writes Brent Staples of the *New York Times*, "into a nation of ex-convicts."

One final example of disfigured produce may be offered—the demise of welfare. The tangled skein of Americans' negative views about welfare is not easily unraveled. Yet racial hostility, mostly toward blacks, appears in the literature as a "major," even a "decisive," factor. In the understated language of one study, racial animosity makes welfare for the poor, who are disproportionately black, "unappealing to many voters."

But rarely have high public officials matched the explicitness of Newt Gingrich. At the heart of Gingrich's successful dump-welfare campaign, linear successor to Ronald Reagan's Welfare Queen and George Bush's Willie Horton, was a stick-figure caricature of the ghetto: "You can't maintain civilization with twelve-year-olds having babies and fifteen-year-olds killing each other and seventeen-year-olds dying of AIDS." The image of the black ghetto was thus instrumental not only in ending decades-old welfare entitlement but also in dropping the jobs, training, and child care originally supposed to have been part of the deal. We don't yet know for sure what effect welfare reform is having on children, although DeParle's recent book, *American Dream,* supplies no cause for optimism. But the concern for maintaining civilization has not led to measures to help the ghetto children—American children, let us remember—who inhabit Gingrich's caricature.

Can these deformed fruits be blamed solely on black ghettos? No, they cannot. Ending black ghettos wouldn't end antiblack attitudes any more than ending Jewish ghettos ended anti-Semitism. But it would be difficult to find many features of American society that match the black ghetto's poisoning effect on attitudes, values, and conduct.

An inference to be drawn from Currie and other criminologists, from Sugrue and other historians, and from Myrdal, Anderson, Yinger, Galster, and other social critics, is that a great deal about how Americans think and act *can* be explained by the black ghetto. What Tom Brokaw and David Rusk perceived about why whites were leaving Matteson is an example of Myrdal's vicious circle, steadily cycling a color-coded poison into our national groundwater, producing such disfiguring results as would seem to compel us to take a searching look at how to dismantle black ghettos before they dismantle us. Disaster may not come in the form of riots and race wars, as Carl Rowan predicts in his book *The Coming Race War in America.* But it will be disaster no less if American values are sufficiently deformed.

5

Which brings us back to the thirty-nine years of Gautreaux and what they can tell us about ghetto-dismantling. "Nothing to be done," says Estragon in *Godot*'s opening line. "I'm beginning to come round to that opinion," observes Vladimir, who then muses that all his life he's tried to "put it from me, saying, Vladimir, be reasonable, you haven't yet tried everything." *Is* there nothing to be done about ghettos? *Have* we tried everything?

Was there was a moment when the holy grail of metropolitan-wide public housing might have been grasped? If Humphrey had won in 1968, and had led the country along the path pointed to by the Kerner, Kaiser, and Douglas reports? Or if Nixon hadn't squelched Romney's initiative? But the moment did pass. The painful history of Gautreaux scattered sites teaches that adamant local resistance to what Nixon was fond of calling "forced integration" through publicly owned housing will not be overcome, even with court orders, on a national scale. History also teaches that even when national politics supports building new housing for poor families, it will not be built for blacks in white neighborhoods. To get the 1949 housing act passed liberals actually had to vote against an amendment that called for integrating public housing. In the 1980s the successor new building program, which works through the tax code and bears the cumbersome moniker Low Income Housing Tax Credits, was enacted without any integration requirements at all; like high-rise public housing, much tax credit housing is located in minority, high-poverty neighborhoods, and the program produces little racial integration. Today, prospects for scattering newly built, publicly subsidized housing throughout America's white suburbs remain nil.

But a different part of the Gautreaux history suggests that there is something we haven't yet tried. We have not yet tried housing mobility on a national scale. That is, we have not tried to dismantle our ghettos by enabling black ghetto dwellers to escape their confines and move into existing private dwellings with housing choice vouchers. This is the "earmarking" proposal I made in 1994 to Henry Cisneros and Bruce Katz, but which—following the Gingrich triumph in November—they pronounced dead on arrival.

Many observers would like to see a "mobility strategy" tried. After canvassing possible solutions, David T. Ellwood says the "obvious" answer is to "move poor people into rich neighborhoods . . ." Says Nicholas Lemann, "For the ghetto kid, making it, 99 percent of the time, goes with getting out of the ghetto." Adds Gary Orfield, "Get them out of the ghettos. This is the most powerful way."

In 2003, in an essay called "A Way Out," subtitled "America's Ghettos and the Legacy of Racism," Owen Fiss, a Yale law professor, argues precisely for a Gautreaux-type program large enough "to relocate all residents of the ghettos who choose to move." The black ghetto, Fiss writes, is an "instrument of subjection" that constitutes the "most pernicious vestige of racial injustice in the United States—the successor to slavery and Jim Crow." Because the ghetto is a deliberate creation of white America, as plainly as were slavery and Jim Crow, Fiss argues that offering the Gautreaux remedy is a matter of simple justice.

> "The state played an important role in creating and maintaining the ghetto, and is thus duty-bound to use its powers to remedy the present-day consequences of that action."

I think Fiss is right, subject, however, to the question of practicality. Does a national Gautreaux Program make sense in the real world, or is it an impractical dream? Yet we don't reach this question if the proposal is rejected as poor policy; practicality aside, not everyone agrees that Fiss's prescription is the right medicine. I will turn first therefore to the arguments that the Gautreaux approach, even if it were doable, is a bad idea.

One of the criticisms is that the approach would do more harm than good. This is the Bovard-Husock contention, discussed in chapter 5, that moving out would be bad for the movers because of the harmful consequences they would suffer, including—a new twist beginning to appear—that suburbia's supposedly better neighborhoods aren't really better after all, that its own problems with drugs and values make life in middle-class suburbia no better than life in the ghetto.

The answer I have already given to Bovard and Husock will serve here as well: Who are "we" to withhold a purely voluntary, escape-the-ghetto opportunity from "them" on the ground that we know better than they what is in their interest? *The Hidden War's* description of children slain in gang wars, or permanently traumatized by the stress of coping with constant violence and disorder, reminds me of what Brent Staples has written about "butchery" in ghetto streets:

> Remember how Britons shipped their children out of London during the blitzkrieg? What American cities need are evacuation plans to spirit at least some black boys out of harm's way before it's too late. Inner-city parents who can afford it ship their children to safety in the homes of relatives. Those who are without that resource deserve the same option extended to parents in London during World War II.

Not to mention that Rosenbaum's studies show that "evacuation" works for many of the families who choose to try it. And, in spite of MTO's flaws, additional MTO analyses are beginning to confirm Rosenbaum. Says one survey, "Rigorous social science research convincingly shows that living in a severely distressed neighborhood undermines the health and well-being of both adults and children, and that moving to low-poverty areas is . . . beneficial."

It is true, of course, that "evacuation" won't work for all participating families. The traumas of moving, severance from familiar support systems, and crossing a "cultural divide" to white or integrated middle-income communities are sure to result in many "failures." But that is hardly a reason not to give those who want it a chance to try. (It can't be emphasized too often that the mobility program I propose is voluntary.) And high-quality, postmove counseling will improve the odds for many families.

A variation on the bad-for-them argument is that dismantling the ghetto will undermine black institutions, political power, maybe even black culture, while destroying valuable communal ties and self-help networks that deserve preservation. As for black institutional and political strength, Italians, Irish, Jews, and others have survived far more mobility than black Americans are likely to experience; and it is absurd to contend that the strong, resilient black American culture has anything to fear from a Gautreaux-type program. Local ties and networks may indeed be (voluntarily) disrupted, even sundered, but the entombment of souls of which DuBois wrote generations ago and the butchery of which Staples writes today make it plain to any objective observer that the bad the ghetto does far outweighs the good to be found there.

Another variation on the bad-for-them argument is that nonmovers will be worse off once some of the ablest and most motivated ghetto residents leave, creating what some critics call a "super-underclass." Even if that were true, it would not be a sufficient reason to reject the approach. Should we not have passed the Fair Housing Act because the departure of better-off ghetto residents may have left those who remained worse off? Moreover, the likelihood that deconcentration will foster redevelopment means that even those who are unable to leave or choose to remain will be benefited over time.

The latter point may raise eyebrows. Why will redevelopment be fostered? And if it is, won't gentrification simply drive out remaining ghetto residents? The answer to the first question is a matter of pressure: when, like a balloon being filled, migrants poured in, the ghetto expanded outward; as deconcentration lets out some of the air, the pressure will be reversed. When ghettos are located near desirable areas (Cabrini-Green is an example), redevelopment pressures will be strong. When they are not, the redevelopment pump may need to be primed with government assistance.

In both circumstances the concern that gentrification will drive out the remaining poor can be addressed. Where government assists the redevelopment process, the assistance should be conditioned on housing for the poor as part of the mix. Where it does not (although usually some form of assistance will be involved), inclusionary zoning can require some low-income housing in all new residential development above a threshold number of units. Additional techniques, for example, deferring or limiting property tax increases in gentrifying neighborhoods, are also available.

Others reject the Gautreaux approach in favor of a preferred alternative. A major one is to "fix up" the ghetto, simply to go in—without worrying about poverty deconcentration through housing mobility—and improve shelter and services for present residents. But with the suburbs having become the locus of metropolitan employment growth, with the opportunity engine the ghetto once was now become a destructive, jobless environment, it is hubris to think that we could reverse decades-old economic forces solely through improved shelter and services. William Julius Wilson concludes, correctly I think, that without reducing their segregation and increasing economic opportunities for poor blacks, programs that target ghettos are unlikely to have much success.

A more sophisticated fix-up approach is "community redevelopment" or "revitalization." With a nonprofit community development corporation generally leading the way, the idea is to attack all of a depressed community's needs comprehensively and simultaneously—not just housing and social services, but commercial development, job creation, school improvement, health and public facilities, credit supply, crime and drug control—the works. This form of revitalization is almost always aided by government funding of one sort or another.

The attraction of revitalizing is considerable. Residents of depressed neighborhoods need hope; the revitalizing possibility may supply it. Cities need redevelopment; the prospect of revitalizing offers it. Democracy requires a strong citizenry; community-based revitalizing builds strong citizens. No wonder community revitalizing is the darling of philanthropy, supported by a growing national movement.

But cautions are in order. First, community development does not generally focus on ghettos, for few black ghettos boast the key instrument of a strong community development corporation. (HOPE VI, limited to public-housing-dominated neighborhoods, lacks the comprehensiveness of revitalizing. HOPE VI's demolition, poverty deconcentration, and mixed-income redevelopment may stimulate other activities, such as commercial development and school improvement, but the other activities are not funded parts of the plan itself because HOPE VI dollars are by law confined mostly to housing.)

Second, even in the neighborhoods in which most revitalizing has been attempted, the record is distinctly mixed. Revitalizing is a difficult, multifaceted, long-term undertaking. Numerous studies make it clear that even after decades of stupendously hard work and much achievement, jobs may still be scarce, neighborhood schools still problematic, poverty still widespread, crime and drugs still unvanquished. One of revitalizing's most enthusiastic supporters, writing about one of its most notable successes—Paul Grogan, on the "renaissance" of the South Bronx, in a book, *Comeback Cities*, written with Tony Proscio—acknowledges that the South Bronx poverty rate did not decline, that employment was mostly unchanged, and that "substantial racial segregation and isolation will continue."

The reason has to do with more than five decades of metropolitan development patterns, which David Rusk examines in his 1999 book, *Inside Game/Outside Game.* The "inside game" is being played in many large cities, and increasingly in many older, inner-ring suburbs as well. Relative to their metropolitan regions, these "inside" places are experiencing declines in their middle-class populations, and in employment, buying power, relative incomes, and tax bases as well. Simultaneously, their poor, disproportionately minority, populations are growing. The "outside game" reverses these patterns, with the newer, farther-out suburbs garnering a steadily larger share of the region's jobs, as well as middle-class families with their incomes, buying power, and tax-paying capacities, while housing a disproportionately small fraction of the region's poor.

Inside Game/Outside Game analyzes the powerful social and economic forces that generate these metropolitan development patterns, and the institutional—including governmental—arrangements that foster them. The result is what Rusk calls the "tragic dilemma" of community-based development programs—"It is like helping a crowd of people run up a down escalator." No matter how hard they run, the escalator keeps coming down. A few run so fast they reach the top, but most weary and are carried back to the bottom.

Is Rusk overstating his point, or understating what community development corporations have accomplished? Consider this from the editor of *Shelterforce,* a journal almost entirely devoted to espousing the work of community development corporations:

> In spite of all our work, more children are now in poverty than have been in years, joblessness is rising, income inequality is obscenely high and racial tensions still exist. Many cities have seen decline for years as manufacturing jobs moved offshore and those with resources left for the suburbs and beyond.
>
> These trends have led to a large number of cities with high rates of housing vacancy and abandonment, joblessness and poverty. With few resources, such cities typically have poor schools and provide limited services. Even with the persistent efforts of [community-based organizations] and others, these cities remain weak.

Edward Goetz, director of the Urban and Regional Planning Program at the University of Minnesota, does not exactly advance revitalizing as an alternative to mobility. In his book *Clearing the Way: Deconcentrating the Poor in Urban America*, Goetz writes that the nation's approach to urban poverty "should include a program of voluntary mobility." Goetz does assert, however, that if mobility is all we do, without moving forward on the broad antipoverty agenda he lays out, mobility will not only accomplish little but may actually be harmful.

It would be a serious concern if Goetz were right about the possibility of harm, for each of the other antipoverty steps Goetz advocates, such as regional revenue sharing and getting rid of exclusionary zoning and housing discrimination, are themselves no less difficult to accomplish than mobility, collectively much more so. It is likely, therefore, that were we able to get mobility under way, it would not be accompanied by many, if any, of the other Goetz recommendations.

Goetz's argument that mobility alone might be harmful is that mobility saps our will to improve the lives of poor people in the places where they presently live, directing our efforts away from the "declining housing stock of poor neighborhoods" and toward "reducing services for lower-income families and attracting more middle-income home buyers." He also fears that the gentrifying consequences of attracting higher-income families will force poor people out.

Yet experience demonstrates that revitalizing can best be achieved through a mixed-income approach that attracts higher-income families to (formerly) poverty neighborhoods, thereby creating an incentive for private profit and investment. Newer revitalizing initiatives are of the mixed-income variety. Attracting higher-income residents is seen as essential partly because of the need to attract private sector resources. But it is also recognition of the crucial point made by Lewis Spence and William Julius Wilson (referred to in chapter 6) that only by integrating the poor with the nonpoor will significant, long-term improvements in the life circumstances of most impoverished families trapped in ghettos be made possible.

To be sure, no effort to improve housing and services for poor families should be gainsaid. Some revitalizing activity may actually prevent marginal neighborhoods from becoming ghettos. Yet Goetz's sap-the-will point can be turned 180 degrees. There is a danger that the appeal of community revitalizing will lead to plans that leave ghettos intact by focusing exclusively on improving conditions within them for their impoverished populations. As Nicholas Lemann argues, we should not be about the business of fostering self-contained communities apart from the mainstream. We should instead be trying to bring the ghetto poor into the mainstream. Like housing mobility, mixed-income development also brings with it the crucial benefit of enabling the poor to live among the nonpoor. Community revitalization should thus be seen not as an opposing or alternative strategy, but as a follow-on, mixed-income complement to housing mobility.

There are those who argue that it is wrong to do mobility before community development because that sequence denies true housing choice; many ghetto residents might choose mobility only because the alternative of remaining in the ghetto is so bad. Revitalize first, the argument runs, and then the choice to leave or stay will be a fair one. But the preceding discussion makes it clear that, with few exceptions, in practice this approach will give us neither revitalization nor mobility. With deconcentration through mobility coming first, we can have both, and a responsible—albeit longer term—means of addressing the needs of those who remain behind because they cannot, or decline to, participate in mobility.

A second alternative to the Gautreaux approach is espoused by Wilson. Echoing the proposals of others, particularly journalist and author Mickey Kaus, Wilson advocates providing a job to everyone who will work, a government job if need be—"public-sector employment of last resort." In the Wilson-Kaus proposal the jobs would pay slightly less than the minimum wage and would be offered to everyone over eighteen who wanted to work and couldn't find a (higher paying) private sector job. The idea is modeled after the New Deal's Works Progress Administration (WPA).

Wilson and Kaus believe "there will be enough worthwhile WPA-style jobs for anyone who wants one"—Wilson's examples include repairing crumbling urban infrastructure, opening libraries every evening and on Saturdays, and serving as nurses' aides. With health insurance, government-funded child care, and earned income tax credits, all of which are part of the proposal, Wilson believes that the government jobs "would enable workers and their families to live at least decently and avoid joblessness."

Live decently on less than the minimum wage? Hardly. Moreover, the jobs approach, though it may sound like a single "program" (Wilson himself, however, includes health insurance, child care, and tax credits), is really nothing of the sort. I spoke about it to Janice Greer, head of an agency which for more than thirty years has run an exemplary, multi-faceted social services program, complete with a school and residential home, on Chicago's South Side. From decades of daily engagement Greer understands the heartbreak, and the occasional triumph, that goes with living and working with ghetto kids, particularly teenagers. Jobs aren't enough, she says firmly. What is needed to give a jobs program a chance to succeed are better schools, with mentors and tutors, after-school programs, day care, better health care, drug rehabilitation programs, neighborhood security, and so on.

Another veteran, Toby Herr, who has for years run a successful, research-oriented program designed to help inner-city Chicago residents get jobs, says, "The process doesn't end when you find someone a job. In some ways, that's only the beginning." Herr explains that it frequently takes two, three, or four jobs. "You have to make a long-term commitment to them, or it doesn't work." So the jobs "program" really rests on layers of supporting programs. It's like pointing to the apex of a pyramid and saying, "build that."

As with revitalization, no effort to provide jobs should be gainsaid. The neo-WPA proposal would certainly help some in the ghetto. But even apart from the time and uncertainties involved in building a pyramid, many ghetto residents suffer from deficiencies in education, skills, and motivation that make them unemployable even by a WPA-type agency. Wilson himself speaks of the need to upgrade the skills of the next generation *before* it enters the labor market.

(A different New Deal model, something we could get up and running more quickly, would be the CCC rather than the WPA. The Civilian Conservation Corps, including remedial education and skill training for those needing it, would have the advantage of providing both jobs and escape from the ghetto because it brings its recruits to where its projects are. Columnist David Broder, quoting historian Stephen Ambrose, writes of the CCC that it "pulled these kids out of the morass of their lives, gave them a sense of identity and discipline and of group purpose—same things they need now.")

Wilson is right to focus on jobs. Work, and all that goes with it, is of the essence, at least in our time, of decent, civic society. If too many of us are without work, society comes apart—the larger society as in the Great Depression, or our ghetto societies of today. When small towns or rural societies fail to provide work, their inhabitants leave, as ghost towns and depeopled rural hamlets attest. People must have the inclination, habit, and opportunity to work if society is to work.

However, a jobs program is not a ghetto-dismantling strategy. During the boom of the late 1990s ghetto poverty rates dropped, and now they have risen again. Throughout, crime, drugs, and violence persisted, and schools stayed terrible. The ghettos remained ghettos, and its children continued to live their formative years under traumatizing conditions. If only for the children, should we not deploy now a remedy that has dismantling potential, and promises, as Staples urges, to spirit at least some children out of harm's way before it's too late?

A third alternative is sometimes proffered: "fix" ghetto children by fixing ghetto schools, hoping that improved schools will somehow lead to radical ghetto improvement. Since 1965, when the federal government began giving money to school districts with large numbers of students from poor families, the nation has poured billions of dollars into inner-city schools. In the process we have "fiddled with practically everything you could think to fiddle with," says James Traub, a contributing writer to the *New York Times Magazine.*

The results are disheartening. In his article "Schools Are Not the Answer," Traub reports that at the end of the 1990s, nearly thirty-five years after the federal billions had begun to flow, two-thirds of New York City's eighth graders failed the state education department's English test, as three-quarters did the math test. In 2003, according to a report issued by a committee of the business establishment, nearly two-thirds of Chicago's eleventh grade students could not meet state standards for reading at grade level, and nearly three-fourths failed to meet state math standards. In both New York and Chicago, strenuous, years-long local reform efforts had supplemented the federal dollars. (The Chicago scores were based on the 60 percent of public school students who remained in high school through the eleventh grade, taking no account of the 40 percent who had dropped out.) While there is no single appropriate measure of school "success," the New York and Chicago data, not atypical of big-city school systems, are sobering.

In the face of the disadvantages that so many ghetto children bring with them to school and return to at home, Traub asks, "How powerful can this one institution be?" His answer to his rhetorical question comes from numerous studies of educational inequality. They show that regardless of the reform strategy chosen, schools will be able to close only a fraction of the gap between ghetto children and those outside. With rare exceptions, writes Traub, the expenditure of all those billions has done "almost nothing to raise the trajectory of ghetto children."

The reasons are not far to seek. They were laid out almost forty years ago by sociologist James Coleman of the University of Chicago in a study still widely regarded as the most important education study of the twentieth century. Pupil achievement, Coleman concluded, was "strongly related to the educational backgrounds and aspirations of the other students in the school." The "educational resources" provided by fellow students were "more important [for pupil achievement] than . . . the resources provided by the school board," indeed, more important than "any school factor." A more recent study concludes that the degree to which poor children are surrounded by other poor children, both in their neighborhood and at school, has as strong an effect on their achievement as their own poverty. A number of studies to the same effect are summed up by James Guthrie, of Vanderbilt University, who writes extensively about education: "If there is one thing that is more related to a child's academic achievement than coming from a poor household, it is going to school with children from other poor households."

A few ghetto schools have succeeded brilliantly. Remember the movie *Stand and Deliver*, about an extraordinary teacher, Jaime Escalante, and his success with impoverished Chicano students? Yet, Traub points out, "Any method that depends on a Jaime Escalante is no method at all." And, indeed, when Escalante left Garfield High School, the number of students taking the AP calculus test dropped from 143 to 37, while the passing percent dropped from 61 to 19.

Some observers believe that growing support for small autonomous schools—run by outsiders under "charters" or contracts from the public school system, or created by the system itself—heralds a new day for improving ghetto schools. Some early evidence is arguably hopeful. But except for the ghetto itself, no institution in our society has been more resistant to significant change than the public school system. To try to change the former by changing the latter is to confront a double hurdle, each of Herculean proportions. As with efforts to improve shelter and services for poor families, no effort to improve ghetto schools should be gainsaid. Yet we should not mistake improvements, should they come, in what Kenneth Clark long ago called instruments "for the perpetuation— and strengthening—of class and caste," for elimination of the class and caste system itself. Ultimately, says University of Chicago president Don Randel, "it will not be possible to fix schools if we cannot fix families or make good [the family deficit]."

A final anti-Gautreaux policy argument remains. It is not really a critique of housing mobility, or a suggested alternative to it, but a philosophical view of the situation of black Americans that rejects a race-specific remedy of any sort. It might loosely be called the self-help approach, and is exemplified by Dinesh D'Souza's *The End of Racism* and Shelby Steele's *The Content of Our Character.* Treating black Americans as victims entitled to redress is worse than useless, the argument runs, because that stifles the individual initiative from which, alone, salvation will ultimately come.

In the view of these writers, black Americans must put their own house in order. For D'Souza, it is the black American's moral and cultural shortcomings, not racial discrimination, that explain the failure of black Americans to make more progress toward economic parity. In fact, D'Souza believes that much "racism" directed at blacks is nothing more than a rational calculation of risks (taxi drivers not picking up black men at night, lenders refusing loans to blacks trying to move into white neighborhoods). When government does step in, as with affirmative action and welfare, it only makes matters worse by undermining black character and initiative. What is needed, D'Souza asserts, is for blacks to "act white," that is, to "embrace mainstream cultural norms, so that they can effectively compete with other groups." Some specific D'Souza recommendations include Big Brother programs, summer camps that teach entrepreneurial skills, credit associations, resident supervision of housing projects, and privately run neighborhood schools.

Shelby Steele sounds a comparable theme. "We black Americans will never be saved or even assisted terribly much by others . . . There will be no end to despair and no lasting solutions to any of our problems until we rely on individual effort within the American mainstream . . . An enormous range of opportunity [is] open to blacks . . ." Uplift will come only when many "millions of blacks seize the possibilities inside the sphere of their personal lives and use them to take themselves forward."

The advice that America should do nothing about black ghettos, except wait for the time when "millions of blacks seize the possibilities," generates a gasp of disbelief. In modern times no one describes the festering sore of the black ghetto more starkly than D'Souza—"the criminal and irresponsible black underclass represents [for many whites] a revival of barbarism in the midst of Western civilization." Are Americans to ignore the festering, while allowing barbarism to spread? More likely, as with our mass incarceration policy, we will try to lance the boil in ways that spread infection to the rest of the body politic. The admonition to do nothing is a nonstarter in the real world. Something, if only building more prisons as we pass ever harsher laws, will be done.

Blacks are in a kind of despair, Steele says, where a "miasma of drug addiction, violence, and hopelessness has already transformed many inner cities into hearts of darkness." Steele's exhortation—"to study hard, pursue their dreams with discipline and effort, to be responsible for themselves, to have concern for others"—will not penetrate the miasma. Recall the saga of the Haynes family, or Kotlowitz's depiction of life in Henry Horner. Recall Popkin's description of the families she interviewed—suffering from substance abuse, domestic violence, serious illness, disability, mental problems, sudden death of friends and family, with at least one family member having a criminal record. These are not families who can be expected to "pursue their dreams with discipline and effort."

It is true that many ghetto-dwelling blacks do not match Popkin's description. Connie Henry lived in Taylor too, alongside Juanita and Johnnie Haynes. But the Connie Henrys face their own daily struggles for survival. It is a minor miracle when they pilot their own children through ghetto seas. Henry's strategy for coping was to tune Taylor out, and to escape from it as soon as possible. It is inconceivable that she would have the will, energy, and resources to perform for the others at Taylor the tasks Steele and D'Souza set for blacks to help other blacks.

Might the Steele and D'Souza exhortations resonate more with middle-class blacks? I have already explained why any hope that the black middle class can break the vicious circle of the black ghetto and white attitudes is forlorn. The greatest problem black Americans face, Steele says, is insufficient development—"this *more* than white racism." Shouldn't Steele, then, be a strong supporter of a Gautreaux mobility program? After all, a major teaching of Rosenbaum's Gautreaux studies is that "getting them out of the ghettos" opens the door to individual development.

Steele recalls a passage by the Italian writer and Holocaust survivor Primo Levi about liberation from the concentration camps. "Just as they were again becoming men," Levi wrote, "that is, *responsible* [Steele's emphasis], the sorrows of men returned." Steele's gloss on the passage is that liberation did not bestow happiness but agency. "And with agency," he writes, "came the responsibility to create opportunities . . . It was precisely this . . . responsibility for their own survival that restored humanity to the survivors."

But liberation from the camp preceded the agency that led to responsibility. So, too, one might expect, liberation from the ghetto will lead to the responsibility to develop the strengths needed to survive outside it. Honor student Jason Bronaugh, considering anesthesiology as a career, not Dantrell Davis, victim of a sniper's bullet at age seven, is the metaphor for that. Yes, Steele *should* support a Gautreaux mobility program.

I conclude that the Gautreaux-would-be-a-bad-idea arguments are unpersuasive. Certainly they do not outweigh the benefits of a national Gautreaux Program that could actually begin the process of ghetto dismantling. Kenneth Clark wrote that the ghetto would not be ended as long as white society believed that it was needed. Yet the Catch-22 of Myrdal's vicious circle is that white society will continue to believe that it needs the ghetto as long as the ghetto continues to exist.

I propose therefore to consider how a Gautreaux mobility program might enable us to break out of the vicious circle and elude the Catch-22. Not instead of revitalizing neighborhoods, or providing jobs, or improving schools, or adopting more sensible criminal justice policies, or doing whatever else can be done to improve the miserable lot of ghetto residents. But separately, regardless of what else is done or not done, as a way to do what Staples, Ellwood, Lemann, Orfield, and others all recommend—to get as many as possible, especially the children, out of the ghettos. Now.

6

Among the Gautreaux-isn't-feasible arguments, one is just wrong—that impossible-to-achieve changes in suburban land use controls would be required. This is a throwback to Bork's argument, fortunately unsuccessful before the Supreme Court, that a metropolitan-wide Gautreaux-type mobility program would "destroy the autonomy and some of the political processes of [suburbs that had] no connection with the violation in Chicago." The Section 8 program, using existing private housing, in fact operates within existing zoning laws. That, indeed, is one of its great strengths, for it makes an end run around the multiple obstacles that would almost certainly block or seriously hamper any new program that sought to build publicly subsidized housing for poor families outside areas of minority concentration.

A second objection is that the Baltimore Debacle proves that the Gautreaux approach would founder on the shoals of local opposition from "receiving" communities. But rarely do those objecting on this ground acknowledge that Baltimore was an aberration. Moving to Opportunity went forward in its other four cities, and ultimately even in the Baltimore area, without significant opposition. Gautreaux families moved into more than one hundred Chicago suburbs with hardly a peep. The Gautreaux experience has generally been replicated in this respect in several dozen small mobility programs operated in other cities. Local opposition will always be a concern, but the low annual ceiling I propose on the number of mobility program families who could move into any single receiving community is likely to extract most of the venom from its fangs.

A third—probably the central—objection is that a Gautreaux-type approach could not operate at the scale needed to make a substantial dent in the nation's black ghettos. Wilson writes that the Gautreaux success is partly a function of its small size. "Since only a few families are relocated . . . each year, they remain relatively invisible and do not present the threat of a mass invasion."

Let me address the scale question with a hypothetical. Suppose that by congressional enactment 50,000 housing vouchers were made available annually, were earmarked for use by black families in urban ghettos, and could be used only in nonghetto communities, distant from high-poverty areas—say census tracts with less than 10 percent poverty and not minority-impacted. Suppose that the vouchers were allocated to the 127 metropolitan areas with more than 400,000 residents—say 125 to make the arithmetic easier. Suppose also that to avoid threatening any receiving community, no more than a specified number of families (an arbitrary number, say, ten, or a small fraction of occupied dwellings) could move—in a dispersed, not clustered, fashion—into any city, town, or village in a year.

If an average of forty municipalities in each metropolitan area served as receiving communities, the result would be—using ten as the hypothetical annual move-in ceiling—that 50,000 families each year, or 500,000 in a decade, would move in "Gautreaux fashion." Notably, the 500,000 moves in a decade would equal *almost half the million black families living in metropolitan ghetto census tracts.* (From census data and Paul Jargowsky's analyses we learned that in 2000 about 2.8 million blacks lived in such census tracts, and the average black household consisted of 2.74 persons.)

We cannot be certain that half of all black families in metropolitan ghettos would choose to or be able to participate (though they might). But it would not require the departure of every other black household to change radically the black ghetto as we know it. Reducing the black ghetto population by a quarter or a third or 40 percent might be enough to initiate radical change. Whatever the time frame (the program could be extended to a dozen or fifteen years if necessary), we would at last be treating a disease that has festered untreated in the body politic for over a century.

The hypothetical is plainly intended only to respond to the objection that a national Gautreaux Program could not operate at a meaningful scale; it is not a real-life working model. Metropolitan areas vary in size— in 2000 the 35 largest of the 331 metropolitan areas contained over half the extreme poverty metropolitan census tracts (1,177 of 2,222). An actual program would be tailored to these variations, operating at greater scale in big ghetto areas and at lesser scale (or not at all) in metropolitan areas with small black ghettos.

(The hypothetical is also limited to census tracts with 40 percent or more poverty. Neighborhoods with 39 percent poverty can be pretty bad places too. Some of the literature even suggests that many neighborhoods in the 30–39 percent range are likely to be on their way to higher poverty. The response is that we must begin somewhere; once extreme poverty neighborhoods are dealt with, the mobility program could be expanded into lower-poverty areas.)

The hypothetical raises several questions. Would 50,000 vouchers a year be feasible? Could such an enlarged mobility program be administered responsibly? Would enough families volunteer to participate? Could 50,000 private homes and apartments be found each year for the program?

The answers are speculative because mobility on such a scale has never been tried, but answers there are. The 50,000 vouchers annually, an arbitrary figure chosen for purposes of the hypothetical, really contemplates 100,000 new vouchers each year with 50,000 of them earmarked for the Gautreaux-type program. The point would be to leave 50,000 new "regular" vouchers for other entering families ineligible for the mobility program or who, for a multitude of perfectly understandable reasons, were unable or unwilling to participate. Fairness to nonparticipants would make the "extra" 50,000 vouchers a necessity. However, 100,000 new vouchers per year is not a fanciful figure; Congress authorized more than that number as recently as the year 2000.

Yet the hypothetical program could be run without issuing any new vouchers at all. Currently about 2.1 million vouchers are in circulation. The annual "turnover rate" is about 11 percent, meaning that for various reasons (for example, a family's income rises above the eligibility ceiling) some 230,000 vouchers are "turned back" to housing authorities each year for reissuance to other families. My imagined congressional enactment could simply direct 50,000 of these turnover vouchers to the hypothetical program (leaving 180,000 "regular" vouchers for new families) each year.

The cost of assisting mobility moves must of course be included in the calculus. But at an average of $4,000 per family—a reasonable, even generous, figure based on the Gautreaux experience—we are talking about $200 million a year, $2 billion total over ten years, excluding inflation. To put that figure in perspective and address the question of whether we could "afford" it, consider that for a single recent year (FY 2004) the Bush administration proposed a military budget of some $400 billion, which—not counting inflation—would amount to $4 trillion over ten years.

It is true that almost any program can be viewed as "affordable" by comparison with our military budget. But we aren't talking about "any" program. We are talking about a program to end the successor to slavery and Jim Crow that is perpetuating a caste structure in the United States and threatening incalculable harm to America. Achieving that, for a negligible fraction (0.0005) of our military budget, would be our best bargain since the Louisiana Purchase.

That negligible fraction is the price tag for mobility assistance only; it does not include the cost of the vouchers themselves. At the current annual cost of about $6,500 per voucher, the ten-year voucher tab for 100,000 new vouchers each year would be just under $36 billion, again not counting inflation. Adding roughly 7 percent for the administrative fee HUD pays to housing authorities brings the total to some $38.5 billion, which is less than 1 percent of the $4 trillion military figure. Our affordable housing crisis is so severe that, entirely apart from mobility and ghetto-dismantling, we should be—and politics will some day dictate—making affordable housing expenditures of this magnitude. Housing expenditures "the Gautreaux way" would give us the double payback of ameliorating both our affordable housing and our black ghetto crises.

Suppose, however, that the country wasn't ready to spend $38.5 billion over ten years for new "double payback" vouchers. Running the hypothetical program with turnover vouchers instead would eliminate entirely the $38.5 billion cost of the new vouchers. This would mean that the only additional tab for my hypothetical program—beyond the costs we are today already incurring for the existing voucher program—would be about $200 million a year, taking us back to that 0.0005 fraction of our military budget. It is mind-boggling to think that, for an infinitesimal expenditure in budgetary terms, we could mount a program that could—to use a storied locution—end the ghetto as we know it.

What about administration? Under a consent decree in a housing desegregation case, in a little over two years the Dallas housing authority assisted some 2,200 families, most of them black, to move to "nonimpacted" areas (census tracts in which few housing vouchers were already in use, but in practice the receiving areas turned out to be predominantly nonblack). Dallas was a case of direct administration by a housing authority. The Gautreaux Program was administered by a nonprofit organization. MTO involves partnerships between housing authorities and nonprofits. These varied and largely positive experiences suggest that, with local administrative arrangements tailored to local circumstances, we could handle the administrative challenge of a nationwide Gautreaux-type program.

One often expressed administrative concern is that moving families will cluster in specific, perhaps "fragile," areas and lead to new poverty enclaves, even suburban ghettos. My proposal that program families move to very low-poverty, nonracially impacted communities, distant from high-poverty areas, and the low annual ceiling on the number of mobility families entering any city, town, or village, makes that unlikely. But this potential problem is easily resolved by the direction included in the Leadership Council's Gautreaux Program contract to place families in a dispersed fashion. In practice, this provision gave the council authority—which it exercised (consistently, indeed, with an "anticoncentration of voucher families" provision in the underlying Section 8 statute)—to avoid clustering of moving families.

Would enough families volunteer to participate? We will not know until we try, but the Gautreaux experience suggests that they may. An average of 400 families moving each year in each participating metropolitan area would be required to reach the hypothetical goal, a smaller average number if more metropolitan areas were used. The 400-per-year number was surpassed more than once by the Gautreaux Program even though the number of entering families was artificially limited, not by lack of demand (remember the thousands turned away in the Leadership Council's State Street fiasco) but by the funding and staff that could be extracted from HUD in the Gautreaux consent decree bargaining process.

Finally, could 50,000 homes and apartments be found each year? The Gautreaux Program was able to place families in more than 100 cities, towns, and villages in the Chicago area, while the hypothetical assumes an average of only 40. The Census Bureau counts 331 metropolitan areas in the country, while the hypothetical assumes that the Gautreaux Program would operate in only 125. Each assumption is conservative with respect to unit supply.

An experience in Massachusetts is encouraging. From 1985 to 1991, a program run by the Massachusetts Department of Public Welfare in a "tight" rental market had considerable success in placing nearly 10,000 homeless persons—predominantly poor and minority—in private housing. Though not designed to foster moves to low-poverty or nonminority areas, the program had that effect for a hard-to-house population.

Most important, the potential supply of units is not a fixed sum. More creativity about addressing landlord concerns, for example, by paying rent for the several weeks it sometimes takes a housing authority to "clear" a family to occupy an apartment being held off the market, can make a big difference. So too with more fine-tuning of fair-market rents (increasing them in low-vacancy times and places, reducing them where they exceed market rents). Finally, for areas in which low fair-market rents remained a serious problem, the law creating the mobility program should direct HUD to approve whatever rents were demonstrated to be reasonable (based on comparable community rents) for program participants. If the 50,000 annual goal were made a bureaucratic imperative, and if administrators were given the right tools, it is possible—indeed likely—that the goal would be achieved.

A different kind of question is prompted by the notion of setting aside 50,000 vouchers each year exclusively for black families. How can one justify denying poor Latinos, poor Asians, and poor whites living in high-poverty neighborhoods an opportunity to participate in the mobility program? Would it even be legal?

A dual justification can be offered. The first is that the proposal is designed to help the nation confront its "most formidable evil," an evil that—if my analysis is correct—results in significant degree from fears and conduct generated by confining blacks, not others, to ghettos. The second is that the country is responsible for the confinement of blacks to ghettos in a manner and degree that is not the case with other groups. This is obviously so as to poor whites, who already live mostly among the nonpoor. Latinos and Asians, for all the discrimination they have suffered, do not have slavery or Jim Crow in their histories. Nor (though segregation of both Latinos and Asians is growing) have they been confined among their own to a comparable degree. Devoting mobility vouchers exclusively to blacks in ghettos can thus be justified both by the purpose of the proposal and by the unique history and current situation of blacks in ghettos.

As for legality, no one can be absolutely certain in a time when 5–4 Supreme Court decisions are routine and "race conscious" remedies are in disfavor. But when in 1988 Congress authorized compensation to Japanese citizens who had been herded into World War II detention camps, no serious legal question was even raised. Though the analogy is obviously imperfect, housing choice vouchers as "compensation" for confining blacks to ghettos is not a bad rationale. It is unlikely that even today's Supreme Court would upset an express congressional determination to make partial amends in this way for a history of slavery, Jim Crow, and ghettoization.

(One can imagine that, for reasons of policy or politics, Congress would choose to offer the mobility program to all residents of metropolitan ghettos. This would require a reworking of my numbers, and possibly prioritizing poverty families. In the New York City area, for example, almost half the population of extreme-poverty areas is Hispanic, and in the Los Angeles area the number is over two-thirds—for the most part, of course, in different census tracts than blacks. Although such an expansion would blunt the programmatic thrust and rationale of ending the *black* ghetto, increase cost and administrative complexity, and probably extend the time frame, it should not affect the basic structure or feasibility of the proposed program.)

A final objection is that my entire proposal smacks of an indulgent fantasy. Don't we clearly lack the political stomach for facilitating the movement of large numbers of black families from inner-city ghettos to white neighborhoods? What on earth makes me think that a nation that has treated blacks as America has throughout its history—the way it still treats the black poor—would give a moment's consideration to the course I am proposing? This very black ghetto issue was instrumental in shifting the political alignment of the entire country just a few decades ago, changing American character in the bargain. We remain today the uncaring nation we then became. Indeed, as this is being written, the Bush administration is proposing to cut back radically on housing vouchers. A Gautreaux-type program would certainly be portrayed as liberal "social engineering." Should it ever be seriously considered, wouldn't some modern-day George Wallace whip up the country's hardly dormant Negrophobia, perhaps especially easy to do at a time when working- and even middle-class Americans are having a hard time?

Maybe. Still, history is full of surprises. England might have succumbed to the Nazis if Roosevelt had not dreamed up lend-lease and persuaded a reluctant "America First" Congress to go along. Truman beat Dewey. Nixon went to China. The Soviet Union collapsed. Each of the academic theories about why whites resist policies to increase racial equality undoubtedly has merit. Yet they bend to the particulars of the right combination of factors assembled at the right moment. We don't necessarily have to be as optimistic as journalist and author George Packer, who believes that throughout American history the desire for a more just society keeps rising to the surface. History does tell us that in one decade the civil rights movement ended generations of seemingly impregnable Jim Crow. In a single fair-housing enactment Congress stripped historically sacred private property rights from American landowners. We have indeed on occasion managed forward steps even with respect to black Americans. National leadership is key, but we will not have a Bush in the White House forever.

(In his book *The Status Syndrome*, Sir Michael Marmot, a professor of epidemiology and public health, relates how for many years a small group of scientists carried out research on health inequalities throughout the world. Marmot calls the research "pure" because the conservative Thatcher administration could not have been more disinterested. When Tony Blair came to power in 1997, the "pure" research was taken down from the dusty shelves to which it had been relegated and a number of its recommendations became national policy.)

If my analysis is correct, it is ghetto fear—anxiety about inundation and antisocial conduct—that explains a good deal (though not all) of white attitudes toward blacks in general, and white rejection of in-moving blacks in particular. If the ghetto were done away with, the fears and anxieties would be ameliorated over time. Gautreaux teaches that the threshold fear of "them" can be overcome by high quality pre- and postmove counseling, by certification from a credible agency that the moving families are likely to be good tenants, and, most important, by keeping the numbers down. No more than a handful of families a year entering any receiving community makes for a different ball game. "They remain relatively invisible and so do not present the threat of a mass invasion," says Wilson. Exactly. The entire national Gautreaux Program I propose would be run in precisely this fashion.

7

We don't know whether the right combination of factors will ever move us to offer justice in the form of a national mobility program to black Americans trapped in ghettos. What does appear certain is that America confronts two courses. The first is to continue to coexist with its black ghettos. The second is to dismantle them.

The prospect along the first course, as Tocqueville prophesied, is that America's black-white race problem will not be resolved. Integration of some middle-class blacks will not change the prospect. Until the vast proportion of black Americans is securely middle-class, says the noted sociologist Herbert J. Gans, so long will whites continue to treat middle-class blacks as surrogates for the poor who might move in behind them. So long as black ghettos exist, entombing black souls within their pathology, white Americans will fear the entry of blacks, *any blacks*, into their communities. And so long as that is the case, America's black-white problem will continue to afflict the nation.

Perhaps the other part of Tocqueville's prophesy—result in disaster—is less certain, depending upon how one defines "disaster." Yet so long as we continue to tolerate the black ghetto, the prospect is for continuation of the two unequal societies described by the Kerner Report, and continued fear of the entombed souls by white Americans. So long as that fear persists, white Americans will continue to treat black Americans as the feared Other. They are likely to continue to act fearfully and repressively, possibly to incarcerate still more black Americans in still more prisons. In that event, the Tocqueville prophecy of disaster—as Currie and the others imply—is where this course may indeed take the country.

The alternative is to dismantle our black ghettos, thereby to lessen the fear and the fearful conduct they generate. Nothing can accomplish dismantling overnight. Any approach will take time, and will be fraught with difficulties and uncertainties. But a national Gautreaux mobility program is a sensible way to begin a task we postpone at our peril.

At the end of the pessimistic epilogue to his book on the black image in the white mind, Fredrickson allows that Tocqueville may have been right in describing the American race problem as insoluble and certain to result in disaster. He then advances the "slightly more hopeful view" that the problem could be solved by a radical change in basic institutions and values—"perhaps because the social anxieties fueling prejudiced thought and action have been removed." If that is possible, he continues, then it is the responsibility of Americans who believe in the ideal of racial equality to indulge in some serious Utopian thinking, for "there is always the slender but precious hope that today's Utopia can be tomorrow's society."

Unless Americans do that serious thinking, and do address directly the social anxieties—major among them the black ghetto—that fuel prejudiced thought and action, the American experiment, which so many have hoped would be a beacon for mankind, may end not in light but in darkness. Mr. Godot may, after all, not come.

ACKNOWLEDGMENTS

Grateful thanks to all those who so generously helped me along the way: to thoughtful readers, too numerous to mention, of parts or all of the manuscript; to interviewees, also too numerous to mention, who suffered through endless hours of remembrance of things past; to the unstinting support staff at BPI—Marissa Manos, Paula Kruger, Mary Rice, and Deborah Johnson; and to three people without whom this book would not have been—Mary Davis, who headed the Gautreaux Program for nearly two decades, Jim Rosenbaum, who told the story, and Len Rubinowitz, who nursed the book as if it were his own.

CHRONOLOGY OF KEY EVENTS

August 1965
The southern civil rights movement culminates with the signing of the Voting Rights Act by President Lyndon B. Johnson. The Watts riot explodes in Los Angeles.

Summer 1966
Dr. Martin Luther King Jr. and the Chicago Freedom Movement march for "open housing" in Chicago in the first effort to extend the civil rights movement outside the South.

August 1966
Gautreaux cases are filed against the Chicago Housing Authority (CHA) and the U.S. Department of Housing and Urban Development (HUD).

November 1968
Richard M. Nixon defeats Hubert H. Humphrey to become the thirty-seventh president of the United States.

February 1969
Judge Richard B. Austin rules that the CHA is guilty of racial discrimination in the Gautreaux case.

July 1969
Judge Austin directs the CHA to begin building scattered-site public housing in Chicago's white neighborhoods.

1969–1971
President Nixon appoints four new justices to the Supreme Court (Burger, Blackmun, Powell, and Rehnquist).

September 1970
Judge Austin rules that HUD is not guilty of racial discrimination in Gautreaux.

September 1971
The U.S. Court of Appeals reverses Judge Austin's decision and rules that HUD is guilty of racial discrimination in Gautreaux.

January 1974
The Supreme Court finally rejects the CHA's attempt to further delay the scattered-site program through technical legal arguments.

Spring 1974
The CHA's scattered-site program begins and runs to 1998, producing fewer than 2,000 new units.

June 1974
The Supreme Court rules (5–4) in Milliken v. Bradley that suburban school districts cannot be required to help desegregate Detroit schools.

April 1976
In Hills v. Gautreaux, the Supreme Court phase of the case against HUD, the Court rules (8–0) that Milliken v. Bradley does not shield HUD from providing relief to Gautreaux families in Chicago suburbs.

June 1976
Gautreaux plaintiffs and HUD agree upon a metropolitan-wide housing mobility program using rent subsidy vouchers as partial settlement of HUD's Gautreaux liability.

November 1976
The Gautreaux housing mobility program begins and runs to 1998; some 7,500 families are helped to move to opportunity areas, mostly in the suburbs.

June 1981
A consent decree with HUD, expanding and formalizing the partial settlement of June 1976, is approved by Judge John Powers Crowley. The decree terminates in 1998 when its numerical goals are reached, ending the Gautreaux case against HUD.

March 1995
Judge Marvin Aspen approves mixed-income units as relief for Gautreaux families, opening the door to demolition and replacement of failed CHA high-rises throughout Chicago.

1995–present
Demolition of CHA high-rises, relocation of families, and development of mixed-income units proceed under the CHA Transformation Plan, subject to Gautreaux conditions.

NOTE ON SOURCES

As in any memoir, much derives from recollection. My memory has been supplemented in a number of ways. BPI's extensive Gautreaux files include a nearly complete litigation record as well as voluminous research, correspondence, and press files. An even larger number of Gautreaux files is lodged with the Chicago Historical Society, which was most cooperative in arranging access, as was the clerk's office of the United States District Court in Chicago for official court files. The U.S. Supreme Court clerk's office supplied an official transcript of the Supreme Court oral argument, and selected Nixon tapes were made available by the National Archives. Both Sue Brady and Lois Weisberg shared their personal files on scattered sites with me, and I conducted dozens of interviews. The bibliography identifies many of the books I consulted for understanding, facts, and quotations. Except for two, one by James Rosenbaum and one by Rosenbaum and Stefanie DeLuca, I chose not to try the reader's patience by including the scores of articles I consulted as well. Newspaper and media sources are generally identified in the text. The chapter epigraphs are from Samuel Beckett's *Waiting for Godot* (New York: Grove Press, 1954).

SELECTED BIBLIOGRAPHY

Abt Associates and National Bureau of Economic Research. *Moving to Opportunity for Fair Housing Demonstration Program: Interim Impacts Evaluation.* Washington, D.C.: U.S. Department of Housing and Urban Development, 2003.

Anderson, Alan B., and George W. Pickering. *Confronting the Color Line: The Broken Promise of the Civil Rights Movement in Chicago.* Athens: The University of Georgia Press, 1986.

Anderson, Elijah. *Streetwise: Race, Class, and Change in an Urban Community.* Chicago: University of Chicago Press, 1990.

Beckett, Katherine, and Theodore Sasson. *The Politics of Injustice: Crime and Punishment in America.* Thousand Oaks, Calif.: Pine Forge Press, 2000.

Cashin, Sheryll. *The Failures of Integration.* New York: Public Affairs, 2004.

Clark, Kenneth B. *Dark Ghetto: Dilemmas of Social Power.* New York: Harper & Row, 1965.

Cohen, Adam, and Elizabeth Taylor. *American Pharaoh: Mayor Richard J. Daley: His Battle for Chicago and the Nation.* Boston: Little, Brown, 2000.

Cole, David. *No Equal Justice: Race and Class in the American Criminal Justice System.* New York: The New Press, 1999.

Currie, Elliott. *Crime and Punishment in America.* New York: Metropolitan Books, 1998.

DeLuca, Stefanie, and James E. Rosenbaum. "If Low-Income Blacks Are Given a Chance to Live in White Neighborhoods, Will They Stay? Examining Mobility Patterns in a Quasi-Experimental Program with Administrative Data." *Housing Policy Debate* 14, no. 3 (2003): 305–45.

DeParle, Jason. *American Dream.* New York: Viking, 2004.

D'Souza, Dinesh. *The End of Racism: Principles for a Multiracial Society.* New York: Free Press, 1995.

DuBois, W. E. B. *The Souls of Black Folk.* New York: Fawcett Publications, 1961.

Ehrlichman, John. *Witness to Power: The Nixon Years.* New York: Simon and Schuster, 1982.

Fairclough, Adam. *Better Day Coming: Blacks and Equality, 1890–2000.* New York: Penguin, 2001.

Fiss, Owen. *A Way Out: America's Ghettos and the Legacy of Racism.* Princeton: Princeton University Press, 2003.

Fredrickson, George M. *The Black Image in the White Mind.* New York: Harper & Row, 1971.

———. *Racism: A Short History.* Princeton: Princeton University Press, 2002.

Galster, George C., Peter A. Tatian, Anna M. Santiago, Kathryn L. S. Pettit, and Robin E. Smith. *Why Not in My Backyard? Neighborhood Impacts of Deconcentrating Assisted Housing.* New Brunswick, N.J.: Center for Urban Policy Research, 2003.

Garrow, David J., ed. *Chicago 1966: Open Housing Marches, Summit Negotiations, and Operation Breadbasket.* Brooklyn: Carlson Publishing, 1989.

Goering, John, and Judith D. Feins, eds. *Choosing a Better Life? Evaluating the Moving to Opportunity Social Experiment.* Washington, D.C.: The Urban Institute Press, 2003.

Goering, John, ed. *Housing Desegregation and Federal Policy.* Chapel Hill: The University of North Carolina Press, 1986.

Goetz, Edward G. *Clearing the Way: Deconcentrating the Poor in Urban America.* Washington, D.C.: The Urban Institute Press, 2003.

Grogan, Paul S., and Tony Proscio. *Comeback Cities: A Blueprint for Urban Neighborhood Revival.* Boulder, Colo.: Westview Press, 2000.

Hirsch, Arnold R. *Making the Second Ghetto: Race and Housing in Chicago 1940–1960.* New York: Cambridge University Press, 1983.

Jargowsky, Paul A. *Poverty and Place: Ghettos, Barrios, and the American City.* New York: Russell Sage Foundation, 1997.

Kaus, Mickey. *The End of Equality.* New York: Basic Books, 1992.

Kennedy, Randall. *Race, Crime, and the Law.* New York: Random House, 1997.

Kingsley, Thomas G., and Margery Austin Turner, eds. *Housing Markets and Residential Mobility.* Washington, D.C.: The Urban Institute Press, 1993.

Lemann, Nicholas. *The Promised Land: The Great Black Migration and How It Changed America.* New York: Alfred A. Knopf, 1991.

Loury, Glenn C. *The Anatomy of Racal Inequality.* Cambridge, Mass.: Harvard University Press, 2002.

Massey, Douglas S., and Nancy A. Denton. *American Apartheid: Segregation and the Making of the Underclass.* Cambridge, Mass.: Harvard University Press, 1993.

Meyer, Stephen Grant. *As Long As They Don't Move Next Door: Segregation and Racial Conflict in American Neighborhoods.* Lanham, Md.: Rowman & Littlefield, 2000.

Myerson, Martin, and Edward C. Banfield. *Politics, Planning, and the Public Interest.* New York: The Free Press, 1969.

Myrdal, Gunnar. *An American Dilemma.* New York: Harper & Bros., 1944.

Orfield, Gary. *Must We Bus: Segregated Schools and National Policy.* Washington, D.C.: The Brookings Institution Press, 1978.

Packer, George. *Blood of the Liberals.* New York: Farrar, Straus and Giroux, 2000.

Pattillo-McCoy, Mary. *Black Picket Fences: Privilege and Peril Among the Black Middle Class.* Chicago: University of Chicago Press, 1999.

Popkin, Susan J., Victoria E. Gwiasda, Lynn M. Olson, Dennis P. Rosenbaum, and Larry Buron. *The Hidden War: Crime and the Tragedy of Public Housing in Chicago.* New Brunswick, N.J.: Rutgers University Press, 2000.

Ralph, James R. Jr. *Northern Protest: Martin Luther King, Jr., Chicago, and the Civil Rights Movement.* Cambridge, Mass.: Harvard University Press, 1993.

Rosenbaum, James E. "Changing the Geography of Opportunity by Expanding Residential Choice: Lessons from the Gautreaux Program." *Housing Policy Debate* 6, no. 1 (1995): 231–69.

Royko, Mike. *Boss: Richard J. Daley of Chicago.* New York: Dutton, 1971.

Rubinowitz, Leonard S., and James E. Rosenbaum. *Crossing the Class and Color Lines.* Chicago: University of Chicago Press, 2000.

Rusk, David. *Inside Game/Outside Game: Winning Strategies for Saving Urban America.* Washington, D.C.: The Brookings Institution Press, 1999.

Safire, William. *Before the Fall: An Inside View of the Pre-Watergate White House.* Garden City, N.Y.: Doubleday, 1975.

Sowell, Thomas. *Race and Culture: A World View.* New York: Basic Books, 1994.

Steele, Shelby. *The Content of Our Character: A New Vision of Race in America.* New York: HarperPerennial, 1991.

Tonry, Michael. *Malign Neglect: Race, Crime, and Punishment in America.* Oxford: Oxford University Press, 1995.

Venkatesh, Sudhir Alladi. *American Project.* Cambridge, Mass.: Harvard University Press, 2000.

Wilson, William Julius. *When Work Disappears: The World of the New Urban Poor.* New York: Alfred A. Knopf, 1996.

———. *The Truly Disadvantaged: The Inner City, the Underclass, and Public Policy.* Chicago: University of Chicago Press, 1987.

Yinger, John. *Closed Doors, Opportunities Lost: The Continuing Costs of Housing Discrimination.* New York: Russell Sage Foundation, 1995.

INDEX

ABOUT THE AUTHOR

Alexander Polikoff served for twenty-nine years as executive director of BPI, Business and Professional People for the Public Interest, a Chicago public interest law and policy center. He is the author of articles on civil rights and urban affairs and of *Housing the Poor: The Case for Heroism.* He lives in the Chicago area with his wife, a writer of fiction for young people, and continues to work at BPI.